DEFENDING THE FAITH

DEFENDING THE FAITH an anti-modernist anthology

Edited and translated by

William H. Marshner

Introduction by C. J. T. Talar

The Catholic University of America Press
Washington, D.C.

The paper used in this publication meets the minimum requirements of American National Standards for Information Science—Permanence of Paper for Printed Library Materials, ANSI Z39.48-1984.
∞

Library of Congress Cataloging-in-Publication Data
Names: Marshner, William H., editor, translator.
Title: Defending the faith : an anti-modernist anthology / edited and translated by William H. Marshner ; introduction by C.J.T. Talar.
Description: Washington, D.C. : The Catholic University of America Press, [2016] | Includes bibliographical references and index.
Identifiers: LCCN 2016042161 | ISBN 9780813228969 (pbk. : alk. paper)
Subjects: LCSH: Modernism (Christian theology)—Catholic Church. | Catholic Church. Pope (1903-1914 : Pius X). Pascendi Dominici gregis. | Catholic Church—History—20th century. | Catholic Church—Doctrine—History—20th century. | Modernist-fundamentalist controversy.
Classification: LCC BX1396 .D44 2016 | DDC 273/.9—dc23
LC record available at https://lccn.loc.gov/2016042161

To the historical Jesus, *qui salvandos salvat gratis*

CONTENTS

EDITOR'S PREFACE

After three decades of teaching an occasional elective on the history and nature of Modernism, I became discontented with the one-sidedness of literary fame. It has continued to cling to the pioneers accused of "Modernism," especially Loisy and Tyrrell, but has largely slipped away from their scholarly critics, such as those whose contributions I have selected for this volume. (Many other critics were not at all scholarly, and they are deservedly forgotten.) But these, I think, still have something to say to us.

They are not easy to pigeonhole. Lagrange was an historico-critical exegete, sharply dismissive of the "conservative" exegesis still practiced in most Catholic seminaries. Batiffol was a critical historian, as was Portalié, as was the latter's fellow Jesuit Grandmaison. None was a professional scholastic philosopher; only Fr. Franon even taught philosophy. So none of them thought the Thomistic revival was the solution to all the church's problems with what calls itself modern thought. And Wehrlé was even a disciple of the anti-Scholastic Blondel.

Yet all of them rejected the Modernist initiatives. And they did so from the beginning, years before Pius X intervened. Why did they do so? I thought it was time the English-speaking reader should see for himself or herself.

Is the history of the Modernist period being seen differently since Vatican II? Then it is time for these pioneers of anti-Modernism to be seen differently, also. Seeing things differently is always a matter of putting them into a new context, in our case the context created by developments since the close of Vatican II. As to what this context is and demands, one can hardly do better than ponder the survey presented by Pope John Paul II in his 1998 encyclical *Fides et ratio*. There in paragraphs 80 through 99, this Polish pope, who had been both a participant in Vatican II and a privileged witness to the entire post-Conciliar situation, renews the critique of relativism, historicism, positivism, and pragmatism begun by the anti-Modernist pioneers excerpted in this volume.

ACKNOWLEDGMENTS

The maker of these selections has the following persons to thank. First of all, the historian Jean Rivière was the author who led me to Msgr. Batiffol, Fr. Portalié, Fr. Franon, and Fr. de Grandmaison, as the most competent critics of the Modernist movement (apart from the already famous biblicist M.-J. Lagrange). Second, Fr. C. J. T. Talar was kind enough to replace my own tentative introduction with his more professional, more comprehensive one. I thank him for his labors. Third, the editors of the Catholic University of America Press have been uniformly supportive, especially the former acquisitions editor, Dr. James Kruggel. I confess also a personal indebtedness to the many students at Christendom College who served as amanuenses on this project, as well as to my summer assistant, Ms. Lila Black. You are individually and collectively the *sine quibus non.*

Besides these proximate debts, I think it would be churlish to pass over a more remote one. It is to the Baltimore City College that, despite its name, was (and is) a public high school. My professional life as an academic was made possible by a small group of language teachers who worked there fifty-five years ago. They gave me the French, German, and Latin that I have been using ever since, daily and avidly. The program in which they taught was politically incorrect in most ways. It was not co-ed; so it must have been sexist. It was an all college-prep program; so it must have been elitist. Therefore it no longer exists. But my gratitude does not fade, and when my own students hear about it, even the "millennials" share my sorrow at the destruction of what was once available as free public education in America.

INTRODUCTION

C. J. T. Talar

"Modernism," as applied to a series of reformist proposals within Roman Catholicism that roughly coincided with the period of the Belle Époque (1890–1914), is an outsider term. It was initially applied by persons alarmed at the directions such proposals were taking, and it was consecrated in 1907 in the condemnations issued by the Vatican in the forms of the syllabus *Lamentabili sane exitu* and the encyclical *Pascendi dominici gregis*.[1]

While surfacing in various regions of the Church, hopes for a rapprochement between Catholicism and modernity were especially prominent in France. The encyclical *Rerum novarum* (1891) encouraged greater involvement on the part of Catholics, especially clergy, in social questions of the day. The following year, in an encyclical to the French, *Au milieu des sollicitudes*, Pope Leo XIII called on French Catholics to rally to the Republic, bolstering progressives' hopes for a change in the Church's stance toward democracy.

These developments lent support to an intellectual ferment in French Catholicism, assuming prominence around the same time. Closely allied with non-Scholastic philosophies, it took the form of a call for a "new

1. The text of both syllabus and encyclical may be found in *All Things in Christ: Encyclical Letters and Selected Documents of Saint Pius X*, ed. Vincent A. Yzermans (Westminster, Md.: Newman Press, 1954).

apologetics" to engage minds shaped by modernity. The work of Maurice Blondel (1861–1949) became a rallying point for Catholics who wished to provide means for the Church to better communicate its message to the time.[2]

Apologetics could also assume a more historical form among those who labored to domesticate the applications of historical critical methods, wresting those from nonconfessional and liberal Protestant biblical scholars to place them in service of a Catholic orthodoxy. Here both Alfred Loisy (1857–1940) and Marie-Joseph Lagrange (1855–1938) became prominent practitioners.[3] Critical methods also made their presence felt in Church history more broadly, especially in the contested area of Christian origins, and in specializations such as hagiography as practiced by the Bollandists. Prominent here were Louis Duchesne (1843–1922), Pierre Batiffol (1861–1929), and Hippolyte Delehaye (1859–1941).[4] Dogma was impacted, as well, and not only the historical development of dogma. The new movements in philosophy and in history placed the very nature of dogma under examination, as exemplified in the controversial article on dogma

2. On Blondel, see Oliva Blanchette, *Maurice Blondel: A Philosophical Life* (Grand Rapids, Mich.: Eerdmans, 2010).

3. A prolific writer in the areas of biblical exegesis and the history of religions, Loisy was no less so in the genre of autobiography; see his *Choses passées* (Paris: Émile Nourry, 1913); English translation *My Duel with the Vatican* [1924], translated by Richard Wilson Boynton (New York: Greenwood Press, 1968); and *Mémoires pour servir à l'histoire religieuse de notre temps*, 3 vols. (Paris: Émile Nourry, 1930–31). Émile Goichot has provided a short biography in *Alfred Loisy et ses amis* (Paris: Les Éditions du Cerf, 2002). On Lagrange, see Marie-Joseph Lagrange, OP, *Le Père Lagrange: Au service de la bible; Souvenirs personnels* (Paris: Les Éditions du Cerf, 1967); English translation *Père Lagrange: Personal Reflections and Memoirs*, trans. Henry Wansbrough (New York: Paulist Press, n.d.); see also Bernard Montagnes, *Le Père Lagrange (1855–1938): L'exégèse catholique dans la crise moderniste* (Paris: Les Éditions du Cerf, 1995); English translation *The Story of Father Marie-Joseph Lagrange: Founder of Modern Catholic Bible Study*, trans. Benedict Viviano (New York: Paulist Press, 2006). Montagnes expanded his earlier study as *Marie-Joseph Lagrange: Une biographie critique* (Paris: Les Éditions du Cerf, 2004). A study of Lagrange by his close associate Louis-Hugues Vincent completed in 1951 has only recently been published: *Le père Marie-Joseph Lagrange: Sa vie et son oeuvre* (Paris: Éditions Parole et Silence, 2013).

4. See Brigitte Waché, *Monseigneur Louis Duchesne (1843–1922)* (Rome: L'École Française de Rome, 1992). Pierre Batiffol awaits a definitive biography. A former student, Jean Rivière, published a brief study, *Monseigneur Batiffol (1861–1929)* (Paris: J. Gabalda, 1929); see C. J. T. Talar, "Le moderniste malgré lui: Pierre Batiffol," in *By Those Who Knew Them: French Modernists Left, Right, and Center*, ed. Harvey Hill, Louis-Pierre Sardella, and C. J. T. Talar (Washington, D.C.: The Catholic University of America Press, 2008), 71–89. Hippolyte Delehaye has received extensive treatment in Bernard Joassart, *Hippolyte Delehaye: Hagiographie critique et modernisme*, 2 vols. (Brussels: Société des Bollandistes, 2000). On the work of the Bollandists, see Hippolyte Delehaye, *L'Oeuvre des Bollandistes à travers trois siècles 1615–1915* (Brussels: Société des Bollandistes, 1959).

published by Édouard Le Roy (1870–1954).[5] The collective impact of these intellectual forces on epistemology and metaphysics went to foundational issues of Catholic belief. In turn, pushing the limits of intellectual boundaries fed back into optimistic hopes for progress on political and social fronts.

All of this contributed to imparting to Modernism a complex character. While intellectual aspects of Modernism raised considerable alarm over their possible consequences for Catholic faith, there were areas of the Church where social and political reforms were of paramount concern.[6] In short, clarifying and defining exactly what Modernism was provided a formidable challenge.

Thus, returning to the Vatican condemnation of Modernism, it is understandable that the consequences of revisionism were judged to be far reaching. *Pascendi* identified the Modernist threat as encompassing multiple areas: the Modernist is "a philosopher, a believer, a theologian, an historian, a critic, an apologist, a reformer" (no. 5). We shall not follow the encyclical's discussion of each of these various facets of Modernist activity, tracing in that order of presentation a natural progression. Rather, it is noteworthy that the inventory begins with the philosopher. If on the level of proscribed doctrine the positions of a Loisy are prominent or the dogmatic revisionism of a Le Roy is implicitly in view, in presenting Modernism as a system the encyclical exposes that system's philosophical foundations, identified as agnosticism and immanentism.[7] In the encyclical's perception of Modernism, if its effects are diverse, its philosophical grounding provides a unifying perspective.

5. Édouard Le Roy's "Qu'est-ce qu'un dogme?" originally appeared in *La Quinzaine* (April 16, 1905). Le Roy republished it in *Dogme et critique* (Paris: Librairie Bloud, 1907), which also contained his responses to the critical analyses of the article by Léonce de Grandmaison, Eugène Portalié, and Joannès Wehrlé that are translated in part 4 of this volume. A translation of Le Roy's article may be found in *Romance and the Rock: Nineteenth-Century Catholics on Faith and Reason*, ed. Joseph Fitzer (Minneapolis: Fortress Press, 1989), 349–73. Guy Mansini has contributed an analysis of the controversy in *"What Is a Dogma?": The Meaning and Truth of Dogma in Edouard Le Roy and His Scholastic Opponents* (Rome: Editrice Pontificia Università Gregoriana, 1985).

6. "For some, social Modernism is the most important, the most innovating, the most 'scandalous,' imposing on Catholic consciousness 'a ferment, a tension, the cause of a radical mutation, as pressing and unstoppable as an error on the origin of the Pentateuch or even of the fourth Gospel'"; André Boland, *La crise moderniste hier et aujourd'hui* (Paris: Beauchesne, 1980), 13.

7. In this context agnosticism referred to a philosophical conviction that God's existence is not scientifically knowable. Kant's *Critique of Pure Reason* is a famous statement of this position.

Pascendi's synthetic, systematic characterization of Modernism remained the standard for several decades following its 1907 promulgation. As with many areas in Catholicism, the period of the Second Vatican Council marked a time when perceptions of Modernism began to undergo a change. By 1970, in *A Variety of Catholic Modernists*, Alec Vidler could write:

> There are at least two distinct and legitimate ways of studying the modernist movement. One is to start from the papal acts which defined and condemned modernism, especially the encyclical *Pascendi*. In that case the system of ideas which the pope called "modernism" would have to be expounded and examined, and the pedigree and profession of those ideas would, as far as possible, have to be observed. This would be a schematic study in the history of Christian doctrine or heresy. The other way is, without presuppositions concerning orthodoxy or heresy, to look at the various persons or some of them who were involved in the movement that provoked the papacy to define and condemn the system which it called "modernism," with a view to ascertaining what they conceived themselves to be doing, whether individually or collectively. While I acknowledge the legitimacy of the former way of studying the modernist movement, my own decided preference is for the latter, and for more than one reason.[8]

Vidler wrote those observations at a transitional point in the historiography of Roman Catholic Modernism. The first of his two approaches had long dominated scholarship and was accepted as setting the terms under which Modernism was to be understood. A major question therefore became, "Who was a Modernist?," since the encyclical did not name anyone specifically and cast its net rather widely. It was not always clear where the boundaries lay.[9] At the time Vidler wrote, there was an emerging sense that a "top down" approach to defining Modernism gave only part of the picture of a phenomenon that was in reality more complicated. The approach adopted in *A Variety of Catholic Modernists* is more of a "bottom up" way of viewing things. At the time Vidler wrote, legitimacy could still be accorded the first approach, even when one opted to pursue the second. In current scholarship on Roman Catholic Modernism, the two approaches Vidler identified are no longer seen as viable alternatives. The papal condemnation of Modernism is now viewed as itself part of the dynamics of a process of de-

8. Alec Vidler, *A Variety of Catholic Modernists* (Cambridge: Cambridge University Press, 1970), 15.

9. For instance, at one point there was some concern that Cardinal John Henry Newman's work on the development of doctrine may have come under censure, and papal assurances were solicited to reassure that Newman was not in view.

fining rather than a standard to be accepted as definitive in itself. Put another way, *Pascendi* is part of the problem of defining Modernism rather than the starting point of any solution to that problem. Increasingly, scholarship on the movement has turned to what those involved in it thought they were doing. Symptomatic of the need to take those views into consideration is the fact that "Modernism" was a label applied to currents of renewal within Catholicism by some who opposed those initiatives and that was canonized by the Vatican condemnation; in general partisans of renewal themselves did not accept the label and defined themselves and their work in other terms.

So then, around the time of the Second Vatican Council (1962–65) the first wave of studies of Roman Catholic Modernism—the one that followed the binary terms "orthodoxy" and "heresy," set out in the Roman condemnation—was giving way to a second wave of scholarship "that read texts and events more closely, demonstrated the complexity of the intellectual controversies, unmasked unsavory institutional politics, and rehabilitated a number of the better-known figures."[10]

The translated articles that form the contents of this volume may seem to vindicate the top-down approach, but they also contribute to the bottom-up approach. They form a complement to the Modernist writings of a Loisy, a George Tyrrell (1861–1909),[11] or an Édouard Le Roy by providing insight into how these writings were judged prior to the Vatican condemnation. In this they not only anticipate criticisms leveled by *Pascendi*, but also manifest the difficulty in achieving clarity on the positions that were advanced. In the somewhat confused state of affairs at the time, opponents of reformist initiatives were not always able to discriminate between legitimate and illegitimate uses of historical method, at times condemning those methods *en bloc* or between theories of doctrinal development that preserved a supernatural truth conveyed by the dogmatic expression and those that conveyed an evo-

10. Stephen Schloesser, review of *By Those Who Knew Them: French Modernists Left, Right and Center* (2008), by Harvey Hill, Louis-Pierre Sardella, and C. J. T. Talar, *American Historical Review* 114 (2009): 1163–64. In his review Schloesser identifies a third approach, now emerging, that is informed by post-structural theories of recent decades, one that is "keenly aware of rhetorical strategies used in producing biographical inventions of others and oneself; of the multiple receptions that any such text might elicit; and the use of such texts as weapons in wars of contested memory." In other words, if *Pascendi* cannot be taken simply and straightforwardly as the definitive word on Modernism, neither can the witness provided by Modernists themselves be taken unproblematically.

11. On Tyrrell, see Maude Petre, *Autobiography and Life of George Tyrrell*, 2 vols. (London: Edward Arnold, 1912), and Nicholas Sagovsky, *"On God's Side": A Life of George Tyrrell* (Oxford: Clarendon Press, 1990).

lutionary naturalism that volatilized the supernatural element. In attempting to meet a Loisy, a Tyrrell, or a Le Roy on their chosen ground, progressives such as Lagrange and Batiffol exposed themselves to the risk of being classified with those they wished to critique. (It is noteworthy that neither of these men emerged entirely unscathed from their involvement in the controversies of the day.)

The critical writings collected here show an emerging clarity in perceptions of key texts that shaped the Modernist Crisis: most directly Loisy's *L'Évangile et l'Église* (1902) and *Autour d'un petit livre* (1903); George Tyrrell's *Religion as a Factor of Life* (published pseudonymously in 1902 under "Dr. Ernest Engels") and his *Lex Orandi* (1904); and Le Roy's "Qu'est-ce qu'un dogme?" (1905). The issues raised in discussion and dissection of these works indirectly engage other writings by Catholics such as Maurice Blondel and Lucien Laberthonnière,[12] by Henri Margival[13] and Marcel Hébert,[14] and by a number of liberal Protestant or "independent" (nonconfessional) scholars. As France was the center of some of the most important and most prominent Modernist writings, it is less than surprising that it should also produce important critiques of these writings. Since a fair number of writings by more or less prominent Modernists have been available in English translation, Professor Marshner's collection contributes toward filling a gap in translating critical rejoinders by their contemporaries. For the most part, the critics gathered here write in rather measured tones, despite the gravity of what is held to be at stake, although on occasion a certain sharpness breaks through.

12. Lucien Laberthonnière (1860–1932) was closely aligned with Blondel during this period. Laberthonnière's philosophy of moral dogmatism was identified with an apologetic of immanence. Several of his works were placed on the Index, and in 1913 he was prohibited from publishing anything further; see *Laberthonnière: L'Homme et l'oeuvre, introduction à sa pensée*, ed. Paul Beillevert (Paris: Beauchesne, 1972).

13. Over 1896–99, in the *Revue d'histoire et de littérature religieuse*, Henri Margival published a series of articles on "Richard Simon et la critique biblique au XVIIe siècle." While ostensibly on Simon, they undertook a defense of historical criticism and of Loisy in particular; see C. J. T. Talar, "Rehabilitating Richard Simon, Legitimating Alfred Loisy," in *The Rise of Historical Consciousness among the Christian Churches*, ed. Kenneth L. Parker and Erick H. Moser (Lanham, Md.: University Press of America, 2013), 47–63.

14. Marcel Hébert adopted a symbolist interpretation of dogma that ultimately denied the attribution of personality to God. Several of his essays are translated in *The Modernist as Philosopher: Selected Writings of Marcel Hébert*, ed. C. J. T. Talar (Washington, D.C.: The Catholic University of America Press, 2011). On Hébert, see Albert Houtin, *Un prêtre symbolist: Marcel Hébert (1851–1916)* (Paris: F. Rieder, 1926).

To appreciate something of the substantive issues at stake and the seriousness with which these critics engaged them, some suggestion of the broad context in which Modernists worked for Catholic renewal will now be given, followed by discussion of major questions that surfaced in intellectual Modernism, as a way of situating both the Modernist writings under examination and their critics' rejoinders to them.

The Context: Modernity

Depending upon one's interests, the beginning of "modernity" can located at different points. A conventional location would be the French Revolution, one that works very well for our purposes, as from the "long" nineteenth century (1789–1914) there emerged currents of thought and events that gave many people a sense that their world had changed appreciably from that inhabited by people in the past, a change summed up in the word "modernity."

In philosophy, in the wake of Immanuel Kant's "Copernican Revolution"—and still more after the contributions of G. W. F. Hegel—knowledge of the world could seem less secure. Awareness of the subjective contribution of the human knower to the process of acquiring knowledge challenged an unproblematic (or relatively unproblematic) objectivity of knowledge. Religious knowledge was not immune and, in some ways, especially vulnerable. Indeed, Pierre Colin has gone so far as to identify acceptance or rejection of Kant as the dividing line between acceptance and rejection of modernity:

> Between Kant and modernity there exists a bond so strong that it may be difficult to gain a deep understanding of modernity without at least passing through Kant.... Reciprocally, moreover, the refusal of Kant can signify the conscious or unconscious refusal of modernity. The anti-Kantian fight of the Catholic adversaries of Kant is an anti-modern fight, at the same time that it is an anti-Protestant fight.[15]

As noted earlier, in the Modernist system as portrayed by *Pascendi*, philosophy played a dominant role. And, while Kant is not explicitly named, it is clear that his philosophy is in view as foundational to that system.

During the nineteenth century one may speak of the development of

15. Pierre Colin, *L'audace et le soupçon: La crise moderniste dans le catholicisme français 1893–1914* (Paris: Desclée de Brouwer, 1997), 466. The author's identification of anti-Kant with anti-modern reflects the situation in France in particular.

"modern historical consciousness." Over that period history achieved a certain preeminence—even hegemony—inheriting philosophy's domain, as philosophy had earlier displaced theology—at least in the secular sphere. On religious terrain the field was still contested. Put in simple terms, what was modern about the sense of the past that emerged at this time was a disruption of an organic connection with the past; in short, a sense that the world had decisively changed, to the point that the connectedness of the present to the past was no longer unproblematic. As change rather than continuity dominated, the past grew more distant. This growing sense of historical distance was reinforced by an ideology of developmental progress. Changes in social and political life were no longer thought of as deviations from an original order of things or as cyclical repetitions. Instead, they were understood as stages in an irreversible process of development. While traces of this intellectual outlook can be found earlier, it is the very pervasiveness of this perspective that marks its newness: "it was not until the nineteenth century that history began to pretend that it could proffer a comprehensive interpretation, and, what is more, on an unprecedented scale."[16]

Against this larger background the sense of the historian's function underwent a change, from basically an editorial and harmonizing one to an approach that treats historical sources like witnesses in a court of law, subjecting them to interrogation. In the former case the testimony of a person who claims to have knowledge of an event is accorded authority and accepted as historical truth. In the second instance, it is the historian who possesses a criterion to which his sources must conform and by which they must be criticized. In short, there emerges a contrast between an ideal of belief and its acceptance of authority and a critical stance that claims autonomy for the historian and interrogates the past while holding doubt to be a virtue and not a vice. This changed mindset had far-reaching consequences for biblical scholarship and for Church history—as evident in controversies over acceptance or rejection of legendary accounts of apostolic origins of French dioceses or lives of early saints. In the minds of defenders of orthodoxy, a defective philosophy inevitably led to a defective approach to history; from the vantage point of would-be reformers,

16. Van Harvey, *The Historian and the Believer* (Toronto: Macmillan, 1969), 38.

at stake was nothing less than the very credibility of Christianity itself to people whose outlook was increasingly shaped by modernity.

A third contested area, already suggested by history's impact on a consciousness of changes in social and political life, is that of Church-state relations. In conversation Georges Tavard once observed that Modernism was "one of the aftershocks of the French Revolution." A great deal is implied in that brief statement, but in a preliminary way it indicates that, while the intellectual aspects of Modernism may have had a limited scope in their impact, the changing social and political fortunes of Catholicism had potentially wide repercussions.

The nineteenth century witnessed the passing of a longstanding set of arrangements by which religion was regarded as a fundamental cohesive force in a society and a given religion was given a privileged role in a confessional state. Calls for acceptance, on the part of so-called liberal Catholics, of a new order of things, in which free exercise of religion would be allowed, were rejected by Rome in a series of condemnations, the most notorious of which remains the Syllabus of Errors (1864).[17] What was rejected in principle often had to be accommodated in practice, although not without varying degrees of tension, depending on the period and place in question. Closer to the time of the Modernist crisis, relations in France between Catholicism and the Third Republic continued to deteriorate, despite Leo XIII's efforts to get Catholics to rally to the support of the republican government. The Dreyfus Affair exacerbated divisions between the "Two Frances," effectively ending any hope of success for the papal policy of *ralliement* and eventuating in the separation of Church and state in 1905.[18] Monarchical forms of government could, however, bring their own problems. In Prussia and other German states, in Austria, and

17. Initiatives by Liberal Catholics in the earlier part of the nineteenth century and Roman reactions to those are set forth in Alec R. Vidler, *Prophecy and Papacy: A Study of Lamennais, the Church and the Revolution* (New York: Charles Scribner's Sons, 1954).

18. In 1894 Captain Alfred Dreyfus was convicted of supplying confidential military information to a German contact. The verdict was based in part on fabricated evidence supplied to the military court, but withheld from the accused and his defense. The ensuing controversy over Dreyfus's guilt or innocence inflamed already existing divisions in France and engaged anti-Semitic, nationalist, and clericalist ideologies. For a succinct account of the affair, see Jean-Marie Mayeur and Madeleine Rebérioux, *The Third Republic from Its Origins to the Great War 1871–1914*, trans. J. R. Foster, Cambridge History of Modern France (Cambridge: Cambridge University Press, 1984), chap. 7. On the separation of Church and state in France in 1905, see Maurice Larkin, *Church and State after the Dreyfus Affair: The Separation Issue in France* (New York: Macmillan, 1974).

in Switzerland attempts to bring Catholicism under tighter state control resulted in the Kulturkampf.[19] While tensions eased under the more conciliatory policies of Leo XIII, there is little wonder that Catholics felt increasingly embattled over the last quarter of the century. The unification of Italy presented its own problems, with the loss of the Papal States and with them the temporal power of the papacy. The pope became the self-declared "prisoner of the Vatican," and various limitations were placed on the participation of Catholics in civil society. Little wonder, then, that social and political issues loomed larger with Italian reformers than intellectual ones, and Modernism wore a somewhat different face there than it did in France or in England.

An appreciation of this broader context makes the forceful reaction to Modernism on the part of the Vatican somewhat easier to understand and the efforts devoted to painstaking analysis of Modernist arguments by critics more comprehensible.

Back to the Modernists Themselves

If one begins with *Pascendi*'s depiction, Modernism emerges from the encyclical as a coherent system, united by the philosophical principles that grounded it, principles shared by its partisans, principles whose consequences are drawn out so that their full impact might be appreciated. Modernism also emerges as a coherent movement, whose apparent diversity and seeming independence of initiatives are the result of a conscious strategy by Modernists. Alternatively, if the work of individual Modernists constitutes the starting point, a somewhat different picture emerges. Modernism appears more as a number of tendencies and its partisans at best loosely coordinated and notably diverse.

In any treatment of Modernism critical biblical scholarship looms large, and Alfred Loisy's contributions are prominent. In the seminary education of the time, dogmatic and moral theology made up the core of the curriculum, with scripture receiving comparatively little attention. Loisy developed an interest in scripture early on, one he was able to develop after being sent to the Paris Institut catholique for higher study. There he

19. The Kulturkampf refers to the attempts of the German Empire under Chancellor Otto von Bismarck to increase the power of the secular state by reducing the social and political influence of the Catholic Church through a series of discriminatory laws.

gained access to the secular university and, with that, exposure to research methods and non-Catholic biblical scholarship. As a result of his mastery of biblical languages and extensive knowledge of both primary texts and secondary literature, Loisy received an appointment to the faculty of the Institut. In his teaching and early publications he pursued a gradualist strategy of introducing a critical approach to the Bible, with the aim of domesticating historical criticism and utilizing that in defense of Catholicism against rationalist practitioners of the method.[20] In a climate highly suspicious of critical methods precisely because of their corrosive effects on the credibility of scripture in rationalist exegesis, Loisy's undertaking was not without risk. Just how risky innovating perspectives in this area of scholarship could be was made evident by the controversy stirred up by an article on the "biblical question" by the Institut's rector, Msgr. d'Hulst.[21] Intended to be a survey of a range of positions on biblical inspiration, it depicted a "broad school" of interpretation on this topic that raised opposition, drew Loisy into the controversy, and served to catalyze the issuance of the encyclical *Providentissimus Deus* (1893) designed to regulate matters. The position that Loisy took on inspiration, and on the relation of exegesis and theology more largely, in an attempt to distinguish his view from d'Hulst's broad school was judged too radical, and, as a result, Loisy lost his teaching position.

While he continued his more strictly exegetical studies, this change of fortune had the effect of turning his interests in the direction of apologetics. Over the next several years he wrote a long apologetic treatise, "Essais d'histoire et de philosophie religieuses,"[22] which engaged subjects such as revelation and faith, the nature of religion, the development of doctrine, and miracles as a motive of credibility. It was from portions of this manuscript that Loisy quarried the articles that appeared in the *Revue du clergé*

20. On Loisy's early formation and teaching at the Institut catholique, see C. J. T. Talar, "Innovation and Biblical Interpretation," in *Catholicism Contending with Modernity: Roman Catholic Modernism and Anti-Modernism in Historical Context*, ed. Darrell Jodock (Cambridge: Cambridge University Press, 2000), 191–211.

21. Msgr. Maurice d'Hulst, "La Question biblique," *Le Correspondant*, n.s. 134 (1893): 201–51. On the background to this article and the ensuing controversy, see Hill, *The Politics of Modernism: Alfred Loisy and the Scientific Study of Religion* (Washington, D.C.: The Catholic University of America Press, 2002), chap. 3.

22. Recently published as François Laplanche, ed., *Alfred Loisy: La crise de la foi dans le temps présent* (Turnhout: Brepols, 2010).

français over 1898–1900 under the pseudonym "Firmin." These formed the substance of *L'Évangile et l'Église* (1902) and portions of *Autour d'un petit livre* (1903).[23] *L'Évangile et l'Église* played a pivotal role in the unfolding of events; it may be said to have precipitated the "Modernist Crisis." It is the center of attention of the two responses by Batiffol and Lagrange that make up part 1 of the translations in this volume. *Autour d'un petit livre*, published the following year, provided the occasion for Loisy's critics to revisit his historical apologetic, with the additional participation of Eugène Portalié.[24]

While Loisy assumes prominence in accounts of Modernism, during the 1890s his reputation as an exegete was rivaled by the Dominican biblical scholar Marie-Joseph Lagrange. Sent to found a school of biblical studies in Jerusalem in 1890, Lagrange combined a textual approach to biblical scholarship with archaeological investigation, creating an outlet for work on biblical subjects with the *Revue biblique*, which began publication in 1892. The *Revue* was intended to meet critical objections to the Bible on critical grounds. Through his own published articles and as a prolific reviewer of scholarly work, Lagrange became an influential voice in Catholic circles on biblical matters. With prominence went a price: advocacy of critical methods, however moderate, could attract suspicion from those who equated their use with rationalist exegesis. Loisy was not alone in attracting censure from those fearful of the results of a critical approach to the Bible.

23. A. Firmin [see bibliography under Alfred Loisy], "Le développement chrétien d'après le Cardinal Newman," *Revue du clergé français*17 (1898): 5–20; "La théorie individualiste de la religion," *Revue du clergé français* 17 (1899): 202–15; "La définition de la religion," *Revue du clergé français* 18 (1899): 193–209; "L'Idée de la révelation," *Revue du clergé français* 21 (1900): 250–71; "Les preuves et l'économie de la révelation," *Revue du clergé français* 22 (1900): 126–53; and "La religion d'Israël," *Revue du clergé français* 24 (1900): 337–63, English translations in Loisy, *Prelude to the Modernist Crisis: The "Firmin" Articles of Alfred Loisy*, trans.Christine Thirlway (Oxford: Oxford University Press, 2010). Loisy, *L'Évangile et l'Église* (Paris: Alphonse Picard et fils, Éditeurs, 1902), English translation *The Gospel and the Church*, trans. Christopher Home (London: Isbister, 1903); repr. Fortress Press, 1976). Loisy, *Autour d'un petit livre* (Paris: Alphonse Picard et fils, Éditeurs, 1903). B. M. G. Reardon translated a portion of the introduction to *Autour d'un petit livre* (v–xxvii, xxxvi) in Reardon, *Roman Catholic Modernism* (Stanford: Stanford University Press, 1970), 98–107.

24. Eugène Portalié (1852–1909) devoted his life to the teaching of theology, first in Jesuit scholasticates and later at the Institut catholique in Toulouse (1899–1909). He has been characterized as a critical, often polemical, but fair-minded critic of Modernist positions, though from an intellectualist conception of the act of faith and its preambles; Henri de Gensac, "Eugène Portalié," *Dictionnaire du monde religieux dans la France contemporaine*, vol. 1, *Les Jésuites* (Paris: Beauchesne, 1985), 217–18. See also the notice on "Portalié, Eugène," by Ferdinand Cavallera in the *Dictionnaire de théologie catholique*, vol. 12, cols. 2590–93.

Though better grounded in theology and thus more moderate in his application of criticism than Loisy, Lagrange also had to tread carefully in the charged atmosphere of the time.

One must be careful not to retroject later positions back into earlier work, and this applies especially to Loisy.[25] It is indicative that, in 1896, Lagrange could solicit Loisy's collaboration with the *Revue biblique*.[26] Two years later, however, Lagrange was having serious enough reservations about Loisy's work to want to distance himself from the abbé and his partisans. The Dominican's writings had become linked with Loisy and his circle, and (more ominously) in that same year the École biblique was accused of harboring tendencies that were "rationalist and even Protestant."[27] Both the school and its director were denounced to Rome, although nothing came of it then.

Lagrange inadvertently became connected with Loisy again, just at the time that *L'Évangile et l'Église* saw publication in November 1902. Early that same month he delivered a series of lectures at the Toulouse Institut catholique, where Pierre Batiffol served as rector. They were published in February 1903 under the title *La méthode historique: Surtout à propos de l'Ancien Testament*.[28] The ideas it contained had been expressed by Lagrange many times before in the *Revue biblique*. The popular form of the lectures and the application of principles to specific cases caused the book to appear as the manifesto of a new direction in exegesis.[29] Moreover, the coinciding of the publication of *La méthode historique* with that of *L'Évangile et l'Église* led some to conclude that this was no mere coincidence, but com-

25. Loisy's autobiographical writings, notably *Choses passées*, have been judged as doing this.

26. Loisy contributed "L'Apocalypse synoptique" published in two parts: *Revue biblique* 5 (1896): 173–98 and 335–59. Lagrange had reservations regarding views expressed by Loisy on the extent of Christ's knowledge and published the articles with a note distancing the *Revue* from opinions expressed by the author. That effectively ended Loisy's collaboration with the *Revue biblique*.

27. Lagrange, *Père Lagrange: Personal Reflections and Memoirs*, 62–64.

28. M.-J. Lagrange, *La méthode historique: Surtout à propos de l'Ancien Testament* (Paris: Victor Lecoffre, 1903). English translation: *Historical Criticism and the Old Testament* (London: Catholic Truth Society, 1905).

29. Bernard Montagnes has observed that *La méthode historique* achieved the status of a manifesto not from the author's intentions, but from the manner of its reception; Montagnes, "La méthode historique: Succès et revers d'un manifeste," in *Naissance de la méthode critique* (Paris: Les Éditions du Cerf, 1992), 67, 68. See also Julien Fontaine: "The veritable author of the historical method, or rather the one who has contributed most to its introduction among French exegetes, is the distinguished director of the *Revue biblique*, Père Lagrange"; Julien Fontaine, *Les infiltrations protestants et l'exégèse du Nouveau Testament* (Paris: Victor Retaux, 1905), 174.

plicity.[30] Thus there was incentive for Lagrange to distinguish his use of historical criticism from that of Loisy, while at the same defending a legitimate use of that criticism in biblical interpretation. If he could not make a convincing enough case on both of these fronts, he risked being identified with the problem rather than the solution.

Pierre Batiffol had known Lagrange in seminary, prior to the latter's leaving to enter the Dominicans. Friendship constituted the basis for professional association; for a time Batiffol functioned as secretary to the *Revue biblique*. His articles and reviews regularly appeared in its pages, and he had arranged for Lagrange's lectures on historical method to be delivered at Toulouse. As a historian of Christian origins Batiffol was no stranger to critical methods in historical research and was acutely aware that he also worked in areas that required a certain delicacy of approach.

Batiffol's own response to *L'Évangile et l'Église* appeared in the *Bulletin de littérature ecclésiastique*, published by the Toulouse Institut catholique.[31] While abstaining from judging the exegete's intentions, he noted the consequences of a philosophy of religion that permeated the book. At base, the problematic nature of Loisy's apologetic stemmed not from the use of critical methods as such, but from the underlying philosophy that informed them. (In his review article on Loisy's book Lagrange had adopted a similar position.)[32]

The appearance of *Autour d'un petit livre* intensified Batiffol's efforts. He gave three lectures at the Institut in December 1903. The first remained unpublished; the second was printed as a pamphlet, *Jésus et l'histoire* (1904); the third furnished the substance of "Jésus et l'église" that appeared in the Toulouse *Bulletin* together with critical contributions by Lagrange and Portalié under the general rubric "Concerning the Foundations of the Faith."[33]

30. F.-M. Braun, *The Work of Père Lagrange*, adapted from the French by Richard T. A. Murphy (Milwaukee: Bruce, 1963), 80.

31. It appears in this volume as selection 1, Batiffol, "The Gospel and the Church."

32. See this volume, selection 2, Lagrange, "Review of Alfred Loisy, *L'Évangile et l'Église.*"

33. Batiffol's contributions are summarized by Émile Poulat, who also draws upon Batiffol's *L'Enseignement de Jésus* (1905) to explore areas of accord and difference between Loisy and his critic; see Émile Poulat, *Histoire, dogme et critique dans la crise moderniste* [1962] (Tournai: Casterman, 1979), 376–92. Lagrange's "Jesus and la critique des Évangiles" appeared in the *Bulletin de littérature ecclésiastique* early in 1904, as did Portalié's more polemical "Dogme et histoire" (translated in this volume as selections 3 and 5, respectively). Batiffol's article appears here as "Jesus and the Church" as selection 4.

Like Lagrange, Batiffol sought to occupy a middle position in these controverted areas. Loisy and the group associated with the *Revue d'histoire et de littérature religieuses* remained to the left: they followed criticism's lead and left it to theology to make whatever adjustments it could in light of critical conclusions. On the other hand, the program statement of the *Bibliothèque de théologie historique*, initiated by the Jesuits, may serve as an indicator of a less adventurous position than the one taken by Batiffol. The statement asserted a fundamental identity of faith between ancients and moderns and thereby defended the principle of interpreting the past via the present. "How many times did the Fathers say or want to say what we do, though seeming to say the opposite or something else?"[34] If the left did not do justice to the integrity of the tradition, the right did not always respect sufficiently the integrity of the texts. It is precisely this attempt to occupy the middle ground that contributes to the interest of these critics. Their critical responses help to clarify the dynamics of the intellectual debates and positions taken at the time of Modernism and to substantive issues that have proven to be of enduring theological interest.

Somewhat in parallel with developments in Catholic biblical scholarship were initiatives in philosophy that affected apologetics from that side. The name of Maurice Blondel became synonymous with an apologetics of immanence, which aimed at overcoming what he saw as limitations of a Scholastic approach. Although George Tyrrell and Édouard Le Roy are the subjects of the remainder of the critical articles that comprise this collection, Blondel's name receives mention, and an apologetics of immanence is clearly in view. A brief suggestion of Blondel's approach and its reception during the 1890s provides a context for understanding criticisms leveled against Tyrrell and Le Roy, as well as raising another major issue that engaged Catholics during the Modernist Crisis: the subjectivity of human knowing.

34. Jean Vanot, "Une grande enterprise théologique," *Études* 90 (1902): 407. The series was published under the auspices of the Jesuits at the Paris Institut catholique. Ironically, in light of the program statement authored by Vanot, the inaugural volume was written by Joseph Turmel and placed on the Index in 1910. Turmel was excommunicated in 1930. On Turmel, see Karl-Peter Gertz, *Joseph Turmel (1859–1943): Ein theologiegeschichtlicher Beitrag zum Problem der Geschichtlichkeit der Dogmen* (Frankfurt am Main: Peter Lang, 1975). Turmel's two-volume autobiography, *Comment j'ai donné congé aux dogmes* (1935) and *Comment l'église romaine m'a donné congé* (1939) has been translated as *"Martyr to the Truth": The Autobiography of Joseph Turmel*, trans. C. J. T. Talar and Elizabeth Emery (Eugene, Ore.: Pickwick, 2012).

On June 17, 1893, Maurice Blondel defended at the Sorbonne his doctoral dissertation, *L'Action: Essai d'une critique de la vie et d'une science de la pratique*.[35] In *L'Action* Blondel is concerned with the problem of human destiny, the meaning of life, a problem of paramount interest to philosophy. Through examination of various possible solutions to this problem, in the course of which the insufficiency of each possibility is uncovered, one arrives at the idea of God and at the logical necessity of a supernatural end. But if this destiny is indeed supernatural, then it is impossible for humanity to reach its necessary end by its own powers—otherwise the supernatural would not be gratuitous, would not be supernatural. Thus while philosophy leads to the idea of the Christian supernatural as necessary, it recognizes that it is powerless to affirm its reality. The philosophy of insufficiency leads to the insufficiency of philosophy.

L'Action provided a focal point for Catholics who were attempting to advance a new method of apologetics as well as those who reiterated the essential soundness of the traditional approach. While intended primarily as a philosophical work, *L'Action* had an apologetic aim. In its analysis of human destiny it took the human subject as its point of departure through the fundamental category of action.

While Catholic reaction to Blondel's thesis was generally favorable, his approach was understood by some Catholics as pragmatic or as psychological rather than resolutely philosophical.

Three years later Blondel attempted to draw out implications of this philosophy of action for Catholic apologetics and to correct misreadings via the *Lettre sur les exigences de la pensée contemporaine en matière d'apologétique*, known more succinctly as the *Lettre* of 1896.[36] In attempting to dispel misunderstandings of his project on the part of those who were looking for alternatives to the traditional approach, he evoked another set

35. Blondel, *L'Action: Essai d'une critique de la vie et d'une science de la pratique*, Ph.D. diss. (Paris: Sorbonne, 1893); English translation: *Action* (1893), trans. Olive Blanchette (Notre Dame, Ind.: University of Notre Dame Press, 1984). Critical expositions of *L'Action* may be found in James M. Somerville, *Total Commitment: Blondel's "L'Action"* (Washington, D.C.: Corpus, 1968) and, much earlier, in Josef de Tonquédec, *Immanence: Essai critique sur la doctrine de Maurice Blondel* (Paris: Beauchesne, 1913).

36. Blondel's *Lettre* was originally published in the *Annales de philosophie chrétienne*, January to July 1896, and reprinted in *Les premiers écrits de Maurice Blondel* (Paris: Presses Universitaires de France, 1956); English translation: *A Letter on the Requirements of Contemporary Thought and on Philosophical Method in the Study of the Religious Problem*, in *Maurice Blondel: The Letter on Apologetics and History and Dogma*, ed. Alexander Dru and Illtyd Trethowan (London: Harvill Press, 1964).

of misinterpretations from some of its defenders. In an early response published in the *Revue Thomiste*, Blondel was labeled by turns "neo-Kantian," "idealist," "subjectivist," "solipsist," and "rationalist," while his study is said to abound with "heretical, erroneous, or audacious propositions"[37]—objections that will be raised repeatedly in subsequent controversy.[38]

George Tyrrell's relation to Blondel and the apologetic of immanence is nicely captured by Oliver Rafferty:

> The idea of immanence was important for Tyrrell and the other Modernists as enabling the communication of Catholic truth in a post-Kantian age. Like Blondel, Tyrrell believed that the will rather than the intellect provided the basis on which to express the inner striving for God. What Tyrrell then actually proposed was a move away from the idea that faith was grounded on unchanging exterior propositions about God which were guaranteed by hierarchical authority. Instead he propounded a view that faith was best seen as an interior response to God predicated on human experience.[39]

In his own day Tyrrell was a popular spiritual writer, and in his earlier theology especially he sought to find a balance between experience and understanding, devotion as the "internal" component in religious experience and theology as the "external" component. He was concerned that the conventional theology and spirituality in the Catholicism of his time were not meeting the needs of "modern" Catholics. In the turn to human experience as a primary and a viable theological category, Tyrrell departed from the neo-Scholasticism then dominant and raised the problem of subjectivity. In seeking an alternative to a propositional view of revelation, in his sensitivity to the cultural contexts in which faith was expressed, he took on issues emerging from modern historical consciousness that were engaging Loisy, Lagrange, and others.

In order to avoid Jesuit censorship Tyrrell published *Religion as a Factor of Life* (1902) under the pseudonym "Dr. Ernest Engels." He described it as "an amalgam of Loisy, Blondel, [Hugo] Munsterberg [*sic*], [Rudolf]

37. M. B. Schwalm, "Les illusions de l'idéalisme et leurs dangers pour la foi," *Revue Thomiste* 4 (1896): 413–41.

38. René Virgoulay, *Blondel et le modernisme* (Tournai: Casterman, 1979) presents Blondel's writings and their reception in detail.

39. "Introduction" to *George Tyrrell and Catholic Modernism*, ed. Oliver Rafferty (Dublin: Four Courts Press, 2010), 11–12; see also David Schultenover, *George Tyrrell: In Search of Catholicism* (Shepherdstown, W.Va.: Patmos Press, 1981), 188–245, for extensive treatment of Tyrrell's philosophy of religion.

Eucken,"[40] and, he could have added, his reading of spiritual classics and secondary works on mysticism. Collectively, these various sources served to emphasize the importance of will and feelings in religion as well as intellect, of the inadequacies of the intellect in representing reality, and of the subordinate and instrumental role of the latter in moral development and in fostering the relationship with God and with others.[41] Situating religion within this constellation of factors opened Tyrrell to charges similar to those earlier directed at Blondel—as the first of the two essays on Tyrrell in this volume by Eugène Franon illustrates.[42] Tyrrell judged *Religion as a Factor of Life* to be of such significance that he revised it in ways to pass Jesuit censorship and was able to publish it as *Lex Orandi* in 1903. Since large portions of its predecessor volume were incorporated into *Lex Orandi*, the identity of Tyrrell as the author of both volumes was patent. Franon's second critical article is a natural sequel to the first.[43]

In stigmatizing Modernism as "the synthesis of all heresies," *Pascendi* (no. 39) was signaling that this assault on Catholic orthodoxy proceeded along a broad front. At stake was not a denial of one or even several dogmas of the Church, but the very nature of dogma itself. Concerns over symbolic interpretations of dogma that had surfaced in the work of Loisy, Tyrrell, and others took on a new immediacy after the publication of Édouard Le Roy's article on dogma that appeared in 1905. As with Loisy, Tyrrell and a number of others who ultimately received ecclesiastical censure, Le Roy did not initially set out to undermine Catholic teaching but to defend it—

40. Letter of January 3, 1902, written to Friedrich von Hügel, cited in Schultenover, *George Tyrrell*, 188, to which he could have added Henri Bergson. Schultenover gives details of what Tyrrell read of their works and what he derived from them.

41. For a careful analysis of Tyrrell's argument in *Religion as a Factor of Life* (Exeter and London: William Pollard, n.d.), see Schultenover, *George Tyrrell*, 208–36.

42. Eugène Franon was director of the seminary of the Institut catholique of Toulouse and a regular contributor to the *Bulletin de littérature ecclésiastique* on philosophical subjects. Prior to his death in 1913 he taught at the Toulouse Institut for thirteen years, acquiring a reputation as a staunch defender of Catholic truth and its moral consequences. He was the principal refuter of Tyrrell's ideas in France; Raoul Gout, *L'Affaire Tyrrell* (Paris: Librairie Critique Émile Nourry, 1909), 93.

43. At the time of the first article's appearance, Tyrrell enjoyed a growing reputation in France. He appeared as the heir to Newman, and his books were translated and read avidly. To those impressed by Tyrrell's gifts as a writer on spirituality, Franon's initial article appeared harsh and exaggerated. The second article, which named Tyrrell explicitly, formed part of the larger defense mobilized by the Toulouse Institut against ideas that threatened to overrun Catholic thought. In a later article, "Le cas du Père Tyrrell," published in the Toulouse *Bulletin* in 1911, Franon found vindication of his earlier critical stance in the condemnations issued by the Vatican in the interval; La rédaction, "Monsieur Eugène Franon," *Bulletin de littérature ecclésiastique* 5 (1913): 176–81.

in his case, defending the faith against a positivism that would render a religious metaphysic superfluous.

Le Roy viewed himself as making common cause with Blondel and, by association, with Lucien Laberthonnière, whose "moral dogmatism" was seen to be closely allied with the Blondelian position. Taking note of a situation in which the very notion of dogma was repugnant to modern contemporaries (a state of affairs acknowledged by Léonce de Grandmaison in his critical response),[44] Le Roy set out to propose an understanding of dogma that would rectify it.

The proposed solution is based on the primacy of action. Dogmas became for him primarily rules of practical conduct, practical guides to the spirit and conduct of the religious life, whose value is religious and not speculative. Contrary to the intellectualist position that placed primacy on dogma as a revelation adding to speculative knowledge, and only consequently and derivatively making claims on life, he stressed the living, active side of Christianity. Thus, for example, the dogma of the resurrection does not add to our knowledge of the new life that Jesus lived after death or provide information on the manner of transformation of the old life into the new. Rather, it prescribes a guide for living, specifically a mode of relationship with Christ in the life of the believer.

Le Roy did admit a theoretical character to dogma, but submitted it to the practical order. Namely, dogmas have a negative value on the speculative level: if they cannot offer positive knowledge, say, of the nature of Christ's resurrected life or of the means by which that unique transformation was accomplished, they are at least able to exclude or condemn certain positions as erroneous. To extend the example, if the dogma of the resurrection of Jesus does not provide positive content, it does importantly deny that his action in the world ended with his death and rejects any notion that Jesus' present action on the world is similar to that of any long-dead figure whose influence remains living and effective.[45]

44. Loisy acknowledged Grandmaison as a fair-minded critic, characterizing his response to *L'Évangile et l'Église* as "quite sensible and moderate, in no way flattering, but written in a dignified manner by a man with whom I could have entered into a discussion"; Loisy, *My Duel with the Vatican*, 229–30. Grandmaison's article appeared in *Études* in January 1903. On Grandmaison, see Jules Lebreton, *Le Père Léonce de Grandmaison* (Paris: Gabriel Beauchesne, 1932).

45. Édouard Le Roy, "Qu'est-ce qu'un dogme?," republished in *Dogme et critique*, 1–35. Guy Mansini relates Le Roy's position to those of Loisy, Blondel, and Laberthonnière in *"What Is a Dogma?" The Meaning and Truth of Dogma in Edouard Le Roy and His Scholastic Opponents.*

As with Tyrrell, this approach to dogma privileges intuition, will, feeling, and action. As such it represents an attempt to overcome at the theological level problems raised by the heavily speculative approach inherent in the dominant theology and at the philosophical level the dualism consequent upon the Kantian philosophy.

Connections between Le Roy's position and those of Loisy and the "philosophers of 'immanence'"—Blondel and Laberthonnière—were not lost on Portalié, who crafted a response to "Qu'est-ce qu'un dogme?" In departing from the secured philosophical foundations of Scholasticism in favor of Bergson's philosophy, Le Roy is faulted for not having overcome Kantianism but instead having fallen victim to its subjectivism.

Among the critical responses to Le Roy, that by Joannès Wherlé is particularly noteworthy, given his close association with Blondel.[46] In the course of a critique of Le Roy, Wehrlé defends the legitimacy of Blondel's apologetic approach. Making a distinction between a doctrine of immanence (which is not acceptable) and a method of immanence (which, as practiced by Blondel, is), Wehrlé contends that it is possible to begin with the subject and yet not compromise the objective transcendent order. He also supports Blondel's opposition to intellectualism, contrasting what he finds to be a one-sided reaction on the part of Le Roy with "a remarkably balanced system which preserves the equilibrium between thought and action, knowledge and practice, metaphysics and morals, dogma and religious experience" in Blondel's work.[47]

✳

Several things occur when we go back, not only to the Modernists themselves, but to some of their more noteworthy critics. The seriousness with which the critiques were undertaken and especially the occasional stridency of tone serve as a reminder of the proportions of the "crisis" in the "Modernist Crisis." In their perception nothing less than the very integrity and future of Catholicism was at stake.

These critics also serve as a counterpoint to the rather monolithic impression of Modernism as portrayed in *Pascendi* and to any tendency to

46. Under the editorship of Henri de Lubac, two volumes of correspondence between Blondel and Wehrlé were published as *Maurice Blondel-Joannès Wehrlé: Correspondance* (Paris: Aubier, 1969). On Wehrlé, see Émile Poulat, *La Question religieuse et ses turbulences au XXe siècle* (Paris: Berg International, 2005), 127–29.

47. See "What Is a Dogma?" in this volume.

view it as a snapshot taken through the lens of the encyclical. Positions developed over time, even over the relatively short span of some two decades prior to 1907. In the 1890s it is still possible to discern a sort of middle ground in biblical scholarship in which a degree of consensus on biblical inspiration, non-Mosaic authorship of the Pentateuch, and a number of other issues is still present.[48] At the point at which the initial critical pieces in this volume appear, a growing radicalization of exegetical conclusions and a more radical reconstruction of Christian origins and development are breaking through in Loisy's work, evoking reservations on the part of Catholic progressives and attempts to distinguish a legitimate use of historical criticism from applications corrosive of Catholic Tradition. In these earlier articles the development of dogma is a prominent issue, together with implications of that development for what dogma represents. While "dogmatic evolutionism" remains a concern, in the later critical responses the emphasis shifts to more professedly philosophical treatments of the nature of dogma itself. Even here, areas of disagreement between Le Roy and George Fonsegrive are brought to light in Portalié's contribution,[49] and in Wehrlé's article precisions on where partisans of an apologetics of immanence stood with respect to Le Roy have been noted.

Despite attempts to discriminate among reformist agendas, partisans of more moderate positions like Lagrange, Batiffol, and Wehrlé were not always successful in conveying important distinctions. *Pascendi* cited "grave reason to complain that there are Catholics who, while rejecting immanence as a doctrine, employ it as a method of apologetics" (no. 37). Batiffol's study on the development of the real presence and transubstantiation in the Eucharist suffered from identification with rationalist treatments of the history of dogma and was placed on the Index in 1907.[50] Although the censure was not made public, he lost his position as rector. Lagrange's writings were subject to strict censorship, a commentary on Genesis on which

48. As Christoph Théobald has argued, the frontiers between Lagrange and Loisy "*were much more permeable, at least between 1890 and 1902, than later polemics let on*"; Théobald, "Le Père Lagrange et le modernisme," *Naissance de la méthode critique*, at 51.

49. George Fonsegrive (1852–1917) edited *La Quinzaine*, in which Le Roy's article on dogma appeared. Fonsegrive's contributions to the issues of the day were multifaceted; they are covered in *George Fonsegrive*, vol. 11 of *Cahiers de la nouvelle journée* (Paris: Bloud and Gay, 1928).

50. Batiffol, *Études d'histoire et de théologie positive*, vol. 2, *L'Eucharistie: La présence réelle et la transubstantiation* (Paris: Lecoffre, 1905); see also C. J. T. Talar, "Newman in France during the Modernist Period: Pierre Batiffol and Marcel Hébert," *Newman Studies Journal* 2, no. 1 (2005): 45–57.

he had labored was denied publication, and the exegete himself was ordered to refrain from publishing anything on the controverted book. Of his situation in 1909 Lagrange later wrote:

> Basically, the danger of our position was that we seemed to be on the same side as those scholars whose abandonment of the faith had saddened the Church. This abandonment was attributed to their critical scholarship, and the conclusion was hastily drawn that there was a premeditated and treacherous plan afoot to drag down the Church to the lowest depths.[51]

The critical essays translated here provide insight into the reception of Modernist ideas in the period just prior to the Vatican condemnations. While Modernism continued to be perceived as a threat after 1907, as is evident from the imposition of an Oath against Modernism in 1910, the First World War brought a different set of concerns to the forefront. In the decades following the war, Catholic interest in Modernism was rather marginal. The Second Vatican Council rekindled interest in the Modernists and their writings, as some of the issues they grappled with resurfaced in conciliar debates and in the council's documents. However, as Ormond Rush points out, "Ironically, just as Roman Catholicism was receiving the elements of modernity judged to be consonant with the Gospel, Western society was entering the yet-to-be-named epoch of what is still vaguely called 'post-modernity.'"[52] The frameworks of meaning have not stood still. This means that the very criticisms surfaced by the critics gathered here themselves have to be recontextualized in the light of theological and cultural changes that have occurred in the interval, and the critics have to be read critically in the light of those changes.

In the end, those involved in the reformist trajectories that constituted Modernism had the courage to grapple with the hard questions, even if they did not always possess resources to answer them adequately. That is worth remembering—and honoring. Moreover, they had the persistence to keep asking the questions and offering solutions, even in face of misunderstanding, discouragement, and sanctions on the part of ecclesiastical authorities. This is as true of some of the critics represented in these essays as it is of acknowledged "Modernists." They personalize the dilemma of the scholar (indeed, of the Catholic) who faces the dilemma of a conflict between fi-

51. Lagrange, *Père Lagrange: Personal Reflections and Memoirs*, 141.
52. Ormond Rush, *Still Interpreting Vatican II* (New York: Paulist, 2004), 20.

delity to one's own integrity and fidelity to one's religious tradition. In that case, what is to be done? The figures who are remembered for their roles in the Modernist Crisis do not present an algorithmic solution so much as a series of *exempla*, each with its own cost. If indeed, as Newman demonstrated in the *Apologia*, truth at times is better demonstrated through narrating a life than through "paper logic," then these lives are worth revisiting by those who seek their own integrity in the midst of a Church still marked by contested frames of meaning.

part 1

critical responses to alfred loisy's *l'évangile et l'église*

Bulletin de littérature ecclésiastique 5 (January 1903): 3–15

1

"THE GOSPEL AND THE CHURCH"

Pierre Batiffol

It is a scholarly thing to distinguish three possible attitudes of a believer toward Christianity, whatever his denomination. First, there is the ecclesiastical attitude. Once the fact of divine revelation has been admitted, it accepts the interpretation that centuries of reflection and experience have made of it, constructing a dogmatic, sacramental, and social system; and it attributes to this construction an authority of divine law. With some fairly deep variations, this is the attitude of all the Churches—of the Church of Rome, for example, and of High-Church Anglicanism.

Then there is the attitude of subjectivistic Protestantism developed after Kant (for one must distinguish this new Protestantism from the Protestant orthodoxy of yesteryear, which, by the very fact that it was an orthodoxy, was more ecclesiastical than it thought it was). The new Protestantism repudiates all metaphysics and takes refuge in the categories of experience and action; it strips Christianity of its "shell" of theory, so as to leave only a practical "kernel," which alone (it holds) is religious. This is the attitude of Ritschl and his school; it is the German formula for evangelical liberalism.

Finally, there is the attitude that wants to give itself the honorific title "scientific." It wants to adopt a purely phenomenal point of view. Christianity is seen as historical in its origins and in all its successive expressions; it is subject to a law of development by which its formation is explained and its future is predicted. Being thus analogous to all the religions that have turned up in past history, Christianity is (like them) nothing more than an ephemeral and symbolic expression of the unknowable. Inspired by [Herbert] Spencer, this attitude is the Anglo-Saxon formula for evangelical liberalism.

Those who have the ecclesiastical attitude (which, if left to its own devices, is "intransigent") are always being solicited these days to go either in the Ritschlian direction or the Spencerian direction—solicited by minds who are troubled to see Christianity "isolating itself" from the general movement of contemporary thought and science. To this religious sense of feeling troubled one must attribute initiatives like that of Mr. Blondel and his friends, aiming to reconcile Kantian subjectivism and Catholicism—as well as the initiative of Mr. Loisy and his group, aiming to reconcile Spencerian evolutionism with the same Catholicism.

I should not like to say categorically that such initiatives are inopportune or in vain. I am convinced that Church doctrine cannot be in conflict with reason and science and that adaptation of doctrine to progress is made by a thousand individual experiments, not all of them successful. One should forbid oneself to see conspiracies and treasons in these experiments; each of them is rather a sort of *irenicon* [an olive branch] and, even if it weren't, charity would always persuade one to think it so. For those of us who demur from these experiments, however, the critical mind retains every right to discuss them.

*

Mr. Loisy's *irenicon* is less new than one might be inclined to believe, since it was anticipated several years ago by Fr. Margival's *Essai sur Richard Simon*,[1] and also by a series of articles in which Loisy himself discussed the principles of a philosophy of religion in commenting on [Prof. August] Sabatier's *Esquisse*.[2] But the book that Mr. Loisy has just published is his most

1. I think I was the first and (apart from a prophetic judgment by Sabatier) the only one to notice where the *Essai sur Richard Simon* was tending; Pierre Batiffol, "À propos de Richard Simon," *Bulletin de littérature ecclésiastique* 2 (1900): 257–68. [The full title of Henri Margival's book was *Essai sur Richard Simon et la critique biblique au XVIIe siècle* (Paris: Maillet, 1900).—Tr.]

2. Alfred Loisy [writing as Firmin], "Le théorie individualiste de la religion," *Revue du clergé*

far-reaching exposition of his principles and their application to Catholicism; it is also the most troubling.[3] If these principles and these views have a future, his little book will mark an epoch in the history of Catholicism. But just as truly, if his little book (along with its more judicious imitators) *misconceives* the Gospel or the development of the Church or the value of Christianity, few things will be more deplorable than these new "memories of Assisi."[4] The alternative is no less drastic.

[Adolf von] Harnack's book, *The Essence of Christianity* [*Das Wesen des Christentums* Leipzig: Hinrichs'sche Buchhandlung, 1900], provided Loisy with a theme and an occasion to write his own.[5] You may recall that the lectures of the great Berlin historian were grouped around two topics: the Gospel within the Gospels and the Gospel in history.[6] Loisy has now taken his turn to treat the same two topics.

On the first, Loisy has too refined a sense of history to grant Harnack's claim that the Gospel can be reduced to a single formula that (as it happens) agrees with the Ritschlian philosophy of religion. In effect, Harnack conceived the essential Gospel of Jesus Christ as limited to affirming God's fatherhood and the infinite dignity of the human soul. This was saying too little, surely; for while this religious minimum matches a certain modern state of mind, it cannot be said to have been identical historically with the faith that generated Christianity. Harnack was arbitrary, then, in reducing the message of Jesus to this abstraction, which is only a quintessence of the message (chosen with the most modern taste).

But is Loisy any less of a systematizer when he wants to see in the message of Jesus a pure and simple apocalypse? We were pleased to see that Harnack continued to place himself among the exegetes who take the

---

français 17 (1899): 202–15. [Prof. August Sabatier's full title was *Esquisse d'une philosophie de la religion* (Paris: Fischbacher, 1897.—Tr.]

3. Loisy, *L'Évangile et l'Église* (Paris: Picard, 1902). [Page citations in the texts and footnotes of this and succeeding selections are to this first edition.—Tr.]

4. [Batiffol is alluding to the "symbolist" pamphlet *Souvenirs d'Assise*, printed secretly by Fr. Marcel Hébert, who was the center of a scandal after his authorship was discovered.—Tr.]

5. [Adolf von Harnack, *Das Wesen des Christentums* (Leipzig: Hinrichs, 1900); a French translation had also appeared: *L'Essence du Christianisme* (Paris: Fischbacher, 1902.—Tr.] See the reviews by the Catholic critics who have spoken out in France: M.-J. Lagrange, *Revue biblique* 10 (January 1901) and 11 (July 1902) and Léonce de Grandmaison, *Etudes* (March 10, 1902). The *Revue du clergé français* contented itself with a synopsis by Mr. Labourt (April 15, 1901).

6. Here and in subsequent selections, the word "gospel" with a small "g" refers to the Jesus-event and its oral transmission prior to the canonical Gospels.

Kingdom of God announced by Jesus to be something *other* than eschatological expectancy. "We have no wish," Harnack wrote, "to strip Jesus' preaching of its tone and color, to transform it into a simple moral outline; but, on the other hand, we have no wish to join those who dissolve his preaching into the popular conceptions of his era. The way Jesus *selected* among the ideas of his time already shows that He spoke with a profound consciousness." Thereupon Harnack, along with some of the weightiest critics of our day,[7] held that the message of Jesus set aside all the popular, apocalyptic representations of the Kingdom so as to unveil for us its arrival as planned by God. Jesus took the consciousness of his Galileans, such as it was, and elevated it, from parable to parable, up to conceiving the will of the Father, conceiving confidence in this attentive will of the One who sees what is hidden, conceiving man's dependence on Him, and the hatred of evil.... There you see already some religious ideas that are stripped of all eschatology. And for the fact that these thoughts were the center of Jesus' preaching, we have undeniable proof in the fact that a text guaranteeing us the *ipsissima verba* of the Savior—the most authentic there can be, the text of the Our Father—adds no further comment beyond entreating the Kingdom to come. But Loisy tries to hold that Jesus had nothing but an eschatology, or conditioned all his preaching upon eschatology. The Savior spoke to a world convinced that it was close to ending. His message did not go beyond announcing the Kingdom as "close at hand" and exhorting people to repentance so as to have a share in the Kingdom as an objective and imminent reality.

Loisy systematizes in a similar way the witness of Jesus about Himself.

7. See *Theologische Rundschau* (November 1902): 437ff. See Harnack, *Das Christentum und die Geschichte* (Leipzig: Hinrichs'sche Buchhandlung, 1906), 16: "Allein es wurde doch nur dann etwas an seiner Giltigkeit und Kraft verlieren, wenn sich nachweisen ließe, daß nun der Kern der Erscheinung und der Sinn und der eigentliche Treffpunkt der Reden ein anderer geworden ist. Ich kann nicht finden, daß die geschichtliche Kritik daran irgend etwas geändert hat. Dasselbe gibt von seinem Selbstzeugnis. Ja, wenn die geschichtliche Forschung nachgewiesen hätte, daß er ein apokalyptischer Schwärmer oder ein Träumer gewesen ist, dessen Wort und Bild erst durch die Sublimierung der Folgezeit auf die Hohe reiner Absichten und erhabener Gedanken gebracht worden sei, dann stände es anders. Aber wer hat das nachgewiesen, und wie könnte es nachweisen?" [The only way the Gospel would lose something of its validity and power would be if it could be proved that the heart of the Jesus-event, its meaning, and the genuine force of His sayings, has become different. I cannot find that historical criticism has made any difference on that score. Ditto for His self-testimony. To be sure, if historical research had proved that He was an apocalyptic zealot or dreamer, whose word and image was raised up to purer perspectives and nobler thoughts by a sublimation process in later times, the case would be different. But who has proved such a thing, and how could it be proved?—Tr.]

Harnack had strongly emphasized that the message of the Kingdom was inseparable in Jesus' mind from the relation of His own person to the Kingdom or to God. It was not possible to separate the message of Jesus from His message about Himself. Harnack had refused to subscribe to the judgment of Wellhausen and other critics, who had doubted that Jesus presented Himself as the Messiah. It is incontestable, indeed, that Jesus saw Himself as the Messiah. But the doctrine of Jesus about Himself, like His message about the Kingdom, had set aside all the messianism of his race and time. "Jesus was and was not the Messiah," Harnack was able to write; "He was not, because He left messianism far behind Him, because He filled it with a content that exploded it." Loisy does not understand things that way. To be sure, he rejects the theory [of Wrede] that tried to make affirming Jesus' messianic status a theme introduced by early Christian preaching and tried to interpret the Savior's reserve in the synoptics as an absolute silence on the question of His messianic status. But because Loisy has given an exclusively eschatological character to the Kingdom, he is obliged to conceive the Messiah eschatologically. "The role of the Messiah," he says, "is essentially eschatological ... in one sense, Jesus was the Messiah, and in another sense he was not *yet* the Messiah. He was, insofar as he was personally called to rule the New Jerusalem. He was not yet, because the New Jerusalem did not exist yet, and the messianic power had no scope for its exercise. Jesus had before him the prospectus for his own future." So, far from setting aside popular messianism (as surely the scene of the temptation in the desert should have made clear), far from exploding this messianism through a consciousness (perceptible to all) of having authority of another order and having a role of another order (as is proved by the memory preserved by the ones who ate and drank with Him), Jesus was the prisoner of an illusion common to him and his poor listeners; he believed himself to be the Messiah on the same terms as Judas the Gaulonite managed to convince himself that he was the Messiah.

There you have "that which Jesus believed and declared himself to be." As for knowing "what interior struggle led him to this conclusion"—that is a point on which "one can only make a guess," Loisy assures us (49). Harnack spoke more religiously: "It is Jesus' secret, and no psychology can penetrate it." But Loisy goes on to penetrate it. And here is the "guess" he makes:

As to the origin of the messianic consciousness in the soul of Jesus, one cannot deduce it with certitude from the texts. The oldest tradition seems to have explained it (or pictured it) by a revelation [the Father's voice saying "This is my son"] that was supposedly given on the occasion of his baptism in the Jordan. This may have been an effect of perspective, although this circumstance of baptism no doubt marked a decisive moment in the savior's career (56).

We hardly dare interpret this sentence; but while Loisy disguises his boldest affirmations under silken phraseology, he did not fail in this case to interpret himself. "The texts," he says,

do not permit a psychological analysis of the notion of "Son of God." Jesus called himself the unique Son of God to the extent that he avowed himself to be Messiah. The historian will conclude tentatively that he believed he was Son of God after he believed himself to be the Messiah (57).

The earliest stratum of tradition puts this moment at the baptism in the Jordan.

It is not our job to pin a label of ecclesiastical censure on this interpretation of the Savior's message and consciousness. It is enough for us to say that Loisy wants to prove a thesis for which he needs the gospel to be reduced to "nothing new" vis-à-vis the religion of the prophets. For him, then, the gospel is reduced to a Judaic datum, purely Judaic. *And the historical implausibility is that this datum is no longer pregnant with Christianity.* If the message and the consciousness of Jesus were to have been what Loisy says, one must search elsewhere than in the gospel for the origin of Christianity. It will have been born (not from imposture, of course, but) from illusion and from the enthusiasm of the disciples.

These disciples, however, and it's a strange thing, were already a society. In an unexpected contradiction, Loisy recognizes that this society was organized in some way by Jesus himself. One can guess that Loisy took pleasure in refuting Harnack on the point that the essence of Christianity was not so abstract as the latter wanted to make it and that already in the gospel there appeared the first outlines of its future catholicization. Indeed, the disciples who surrounded Jesus formed a society no less visible, no less real than the Roman Church, says Loisy, in a spiritual vein. This society was not "formed of pure spirits who had no other bond between them than shared sentiment," be it the sentiment of God's fatherhood and the infinite value of the human soul, or be it (we should like to add) the sentiment of religious dynamism that Jesus had initiated. This society was a visible group, centralized, even hierarchicalized, in which Jesus was the center and the "undisputed authority"; Jesus had joined the Twelve to his ministry; and among the Twelve, "there was one who was first ... by a sort of designation from the master, who had accepted this role and whose consequences are still being felt in history." That was a de facto organization, but "a certain time before the passion, it saw itself as finished and ratified by Jesus ... it was a society of men, a society that bore the gospel and that had to become the Kingdom" (91). When Loisy grants us this de facto organization, when he grants that this de facto organization was ratified—was it only ratified?—by the Savior, when he grants that it bore the gospel and was the preparation for the Kingdom, aren't we entitled to say that Loisy is right, but that he is now discovering in the gospel an element for which his own analysis of Jesus' thinking about the Kingdom and Himself provided no clue?

It is true that Loisy erases these outlines almost as soon as he lets us see them. But how else can we understand what he says about this embryonic Church—namely, that she had "from her faith in Jesus" the source of the "distinctive life that is in her and gives her subsistence." She is thus exterior to Jesus. And if I am understanding him right, the Savior will have endowed her with a religious current of incalculable energy, while being Himself a current in the opposite direction! "Jesus announced the Kingdom, and the Church is what came" (111).

Quite clearly, then, what made for continuity from the gospel to the Church was not a sameness of thought. The gospel of Jesus was an eschatological expectation, while the Church was a society that organized itself to last. I *do* see in the Church a continuation from the hope of the Kingdom, a continuation of faith in the Messiah, a continuation of preaching and the apostolate—no doubt. But [according to Loisy] the object of this hope, of this faith, and of this preaching was not the object announced, affirmed, and preached by Jesus. Continuity of life was achieved without continuity of what Newman called the "original type."[8] "Jesus announced the Kingdom, and the Church is what came."

This gap is not an obstacle for Loisy, because he does not have the same

8. [What John Henry Newman meant by "type" and how continuity of type functioned as one of his criteria for the genuineness of an alleged development; see his *Essay on the Development of Christian Doctrine* (London: Toovey, 1845), republished by Penguin (Baltimore: 1974), 116–24.—Tr.]

theory of development as Newman had. We shall try to sketch his theory as objectively as possible.

"Let us not grow weary of repeating," he wrote, that "the Gospel was *not* an absolute and abstract doctrine directly applicable to all times and all peoples thanks to its own power; it was a living faith engaged in all its parts with the era and the environment where it was born; a work of adaptation was and will always be necessary if this faith is to preserve itself in the world" (124). This living faith cut itself loose from the Jewish eschatology within which the thinking of Jesus had moved. "The first change, the most decisive and the most important change, and also perhaps the most rapid" that gospel Christianity underwent "is the one that turned a Jewish movement based on the idea of a Messianic reign into a religion acceptable to the Graeco-Roman world and to humanity" (134). "The Pauline theory of salvation was indispensable in its time, if Christianity was not to remain a Jewish sect with no future" (136). Then, "Progressively but early on ... the Greek interpretation of Christian messianism appeared, and the Christ ... became the Word made flesh. The divinity of Christ, the incarnation of the Word, was the only suitable way to translate the idea of the Messiah into Greek understanding" (140). "The dogma of grace is no more explicitly taught in the gospel than the Christological dogma" (155). "The dogma of grace is an interpretation of messianic salvation and of heavenly-kingdom theology" (156). "The conceptions which the Church presents as revealed dogmas are not truths that fell from heaven and were kept by religious tradition in the precise form in which they first appeared. The historian sees here the interpretation of religious facts, acquired by a laborious effort of theological thought" (159). These quotations, which we could multiply, can be defended, because they contain a part of the truth insofar as they express the development of revelation in the New Testament and the development of dogmatic formulae in the Church. Within these limits, Cardinal Newman (or a theologian of his school) could accept them.[9] But Loisy, who in this respect is faithful to a rather Scholastic methodology, admits separate doctrinal strata, not only in the Apostles' theology but also in that of the

9. Rev. Fr. [André] de la Barre [SJ], *La vie du dogme catholique* (Paris: Lethielleux, 1898), 145ff; Archbishop [Eudòxe-Irénée-Edouard] Mignot, "L'Évolutionnisme religieux," in the *Correspondant* (April 10, 1897), 85ff; Msgr. [Louis-Marie-Olivier] Duchesne, *Témoins anténicéens du dogme de la Trinité* (Amiens: 1883), 4ff.

synoptics and even in the gospel parables, and so he has blocked himself from admitting a development of Newman's kind.[10] For him, soteriology and Christology are just so many *dated* theological interpretations of the initial idea of "messianic Kingdom" expressed by Jesus. (It would be a good exercise to attack this stratification idea from a historical point of view.) Hypothetically, we could say *transeat*—but on one condition—namely, that there was not more in the interpretation than there was in the original, and that Jewish imagery was not poorer in content than the Hellenic metaphysics that "translated" it. After all, if you do not wish to see anything but "adaptations" in the New Testament or in the Church, then if the original datum has been denatured in this laborious effort of adaptation, the latter is no longer "development" in Newman's sense, but transformism.

What confirms our thinking that there has been a misunderstanding between Newman and his subtle interpreter [Loisy] is the fact that the latter does not repudiate the total relativism that transformism implies. The laborious effort of adaptation that Loisy describes, by his own admission, comes to nothing but representing "religious facts" intellectually, and every intellectual representation is, of itself, provisional and imperfect. Our most abstract concepts are but metaphors in some fashion, and we recreate our logic and our metaphysics continually. "A considerable change in the state of science can render necessary a new interpretation of the ancient formulae, which, since they were conceived in another intellectual climate, are no longer found to say all that they must, or no longer found to say it suitably" (164). One will be distinguishing, then, between the real sense of the formula and its "properly religious and Christian significance." The "intellec-

10. In his article "An Irenicon from Culture," *Journal of Theological Studies* 3 (January 1902): 229–30, William Sanday summarizes very well what is Scholastic about this method: "It would be wrong to blame Dr. [Percy] Gardener for doing what theologians and critics generally have been in the habit of doing. It has long been their custom to map out the New Testament into a number of *Lehrbegriffe* or strata of doctrine, Pauline, sub-or Deutero Pauline, Petrine, Johannine; to give elaborate analysis of each of these, but to leave the whole of which they are the parts, the common Christianity which they go to form, to take care of itself; and least of all to trouble about the Christianity of the rank and file as distinct from that of the leaders. Only of late is it beginning to be seen that this is a mistaken procedure." Harnack, in *Christentum und Geschichte* [see footnote 7], 16, had already said quite rightly, "Außer den vier geschriebenen Evangelien besitzen wir noch ein fünftes, ungeschriebenes, und es spricht in mancher Hinsicht deutlicher und eindrucksvoller als die vier anderen; ich meine das Gesamtzeugnis der christlichen Urgemeinde." [Besides the four written Gospels, we also have a fifth, an unwritten one, and in many respects it speaks more clearly and impressively than the other four: I am talking about the collective witness of the original Christian community. —Tr.]

tual representation" of the belief, its "verbal expression," is not strictly immutable (166). Otherwise, the living faith would become overloaded with the dregs of the past. "The best apology of a living thing is in its very life" (170). The Gospel was a "living religion," a "movement of limitless power such that those who carried it and those whom it carried had only a partial consciousness of it, and those who try to analyze it today are unable to penetrate all its depth." The "doctrinal efflorescence" of this great life "has gotten to look wilted," but the old tree will be able to "rejuvenate its leafy finery for a new age, as for a new springtime" (171).

What one says in this vein about dogmas one will also say about sacraments and forms of worship. The whole sacramental system of the Church arose spontaneously from the living religion that is Christianity, and it developed like the dogmatic system. Loisy proclaims by analogy that this development is not at an end: "The end is yet to come, since sacramental development can only stop when the Church herself ceases to live." Without predicting otherwise, if we just do not "exaggerate the importance of the work done by Catholic theologians" ... we are permitted to glimpse the future of sacramental theology in the direction of symbolism, as the future of dogmatics is augured in the same direction.

> Christianity has not escaped the need for symbols, which is the normal form of worship as well as of religious knowledge (204).

And elsewhere we read:

> The number, the variety, and even to some extent the quality of the symbols are indifferent things, or secondary things, in themselves; their value lies in the meaning one attaches to them (188).

*

Thus the gospel was an eschatological "expectation." As for the Church, it was an adaptation, a living and continuous correction of this gospel. This adaptation has not said its last word, which will be symbolism. To these three claims one can reduce the doctrine of Loisy's book, as well as the conditions under which he reconciles the gospel, the Church, and contemporary consciousness. "Jesus," he said elsewhere,

> was much less the advocate of a doctrine than the instigator of a religious movement. The movement he started has been perpetuated under the normal conditions of every movement which is fertile within humanity. And while it is still pos-

sible today to feel its influence and spread it, it was impossible even in apostolic times to relive its point of departure.[11]

We think we have indicated sufficiently in the course of our analysis the historical reasons that forbid us to see the "gospel" as a simple apocalypse. As for symbolism, the case for it does not arise from history. It is the temporary refuge in which positivists park their emotion toward the unknowable. As for the work of the Church as Loisy conceives it, a work of collective adaptation, over centuries, anonymous, I must say that I do not see how it differs at bottom from the individual work attempted by Harnack, when he pretended to adapt Christianity to a formula acceptable to students in Berlin in 1900, for which he is so much chided by Loisy: the Church will have modernized the gospel continually by moving away from it. There's nothing left for us to do but move away from it completely, by going over to agnosticism.

With the best will in the world, we will not relive the point of departure—that is, the thought of Jesus. The Master, if we dare still call him by that name, inaugurated a movement that has spread, but not a doctrine that has continued faithful to its original type in the growing specification of its essential traits. If its energy is not exhausted, the movement will pass through the orthodoxies in which tradition once thought to fix it forever. If Catholicism accepts this new dogma, the last dogma, the dogma of development thus understood, it will join up with Sabatier's "faith without belief," with Dreyer's "*undogmatisches Christentum*," and (better yet and for good reason) with the Spencerian agnosticism of Caird.[12]

I shall stop here, and I do not have the courage to put a label on this (I won't say historical criticism—because historical criticism is no longer the issue—but) philosophy of religion.

Christmas 1902

11. Loisy, *Études évangéliques* [Paris: Picard, 1902)], xiii.

12. [The "Caird" meant is the philosopher Edward Caird (1835–1908). He and his older brother John, a clergyman, were important voices for "liberalism" in British Protestantism. At the time of Msgr. Batiffol's writing, Edward was famous for his book *The Evolution of Religion* (Glasgow: James Maclehose and Sons, 1893).—Tr.]

Revue biblique 12 (1903): 292–313

2

REVIEW OF ALFRED LOISY, *L'ÉVANGILE ET L'ÉGLISE*

M.-J. Lagrange

This book is a daring attempt. To engage a great Protestant theologian in debate on his chosen ground, to be even more exacting than he in literary criticism and nevertheless prove to him that the true Gospel of Jesus, in its essence, is found in Catholicism and cannot be defined apart from tradition—in other words, to reconcile the most audacious moves of biblical criticism with the justification for Catholic customs, including popular devotions, like asking St. Anthony of Padua to find lost objects—it is an interesting paradox, carried off with gusto, and many believe victoriously. The edifice of the Berlin theologian, a master in Germany, is supposed to have folded like a house of cards under the blows of a Catholic priest, and this striking triumph is supposed to have been won cheaply enough, at the cost of a few little changes in traditional opinions. It is refreshing to look upon the faith not as an abstract formula but as the ever-expanding religious life of humanity!

In reality, however, no matter how pure the author's intention may have been, Christianity in its entirety has been put in jeopardy and gravely compromised.

This is what several reviewers have tried to make clear.

The *Revue biblique* cannot avoid the same task, unpleasant as it may be. If Mr. Loisy were the only person in question, one would abstain from speaking out altogether. To criticize the work of a Catholic priest who has been condemned by his ordinary—isn't this persecuting a man already smitten? And if this priest has submitted, it is even more odious to attack a person whose character demands as much respect as his learning. But Mr. Loisy, and no doubt he deplores it, has a large following, which is not at all moved by the condemnation placed upon his book. According to his friends, the bishops could condemn him but could not answer him. Each of his opponents is being derided. People even say that Mr. Loisy is the only one writing in pure obedience to his conscience. Hopefully, these partisans will not reproach me for lack of due regard toward an unfortunate man. They are free to pretend, of course, that I have not understood the book (whose secret key they alone seem to possess) any better than others.

In the camp of Loisy's followers, one is not even allowed to mention his theological mistakes—on the ground that Loisy had no intention of doing theology, but rather history. One could smile at this jab at theologians, if it were a question of Babylonian myths. But the best jokes are the shortest, and in order to overlook the invincible fascination that draws Loisy toward theological problems, one must never have read two lines by him. Indeed, one of the seductive traits of his marvelous talent is the instinct that draws him toward divine things. One must say the same to the people who consider Loisy an able exegete but think it deplorable that he did not craft a better theology. If only he had been their pupil! They take pains not to notice that Mr. Loisy knows Scholastic and even positive theology as well as they do; but he has learned many other things as well, and it seems to him that these other things, which he thinks solid, require considerable changes in theology. This he lets us know while paying boundless respect to the edifice of theology as we have it, as the best that could have been built (on certain premises and given certain needs). Loisy will permit us, then, to try to clarify the theology that his book contains. We can only do so by deductions, and he has announced that one should not judge him by what one deduces from his book, but by his own words. It is just too bad that we have at our service no other intellectual tool but reasoning. Loisy's own historical views seldom are, and seldom can be, anything but deductions drawn from the texts, and it must be allowable to treat his own text in the same way.

*

Loisy never says what, for him, the person of Jesus Christ *is*. One should therefore presume that he recognizes Christ's divinity, as the whole Church does. On the other hand, he has neatly determined *what* Jesus *could not* have been—given the idea that He fashioned of the Kingdom of God, of which He was the principal vicar—given what the title "Son of God" meant for Him—given the primitive Church and the writings of the New Testament. (Loisy insinuates here and there what Jesus could still be for us.) The apparent upshot of all this, unfortunately, whatever the personal faith of the author, is that divine status landed upon Jesus Christ only belatedly, as a development (oh, very legitimate), and without a substantial change of dogma! People less versed in the subtleties of exegesis will conclude that He was not God at all.

We shall go through these points in order to examine in reverse the proofs that Loisy has brought forward. This is most assuredly the main part of the book. We do not intend to examine all its propositions, and especially we shall not linger over the chapters on the Church and on worship, whose entire content depends upon these prior issues. What does the façade matter if it has no foundation?

The Kingdom.—At a certain point Loisy makes this remark:

> Shouldn't we say that all heresies are born of deductions pursued one-sidedly, from a point of tradition or of knowledge isolated from all the rest, set up as an absolute truth, and upon which one has built up conclusions incompatible with the general harmony of traditional religion and teaching?[1]

Aside from the talk of heresy (which one ought to reserve for those in authority), this is exactly the procedure followed by the author. The point of tradition isolated from all the rest, set up as an absolute truth, and to which everything else is subordinated (not by speculative reasoning, but by practicing historical criticism one-sidedly) is *the eschatological idea of the Kingdom of God*. And it is here, in this deductive rigor, wrapped in a clear and pleasant style, that one must look for the success of this book. The young

1. Loisy, *L'Évangile et l'Église* (Paris: Picard, 1902), 143.

readers who have thought they could applaud the author's biblical criticism—have they given themselves the trouble to follow his arguments with the Gospels in hand? It is rather to be feared that they have yielded unwittingly to the influence of an aprioristic education. What has seduced them is a new theology nicely deduced, and they will no doubt find it ugly to combat this theology with the nitpicking of meticulous biblical criticism!

Still, let us go back to the "Kingdom of God," which contains the very essence of Christianity.

It is hard to get one's hands on the author's thought. When he is proving to Harnack that the Kingdom of heaven is not entirely interior, the argumentation seems to be based completely on an exegesis [of the Gospels] that is not only traditional but almost popular: one reads "the Kingdom of God" while thinking of Paradise; it was for the sake of this blessed Kingdom that Jesus preached renunciation and love. One notices also at the beginning of the chapter an excellent formula:

> In the Gospel, the national element has disappeared; being an Israelite is no longer, of itself, a title to the Kingdom; the eschatological element ceases to fill the entire horizon, and the religious and moral element is seen to predominate.[2]

But one has to read between the lines: "the Gospel" is not synonymous with "the thought of Jesus." So one need not be surprised that, after this passage, the author accentuates beyond all measure the eschatological character of the Kingdom, considered as the imminent arrival of the Messiah on the clouds. As if he enjoyed emphasizing that Jesus Christ's expectation was a fantasy, since it was not realized, Loisy insists that during the first stage, and up until the eve of His death, Jesus did not understand that "coming on the clouds" meant His glorious resurrection, because He did not originally foresee that He had to die before the coming of the Kingdom.

> The gospel as such was just a religious movement that occurred in the bosom of Judaism, to fulfill perfectly its principles and hopes. It would have been inconceivable, therefore, for Jesus to formulate ritual prescriptions before his last hour. He could only have thought of this at the supreme moment, when an immediate accomplishment of the messianic Kingdom was seen to be impossible in Israel, and a different accomplishment (mysterious in his eyes, obtained through the death of the Messiah) remained the last chance for the Kingdom of God on earth.[3]

2. Ibid., 2.
3. Ibid., 181.

So Jesus is supposed to have believed initially that the Kingdom's imminent coming would precede His death, and this is why the author calls into doubt the passages in which Jesus made allusion to that death.

> It is true that, after the confession of Simon Peter, Jesus is represented as instructing his disciples on several occasions about the fate that awaited Him as the Messiah; but, since the general tenor of these discourses (where not a single sentence appears as a formal quotation from the Lord) is based on past events and on the themes of primitive Christian preaching, such an assertion deepens the difficulty rather than clearing it up.[4]

The difficulty is one that the author posed to himself, but he accepts its full force—Jesus never foretold His death as the Messiah, and the reason (as we noted before with this author) is that He believed in His imminent coming as the Messiah, which excluded the very idea of His death. On the very eve of dying, He understood that another prospect was opening up before Him; but until then He had joined His coming inseparably with the end of the world. From this imminent end there proceeded "that supreme indifference towards human interests which is the very foundation of the Gospel." Jesus "was not in revolt against Caesar, but He knew that the power of man was just about finished."[5] This is how the Gospel gets from Loisy a wholly simple and unnuanced character,[6] which one is amazed to find from the pen of a writer who has demonstrated so well elsewhere the complex character of nascent Christianity.

From this first understanding of the Kingdom of God, it follows quite logically that Jesus in no way foresaw the Church, unless it was on the eve of His death, perhaps, in the mysterious prospect into which He plunged, trusting in God. The author has said in clear terms:

> Jesus' horizon did not include directly the idea of founding a new religion, or founding a Church, but always the idea of realizing the Kingdom of heaven.[7]

Since the Kingdom consisted in the glorious arrival of the Messiah upon the clouds, prior to this event there was, properly speaking, no Messiah. It is quite logical.

The Messiah Son of God.—When one asks oneself "what Jesus thought

4. Ibid., 51.
5. Ibid., 31.
6. Ibid., 26.
7. Ibid., 182. "Directly" is a theological precaution that does not go far enough.

He was and declared Himself to be—critical discussion of the gospel sources can furnish indications that are sufficiently solid."[8] Sufficiently clear, too. All things considered, the upshot of the texts is that Jesus believed Himself to be the Messiah. He also believed Himself to be the Son of God. But if Jesus had an exceptional filial sentiment toward God, He did not have a special filial consciousness apart from his messianic consciousness. "Jesus called Himself the unique Son of God to the extent that He avowed Himself to be the Messiah."[9] "He is the Son *par excellence*, not because He has learned to know and reveal the goodness of the Father, but because He is the unique vicar of God for the Kingdom of heaven."[10] What was the Messiah according to Jesus? He was the unique vicar of God for the Kingdom of heaven. This title indicates a function, an employment; in no way does it imply anything supernatural in the man Jesus prior to the moment when He would be invested with this honor.

> The Savior admits that He is the Christ, but to explain His assertion He adds at once: "And ye shall see the Son of man seated at the right hand of the power [i.e., of God] and coming on the clouds of heaven." What identifies the Messiah is precisely this place of honor and this coming on the clouds. Jesus is declaring that He is the Son of man who is to come.[11]
>
> In a sense, Jesus was the Messiah, and in another sense He was not yet. He was, insofar as He was personally called to rule the New Jerusalem. He was not yet, since the New Jerusalem did not exist yet.[12]

All of that is quite clear. Jesus suspected nothing supernatural in His person, unless it was his being *called* to be the Messiah—that is, to be invested by God with the title of the principal agent and vicar of His Kingdom. Strictly speaking, one has to admit that this theory does not amount to a negation of the divine nature of Jesus, since, absolutely speaking, one can conceive of a personal union that was not known to the human understanding of Jesus. On the other hand, Loisy not only denies that the knowledge of Christ was as flawless as the medieval doctors maintained—and one can cite many Fathers on this point—but he also gives Jesus no knowledge of His divine sonship. This is a position that the theologians will know how to censure. But we are not yet at the bottom.

8. Ibid., 49.
9. Ibid., 57.
10. Ibid.
11. Ibid., 54.
12. Ibid., 53.

The faith of the primitive Church.—If Jesus did not suspect His divine sonship other than as a traditional and honorific equivalent of His messianic vocation, how would the primitive Church have pictured it? She herself taught only what emerged from the thinking of Jesus.

One comes to see also that the apostolic Church taught that Jesus became Christ and Lord through the resurrection, that is to say, through His entrance into celestial glory; one also comes to see that the apostolic Church would have awaited His *coming*, that is to say, His coming as the Christ, and not His *return*, since His ministry on earth had not yet been envisaged as a messianic success.[13]

We shall be coming back to this text. We just note here that it excludes from the primitive community all belief in the divinity of Jesus. He became Messiah and hence Son of God through His resurrection—which is not even an implicit faith in the divinity of Jesus. How could this faith have emerged in the primitive Church—which no writings of the New Testament still present in its genuine form? [Loisy answers:] By worship and prayer. This we are told on a page that would have conveyed a very good meaning, if its interpretation had not been conditioned by what preceded it:

Christian piety was always putting the Savior at the highest level of glory, seeking God in him and finding God, adoring him in heaven and trying to imitate his example on earth, drawing its force from this double character of the object worshipped: the divine and the human.[14]

That is the point Christian worship got to. Its point of departure was the Messiah's being invested after the resurrection with the government of the Kingdom.

It was thus quite natural that one would pray to God through Jesus, with Jesus, in Jesus, and it did not take long to pray to Jesus himself (if people were not doing so from the beginning) because he was always with his own, ready to hear them, and he had the power to answer them. There is no conceiving how Christianity could have failed to be the cultus of Christ, and it is in no way temerarious to think this cultus preceded in some measure, sustained, and inspired the work of Christian thought about the person of the Redeemer.[15]

The writings of the N.T.—Up until a certain point, Jesus' resurrection served as the first moment of his messianic dignity. But soon one had to

13. Ibid., 55.

14. Ibid., 207.

15. Ibid., 206f.

go back further and ask oneself whether Jesus did not have already in the course of His mortal life some supernatural quality other than that of "Messiah-designate" and "Messiah to come." People answered in the affirmative. And this is the testimony of Christian consciousness that the New Testament records, the consciousness of Paul and John, passing through Mark and the other synoptics.

From the resurrection, St. Paul goes back to the death. "Paul discovers in the death a meaning and an efficacity that can count independently of the resurrection while still being coordinated with it."[16] This was something new, as the author takes care to tell us in several places.

> But if Jesus was proclaimed Christ and Lord by the first disciples, it was not because of His death,[17] but because of the resurrection, which introduced him into the glory of his messianic vocation;[18]

and again:

> as best one can judge by testimonies more or less influenced by Pauline theology, it was the resurrection alone that made him the Christ and put him on his throne of glory.[19]

The resurrection that made Him the Christ—underline that. In Paul, there was something more: the efficacity of His death. This efficacity presupposed in the living Christ something more than a mere man. Mr. Loisy does not delve into the modalities of this transformation; he told us in his introduction that it was not his intention to be complete on the topic of Christ's divinity. He says, however, "The Pauline theory of salvation was indispensable in its time, if Christianity was not to remain a Jewish sect with no future."[20] Every allusion to a redemption in Mark, then, is attributed to the influence of Paul's theology.

St. John, or rather the Gospel that bears his name, made an even more important step with its doctrine of the Logos. This claim also is none too clear. If it were only a question of [the title] "Logos," one could say in a perfectly good sense, "This is how ... the Christ, Son of God and Son of man, predestined Savior, became the Word made flesh."[21] A theologian dwells

16. Ibid., 73.
17. The point is quite evident, but is there no option but the "horns" of this "dilemma"?
18. Loisy, *L'Évangile et l'Église,* 73.
19. Ibid., 69.
20. Ibid., 136.
21. Ibid., 139.

at length on this "became" as smacking of heresy. If one were to read the phrase in one of the Fathers, one would not be embarrassed and would distinguish "became *quoad nos*." There is no denying that the doctrine of the Logos marked a step forward in the development of Christian doctrine. It seems that the term was unknown to the New Testament writers prior to John's prologue. But what we need to know is whether the new thing here is just the expression "Logos" (as an explication of Jesus' divine person) or is His divinity itself. People were able to go quite correctly from faith in the Son of God to the concept of the Logos, whereas for Mr. Loisy, or rather for the primitive community, the Christ was only the Christ after the resurrection, and was only the Son of God insofar as He was Messiah, and was only the predestined Savior thanks to St. Paul. So where does His being the Word come from? Loisy tells us fairly clearly:

> At the same time, the divinity of Christ, the incarnation of the Word, was the only suitable way to bring the idea of the Messiah into the Greek understanding.[22]

Nevertheless (and for consumption by theologians), the author notes without smiling that if dogmas are divine in origin, they are human in structure, and that this development of dogma entails no substantial change. Will the theologians listen to this song? Simple good sense will conclude with Loisy that this process was "a vital manifestation, a great effort of faith and understanding, which permitted the Church to join together her own tradition and the science of the time."[23] The process was no doubt divine, like everything that happens in this world, but could it have been so substantial!

> The first, the most decisive, the most important, and perhaps also the most rapid change which it [Christianity] underwent is the one that took a Jewish movement based on the idea of the messianic reign and made it a religion acceptable for the Graeco-Roman world and for humanity as a whole.[24]

After that, one is edified to see the author making every Christian doctrine go back to the New Testament. The impassable gap is between Jesus and the New Testament. Jesus inaugurated a Jewish movement; a marvelous instinct of faith made it a universal religion. Where is the divine? In the Jesus who preached as imminent the realization of the Jewish ideal, which the facts showed to be a fantasy? Or is it in those who sensed, not

22. Ibid., 140.

23. Ibid., 137.

24. Ibid., 134.

by calculation and worldly wisdom (we are told aloud), but by instinct that the only way to escape this false position was to accommodate the Jewish Christ to the ideas of the Gentiles, consecrating Him Savior, Son of God in the proper sense, Incarnate Word? And how did this seed bear such fruits simply by being transplanted?!

Christ for the Church of tomorrow.—If such was the marvelous creative energy of the primitive Church, there is no need to despair of the current Church, once she has understood that such changes are not at all substantial and do not compromise the divine origin of dogma. As for dogmas:

The historian sees in them the interpretation of religious facts acquired by a laborious effort of theological thought; let the dogmas be divine by origin and substance, they are still human in structure and composition. It is inconceivable that their future should not correspond to their past.[25]

Mr. Loisy, who tries hard not to break with tradition and tries to keep its chain uninterrupted, without substantial changes, would have no wish, of course, to renounce the divinity of Jesus Christ. He insinuates vaguely how one could preserve it without discontenting anyone.

Thus, Jesus reveals to men the secret of God and of religion, because God was in him revealing Himself to men; thus men sense that they possess in Jesus God revealed.[26]

Notice the phrases that one finds running in the Johannine matrix, and here no doubt is how modern people should interpret them:

The worship of Jesus and the cult of the saints proceed nevertheless from what one can call in all truth the primitive revelation, the revelation which was never specified in formal teaching and which man carries at the bottom of his religious consciousness, written in faint characters. The one article that constitutes this unexplicated revelation, and which Jesus manifested in His person and in His life as well as in His teaching, but which He manifested first in a clear and intelligible fashion because He bore it realized in Himself, is that *God reveals Himself to man in man*, and that humanity enters into a divine society with God. Man had always believed this and only vaguely understood it. Jesus makes man understand it, and one can say that from this moment on, the orientation of prayer has been changed, the clouds of mythology have been dissipated, at the same time as the barrier of legalism and of verbal revelation has been overthrown. The most divine thing in

25. Ibid., 459.
26. Ibid., 224.

the world is not the crash of thunder, nor the light of the sun, nor the spread of life over the earth; it is the beauty of souls, the purity of the heart, the perfection of love in sacrifice, because all that is the sovereign gift of God to man, who is the greatest work and the supreme manifestation of God in the universe.[27]

The gift of God! Decidedly this is a travesty of St. John. But haven't we come back to the conclusions of Herr von Harnack? Nothing is missing but the heavenly Father; He has been replaced by "the beauty of souls," which replaces in turn "the infinite value of the soul."

*

People have not failed to say that Mr. Loisy's book is a sad sign of the times. But a scholar, however high his profile, does not make an epoch all by himself. The sad sign of the times is the *welcome* that his book has received and the disarray that it has brought to light. Msgr. Batiffol, who has been following the movement now afoot for a long time and with rare perspicacity, has brought the issue to its real point from the first.[28]

Others have thought the time was ripe to put all forms of criticism under reprobation under the label "the critics." In this way Mr. Gayraud, a good Scholastic theologian, after having rightly pointed out some of the book's consequences, has been driven to condemn the message of "the critics" wholesale.

> Perhaps people will reproach me for exposing the error without refuting it. My excuse is a ready one: it is that when affirmation of the error is supported by no proof, the wisest strategy, in my opinion, is just to expose the error to the light of day.... Before we answer hidden arguments, let us see what they produce. A critic, they say, is guided by his intuition and does not reason at all.[29]

The intuition of dogs is no illusion; it permits them to follow a trail where others detect nothing. The intuition of critics is not an instinctive impression, however; it is the light that is added to good sense by long, specialized studies in matters of fact, where good sense and philosophy are equally powerless. A critic who allows himself to argue from his intuition without giving the reasons that determine it will not survive two days without being ridiculed by his colleagues. The works of Mr. Loisy are nothing

27. Ibid., 223f.

28. Batiffol, "The Gospel and the Church," *Bulletin de littérature ecclésiastique* de Toulouse (January 1903): 3–15. [See selection 1 in this volume.]

29. Hippolyte Gayraud, OP, "L'Évangile et l'Église," *L'Univers* (February 15, 1903).

but a tissue of reasonings. In order to see them, must one count them up, or does one have to banish reasoning a posteriori from factual studies, so as to replace it with reasons of convenience a priori? This injustice and this disdain for critical procedures are perhaps among the reasons for the enthusiasm that the book has excited among young people. One might have expected it: after so many years of revival, Scholasticism is less in credit than ever among the younger generations—and (here is a remarkable phenomenon) especially where it seems to flourish the most absolutely all by itself. This discredit has less to do with Scholasticism itself than with the manner in which it is practiced. Too often, theologians have considered exegesis and history to be noisy rivals, without realizing that by eliminating them they would destroy their own foundations. The young people have good reason to think that before we elucidate the agreement between Suarez and St. Thomas over the question *utrum in Christo sit unum esse*, it would be a good idea to teach them how one establishes the divinity of Christ from the sources of Christian revelation.

It is not enough to make criticism responsible for all the evil. Mr. Gayraud would have been better advised to declare that only criticism can combat criticism. If the arguments of Mr. Loisy do not reach their conclusions—for he never stops arguing—one should be able to prove it. In this review, we cannot undertake to follow him step by step; it will be enough to show that each of the main positions that we have previously distinguished is ill-supported or clashes with texts whose authority has been rejected without good reason.

We do not refuse to place ourselves on the author's chosen ground. He himself, in arguing against Harnack, could not use the Gospel of John without long preambles; and quoting John with both hands without paying any attention to the dogmatic development of the Fourth Gospel is not answering him. For there is a dogmatic development within the New Testament itself, and it is even in the nature of things that this development should have begun prior to the epoch to which the Gospels are dated. "For me," says Mr. Gayraud,

> I think it much more reasonable to see in the apostolic writings the value of real testimonies, in which the personalities of the writers virtually disappear, so as to make room totally for the One whose words they report faithfully and whose acts they narrate scrupulously.[30]

30. Gayraud, *L'Univers* (February 15, 1903).

But it is not a question of preference, or of reasonableness, but of fact. Differences exist in the discourses and in the stories, and these differences must have their reason for being there, be it in the conditions of oral transmission or be it in the literary activity of the writers. The sayings and stories were collected with care and analyzed with finesse, and one must admit that often we cannot discern the motive for the divergences, nor the precise quotation, nor the concrete circumstances that lay at the origin. It is a matter of due degree, between an exaggerated distrust and a naïve confidence. Harnack had the merit of recognizing this difficulty. In reading Mr. Loisy, one has much more the impression that "criticism" has pronounced its verdict, that "science" has spoken—which is a serious drawback. And if it is really the case that Mr. Loisy only had to blow on Harnack's edifice to make it collapse, we are even less impressed by the solidity of the critics' *positive constructions*, since the scientific credentials of the Berlin scholar are no less than those of the French scholar.

Since the detailed arguments of historical criticism are so tenuous and its conclusions are so uncertain, it is legitimate to take general indicators to mark out the path. May one not assume the faithful attachment of the primitive community to the teaching of Jesus? That His words were transmitted with variations, that they were even explicated by tradition, and that certain rudiments of interpretation penetrated into their style even among the synoptics—this is difficult to deny—but that people composed an allegory out of whole cloth or composed a dogmatic teaching so as to put it into the mouth of Christ, from synoptic times onward—that is what one cannot concede—certainly not on the basis of more or less subjective constructs.

Above all, one must not consign all the questions to the short period for which we have no documents, so as to settle them the more easily by conjecture. The time has passed when people saw neither in Paul nor in the synoptics any formal proofs for the divinity of Jesus Christ. According to Wrede and Bousset, the Gospel of Mark is not so remote from the Gospel of John as people have imagined.[31] For Mark (and we know that according to the critics it is the oldest of the Gospels we possess), Jesus is no longer

31. Wilhelm Bousset, "Review of Wrede's *Das Messiasgeheimnis*," *Theologische Rundschau* (August. 1902): 314. [The book under review was Wilhelm Wrede, *Das Messiasgeheimnis in den Evangelien* (Gottingen: Vanderhoek and Ruprecht, 1901).]

the Messiah in the Jewish sense but the miraculous Son of God endowed with a supernatural essence. The devil loses nothing by this concession, because the critics conclude that "Mark no longer has any real grip on the life of Jesus."[32]

That at least is clear enough, but then one must recognize that these gentlemen are living a fantasy in their attempt to recover his "real life" from a book that disfigured it. There you see Mark having become almost as suspect as St. John, and they start to demand that Catholics no longer quote Mark in order to prove the divinity of Jesus!

So when was the image of the miracle-working Son of God formed? Not between Paul and Mark, because it is in Paul. Was it perhaps Paul himself who forged it? There has been no suspicion of this. We still think that Paul adopted the ideas of the Christian community, that he abandoned his pharisaic ideal of the Messiah in order to adopt the one that was imposed upon him in a vision and that he found to conform to that of the other disciples. It is impossible to call this point into doubt. We are thus carried back still further. But from the very first days, the Christian communities were multiplying. Persecution dispersed Christianity far and wide. Where did people form an idea of the Christ so different from the one He supposedly gave of Himself? In what locale did Jewish monotheism bend? How did the other Christian communities accept this change in the gospel, which one has to call substantial? Why did the protest of the Ebionites arrive so late and remain so isolated? Everywhere we meet the faith of the Church. She cannot have mistaken the whole of Jesus' teaching. She cannot have been unfaithful to His spirit in adoring Him as God, and she would not have had the right to do so if He had not (as she affirms through the Gospels she has received) compelled her credence by His miracles and His affirmations.

It is upon this faith of the primitive Church that believers can rest in peace, while the critics agitate their problems. If they maintain that this faith was transformed, we at least ask them for decisive proofs. And we shall be thoroughly astonished if they can furnish them, since their conclusions will be drawn from documents composed to teach the contrary, and since by that very fact the critics' conclusions can have no other status than

32. Ibid., 315.

that of conjectures. By knocking down the authority of the Gospels, the critics preclude themselves from constructing anything solid on this moving terrain. For us, the Church guarantees the authority of the Gospel.

Nevertheless, let us take a look at Loisy's conjectures on this transformation, taking as our basis the New Testament writings.

The N.T. Writings.—An important transformation is attributed to St. Paul. We note here (and not for the last time) Loisy's tendency to exaggerate the certitude and the scope of his initial insinuations. We read on page 69:

> The word of Paul to the Corinthians: "I have transmitted to you that which I have received, namely, that Christ died for our sins . . . and was raised on the third day,"[33] in no way guarantees that the idea of an expiatory death existed from the beginning with the clarity that Pauline teaching gives us, nor that it contributed as much as the resurrection to the founding of Christology.

The statement has been attacked; it is quite defensible. The word "clarity" saves it. After Paul, the point is clearer—so be it. But the text of St. Paul does guarantee, absolutely, at least the point that Paul got this idea from the tradition. Harnack stopped himself in loyalty before this text. It is the rock on which one builds genuine history. But on page 73, the qualifier has disappeared completely:

> Paul discovered in the death a meaning and an efficacity that could count independently of the resurrection while being coordinated with it.

Paul *discovered*. But Paul tells us that he was taught it, and he is the one we should believe. When we find in Mark that Christ came "to give His life as a ransom for many"[34] instead of saying that this text "has every likelihood of having been influenced by the theology of Paul,"[35] we have to say that this text, placed by the evangelist in the mouth of Jesus, represents precisely the tradition that Paul received. Likewise in connection with the Eucharist. If Mark says, "This is my blood of the covenant shed for many" (14:24), these are not exactly the words that one may read in Paul (1 Cor 11:25). They are equivalently in Luke and in Matthew. The critics pretend that these words in Luke have been added afterward, thanks to the teachings of Paul. The word "teaching" suggests at once a theological doctrine. Things get even worse when all three evangelists are supposed to have bor-

33. 1 Cor 15:3–4.

34. 1 Cor 10:45.

35. Loisy, *L'Évangile et l'Église,* 72.

rowed from the text of Paul, but there again Paul recites a tradition that he *received*.[36] If apostolic tradition did not at least hang onto the general sense of the most solemn words of farewell pronounced by Jesus, one has to renounce all certitude. And yet Loisy concludes that for the first generation "the death was merely the providential condition for the resurrection."[37]

The faith of the primitive Church.—Allegedly, for the first generation, "it was the resurrection alone that made the Christ."[38] Loisy's text runs thus:

> One comes to see also that the apostolic Church taught that Jesus had become Lord and Christ through the resurrection, that is, through His entry into heavenly glory, and that she was at the same time awaiting His *coming*, that is, His arrival as the Christ, and not His *return*, since His earthly ministry was not yet envisaged as a messianic success.[39]

Herr Bousset wrote thus:

> He (Wrede) finds an analogous idea in the conception which one certainly finds in the bosom of the primitive community, particularly in the author of the Acts (but one can also show it in Paul), namely, that Jesus only became Messiah and Son of God through the resurrection and being taken up into heaven (Acts 2:36; Rom 1:4, Phil 2: 6ff). This viewpoint, according to Wrede, is certainly the oldest viewpoint of the community of Jesus and shows itself, for example, in the fact that one did not speak of a return but of a coming (*parousia*) of Jesus in messianic glory.[40]

These two passages resemble one another far more closely than the logion *Confiteor tibi, Pater* [Mt 11:25; Lk 10:21] resembles chapter 51 of Ecclesiasticus. It is possible that Loisy just had Bousset's text somewhere in the back of his memory, which would excuse him for not footnoting it. But how much more emphatic the claim has become in the French scholar, and how much less justified! The German scholar cites texts; he concludes to "a viewpoint" in the primitive community; each reader can form an opinion. Loisy cites no texts but pronounces squarely that the apostolic Church (i.e., the supreme authority for us) teaches (i.e., maintains as a point that is certain) that Jesus became Christ through the resurrection. And this is how he imposes his claim on the credulity of the reader—so serious because it contains implicitly this other proposition—namely, that the apostolic

36. 1 Cor 11:23ff.
37. Loisy, *L'Évangile et l'Église*, 70.
38. Ibid., 69.
39. Ibid., 55.
40. Bousset, *Theologische Rundschau* (August 1902): 315.

Church did not consider Jesus the Messiah while He was still on earth, nor therefore the Son of God, if we follow the author's previous reasoning.

To be fair, one must acknowledge in the two authors an open contradiction. Thanks to the resurrection at least, Jesus *was* Christ, and the community was still waiting for Him to become Christ! Loisy has done us the service of putting the matter into a clearer light, thanks to his French clarity.

Elsewhere Loisy does cite a text.[41] It is Acts 2:23–24. He cites it with a "*cf.*," which shows that he does not consider it decisive. One only has to read it. The better argument is that of Bousset, drawn from Acts 2:36: "Let the whole house of Israel know, then, for a certitude that God hath made both Lord and Christ this Jesus whom ye crucified."[42]

One has to pay attention to this text and observe that, for the first generation, the resurrection of Christ was truly His entry into messianic *glory*. But was He only then invested with an inner status that He had not had before? In the same discourse, Peter remarks that Jesus was authorized by God for a special mission involving the miracles that God had done through Him, and that it was not possible for death to overcome Him.[43] At verse 31 he speaks of "the resurrection *of* the Christ" [rather than *as* the Christ]. His intention, then, is not to teach formally that messiah-status is posterior to the resurrection. The same Peter, in the same book of Acts, sees these things in a quite different order: "Jesus of Nazareth whom God *anointed* with the Holy Spirit and power, who went about doing good and healing... because God was with Him."[44] As for the other two texts, it suffices to note that they are from Paul. No one underscored more strongly the consequences of the factual resurrection, but as a declaration, a manifestation, which brought into full light the divine element that Christ possessed already, even before His birth.

Besides, how could the apostolic Church have taught that Jesus became Christ through the resurrection, when Jesus had confessed before the high priest that He was the Christ, and when Peter had solemnly attributed to Him this credential? Loisy foresaw these arguments and tried to break them. One must say that the result is not history but the subtlest sort of

41. Loisy, *L'Évangile et l'Église,* 73.
42. Loisy also makes reference to this, citing Acts 2:22–36; ibid, 206.
43. Acts 2:22–24.
44. Acts 10:38ff.

casuistry, imposing on the texts the sort of treatment they have received all too often in ultraconservative exegesis.

When John [the Baptist] asks, "Art thou the Christ?" [Lk 7:19], he is not asking [according to Loisy] a present-tense question, because the Kingdom of heaven is not yet realized and Jesus is not yet in the role of Messiah. He is asking rather [says Loisy] whether Jesus is going to be the Christ. But Jesus answers him in a way that will make him understand that the one who is presently preparing the coming of the Kingdom is the one who must come with the Kingdom.[45]

In reality, John had learned in his prison the *works* of Jesus and did not know if they were preliminaries to the arrival of the Messiah or were the very role of the Messiah.... Jesus answered with the signs predicted in Isaiah (35:5–6; 61:1), as signs of the great event awaited when God Himself would come to save. The great work has begun; the Messiah is in act.

When Peter says, "Thou art the Christ," it does not mean that the Savior is already exercising the messianic function but that He is the person designated for this function.[46]

This is very clever of St. Peter, and absolutely contrary to the text. The works of Jesus are such that everyone is attributing to Him an extraordinary identity: Jeremiah, Elijah, a prophet. Peter, enlightened from on high on the true character of Jesus, declares that He is the Messiah, by which he does not mean a function but the true identity of Jesus, as Matthew underscores so strongly.[47]

Finally, in front of the high priest, when Jesus says so clearly that He is the Christ, Loisy will explicate—that is, attenuate—this declaration by specifying that He was the future Messiah. "Jesus declares that He is the Son of man who is to come."[48] So He was not guilty, except prospectively. It would have been better to say with Bousset that this declaration included more than a simple avowal of pretending to the Jewish messiahship.[49] Jesus was acknowledging Himself as Son of God in the supernatural sense, and this is the reason He is condemned as a blasphemer. For to call Himself the Messiah in the Jewish sense, and in the future, would not have been a blasphemy.

45. Loisy, *L'Évangile et l'Église*, 54.
46. Ibid.
47. Mt 16:13–16.
48. Loisy, *L'Évangile et l'Église*, 54.
49. Bousset, *Theologische Rundschau*, 314.

One cannot omit here a purely critical remark, which can only be taken *ad hominem*. If the evangelists so strongly "retouched" the sayings and the facts in the direction of their own dogmatic preoccupations, is it not even more improper to take their expressions in a conjectured primitive sense? For Mark, the Christ is certainly the supernatural son of God. How then could he have presented the facts according to a contrary supposition? The German critics are the only consistent ones. If one grants their premise, one must follow it all the way to the end.

Jesus' opinion of Himself.—The capital point, of course, is "what Jesus believed himself to be and said he was." Loisy, in a remarkably systemizing spirit, eliminates all the texts in which Jesus says more or less openly that He is the Son of God in the supernatural sense; Jesus believed He was the Messiah to come—that is, the predestined agent of a Kingdom of God that was supposed to come, without any clear vision of the Church that did come. We have here two distinct issues: the Son of God and the Kingdom of God.

Let us go back to the documentary situation. Let us take as our point of departure the Gospel of Mark, because people acknowledge it as the earliest in date. What we shall say about this Gospel will hold a fortiori for Matthew and for Luke, who also had the supernatural conception. One may say rightly enough with Wrede and Bousset that Mark in its entirety presents the following double point of view, which might seem contradictory:

—Jesus manifests continually His messianic glory (and thereby one must understand His supernatural status as son of man/Son of God, since Mark hardly uses the term "messiah"),

—and yet this status remains a mystery: the disciples do not understand it.

From the beginning, Jesus is teaching as one having the power to teach and not as the scribes did (Mk 1:22). It was the demons, because of their acquaintance with the supernatural world, who recognized Him as the holy one of God (Mk 1:27), the Son of God (Mk 3:11). He forgives sins without denying that the right to do so belongs only to God, and He performs a miracle to show that He has this power (Mk 2:10). He exercises a sovereign control over the elements (Mk 4:35ff). There is no point in rehearsing His many, many miracles. Mark underscores the general astonishment. People asked themselves who this was (Mk 6:1ff). Jesus is amazed at the unbelief of His disciples (Mk 6:6), and so they should have recognized Him, since He congratulates those who attribute to Him the power to heal. The disciples did not know how to appreciate the multiplication of the loaves (6:52); the walking on water did nothing but plunge them into stupor. Jesus again laments the inability of His miracles to open the eyes of His disciples (8:17ff); He foresees that the Son would be rejected like the servants (parable of the vinedressers). Finally came the solemn confession that produced such a shocking effect on the Sanhedrin and the confession of the centurion who recognized the Son of God (15:39). Even the most superficial reading of Mark leaves the impression that Jesus imposed Himself upon the faith of His disciples through His miracles, despite a long resistance on their part, without noisy and untimely pronouncements. Refusing even the help that the devils were offering Him to reveal His true identity, He still showed clearly that He was the Son of God. This point is so well confirmed that the most independent criticism agrees here with the traditional conclusions. The critics add, to be sure, that "Mark no longer has any real grip on the life of Jesus,"[50] and this they say because miracles, in particular healings of the possessed, cannot be historical events.

Without going so far as to say that, Loisy tries to attenuate and even extenuate the vigor of the tableau traced by Mark. Everything in the mouth of Jesus that seems to echo His consciousness of Sonship is carefully eliminated from the primitive tradition. An example is the parable of the vinedressers (Mk 12:1–12). Here let us go back to the author's work on the parables, which is supposed to give the scientific support for the bold theories expounded in *L'Évangile et l'Église*.[51]

First of all, it is not a parable [he says] but an allegory, and on this ground alone it is excluded from the teaching of Jesus because He only told parables.—No doubt it is very opportune to distinguish, with [Adolf] Jülicher, parable from allegory. But can one say that Jesus never used allegory, in a time when it was in vogue everywhere?—"Like many allegories, this one has no value but that of a theoretical and theological conception."—What suffices to exclude this parable is the principle that Jesus is not supposed to have taught any doctrine about His Person.—"Prior to the event there was no good reason to show the death of Jesus as the full term of

50. Ibid., 314.
51. Loisy, *Études évangéliques* (Paris: 1902), 52ff.

divine patience."—There was no good reason!—[The story is not historical, because, if it were]

Jesus would have had no intention of winning over those whom he was addressing; he would be declaring them lost and condemned, not to bring them into repentance, but to manifest the knowledge which he had of the divine decrees, so as to furnish an argument for His apologists in the future. Such an attitude, especially in the case of the Christ, is not that of a living and acting person.

Say rather: it is not the attitude of a mere human without any special or prophetic light. Why is not a threat sometimes the best way to win back souls? And why would Jesus not have tried to forearm His disciples against the discouragement they would feel because of the stubbornness of the Jews?—"It is very strange that the discourse should excite the hearers to commit the crime whose consequences had just been indicated to them."—How many warnings have had no other result!—"If Jesus proclaimed Himself Son of God in front of so many witnesses who knew what He was saying, one does not see why His cause was so difficult to put across before the high priest."—But if it was just an allegory?

One can read the entire passage in Loisy. When he piles up reasons like these, it is because he has no good reasons. Indeed, these are not at all compelling proofs for rejecting a parable (or an allegory) that is found in all three synoptics. Criticism establishes that this passage presents itself in the best literary conditions; the key traits are the same in all three; the little differences prove that Matthew (21:33–46) and Luke (20: 9–19) did not content themselves with following Mark word for word.

Such is the treatment one has to inflict upon Mark in order to extract a portrait absolutely contrary to the one he painted: Jesus doing nothing to make people believe He was Son of God. One may say of this exegesis what Renan used to say about the harmonizing solutions of ultraconservative exegetes: one can justify it once, twice, three times, but not every time.

In *L'Évangile et l'Église*, Loisy tries above all to exclude from the tradition the famous passage "*Confiteor tibi, Pater.*" Harnack had respected it, because it is found in Matthew (11:25–27) and in Luke (10:21–22). Their agreement is very significant because Luke and Matthew are literarily independent in their current form. What Luke did not borrow from Mark, he owes to the tradition or to the earliest written documents; since the passage is in Matthew, it is probable that it was part of Matthew's underlying document, which people rightly or wrongly (and mostly wrongly, in our view) have called the *logia*.[52] Nothing has higher standing in the Gospel tradition. And here Luke and Matthew are very specifically in agreement on the wording, as if it were understood that such an important text should be reproduced word for word. It is in any case impossible to distinguish a more original form from a secondary form of it.

Loisy first puts the saying under suspicion in a moderate way: "It is difficult to see here the literally exact expression of a declaration made by Christ before His disciples."[53] "Literally" saves everything. Then,

> it is quite probable that, despite its presence in the two Gospels, the section where the text brought forward by Harnack is found, at least in its current form, is a product of the Christian tradition of the early times.[54]

"In its current form" is a nice precaution. And indeed the arguments brought forward against the text would prove at most that it has been put into a certain literary form. They do not even prove that much, because the resemblance with chapter 51 of Ecclesiasticus is very slight,[55] and the section does not have the rhythm of Luke's canticles, and Luke probably borrowed the passage anyway from the *logia* of Matthew. Finally, when the Savior says that all things have been entrusted to Him by His Father, it is not fair to say that these words do not suit "strictly speaking" anyone but "the glorious Christ," because there is no assessing the "strictly speaking" without the context that marks a revelation, and because the words of Matthew 28:18, "all power has been given to me in heaven and on earth," are not at all "wholly similar." But at the end, all that Loisy concludes from his literary analysis is that very probably this section is, at least in its current form, a product of the Christian tradition. This leaves untouched the underlying form. If the underlying form remains, if Jesus gave us to understand that He was the Son of God thanks to a direct relation with the Father, apart from a future messianic event, then one simply cannot say, "The idea of divine filiation was tied to that of the Kingdom; it had no meaning of its own, as ap-

52. [It is no longer customary to call this underlying document *Logia* but rather Q." Fr. Lagrange did not approve of "Logia" because, as of 1903, he still thought the source behind the canonical Gospels was a full-scale Gospel in Aramaic.—Tr.]

53. Loisy, *L'Évangile et l'Église,* 45.

54. Ibid., 46.

55. See the article by Rev. Fr. Léonce de Grandmaison in *Études* (1903).

plied to Jesus, except in relation to the Kingdom to be established."[56] Here again, Loisy's conclusions obviously go beyond the premises of his literary analysis, which in any case is overly convoluted.

We come at last to the notion of the Kingdom of God, which is the basis for all of Loisy's theological construction. To hear him tell it, nothing could be simpler: "The qualities of the gospel hope are as easy to determine as its object."[57]

If he [Jesus] never gives his definition of the Kingdom of God, it is because the Kingdom, whose messenger and agent he was, is identified in his thought, as in the thought of his auditors, with the one which the prophets had announced.[58]

In the *Études évangéliques* we read:

The Kingdom of heaven in the gospels and especially in the parables, as in Isaiah, Jeremiah, Ezekiel, Daniel, is a collective hope, an objective reality, an eschatological event.[59]

Loisy says not a word about the considerable differences one can easily point out between Ezekiel's ideal and that of the second Isaiah, between Jeremiah and Daniel; he says not a word about the popular hopes for a kingdom that would be above all temporal and that could create so profound a misunderstanding between Jesus and His hearers. "The gospel as such was nothing but a religious movement which emerged in the bosom of Judaism so as to fulfill its principles and its hopes."[60] If the word "Judaism" is taken in a narrow sense, how does one reconcile this with the universalistic hopes of the second Isaiah? If the word really means Old Testament Scripture, why not take into account the very real influence exercised or manifested by other writings? If the word represents the whole movement of ideas that emerged around Jesus, what a chaos—and how can one fulfill so many confused hopes and so many divergent principles?

Frankly, Loisy's conception is too simplistic. The idea of the Kingdom of God among the Jews, and this idea in the thought of Jesus, is a topic for further study (or rather for study, because Loisy did none). We also do not intend to capture in a few lines this highly complex problem; we are reviewing a book, and it is enough if we indicate what we consider the weak points of Loisy's argumentation.

56. Loisy, *L'Évangile et l'Église*, 57.
57. Ibid., 7.
58. Ibid., 13.
59. Ibid., 105.
60. Ibid., 161.

First of all, in the system proposed, Jesus, being convinced that He was called to be the Messiah, is not supposed to have foreseen that His death would occur between His hope and His glorious arrival. Therefore, He did not announce His death as Christ through "a quote formally retained as a word of the Lord."—That is not accurate, since one finds the direct quote in Matthew (16:23) and in Mark (8:33), in a very lively saying addressed to Peter, which can only be explained by this context. Also, in one of the most picturesque parables, Mark showed clearly that Jesus had from the beginning a presentiment of His death (2:19f). According to Wrede, a child would have understood that Jesus was presenting Himself as the groom and prophesying His death.[61] Loisy prefers to hunt for a more primitive sense of Jesus' words, using Jülicher.[62] Here is how he interprets the text:

> But if Jesus had been pointing to Himself as the groom, His argumentation would have had no probative force; He must have been just affirming that His disciples could not fast as long as He was with them.

He must have affirmed this by way of a comparison, as is done in every parable, and the probative force lay precisely in the fact that He was the groom.

> The oldest sense of the response seems to have been this: the groomsmen at marriages cannot fast as long as they are in the feast with the bridegroom; if the groom is unexpectedly taken away, the feast is finished, the groom's companions are saddened; thus the disciples of the Baptist fast, since they no longer have their master, and those of Jesus do not fast, since they have him with them.[63]

The spice of this little subtlety is that it takes away from the parable any allegorical nuance so as to make it fit the primitive words of Jesus in the tight circle that Jülicher draws. Well, even in this "primitive" sense, who could stop himself from concluding that Jesus was the spouse whose departure would plunge His disciples into mourning?

The Kingdom of God did not consist uniquely in an imminent advent upon the clouds—so much so that it had already begun. This is something that Loisy was forced to recognize.

61. Wilhelm Wrede, *Das Messiasgeheimniss in den Evangelien* [Göttingen: Vandenhoeck and Ruprecht, 1901], 20.

62. Adolf Jülicher, *Die Gleichnisreden Jesu*, 2nd ed. [2 vols. (Tübingen: Akademische Verlagsbuchhandlung J. C. B. Mohr, 1888f.)], 89.

63. Loisy, *Études évangéliques*, 43.

But he made this concession grudgingly, and his ill humor fell upon the evangelists. Luke is explicit: "The kingdom of God is among you."

> The whole of this introduction is in the style of the evangelist, who freely creates the setting for the discourses which he reproduces; and the idea of a present kingdom is out of accord with the discourse itself.[64]

Luke was clumsy: he created a quite explicit setting, and it did not agree with the text for whose sake he created it! (A less systematizing critic would have concluded rather that, if the introduction does not sit well with the main discourse, it is because it contains a misplaced piece of the tradition, clumsily moved by Luke.)

> Unless the assertion, "the kingdom of God is among you," should be understood as a prophecy which would mean: "the kingdom is very close to manifesting itself among you."[65]

Naturally, as "thou art the Christ" means, "thou art the future Christ"!

So little does the Kingdom of God assume a general destruction and an end to society that each person has it in his grasp. It is enough to seek it with good will. This is what the parable of the sower, and the parable of the pearl, and the parable of the hidden treasure, among others, show very clearly, as Harnack had the good sense to recognize.

So little is the Kingdom of heaven an event that comes ready-made from heaven with all its involvements and consequences—which Loisy does not say in these exact words, but which emerges well enough from his insistence on the Kingdom's unique arrival on the clouds—that it develops by its own strength up to its own full expansion. One can put the parables on Jülicher's Procrustean bed, but there is always enough left over to make the message come through. Read again the charming parable of the seed that grows day by day until the moment of the harvest [Mk 4:26–29]. "So is the kingdom of God, as if a man should cast seed into the ground and should sleep and rise, night and day; and the seed should spring and grow up he knoweth not how. For the earth bringeth forth fruit of itself, first the blade, then the ear, then the full corn in the ear; but when the fruit is ripe, immediately he puteth in the sickle, because the harvest is come."[66] Loisy

64. Loisy, *L'Évangile et l'Église*, 20.

65. Ibid., 20f.

66. [Fr. Vincent] Rose, *Études sur les Évangiles* [Paris: H. Welter, 1904], 114. Fr. Rose rightly

concedes that this seed "can evoke the idea of a moral progress occurring in souls; in reality, the comparison concerns the Kingdom as preached and the Kingdom as manifested, the former corresponding to the sowing, and the latter to the harvest; between the two comes the time when the seed grows and the Gospel expands."[67] To be sure, Loisy's concession to the obvious meaning is as small as possible, and yet it is already a great deal that this "Kingdom preached" emerges, whose effects cannot be denied. What is to come, then, is not so much the Kingdom in its wholeness as the *manifestation* of the Kingdom, which no one denies.—Loisy makes the same desperate effort, in the same perspective, to take away the obvious meaning of the parable of the mustard seed and the parable of the leaven. It is impossible not to recognize that Jesus chose the leaven and the mustard to indicate a powerful energy of continuous development within a small germ. But that would be allegory! Hence

> the parables of the mustard seed and of the leaven, which bring out the contrast between a small beginning and a large final result, also apply to the antithesis between the Kingdom sown by evangelical preaching and the Kingdom developed in its definitive manifestation.[68]

Even so, Loisy speaks of a *result*: was it then contained in its cause? Was the Kingdom of God the same in any case from the beginning to the end? But let the obvious meaning go by the board, rather than forsake Jülicher and his system! It would have been more effective to say simply that, since these parables are allegorical, they are merely the work of the early community, like that of the vinedressers. Surely some writer could be found to say this.

What can give Loisy's argumentation the appearance of solidity is the fact that the proximity of God's Kingdom, bringing with it the end of the world, *can be* the explanation of certain teachings of Jesus. It is certainly the case that if the world must soon come to an end, renouncing the cares of the world is obligatory. But one *can also* read Him as just comparing the interests at stake: on the one hand a world that quickly passes for each person, on the other hand eternal life. This is why Harnack is not wrong to

remarks that nothing is more opposed than this parable to the idea that the Kingdom is established by a sudden intervention of God, by an irresistible manifestation of His power.

67. Loisy, *L'Évangile et l'Église*, 16.

68. Ibid.

say that Jesus insisted so much on the price of the soul. When Jesus recommends to His disciples that they submit to Providence, it is not because the world is about to end, but because concern for the things of the world, even the most necessary ones, must come after seeking for the Kingdom of God. But once one has put the Kingdom of God and His righteousness *first,* which is [prioritizing,] the hallmark of moral action, rather than the prior arrival of this kingdom, all these things will be granted by way of surplus ... no doubt, in the world where one needs them.[69]

Yes, Loisy remarks correctly that the gospel is subordinate to the Kingdom, that the thought of Jesus is always moving to this definitive consummation, which alone gives human efforts their value. But is Jesus then awaiting strictly an imminent arrival on the clouds? Or does He not envisage the Kingdom in Himself, independently of its glorious inauguration? To make a quick sketch, the three ideas of

> a Kingdom of God on earth through the practice of righteousness,
> a glorious advent of the Messiah, and
> eternal life in a world to come,

were already to be met with in the Judaism of the time, and it would be quite natural for them to be represented in the gospel of Jesus. The sudden coming is not necessarily a menacing prospect for the world—it was not so at all for the Second Isaiah. The fact that Jesus showed clearly that He did not subordinate His idea of God's kingdom to an apocalypse is enough, in any case, to show that the Gospel did not have the wholly simple character that Loisy wants to attribute to it.

In the first place, one is struck by the fact that Jesus taught people to pray "Thy Kingdom come," and this seems to fit well enough into the eschatological system. Loisy even concludes that "it was in view of the Kingdom to come, and soon to come, that one asked not to lack one's daily bread!"[70] In reality, this petition does not assume a thunderous advent any more than these other prayers do—that Thy name be hallowed, that Thy will be done on earth as it is in heaven. All of this was not an absolute novelty. Judaism turned all its thoughts toward the Kingdom to come, but did not overlook the fact that God was already reigning for a very long time. The more criti-

69. Mt 6:32.
70. Loisy, *L'Évangile et l'Église*, 16f.

cism does its homework, the more nuances it will discover in the notions that Loisy has portrayed as so simple, assuming an easy common ground between Jesus and his hearers.

But didn't Jesus prophesy to the high priest His coming on the clouds? It seems that people put a lot of weight on this saying. This one was not altered by the evangelists! It represents the *total* thought of Jesus on the Kingdom and on His own person!—So be it; we respect this saying like anyone else. But in the end, it is a citation, or at least a very clear allusion, to two passages of scripture: Daniel 7:13 and Psalm 110:1. So criticism has no objection to these cases of erudite recollection, unlike the case of the *Confiteor tibi, Pater*? When He quotes this, it is to find a common ground; or it is making an appeal to authority. Jesus affirms His messiahship by reminding the scribes of a text that leaves no room for doubt. What He expected to be is exactly the Messiah as people awaited Him, according to the scriptures. One would still need to know whether these two texts exhausted the notion of the Messiah, whether Jesus knew no further notion, whether He now,[71] intuiting that His death would count for something in the coming of the Kingdom, would have expressed in this way the entirety of His conception of the Messiah.... Sound criticism could then object, while respecting this text boundlessly, that it should not be isolated and serve as the only text that counts, so to speak.

There is no mistaking the fact that for a long time, one generation of exegetes has followed another without succeeding in clearing up the eschatological problem definitively—because, in reality, different perspectives are strangely blended in the Gospel. This was a legacy of the Old Testament, where the perspectives are even more confused. The wisest thing to do in such a case is not to construe everything in light of certain isolated texts by forcing their meaning upon all other texts, but to accept all the texts while trying to distinguish what is traditional in them (and hence a matter of convention, as far as idea and image are concerned) from what new content they include, which one can attribute only to Jesus. This is what Harnack tried to do, though he did so with an all-too-evident program of reducing everything to a quintessence. The grave mistake of Loisy, in our view, has been to leap to the opposite excess and to substitute for Harnack's essence of Christianity (which contained at least a sound idea soundly attributed to Jesus) an idea that, while traditional, has been so isolated and so badly

71. According to Loisy.

understood by Jesus that nothing was left of it but a fantasy. Happily, one cannot attribute this mistake to Jesus without stumbling over texts that express most surely His genuine thought.[72] Loisy does not give us his opinion on this point. It is quite remarkable that "the new creation," which sounds so neatly eschatological, is viewed by St. Paul as something already acquired (Gal 6:15; 2 Cor 5:17), whereas the Kingdom is sometimes already here (1 Cor 7:21; Col 5:13, 4:11) and sometimes still to come (Gal 5:21; 1 Cor. 6:9, 11); some verses are hard to classify.

Did Christ Himself belong to the essence of Christianity? Wellhausen, followed by Harnack, says yes, since the time of St. Paul.[73] Paul is the one who transformed the gospel of the Kingdom into a Gospel of Christ. And people add, following Renan, that Tiberius would have been astonished if people had told him that this little Jew was going to be his best collaborator in the preservation of the Empire. St. Paul would have been no less astonished, if people had told him to his face that he, and not Jesus, was the founder of Christianity. All the novelty of his doctrine—he saw it in the person and the teaching of Christ.

Loisy claims, on the contrary, that Christ "did not present Himself as the revealer of a new principle"; "by enlarging and perfecting, He intended to conserve."[74] This again can be understood in a good sense. But Loisy goes much too far when he adds:

> To search in the gospel for an element entirely new vis-à-vis the religion of Moses and the prophets is to search for what Jesus did not want to put there, and what, by His own statement, is not there.[75]

Perhaps the author is leaving himself some room to maneuver with the word "entirely." But his readers will have lost all memory of it when he tells them so crudely: "Christian thought, at its beginnings, was Jewish and could not be anything but Jewish, even though gospel Christianity contained the germ of a universal religion."[76] The critics also make much of Jesus' declaration "*Non veni solvere sed adimplere*" [I have not come to abol-

72. What proves that the Kingdom had in itself an eschatological value, independent of the Messiah's arrival-in-glory, is that it preserves this value in Paul. Wellhausen and Harnack tell us that Paul changed the gospel of the Kingdom into the Gospel of Christ by presenting the prophecy of the Kingdom as fulfilled by Christ; Harnack, *Das Wesen des Christentums* (Leipzig: Hinrichs'sche Buchhandlung, 1900), 114.

73. Ibid.

74. Loisy, *L'Évangile et l'Église*, 12–13.

75. Ibid., 13.

76. Ibid., 134.

ish but to fulfill]. Here again is a saying that has nothing to fear from the critics! It is an untouchable saying, which must have come word for word from the lips of the Savior! But they isolate it from the context in which it clearly indicates a whole new program of religious perfection. No doubt, Jesus would never have consented to detach Himself from the Old Testament; but St. Paul professes the same respect for the scriptures and for the revealed truths, and yet we know that for him Christianity is a new thing. There was no question of transforming or rejecting monotheism, but rather of making people understand how far the love of God extends. Even on the assumption that the speculative teaching did not change, the truth took on an entirely new force in the religious sphere. God did not reveal anew that He was a Father (people knew it already), but He showed to what an unheard-of extent He was a Father, by sending His Son. It was known that He pardoned sins, but who could have suspected that He would give His Son as the ransom? There emerged from these facts a new teaching on the divine nature, but this teaching penetrated first on its purely religious side—that is, insofar as it brought God and man together. This is why it seems at first sight that there is so little "theology" properly so-called in the words of Jesus. What no one could doubt any longer (after God had given such signs and what so struck St. Paul as an objective truth received by all) was the great *novelty* of salvation. He established this fact not in the dogmatic developments of his letter to the Romans but by quite simple allusions: "God hath willed to save us through our Lord Jesus Christ, who hath died for us";[77] or indeed, "the weak man will perish because of thy knowledge, and he is a brother for whom Christ died."[78]

If this law of love, which conquered so many souls, sprang entirely from the mind of St. Paul, one would have to suppose that he pulled the whole Church with him. Then there would be no more talk of Petrinism and Paulinism; there would be nothing other than Paulinism through and through. The supposition is as contrary to history as it is to the witness of St. Paul himself.[79] St. Paul preached the Gospel of Jesus Christ? So be it. But this is also the title that the Gospels themselves bear. Jesus did not choose to bear witness of Himself in writing. It is the Church that does so.

✳

77. 1 Thess 5:9f.

78. 1 Cor 8:11.

79. Gal 2.

And yet people say that Loisy has rendered a service to the Church by triumphing over Harnack. He has made tradition and the Church prevail over Protestant individualism and a mere critique of texts. People quote Protestants who have been touched by reading it and have appreciated Catholicism better ever since. Certain learned persons affirm that Loisy's little book, while bad for the Catholics, can do some good for the German rationalists.

We need to get along.

It is certain, however, that no polemical advantage can compensate us for the losses we have sustained. At the end of the day, it is rigorously true that the critical theories of Loisy are as fatal to the Christian faith as those of Herr von Harnack. Plus, the advantage Loisy brings to the Church's side will amount to nothing solid; for who will agree to accept the yoke of the Church—and it is a yoke—if she was not instituted by Jesus Christ, and if nothing proves that Jesus Christ is God?

1. Harnack maintains forcefully against Jewish scholars the originality of the teaching of Jesus. If one can cite among the rabbis traits analogous to the traits of the Gospel, Jesus preached the truth already known with such a purity and such a power that it was really something new. If He accepted the popular tradition of the Kingdom of God awaited as an apocalypse, He introduced into it the new idea of an interior renewal that commences the Kingdom. Thanks to this factor, His religion is not just for despairing persons who, feeling the world slip away from them, cling to heaven; it is a religion that, beyond historical forms and above them, can apply to the people of every age.

Loisy is more concerned to stick to the pure domain of history, but to the point of overlooking the ever-present human foundation that corresponds to the Gospel's immutable foundation. What Loisy describes to us—what is it but a religion for the despairing? Listen to this:

> The comparison of the disciples with the birds of the air and the flowers of the fields shows that what Jesus forbad or advised people against is not just worry over bodily goods but work itself.[80]

If the Gospel for Harnack, then, is not a social program or a political code, the reason is that it dominates all ages through its moral value; but

80. Loisy, *L'Évangile et l'Église*, 25.

for Loisy, Jesus saw no need to trace a program for a society that was about to disappear.

2. Harnack admits that Jesus called Himself Son of God in a unique fashion. This is what Loisy refuses to grant. He shows well enough that the text *Confiteor tibi, Pater* should not be understood in a psychological fashion,[81] and he gives it back its genuine meaning. But [then he adds] Jesus probably never said these words, and He never believed or said that He was Son of God in a special fashion—and it is meager compensation to dwell on the role He had as agent and vicar of the Kingdom as the Jewish Messiah!

3. Here is something still more serious. According to Harnack, the earliest community regarded the death of Christ as a sacrifice offered for the remission of sins; it is historically certain that St. Paul got this idea from the community and developed it theologically. According to Loisy, the whole idea was invented by Paul.

4. Finally, the Church. The two scholars do not seem to agree on their philosophy of history. For Loisy as well as for Harnack, the Church developed in a certain line according to the impulsion of the spirit of faith and under the pressure of circumstances. Her movement was thus, in some ways, inevitable. But it seems that for Loisy, everything inevitable is legitimate: "Christian doctrinal development was fated, hence legitimate in principle,"[82] and again, "At the same time each step of progress is explained by a necessity of fact accompanying the logical necessities."[83] Harnack, however, allows history to have regressions and relapses in it. His system is incontestably more in conformity with the theory of human liberty. Be that as it may, Herr von Harnack, who is Protestant, saw the Church in colors too dark, and it is a merit of Loisy's to have opposed this dark picture with admirable pages on the deep congruencies of ecclesiastical development. His attachment to the Church has served him well and has allowed him to put forward a felicitous reason for many a usage condemned by the Protestants. The author's tone is genuinely filial; nowhere did his erudition inspire him so well as in his heart.

81. Ibid., 44; "Does the Father, who alone knows the Son, as the Son alone knows the Father, also receive from the Son a revelation which He will interpret? Is He only the Father because He has known the Son?" See *Revue biblique* (1901), 114: "But then, we shall object, it follows from the parallelism that God is the Father because He knows the Son. The conclusion is ridiculous."

82. Loisy, *L'Évangile et l'Église*, 160.

83. Ibid., 110.

Why, then, must the foundation of his grand scheme ruin us? Harnack, who extracted from the Gospel certain propositions having an eternal truth to them, can still pledge allegiance to a Gospel. But what is left for Loisy? The moral teaching of Jesus—was it not almost the same as everyone else's? Of course, His moral teaching was directed toward the Kingdom, and hope for the Kingdom might remain for us—but on what foundation, if the "agent" of the Kingdom was no better informed than anyone else? Is there nothing left but the vague hope of the human race for eternal life, belief in which Jesus borrowed from His people, and this people supposedly borrowed from the Persians or the Greeks? And while we are talking about the Church of Jesus Christ, what is this Church, if Jesus is no longer the center of its cultus? Loisy stops himself at this very point: "Christianity without this cultus is nothing but a philosophy—you may say, if you like, a mystical philosophy—which would like to call itself a religion and yet has no right to do so, because it keeps no definite religious form."[84] But who will fail to realize that Harnack is the more logical? No doubt, if we no longer believe that Jesus was God, we still have the option to adore God in Him.[85] It is a matter of taste. But since this can be done without sacraments, we can do without the clergy. Assuredly, these extremes are far from Loisy's intention. People will criticize us for having even hinted at them, and for having translated Loisy's very nuanced insinuations into brutal propositions. But even if the insinuations had been less clear than we have understood them to be, does one have the right to proceed by insinuation in a matter like this? No doubt Loisy will try to reassure Catholic opinion, which he has truly moved. In all good faith, his book is not a work of purely negative polemic; the author took advantage of the occasion to sketch out his own views. In such a case, ambiguities can arise. Why not dissipate them?

Rome

84. Ibid., 209.

85. Loisy has Harnack saying the following: "Did the apostles adore Christ even though they *acquired* their faith from His resurrection? Was Jesus not, for the first Christian generation, just a mediator with God, the one with whom and through whom one usefully prayed to and adored the Father, and not the one who was adored?" Loisy then answers at once: "But these circumstances only highlight the need for a cultus deifying the humanity, since from a strict monotheism (whose formulation had been strengthened rather than attenuated) there emerged the cultus of a human being, whose human character no one ever wanted to deny, even while proclaiming His divinity." Where is the logic? Where is the clarity of what we call "a French mind"?

part 2

critical responses to alfred loisy's *autour d'un petit livre*

Bulletin de littérature ecclésiastique 5 (November 1903): 1–26

3

"JESUS AND GOSPEL CRITICISM"

Part 1 of "Autour des fondements de la foi"

M.-J. Lagrange

To Msgr. Pierre Batiffol,
Rector of the Institut Catholique of Toulouse.

My dear friend,

If there is a time to keep silent, people say, there is also a time to speak; and since writing open letters is all the rage, why should I not write one to you, to say in public what you have known all along? It would be more elegant, perhaps, for us to pay no further attention to Mr. Loisy; but neither his own silence (especially with the reason he has given for it) nor the comments of his friends have served to make clear what line of conduct we ought to follow.[1]

When *L'Évangile et l'Église* appeared, we "spoke plain." You were one

1. "To the attacks directed against his book in many Catholic journals and reviews in our country, the author has nothing to say except that he will not answer them. For his part, he wishes to have no share in the views or in the spirit that characterizes the main documents of this polemic"; [Loisy,] *Autour d'un petit livre* [(Paris: Picard, 1903),] xxxi.

of the first to raise your voice.[2] I was in Rome at the time, and I hesitated a great deal before speaking up. I was far from sharing the ideas of such-and-such [Scholastic] opponents of Loisy, and I was repulsed by their polemic, ignorant as it was of the very basics of the subject. Then, too, I had just been named a member of the Biblical Commission. Wouldn't speaking out show too much anxiety and too much zeal? Nevertheless, essential points of the faith were at stake. Silence would have been interpreted as assent. Hence I wrote.[3] You know how Loisy's admirers have treated those of us who have posed fair and well-grounded objections. We never suspected *his* intentions; his admirers have travestied ours. You are the rector of the Institut Catholique; you were doing your job. As for me, I sought the honor of hand-to-hand combat. But these matters have little importance.

People have been saying—and this is more serious; it comes from writers with credentials—that we have not understood the author's thought. He was refuting [Harnack] and did not wish to do anything else. We had no right to put his own thought under scrutiny, nor to attribute to him a "system" he had not conceived.

But by his second red book [*Autour d'un petit livre*], Mr. Loisy has taken in hand to blow these smokescreens away. He continues to say that he did not put forward a system of theological doctrine, that his book was rather "a modest attempt at historical construction."[4] (As to his intention, we shall do no wrong by assuming he is being perfectly honest.) Beyond that, it was an attempt at apologetics. Given the current situation in philosophy and historical research, the business at hand was to highlight the points that absolutely must be explained in or translated into contemporary language, under penalty of losing contact with modern thought. Modestly, the author left it up to the Church to find the formulations that will best meet the needs of the moment and the future. But he did venture in broad outlines a sketch in defense of tradition and the Church, or at least so he believes.

For our part, we think the ground he has chosen is ruinous. With anxiety, we observe that Loisy is the only one who has occupied that ground without ending up in the most liberal sort of Protestantism. But one must recognize, my dear friend, that there is, in his sketch, something great and

2. Batiffol, "The Gospel and the Church," 1–15 [translated as selection 1 in this volume].

3. Lagrange, Review of Alfred Loisy, *L'Évangile et l'Église, Revue biblique* 12 (April 1903) [translated as selection 2 in this volume].

4. Loisy, *Autour d'un petite livre*, viii.

almost tragic. Rest assured that it impresses undecided readers who sympathize with this lonely figure; rest assured that certain Catholics pin their hopes on him. This sincerity he has, this boldness, this erudition, this very virtuosity in writing style, have produced a great effect. A certain Catholic journal printed the following words: "His latest book, which the conspirators have not been able to get condemned by Leo XIII, is the most magisterial work to come from the hands of a priest in a long time."[5] If one objects that Mr. Loisy has put himself in contradiction with the faith of yesterday, they respond that he is appealing from today to the faith of tomorrow. So firm a grip do the ideas of evolution and progress have on the modern world!

Unfortunately, it remains the case that his attempt touches imprudently upon vital parts of Christianity. Many have concluded already that if his historical construction holds up, dogma is pulled down. Despite Loisy's good wishes for harmony, one gets the feeling after reading him that he sees an irreducible opposition between history and dogma.

In this situation, it seemed to you that those of us who proclaim the need to take the results of historical criticism into account (no less energetically than Loisy does) and who proclaim the need to *improve the methods* of those who esteem such criticism (as much as Loisy does) have the duty to say what they think of his "sketches."

For my part, without discussing the texts, I should like to give an external survey of the current situation in historical criticism vis-à-vis Jesus.

If Mr. Loisy thought it was his duty to highlight a change that had to be made in our ideas, under penalty of losing touch with modern science, it is perhaps my right to say that the matter is *not that urgent*. Nothing in the pretensions attributed to philosophy justifies this attitude. Critical exegesis is not sure of its methods, especially in a matter of historical reconstruction, and the scholars are not in agreement. Is it really necessary to disturb the masses of the faithful on points that are the very life of Christianity (like the divinity of Jesus Christ) or the very life of Catholicism (like the divine institution of the Church) or the very life of piety (like the real presence of Christ in the Eucharist), in favor of a few troubled souls who would feel better off with some neo-Catholicism? (They will not even get that result, because what they propose is still too much. If they push the critical

5. "Tribune libre," *Annales de philosophie chrétienne* (October 1903): 85. [A *tribune libre* was a cross between what we call a letters column and an op-ed page.]

method to the limit and go on demanding a submission of mind, it will no longer be justified.)—This is what I shall undertake to show.

*

Of Loisy's position on dogma, I shall say but a few words. It has become quite clear. Mr. Loisy accepts from the Church everything she intends to impose upon him, the divinity of Jesus Christ, His real presence in the Eucharist, the divine foundation and authority of the Church. But he asks her to weigh these articles well and to conform them to the requirements of criticism and history. From this criticism-and-history, it becomes evident to his eyes that *transformations* are imperative, and not just explications. He thinks he is exercising his rights and even fulfilling his duty by pointing out the danger to which the Church is now exposed. The transformations will not alter "the substance of dogma" [he says]. They will continue the history of the seed, and haven't people always compared the development of dogma to that of a seed?

Mr. Loisy thinks his own experience in this area is a harbinger of the future. Theories he defended on the literary history of the Old Testament are now being received without difficulty, despite the blows people gave him at the time; so, it will be the same, he wants to hope, with his historical account of the Gospel, which the Church will know how to reconcile with the ancient faith.

For our part, we see a difficulty here: when it is a question of dogma, the Church is bound by her past. She has not only defined her dogmas but also defined that they cannot be reinterpreted.[6] Almost all Loisy's statements about dogmas developing may seem inoffensive, but only because he does not understand what is "substance" and what is "essential" the way the rest of the world does. What looks to other people like a repudiation of the past he calls a "legitimate development." It will be up to the Church to decide if she wants to embark on this road to relativism.

Take Christology, for example, as a topic on which Loisy invokes the demands of modern thought. Among these, I was a bit astonished to find

6. "Si quis dixerit fieri posse ut dogmatibus ab Ecclesia propositis aliquando secundum progressum scientiae sensus tribuendus sit alius ab eo quem intellexit et intelligit Ecclesia, anathema sit"; Vatican Council I, Constitution *Dei filius*, c. 4, canon 3 *de fide et ratione*. [In recent editions of Henricus Denzinger and Adolphus Schönmetzer, *Enchiridion Symbolorum, Definitionum et Declarationum* (Rome: Herder, 1976ff), this canon is no. 3043. This work will be cited hereafter as "Denzinger" with a paragraph number.]

first and foremost the demands of philosophy—a point we will never emphasize too much, and that we have to thank the author for having said—but I am relieved to read what the bottom line turns out to be:

If the [Christological] problem ... is posed anew these days, it is less because history is better known, than because an integral renewal has arisen and is continuing in modern philosophy (128f).

Now here is what Loisy thinks the new difficulty is:

If one maintains, and I think one must maintain, the personhood of God as a symbol of His absolute perfection and of the essential distinction that exists between a real God and the real world, isn't it obvious that this divine personhood is of another order than human personhood, and that the presence of the personal God at a given moment in human history under the form of a human being is a concept which makes an apparent unity out of two ideas which are incommensurable, that of personhood in God and that of personhood in man? Is God personal in the human fashion? ... Isn't it true also that the theological notion of a person is metaphysical and abstract, while in contemporary philosophy this notion has become real and psychological? ... At bottom, dogma has defined only a metaphysical relation between Jesus and God, and has defined it above all in line with the idea of a transcendent God.... However, the development of modern philosophy tends more and more to the idea of an immanent God, who has no need of an intermediary in order to act in the world and in man (151ff).

One relaxes. A God who is personal in the same way as a human being, a common measure between Him and us, a God who needs an intermediary—when did Christian philosophy *ever* accept such aberrations?[7] And who can imagine that these difficulties are new, that the ancient doctors

7. Perhaps Loisy is thinking of the first centuries of the Church. The objection would come from the history of philosophy and would consist in saying that the Church (particularly St. John) would not have arrived at the idea of "incarnate Logos" if it had not already known the idea of "logos as intermediary." On page 152 we read, "the Word was conceived originally as a sort of indispensable intermediary between God (absolute and immutable) and the world (finite and changing). God was (so to speak) exterior to the world, and the Word stood between the two, like an emanation of God on behalf of the world. *It was in this way that* the Word in John became the Creator in the cosmic order and the Revealer in the human order." All of this is quite right, if one changes "it was in this way that," which I italicized, into "*although on the contrary*." Of course "Word incarnate" is a theological adaptation, but it could not have been made by John except on the already formed conviction of Jesus' divinity, which permitted John to give the Logos his true character. The history of "consubstantial" is that of the more and more complete victory of the Johannine idea over the older notion [of logos]. [Loisy assumed St. John's logos-doctrine was descended from the one in Philo of Alexandria; Lagrange disagreed.—Tr.]

doubted the realness of a person, or did not understand the psychology involved in being a person, when "personal union" was the exact formula chosen to indicate that all the actions of Jesus were at once divine and human, having the same source (divine agent) acting in two natures? Would it not be grotesque to appeal here to *ens analogum* and the rest of the conceptual apparatus we use to indicate that, although we have being, we are very far from the true Being?

If modern philosophy has this low an estimate of Christian philosophy, it needs somebody to explain our formulas to it; for I hardly think they need a translator!

✳

Even if we leave aside the formula of "personal union," there remains the point that Jesus is God. Mr. Loisy asks modern man to affirm with the Church that Jesus is God. Can he?

Our old apologists customarily put at the top of their proof-from-Scripture the witness of Jesus. Jesus called Himself a man, and He acted as a man, but He spoke and acted in the capacity of God. One has to take sides on this testimony. One has to suspect imposture, take pity on a hallucination, or adore. For Mr. Loisy, however, the witness of Jesus reduces to His saying that He is the future Messiah.

Granted, this idea of the Messiah implies, according to Loisy, "a quite particular relation of union between God and the man-Christ, a relation which is not just a simple knowledge of the good God, but something infinitely more mysterious and more profound, a kind of intimate and ineffable penetration of the man-Christ by God, which is given sensory imagery by the decent of the spirit upon Jesus baptized" (134).

Well, no; that is not in the Gospel, because this intimate and ineffable penetration is a modern conception designed to replace the notion of personal union. At the moment of the baptism, a voice from heaven explains the symbol with these words: "This is my beloved Son." There is no talk of intimate and ineffable penetration, any more than there is of personal union. "Intimate penetration" is at best a modern theological conclusion, then—not one that makes the truth embarrassing for the mind, but one that the mind remains quite free to accept or reject, and that in any case does not follow necessarily from the idea of "future Messiah," which is what Jesus is supposed to have been aware of being.

And now what? How does this "intimate penetration" lead us to the formula that Jesus is God? Once Christ's testimony is ruled out, along with that of the first witnesses to His life, whom can we persuade to accept the divinity we find sketched by Paul and affirmed definitively by that "poor John," as Julian the Apostate called him? Among us [Frenchmen], I see nobody. One may find somebody abroad, however, because this sort of religion resembles what one of my English correspondents calls "professorial religion," a religion for the use of Protestant professors of theology who (you must understand) are no longer obliged to believe by anything but social preferment. *Irreligious* rationalism has been hard to put up with since Kant, and especially since Albert Ritschl. People want to have a religion; the Christian religion is the only one that deserves the name; it is *the* religion, as Herr von Harnack says. But in Germany, this does not take one all the way to admitting the divinity of Jesus Christ. One is content to savor the sage (like Wellhausen or Harnack) or to admire the prophet (like Johannes Weiss). The English are ordinarily more conciliating. They are pleased to proclaim "true God" a man who practiced righteousness perfectly. But this "professorial religion," rich in nuances, cannot exist among us, simply because this religious mentality does not exist outside of Protestantism. There is yet a second reason: the French mind has no taste for equivocations.

*

So we do not accept the terms in which Loisy presents the divinity of Christ. But we have seen (with considerable pain) that he resorts openly to threats. If his solution should happen to be insufficient—and his excuse is that he does not for an instant admit a basis for this hypothesis—Christianity will be condemned, because criticism cannot get things wrong.

Enter, stage left, the infallibility of criticism!

> People object that under these conditions the Christ of history will be far below the Christ of faith, that the faith will not be the same, that the gospel of Jesus and the faith of the Church will be one illusion on top of another. But if these conclusions were well founded, the historian would not be the one to blame, and those who express such thoughts would be very imprudent. The facts are the facts, and the first conclusion to draw, if they are such, is that they are not otherwise. In nature, a mountain of syllogisms cannot budge a grain of sand (114).

No, and permit me to draw a distinction here.

The facts are the facts, obviously; but historical-critical constructions are not always facts, and nothing serves better than a syllogism to reveal their fragility. When there is really a question of *fact*, historical or topographical fact, Loisy moves on rapidly; but he slows down and pores over the texts to extract an *idea*. Especially when dealing with a Gospel problem, the task for him is to rediscover the genuine *thought* of the Savior behind the Gospels, which did not have precise reproduction of His thought as their exact purpose, and whose editors arranged the gospel material according to the needs of their time and their audience. One will agree that the critic's lot is not a happy one. He always has to discern what comes from the Church and what comes from Jesus, *on the assumption* (erected into a strict rule) that Jesus never foresaw any of the later needs of His disciples or any of the situations in which they would find themselves. The resulting game is interesting; one can have it come out so neatly that the spectators are charmed. Mr. Bugge thought he could say that the way the critics behave (all too often) is a game of *canon* [a form of billiards]. Given the position of the balls, it is rare that one cannot rearrange them in many ways. When one has succeeded, the solution is no doubt a neat one, but someone else could have proceeded differently with equal success.[8]

*

This explains why Loisy's arguments have made less impression on critical minds than on others: the critical minds are accustomed to the flux and reflux of theories, and they know how dangerous it is to let oneself be seduced by a particular point of view. Those outside the field are the ones who will be afraid, perhaps, thinking they are in the presence of firm results, a unanimous agreement among the specialists, in a word: a *verdict of science*. We need to tell them that it is no such thing.

Even if we consult only the opinions of those who are not Catholic—which is already a grave injustice—we have to distinguish between [critics in] Germany and [those in] England, and Germany itself still has many critics who are quite solid and relatively conservative.

Even in liberal circles, one does not deny that Jesus acted and spoke with a superhuman consciousness as well as with a human one. Wernle,

8. One example out of a thousand. According to Loisy, Luke [12:31] suppressed the word πρῶτον in Matthew [6:33] because it seemed to permit one to occupy oneself secondarily with the goods of the body; so said Holtzmann. But he adds in a footnote, "Wernle accepts the opposite hypothesis; he thinks that the πρῶτον [was originally absent but is inserted] in Matthew [with the effect that it] weakens the sentence"; Loisy, *Le discours sur la montagne* [(Paris: Picard, 1903)], on Mt 6:33.

for example, who is very hostile to the divinity of Jesus, declares that "the amazing thing in Jesus is the combination of His consciousness of being super-human with His very profound humility towards God; and this is even more remarkable in the Synoptics, because in them He rather hides the 'I' which he flaunts in John's Gospel." So we are still face to face with the same dilemma: God or what? And those who do not answer, "God," are still looking for the alternative.

It is true that, for about a dozen years, we have been observing the rise and spread of the "future Messiah" theory. Jesus thought He was destined to be the Messiah. This is perhaps the system currently most in fashion, and it is the one Loisy has sketched. Doesn't it seem to you just as contrary to the Gospel facts as Ritschl's notion of a Kingdom of heaven that is purely moral and interior? Also, the apparent agreement within this group ceases as soon as arguments come up. Johannes Weiss, who appears to be the godfather of the new opinion, does not exclude the witness Jesus gave to Himself in the saying "*Confiteor tibi Pater*" [Mt 11:25–27 and Lk 10:21–22]; Loisy is almost the only one to reject it (along with Wrede, Brandt, and in part Wernle), but he understands it far better than those who do not suspect its authenticity.

If Jesus is the future Messiah, it needs explaining why, during His whole life, he took the title and fulfilled the function of "the son of man," which was precisely a predicate of the heavenly Messiah. And on that, there is far from being agreement!

Those who advance difficulties against the new theory are not only the experts of a decade or so ago (among others, Bernhard Weiss). There are also those who want to go beyond it. And one sees appearing now some scholars who do not see in the primitive gospel any saying in which Jesus affects to be more than an ordinary man. This is the system proposed in the *Encyclopedia Biblica*. Wrede is amazed that J. Weiss has so much confidence in his theory. If, in the mind of the early Church, the idea of a glorious Messiah was predominant over every other way of understanding the life of Jesus, is one quite sure that He Himself had the strange idea of declaring himself the Messiah-in-waiting? Who guarantees us that He had this firm hope (whose source is impossible to discover)? The primitive Church, which allegedly attributed to His death a redemptive value of which Jesus himself (they say) never dreamed—could *she* have imagined His Messiahship in the mode of anticipation? And by an abuse of logic to which no one seems able to object (once the premises have been admitted and the method), Herr Wrede affirms that the sayings about the *parousia* that the evangelists attribute to Christ presuppose the Christian idea of the Messiah. He reasons thus: when the talk is of coming, the issue is coming to earth, and Jesus was here; so he must have known he was supposed to resurrect in order to speak of coming (!?); and doesn't the talk of a *parousia* fit better in the mouth of the community than in His own? After all, He would have spoken of *returning*. From a critical point of view, one really does not see why the sayings of Jesus on the *parousia* should be the only ones that subsequent Christian fact was able to influence.

We are touching here upon a famous difficulty, very old, and which in Loisy's powerful expression has been able to make something of an impression.

✳

"An historian," he tells us,

> will not take pains to torture the Gospel documents and his own intelligence to find that, when Jesus spoke of the imminent coming of the heavenly Kingdom, he was keeping back the fact that there would be endless centuries before the end of the world. And while an historian will take account of the part primitive tradition could have added to Jesus' sayings on this point, he will stop short of claiming that the Apostles created the prospect of an imminent Messianic event from whole cloth. An historian knows that on such a view, practically all of the Savior's discourses would have to be regarded as apocryphal, with the result that the Apostles, for all they wanted to reveal Christ's knowledge, ended up no longer knowing anything of what he had taught. One would be attributing to the disciples a different faith from the one he had preached; and one would be founding the Church on an enormous contradiction. Let him who will, embark upon this road to nowhere (141).

You recognize here again the alternatives mentioned previously once you strip them of the nuances that so naturally compose the face of history.

A more moderate and sober critic, however, would refrain from claiming that the apostles created out of "whole cloth" the imminent prospect of a messianic event. It was imminent in the sense that it had begun with Jesus, who announced it. Then the discourses of the Savior retain all their value and import, independently of the date of the end of the world, although all His teaching leads people to live in such a way as to be ready to enter the Kingdom. Such a critic will not claim lightly that Jesus "kept back" news of endless centuries before the end of the world, because Jesus said very clearly that He had to do His work without making apocalyptic calculations, about which He wished to know nothing. Such a critic also will not say (with Loisy) that Christ's exhortations carried the sense of imminent peril because He was urging detachment from a world that was on the point of disappearing.

But the knowledge Christ had? This is a very grave question, which occupied me a great deal during the period when Loisy was writing his articles on the "Synoptic apocalypse."[9] Since then, I have noted the texts of authorized Church Fathers who did not hesitate to limit the human knowledge of Christ; and since I personally am not able to abandon the Thomistic opinion, I wanted to ask theologians—maybe the question is naïve—if one could perhaps "see the essence of God without penetrating the secrets of His will." I had to add that they should want to study these questions anew.[10] They have done nothing about it, people assure us, and Loisy reproaches them for it severely. Nevertheless, isn't his way of posing the question overblown and declamatory? He says historical criticism could not attribute to Jesus

> limitless knowledge, except on an assumption which is historically inconceivable and morally disconcerting, namely, by admitting that Christ as man had the divine knowledge but deliberately left his disciples and posterity in ignorance and error, on ever so many things which he could have revealed without the least impropriety. A conjecture which would dishonor a man of genius, if it were made about him, does not recommend itself to an historian when the topic is Christ. A theologian can be content with it, if he thinks it indispensable. He can present the Savior as dissimulating his infinite knowledge and keeping His followers in ignorance … (*Autour*, 139).

What "ever so many" things is he talking about? Does Loisy think (with yesterday's conservatives) that it would have been appropriate for Jesus to clear up the question of who wrote the Pentateuch? Did He not cry aloud everything that mattered for salvation, and wouldn't the least remark irrelevant to that have turned souls away from this all-important thought? It looks as though Loisy here (inadvertently, no doubt) is comparing Jesus as just one great man to another. But for one who admits His divinity, the difficulty melts away, because Jesus did not have to reveal as man that which

9. See my review of Loisy, "L'Apocalypse synoptique," *Revue biblique* 5 (1896): 454.
10. Ibid.

God made it a rule not to reveal. This would be the place to recall that there is no common measure between the personhood of God and that of a man. A man of genius, however great, searches for the truth amidst obscurity and is driven imperiously to communicate to his fellows what little light he perceives. He does not avoid debates that will let him establish the superiority of his opinions. Jesus does not debate, does not refute. He teaches, and His point of departure is not His own knowledge but that of others. Among souls of good will, He pronounces sovereignly. We would experience a sort of confusion if we saw Him using His deeper knowledge to triumph over His adversaries. He gently sets prejudices and sophisms aside; He uses everything people offer Him to elevate further their minds and hearts. The Messianic mission is, above all, the arena for this divine pedagogy.

Whatever the case with physical and historical truths, it is quite necessary to recognize that Jesus had a supreme knowledge of religious truths, at least. He did not owe it to visions, since He did not claim to have had any, as the prophets did; He was not suddenly illumined, like the Buddha, after long meditations. He knows because He is the Son who alone knows the Father (Mt 11:27). Most decidedly, one has to get rid of this embarrassing text; otherwise, one might as well conclude that John's description of Christ's knowledge was being echoed in the synoptics, too. And this is what matters for us, since the witness given by Jesus to religious truth is the basis for our faith. It is easy to show also that Jesus devoted special efforts to training His disciples for the future; but this brings up the institution of the Church, of which I am not speaking here. As for His knowledge of the past and of natural truths, it is just as irrelevant to Gospel exegesis as Adam's knowledge is to a commentator on Genesis, or the manner in which he would have transmitted original justice to his descendents, if the case had presented itself. If Jesus was only a man, He possessed only the learning of His time, obviously, and in limited measure; if He was God, it was not suitable for Him to use, as man, the infused knowledge that He could have received. These are questions of appropriateness and psychology, which affect nothing in the explication of the Gospels.

*

The nineteenth century was not always happy in its apologetical experiments. Perhaps it was not sufficiently understood that the best apology is an integral pursuit of the truth, with no other preoccupation than to discover it. One must also say, however, that nineteenth-century apologists were face to face with adversaries who attacked just for the sake of attacking; so we defended just for the sake of defending. The objection was made that the authority of scripture rests on the authority of the Church and that of the Church rests upon the authority of scripture: a vicious circle. Catholics answer by distinguishing two aspects in the evangelists. For apologetical purposes, one could quite freely envisage them as ordinary historians, like secular historians, but truly extraordinary for their fidelity, their ingenuity, and (what is more) for being eyewitnesses (at least St. Matthew and St. John). Thus they provide (and provide to a fare-thee-well) everything historical criticism can demand to establish the facts. Among these facts stand the witness Jesus bore to Himself and the witness that He received as the true Son of God (His resurrection and the institution of the Church). In the presence of these facts, rigorously established by history, a mind perhaps inclined to believe by other considerations concludes to the divinity of Jesus Christ and the divine institution of the Church; subsequently the Church declares the canonical status of the scriptures.

In its broad lines, I think the argument is still sound, and this is where I part company with Mr. Loisy, for whom history is incapable of proving these things. I shall come back to this. But at this point I am obliged to insist on the gaps in our old argumentation and on the impossibility of giving the witness of the evangelists all its value, if one divides them in two, splitting off their character as historians. On this point, Loisy is the one who is right: the evangelists were not ordinary historians at all; they assumed the faith and wanted to spread it.

Their sincerity is no longer put in doubt, and it would be a waste of time to defend it. But when one wants to do apologetics, can one usefully begin by presenting them as eyewitnesses? Such was not the case for Mark and Luke, two disciples, and Luke says so quite clearly. One also cannot claim it for the Gospel of Matthew, because our canonical Gospel was written in Greek, and tradition has it that Matthew wrote in Hebrew or in Aramaic.

Moreover, one need only read his Gospel to recognize that he does not present himself as an eyewitness. As far as John is concerned, you, my dear friend, have said it with perfect justice:

> the historians who are inclined to see in the fourth Gospel a mixture of John's own thought with his objective and personal memories of Christ must admit the diffi-

culty they meet (and people have thrown this up to them) in trying to disentangle the two strands. I would not attempt to justify their view, but I personally believe it to be legitimate.[11]

This suffices, does it not, to make us unable to have full assurance, when we bring forward the witness of John as that of a pure historian and nothing else.

These alleged historians, writing with the accuracy imagined—did they attend closely to the *order* of the facts? Luke seems to have had this concern, but was the order he envisioned purely chronological? That is not obvious at all; and without this intention, one is not an "historian" in the proper sense of the word.

Finally, it is a law of history that the words people say cannot ordinarily be transmitted with perfect fidelity and that facts look different with the passage of time. Yes, there are words so well said that they come down through the centuries, and there are facts that are absolutely certain. But the issue here is the whole body of historical material. Well, a comparison of the evangelists (all equally inspired and canonical) proves that inspiration did not preserve them from these features of humanity's common lot and proves further that they obeyed another law, which holds that an historian deeply into his work brings into his narrative something of his own ideas and those of his group—hence their divergences.—At the same time, the resemblances between the synoptic evangelists have proved that they made use of written sources, a new element in the Gospel problem, and the most delicate one to appreciate. Criticism appears to have reached genuine agreement on the point that Mark, together with another document critics call the *Logia*, are to be considered a source for Matthew and Luke. St. Luke had other sources, and one can conjecture that Mark also used anterior documents. One cannot reproach Loisy for taking this hypothesis to build upon. You yourself, dear friend, have accepted it in your lectures on the Gospels, because it is generally admitted.[12]

What should we conclude from all this, when the task is to be more precise about history and its apologetical bearing?

Very often, it will be impossible to know the chronological order of our Lord's discourses and deeds. Very often, too, let us say most often, it will

11. Batiffol, *Revue biblique* 12 (1903): 513.

12. I would *not* conclude like Loisy that Matthew is later than 70 A.D. But that is a special question.

be impossible to know exactly what words Jesus used, unless it is a case of solemn sayings that would have imprinted themselves deeply on people's minds. Several situations may arise. The agreement even of all three synoptics does not prove that Jesus pronounced precisely these and those words to heal a sick man, for example, because this agreement can come from the fact that none of them felt a need to modify their one source, which, perhaps, did not care about scrupulous accuracy. If the three do not agree, the doubt goes further. His exact words may be found in one of them, but it may be the case that they are not reproduced anywhere. Nevertheless, precisely because they were following older sources, their witness goes back to older witnesses, these having been eyewitnesses, and because the evangelists followed them freely, one cannot argue from their silence that the parallel passage was not found in the source. Because had each his own purpose, they could omit a fact they knew about and that did not seem suspect to them, but that they judged not to be useful for their exposition. Finally, when one speaks about Luke's special source, for example, this does not indicate an aftergrowth of the tradition but simply a feature that the sources of Mark and Matthew did not contain and that Luke (according to his promise) would not have accepted without being sure of its authentic origin. Thus one sees the most liberal critics recognizing *here and there* that Luke had an older source and that he interpreted the tradition better. Not even Matthew itself, which is accused of having developed the Christian point of view more than the others, fails to contain very archaic features; it has preserved especially faithfully the Palestinian and Semitic coloration that Luke had to attenuate for his Gentile readers.

Isn't the upshot of all this that it is easier to extract a religious doctrine from the evangelists than to put them side by side to compose a history properly so called? The wrong move of the critics, once they recognized these facts, was to try to write this history themselves. What happened to the evangelists (on a small scale, one may say) has now happened on a grand scale. Each critic has reconstructed the life of Jesus according to his own idea of Jesus. When one of them despaired of getting all the way back to Jesus, he at least wrote up some new wrinkle on the hypothesis of the primitive source! Each one thought he knew why such-and-such an evangelist added or omitted such-and-such a word, which then had to be omitted from or added to the primitive source. I have already tried to describe this game; sometimes it comes out right, other times it fails. But necessarily, a history composed entirely of these particular reconstructions has every chance of being false. It is certainly subjective, because it is impossible for the critic not to be guided, in his choice of what to remove or leave standing as the primitive tradition, by his own ideas of how the history developed.

Is it not safer and more objective to take as one's guide here the tradition of the Church? If it is, then how are we to understand the relation of the synoptic evangelists to history and to the Church?

We have already put beyond all cavil their absolute sincerity. It is to the credit of contemporary criticism that it does not doubt it. It is thus agreed that the evangelists did not write anything that they did not believe to be true. One cannot suppose that they would have told a story about the life of Jesus without believing it, nor can one suppose that they would put a teaching into His mouth simply because they wanted to address the Church under the cover of His authority. Furthermore, if they did not pretend to be historians in the manner of Thucydides—probably having no inkling of that way of writing history—they certainly wanted to recount real facts, and facts that they considered the basis of their faith, and their intention was that people should take these facts for sure and certain, on their testimony. If they were not eyewitnesses, they had access to sources. As far as essential facts are concerned, they did not advance any claim that was not publicly famous in the Church, with the result that their testimony is not isolated; it is that of the first Christian generation; it is that of the generation that instructed Paul on the deeds of the Savior. It is certain that, for them, the facts did not present themselves outside of their supernatural character. But did this character rob the facts of their phenomenal, historical aspect? [Most critics think so, and] this is what I cannot understand. One can say *in a certain sense* that the incarnation is not a historical fact, nor is the resurrection of Jesus Christ insofar as it established Him in His glory, and it is certain in any case that history is powerless to establish His divinity. But it can fix the facts of His life, and these can serve as the basis for the act of faith.

The supernatural character of the facts and the faith's affirmation of their religious meaning do not change the conditions for examining the phenomena. If an outward phenomenon can be established, one does not see why the evangelists (whose testimony is corroborated by the whole Church) should not be acceptable witnesses.

It remains to pin down the critics' method. Because historical criticism has recognized that precise historical knowledge of the details is impossible in such a large number of cases, the best the critics can do is *select* some primitive details, after comparing the texts, under the control of a preconceived theory.

Would it not be wiser to first take up the documents as they are, study each Gospel very closely to disengage the principal claims made by Jesus, the features of His teaching, and the broad facts of His life? Then one is only comparing one evangelist to another on these broad lines; the synoptics would fit together quite well and would furnish an indisputable basis for the developments found in John. Finally, one would be putting the written Gospels together with the Church herself. Though they were in part her organs, the evangelists lose nothing of their value as witnesses. Without being eyewitnesses, they still inspire full confidence because their testimony is that of everybody. It is the authority of the Church or just ecclesiastical fact that, at the end of the day, closes the question.

For example, my dear friend, in your study on the Eucharist,[13] you encountered the following fact: Paul (1 Cor 11:24) and Luke (22:19) are the only ones to have Christ say at the last supper, "Do this in memory of me." Mark and Matthew are mute on this. Obviously, it is far too arbitrary to conclude that "therefore" the sources said nothing, and this is a Pauline addition. But what settled the question, as you show very well, is the fact that the Church *did* reenact the supper, and it is impossible to explain her conduct if she had not received this order to do so. The ecclesiastical fact and the Gospel texts provide mutual support and constitute, when put together, an unshakable witness.

Anyone wishing to make an attentive comparison of your sharp discussion with the pages in which Loisy "shows" the origins of the Eucharist in faith in Jesus risen and present for His own in the supper of the community (eventually, the Eucharistic banquet) will understand the difference (I think) between these two methods.

*

13. Batiffol, *Revue biblique* 12 (October 1903).

According to Loisy, it was only after the resurrection that the prospect of an imminent arrival was abandoned for good, and so "the texts which really concern the institution of the Church are words of the glorified Christ." From Loisy's historical point of view, it is particularly important to put the whole institution of Christianity into the resurrection era. From the Catholic point of view, this is less important, because the risen Christ is no less real, no less living, than Jesus during His mortal life. But the issue here is history and the evidence it can furnish. It is doubtful whether many historians take the middle position at which Loisy stops. When he denies to history the power to furnish "complete and adequate" proof of a supernatural fact, the precautions expressed by these adjectives seem to me sufficient guarantee for the exactitude of his thought. But if the historian goes further—assuming the terms here have their normal sense—and holds back from endorsing "the objective realness of the apparitions," I do not see how he can judge the *fact* of the apparitions incontestable without immediately giving them the status of probable illusions.[14] Even this will be difficult for him, because the texts speak so clearly of sensory contact that the fact of a return to life must be either accepted or rejected. A historian who is determined not to admit the supernatural will reject it plainly and simply. Instead of saying that the faith of the apostles was stirred up by apparitions, he will much rather suppose that the "apparitions" were due to the over-excitement of their faith.

In any case, if the objective realness of the apparition is in doubt, one sees what must become of the objective reality of the words said by the apparition. Everything evaporates into the *chiaroscuro* of faith, and the message of Easter has no genuine value. We have all the more right to demand that the historian explain to us the fact that the Church had this faith—a fact that, for him, is not an apparition whose reality he can't confirm.

Jesus died having proclaimed that He was the Messiah; the apparitions themselves would not have been a sufficient reason to believe in His divinity, if they were isolated from all the rest. When, then, will the conviction that Jesus was God arrive? With St. Paul? With St. John? . . . And they brought with them the *whole Church*? Here is where genuine historical method protests against such a fragile solution. The three synoptics, with different points of view, agree in showing how far the status of Son of God

14. Loisy, *l'Évangile et l'Église*, 75ff.

burst the limits of the messianic idea, to the point that this filiation can only be understood in the natural sense. Their opinion is undeniably the faith of the Church. After all, they had sources. This idea circulates everywhere in the Gospels, although discreetly, almost veiled. It had to be extracted, so to speak, from the simplest and most authentic sayings of Jesus. How could Paul, who did not know Jesus, bring it about that people retailored His history, transposing it according to Paul's own peculiar idea of the risen Christ, and how could the first disciples have assisted mutely in this transformation? We demand that people show us Petrinism, which is supposed to have marked at least a step in this direction; and if it was not recognized as viable, then Paulinism did not exist in this fashion, either.

*

But the time to examine the facts has not yet come. The task is just to compare methods. Some people wanted to isolate the testimony of the evangelists and see in them nothing but historians (almost historical critics) who established nothing but facts, so as to recover them afterward as canonical and inspired authors, whose every word is the exact expression of the truth. Against this, other people objected with good reason that the evangelists are witnesses to the faith. But when one concludes that they teach us practically nothing about the real life of Jesus because they wrote it up as the faith of the Church had transformed it, and when one concludes that they are no longer witnesses to facts because they envisaged the facts in their supernatural aspect, we reply that the faith of the Church cannot have rested upon nothing, but must have rested upon facts whose objective realness had been sufficiently established and that the evangelists (for all that they were witnesses to the faith) did not cease to be witnesses to facts.

This middle road will permit us, we think, to give good reasons against a premature solution whose consequences would be very grave. People say that Jesus believed He had no other mission than to prepare the world for the judgment that was coming to end it, nor any other title than that of being predestined to be a Messiah such as the Jews were expecting. For Loisy, that much is so well established that Catholicism has no alternative but to reconcile itself with this "verdict" of history. But this is certainly not what the synoptics thought, or what the Church thought, or what St. Paul thought. No artificial construct can withstand this threefold testimony.

We still need to study more closely, however, the idea of the Kingdom of God and Messianism. We need to know whether the idea of the Messiah was as restricted as people nowadays want to think it was, and whether Jesus Himself had a consciousness that His mission and person transcended the general expectation of His time. I leave it to you, my dear friend, to treat this subject, but criticism and history are still what we must call upon in studying this difficult problem.

M.-J. Lagrange
Jerusalem, November 8, 1903

Bulletin de littérature ecclésiastique 5 (November 30, 1903): 27–61

4

"JESUS AND THE CHURCH"

Part 2 of "Autour des fondements de la foi"

Pierre Batiffol

To Dom Laurant Janssens, OSB
Rector of the College of St. Anselm, Rome

Dear Reverend Father,

The pages you wrote about *L'Évangile et l'Église* from your cell on the Aventine[1] seemed to bring me an echo from Rome of my own small voice;[2] and I was sufficiently aware of the rebuffs, insults, or even fond replies that my friends and I have encountered that I attached a particular value to your judgment.

Together we'll have been able to measure—and *la Civiltà cattolica* will have done the same—how little the ecclesiastical public in Italy, France, and England was prepared for the controversies that have just broken out. Some people have jumped in with complete ignorance of the method and attitude such controversies require: "to the defenders of Christianity in our day," the

1. Laurant Janssens, OSB, *Revue bénédictine* (April 1903).
2. Batiffol, "The Gospel and the Church."

Civiltà has said, "one cannot repeat often enough that Christian culture is currently undergoing an historical phase, as it underwent a dogmatic phase in the age of the Fathers, as it had a philosophical phase in the age of the medieval doctors.... In somma, pare che, come tutte le scienze naturali a nostri tempi rifanno i loro calcoli e i loro conti, cosi la scienza religiosa."[3] But on the other side, in the ecclesiastical circles won over to historical criticism, what ignorance of (what we in theology call) the history of the question, and even the state of the question! What naïve snobbery it is to embrace theories, when one has never bothered to learn either their tenets or their results! What intolerance for anyone who isn't thrilled to be full of their favorite book! And in a word, what poverty of mind for science and theology!

Even though some of the new ideas are already refuted, the efficiency with which their promoters have popularized them in France (and even earlier in Germany) has given some people the illusion that they are getting the last word of science, hot off the presses. With no preparation, these people have been introduced to the paradoxes of Johannes Weiss on eschatology, those of [Wilhelm] Wrede on Messianism, those of [Adolf] Jülicher on the parables—much as years ago the early books of [Ernest] Renan initiated the French public into the fragile paradoxes of the Tübingen school.

I have tried, like you, Reverend Father—as has the *Revue biblique* (under the expert pen of Rev. Fr. Lagrange), as has the *Civiltà* (through the voice of Rev. Fr. von Hummelauer), as has the young *Biblische Zeitschrift* (in several severe reviews), as has the *Études* (in a recent study by Rev. Fr. Prat), as has *L'Ami du clergé* (in an article dated last November 26)—I have tried to warn public opinion, to undo the damage done by journals like *The Month*, the *Studi religiosi*, the *Revue du clergé français*.... But even in recovering its balance, public opinion in the Church remains troubled. The Church wants to see clearly along what historical lines people are inviting her to reform herself. The moment seems to have arrived for us to leave polemics aside and turn to constructive criticism.

This is what I want to attempt in the present essay, at the top of which I wanted to inscribe your name, Reverend Father, as a testimony to the unanimity animating our teaching—yours in front of the young Benedictines, mine in front of the young clergy.

*

3. *Civiltà,* March 1903, 717. [The portion left in Italian reads, "In sum, just as all the natural sciences of our day are refining their calculations and their explanations, so, too, is religious science."—Tr.]

Was the Church founded by Christ?

We have to answer this question by pure and simple observation of texts and facts. [Jacques Bénigne] Bossuet (who is not to the taste of all our contemporaries) wrote at the beginning of his *History of the Variations* [*of the Protestant Churches*] [1688]:

> In the end, people know what my opinion is, because I am most assuredly a Catholic, every bit as submitted to the decisions of the Church as anyone else, and so disposed that one may have no fear of my preferring my own judgment to the universal judgment. After saying that, if I went on to act neutral or indifferent to the cause whose history I am writing, or if I hid what I am (when the whole world knows it, and I glory in it), I would be giving the reader too gross an imposture. But with this sincere avowal, I say to the Protestants that they cannot refuse me their credence.

Likewise, when I am discussing points of criticism with critics, I must wear the hat of a critic; I must follow our adversaries onto their own ground and apply their own methods to them. Dogmatic theology builds upon history, having the mission to explain it to our thought and faith. In the pages which follow, history alone will be speaking; but it will be sufficiently visible, I hope, how well dogma fits the history, far from being an arbitrary and blind interpretation of it.

I

People have sought to attribute the founding of the Church to the ministry of the resurrected Christ. I do not wish to get into the earlier thinking that may have inspired this theory. But I must say that, in the Savior's statements after His resurrection, as the four Gospels report them, the Church as such is not even mentioned. We shall have occasion to see that the Savior thought of the Church from the time of His Galilean ministry.

The fourth Gospel shows us the risen Jesus appearing to the disciples in the house where they were staying with the doors shut, for fear of the Jews. Jesus makes Himself recognized by showing them His hands and His side, and He says to them, "Peace be unto you. As my Father hath sent me, even so send I you," and in saying this He breathed upon them: "Receive ye the Holy Ghost. Whosesoever sins ye remit, they are remitted unto them; and whosesoever sins ye retain, they are retained."[4] So runs the story that

4. Jn 20:20–23.

supposedly expresses the positive institution of the Church in the fourth Gospel.—I confess, I see nothing there but the mission of the Apostles. For by the word 'disciples', it is customary to understand the eleven Apostles, as verse 24 makes clear: "but Thomas, one of the Twelve, was not with them when Jesus came." The fourth Gospel is unlike the synoptics in having no account of the selection of the Twelve nor an account of Christ's instructions to the Twelve on their mission (as the synoptics report), but it has this story of this appearance to the disciples and expresses in it, in the most bare-bones form, the essentials of that selection and mission. Jesus does not confer solemnly upon the disciples powers that they had not received before; the proof is that Thomas, who was not present, nevertheless counts as an Apostle. Jesus is proclaiming powers that He had already bestowed. They have the Holy Spirit; they get Him from Jesus, since Jesus already "cast out devils by the spirit of God."[5] They will forgive sins as Jesus did and as He meant them to do: "Verily, I say unto you, all sins shall be forgiven unto the sons of men."[6] But if the fourth Gospel expresses in this way the mission and powers of the Apostles, where does one see it speaking explicitly of the *society* that is the Church?

Mark's account seems to have been inspired by the same datum we have just found in John. The risen Christ appears to the eleven when they are at table: "Go ye," he tells them, "into all the world and preach the gospel to every creature. He that believeth and is baptized shall be saved.... And these signs [miracles] shall follow them that believe: in my name shall they cast out devils.... They shall lay hands on the sick, and they shall recover."[7] Let us leave aside the difficulties that have been raised against this ending of Mark's Gospel; for, whatever the textual authenticity people attribute to it, do we need to adduce this story? We are looking for a text in which the risen Christ institutes the Church; is there a question of such institution in this ending of Mark? Strictly speaking, no. Here again we see only the Apostles on stage. The Savior sends them to preach the good news to every creature throughout the world; whoever believes will be saved. Where does one see the Church directly discussed?

The same goes for Luke, because the datum is always the same: the risen Christ appears to the assembled eleven and speaks to them as in John:

5. Mt 12:28.

6. Mk 3:28.

7. Mk 16:15–18.

"Peace be unto you." Jesus makes Himself recognized, shows His hands and feet, and then adds: "And behold I send the promise of my Father upon you ... power from on high." And in vague terms the mission is expressed: "Thus it is written and thus it behooved Christ to suffer and to rise from the dead the third day, and that repentance and remission of sins should be preached in His name among all nations beginning at Jerusalem. And ye are witnesses of these things."[8] Let me repeat that the Apostles alone are on stage and that only their mission to be preachers of the good news is affirmed.

Finally, here is the most explicit of all the texts about the founding of the Church (or so the critics tell us): that of St. Matthew. The eleven are in Galilee on the mountain where Jesus told them to meet Him: "All power," the Savior tells them, "is given unto me in heaven and in earth. Go ye, therefore, and teach all nations, baptizing them in the name of the Father, and of the Son, and of the Holy Ghost, teaching them to observe all things whatsoever I have commanded you. And lo, I am with you all days unto the end of the age."[9] People want this "end of the age" to be an absolute date of expiration; they want the conquest of all the peoples to have to precede this "end of the age"; they want this conquest to go hand in hand with the organization of Christian society; they foresee a long life of Christ invisible and present in the Church, which becomes His kingdom on earth.... Thus they are stretching immoderately, and indeed tendentiously, the solemn terms of the evangelist; but above all they are denaturing the text's content, which in its totality is no different from what the other evangelists said, and which always reduces to the mission of the Apostles without any mention of the society that the souls of their converts might form.

Hence, we do not accept the claim that the founding of the Church is being presented as an act of the glorified Christ.

But the negative thesis just maintained does not prejudge what answer to give to the fundamental and prior question, which is whether the idea of the Church was an idea foreign to the teaching of Jesus. This question itself should be divided, so as to answer the two distinct difficulties that the critics have posed to us. The first is posed by a theory assuming that the preaching of Jesus was purely eschatological; this is the theory of Johannes Weiss,

8. Lk 24:46–48.
9. Mt 28:18–20.

popularized by Loisy. The second is posed by the theory claiming that Jesus never spoke of converting the Gentiles, but only the Jews, a theory recently expounded by Harnack.

II

When one tries to do as the current critics are doing—that is, give a historical analysis of the doctrinal content of the Savior's preaching, with no regard to any tradition of the Church, and drawing only from the same source as the synoptics did[10]—one sees that the Savior's doctrinal affirmations cluster around a small number of basic themes. The first and simplest of these is the affirmation of the Father who is in Heaven. Jesus advances this affirmation against the harsh theism of Judaism. Jesus transforms the traditional theodicy; He infuses it with a sudden tenderness—not that this revelation of God's fatherhood is utterly new, but in the sense that it becomes henceforth dominant and is at the heart of His message. But after this luminous first theme has been presented, those that follow seem difficult to reduce to a simple statement. The reason is that the Savior's teaching emerged in the midst of an already existing belief system and that His teaching aimed to transcend this system by transforming it. Thus there is in the gospel a duality of what is dying and what is being born—but each is affirmed on the same level by the synoptics, who did not have to take account of the perspective imposed upon us [by the course of later events].

Thus there is the theme of the Law. Jesus did not want anyone to think He had come to abolish the Law or the prophets, so much so that until heaven and earth passed away, not a jot, not a tittle will disappear from the Law; he who transgresses the least of its commandments, he who teaches others to transgress them, will be called least in the Kingdom of heaven. At the same time, who condemned the formalistic and legal piety of the Pharisees more strongly than Jesus? Who more sovereignly than He subordinated the precept to the spirit, and sacrifices to love? Man was not made for the Sabbath, and the Son of man is master of the Sabbath; there is no greater commandment than to love God with all one's heart, with all one's

10. We are referring mainly to [Hans Hinrich] Wendt, *Die Lehre Jesu* [Göttingen: Vandenhoek und Ruprecht, 1901]; Adolf von Harnack, *Dogmengeschichte, vol. 3* [in first part of Harnack's work] (Freiburg im Breisgau: Mohr, 1888); H. J. Holtzmann, [*Lehrbuch der*] *Neutestamentliche*[*n*] *Theologie*, vol. 1 (Freiburg im Breisgau: Mohr, 1896); Paul Wernle, *Anfänge unserer Religion* (Tübingen: Mohr, 1901).

mind, with all one's soul, with all one's strength, and to love one's neighbor as oneself, and this is worth more than all the holocausts and sacrifices.

Jesus did not turn anyone away from piety toward the Temple, not even the Pharisee and publican of the parable. He Himself went up to the Temple as to the house of prayer, and He was infuriated to see merchants there. He said, "And whoso shall swear by the Temple, sweareth by it and by Him that dwelleth therein, as he that shall swear by heaven, sweareth by the throne of God and Him that sitteth thereon."[11] At the same time, Jesus regards Himself and His followers as free of the Didrachma tax due to the Temple, because the children are exempt from it.[12] He knows that there is something greater than the Temple. This Temple made by human hands will vanish; Jesus will build another one that will not be made by human hands. The fact that two or three are gathered together in His name will suffice for Jesus to be among them, as if He Himself were the future temple, the true and definitive temple.

As He observes the Law and reveres the Temple, Jesus accepts the Scripture. He quotes it and draws arguments from it with the same piety as traditional Jews. "What is written in the Law? What do you read therein?" is the question He puts to the scholar to whom He then tells the parable of the Good Samaritan. In the Nazareth synagogue where he entered "as His custom was ... on the Sabbath day," He commented on Isaiah: "This day is this scripture fulfilled in your ears."[13] And yet the Bible whose words are in His memory and come so often to His lips seems somehow a bit strange or "external" to Him. How far Christ distances Himself from the scribes! And how very different in tone the crowd recognizes Him to be! "Ye have heard that it was said by them of old time ... but I say unto you...."[14] He treats the Scriptures with a regal freedom, and if any dictum of Paul could have come from Jesus, it would have been this liberating one, "The letter killeth." Thus the gospel was born and superimposed itself upon the Jewish Bible.

As a liberated Pharisee, Paul showed a marvelous grasp of this duality in the Savior's preaching when he wrote to the Galatians (hapless folk who were close to losing the sense of their liberation), "God sent forth His Son, made of a woman, made under the Law, to redeem them that were under the Law."[15] In the gospel themes of Law, Temple, and Scripture, we sense

11. Mt 23:21–22.
12. Mt 17:25.
13. Lk 4:21.
14. Mt 5:21–22.
15. Gal 4:4–5.

the duality of the present (which God has made) and the future (which He wills to make)—the duality of the present that is a shadow (*umbra futurorum*, St. Paul will say) and the future that is the dawn to which Jesus lifts up His eyes. No doubt we should like it better, for purposes of our logical constructions, if the thought of Jesus were all of a piece, all clear. But it isn't, and the tradition that transmitted it to us in the Gospels did not know it any differently. We may even say that the first generations were pulled in opposite directions. While the disciples were required by the Savior to have faith in His person, some of them understood His message to imply a continuing and strict fidelity to the Temple, to the Law, to circumcision, to the purifications. Didn't the "elders" require St. Paul to go up to the Temple and perform an act of observing the Law? The "elders" were the type who put their hand to the plow and looked back; they understood the language of the Savior without forgetting that of the Pharisees.

I have chosen the topics of Law, Temple, and Scripture, because the principle of interpretation that I am proposing—namely:

(1) a duality inside the teaching of Jesus,

(2) a total absence of perspective in the synoptics' editing,

(3) the possibility of a reaction in some early Christian circles refractory to the novelty of the gospel—is quite well verified in these initial topics. No doubt it will also apply to other, more difficult topics in His teaching as well, such as the Kingdom of God.

III

Critics agree in seeing the Kingdom as the standard theme in Jesus' preaching; but the agreement ceases as soon as one has to define the Kingdom's nature. I have already called attention to the theory in which

—the message of Jesus was limited to announcing the "coming" of the Kingdom as "at hand," imminent and catastrophic;

—Jesus was the last precursor of the kingdom, the agent bringing it in;

—He identified it in His thought with the Kingdom His audience was expecting by their faith in the prophets;

—the times had been fulfilled; the coming had to be a matter of days.

The reality seems to me much less simple.

Yes, the Savior found in the popular mind of His era the lively expectation of Israel's restoration. "Where is the king of the Jews who has just been born?" asked the Magi, and the question would not have surprised any believing Jew. How many were there who, like Anne, or like the disciples in Emmaus, "awaited the deliverance of Israel"? But in the thinking of the Savior, the "kingdom of Israel" was no longer anything more than the throne of which Zebedee's wife dreamed for her sons. The story of the temptation in the desert shows in what striking terms Jesus worked to detach His disciples' higher imagination from that sorry old dream of Israel's political rebirth and dominance over all the kingdoms of the earth. The kingdom that Jesus announces is the Kingdom of God, the Kingdom of Heaven, and thereby Jesus transforms the national hope into a purely religious aspiration.

This transformation was already underway in the preaching of John the Baptist. But how did Jesus Himself indicate where the Baptist's preaching was incomplete and "old" in comparison with His own? There is no greater prophet than John, but "he that is the least in the Kingdom of God is greater than he."[16] The critics want it to be the case that Jesus expressed nothing flatly new vis-à-vis the religion of Moses and the prophets, and that looking for such an element in the Gospel is looking for what Jesus never sought to put there and that by His own avowal is not there. But is not Jesus Himself the one who said, "The Law and the Prophets were until John; since that time, the kingdom of God is preached, and every man presseth into it"?[17]

So what is the Kingdom of God?

Jesus answers, "Except ye be converted and become as little children, ye shall not enter into the Kingdom of Heaven. Whosoever therefore shall humble himself as this little child, the same is greatest in the Kingdom of Heaven."[18] As the fourth Gospel will say admirably, a new birth is possible for a human being. The new life available is the one that the Beatitudes define in the Sermon on the Mount: "Blessed are the poor, for theirs is the Kingdom of God..." The Kingdom is first off conversion, repentance; then it is the fulfillment of righteousness; it is also mercy, love of neighbor, love of God.... In a word, it is a religious and moral way of life. In contrast to the sour-tempered and formalistic piety of the Pharisees, it is an easy yoke and a light burden. It is a task, and it is also a gift, a gift of God: "Seek ye first the Kingdom of God and His righteousness" and "fear not, little flock, for it is your Father's good pleasure to give you the Kingdom."[19] The King-

16. Mt 11:11.
17. Lk 16:16.
18. Mt 18:1–4.
19. Lk 12:31–32.

dom is like a treasure hidden in a field: happy the man who knows to buy that field. The Kingdom is like a pearl of great price: happy is the merchant who will sacrifice all he has to buy the incomparable pearl.[20]

The critics ask us: is the Kingdom an interior life now occurring, or is it the eternal life to come? But in the teaching of Jesus, the Kingdom is both by turns, and it must be both. Wellhausen wrote, "Jesus sets up the kingdom of God as the goal of our efforts; the kingdom will only be realized by God in the future, no doubt, but it is already anticipated in the present." If the way is narrow that leads to life, the disciple still enters upon that way, and his entry is occurring now. "Good Master," asks the rich young man, "what shall I do that I may inherit eternal life?" Jesus answers, "Thou knowest the commandments.... [But] one thing thou lackest; go thy way, sell whatsoever thou hast, and give to the poor, and thou shalt have treasure in heaven; and come ... and follow me." And as the young man went away sorrowing, Jesus said to His disciples, "How hardly shall they that have riches enter into the Kingdom of God!"[21] The Kingdom, like the treasure, is in heaven, then; but the kingdom is also on earth, and one enters it gradually by righteousness, by renunciation—that is, by a disposition of the soul acquired now. The critics quibble with us over the meaning and authenticity of the answer Jesus gave to the Pharisees (when they asked Him, "When cometh the Kingdom of God?")—namely, "The Kingdom of God cometh not [with observation, that is,] in a way that strikes the eye, neither shall they say lo, here or lo, there. For behold, the Kingdom of God is within [or among] you."[22] But this statement, this *logion* of Jesus, harmonizes perfectly with the parable of the grain of mustard seed[23] and with the parable of leaven.[24] The statement and the comparisons reveal to us a kingdom that does *not* burst forth suddenly in heavenly glory, but one whose beginning is as low-profile as the germination of a seed or the working of leaven, because it germinates and ferments in the heart of a human being.

In the preaching of the kingdom there reappears, then, that duality that is the regular thing in Jesus' teaching; popular belief in a kingdom to come is preserved but transformed, spiritualized, into a moral aspiration for the present life and a transcendent hope for Heaven. But this sublime elevation

20. Mt 13:44–46.

21. Mk 10:17–25; Mt 19:16–23; Lk 18:18–24.

22. Lk 17:20–21.

23. Lk 13:18–19; Mk 4:30–32; Mt 13:31–33.

24. Lk 13:20–21; Mt 13:33.

remains very much entangled [with the popular ideas] in the Gospel texts, due to classification and perspective. And those who heard Jesus—did they have a clear grasp of it? "This is Jesus, the king of the Jews," is how the inscription on the cross will read. I should like to think that this is an insulting piece of irony written by the Romans; but wasn't it His own disciples who asked Jesus after the resurrection, "Lord, wilt Thou at this time restore again the kingdom to Israel?"[25]

IV

Talk of a kingdom means talk of a king. If Jesus transformed the popular notion of the "kingdom" of Israel into the religious idea of the "Kingdom" of God, can one suppose a parallel transformation did not affect the idea of the king himself—I mean, the Messiah?

Let us avoid at the outset the confusion that would mix the texts of the Old Testament (in which the Fathers saw the Savior prefigured or predicted) with extrabiblical texts coming from the two centuries before the Christian era, where belief in the "Messiah" strictly so-called developed. Messianism in this strict sense is a very particular doctrine, very late, and (we may say) entirely extrabiblical and popular.[26]

In the Bible itself, this Messianism is barely indicated. When Daniel saw coming "upon the clouds of heaven one like a son of man," who was advancing toward the Ancient of Days, he was personifying under the image of a son of man "the people of the saints of the Most High."[27] He was personifying the people under the traits of a man, because he had represented the four enemy empires under the form of four beasts; he was seeing the son of man coming on the clouds, because the scene described by the prophet was taking place in heaven before the throne of the Ancient of Days. To this people of the saints, symbolized by the son of man, justice would be given by God: on the empires persecuting Israel, judgment would be pronounced, and on Israel

25. Acts 1:6.

26. I call attention to a very apt remark of Brooke Foss Westcott, *The Epistles of St. John* (Cambridge: Macmillan, 1886), 198, on the expression "Anointed" (χριστός, משיח): "It is not a characteristic title of the promised Savior in the Old Testament. It is not even specifically applied to Him, unless perhaps in Daniel 9:25ff, a passage whose interpretation is very doubtful"; quoted by Herbert E. Ryle and Montague R. James, *Psalms of the Pharisees Commonly Called the Psalms of Solomon* (Cambridge: 1891), liv.

27. Dn 7:13; see verses 25 and 27.

would be conferred finally "the kingship, the dominion, and the grandeur of all the kingdoms," in an "everlasting reign." Such was the biblical datum.

But after the crushing humiliation of Israel in the time of Antiochus Epiphanes (175–64 B.C.), this datum had a destiny that would become all the more inevitable as the promised justice became more desirable. Certain Palestinian texts dating from the period 110 to 100 B.C., which were not well known until a few years ago, the apocryphal *Psalms of Solomon* and the apocalyptic book of Enoch, have made us aware of this Messianism, which always and increasingly had Israel's revenge in view, but which was confined to personifying the "Anointed one" by whom this revenge would be accomplished. The "Anointed," the "Christ," the "Messiah" (the three words mean the same) would come at a moment known to God alone; God would raise Him up, but He would be a descendent of David; He would overthrow the domination of the gentiles—that is, the Romans; He would drive them out of Jerusalem and the land of Israel. The kingdom of the "Anointed" would establish itself in Israel; it would regather the scattered tribes; it would restore Jerusalem and the Temple; the gentiles would pay it tribute. The Lord would be its power; its subjects would be "children of God," which is to say that there would be no sinners among them; it would be just and wise. The Anointed would be the lieutenant of the Lord (who is the true king of Israel), but he would be just a human being, without preexistence in the bosom of God, without a supernatural birth. He is not the Lord but "the Anointed of the Lord." Such are the terms in which the most expressive of these Messianic texts describes him, Psalm 17 of the *Psalms of Solomon*.[28]

In the popular mind, such as it expressed itself about Jesus, the Messianism is no different. How many were there like Simeon, who had faith that they would not die "before seeing the Anointed of the Lord"? The whole crowd acclaimed Jesus entering Jerusalem with cries of "Hosanna to the son of David! Blessed be he that cometh in the name of the Lord! Blessed be the kingdom of our father David, which now cometh!" Popular enthusiasm (in its human fashion) found no other acclamation with which to express itself and to understand the Messiah. Did Jesus suppress these

28. Cf. Ryle and James, *Psalms of the Pharisees*, lii–lviii. [The now standard edition of the *Psalms of Solomon* is in R. H. Charles, *The Apocrypha and Pseudepigrapha of the Old Testament*, vol. 2, *Pseudepigrapha* (Oxford: Clarendon Press, 1913; reprinted 1964). The relevant portion of Ps. 17 is on 640–41.]

cries? The Pharisees asked Him to do so, but He replied, "I tell you that, if these should hold their peace, the stones would immediately cry out."[29]

Nevertheless, to this popular and altogether fleshly hope, Jesus is going to oppose and substitute a transcendent spiritual affirmation. Son of David He is, to be sure; but this is a title He never gives Himself. And if He voices a positive teaching on this point, is it not rather to make people understand that He is, in a mysterious sense, greater than David? "If David calls the Christ his lord, how is He his son?"[30] The very title of "Christ," the Anointed or Messiah, in the particular meaning that the people gave it—only once does Jesus claim it, and that with solemnity, when He answers Caiaphus's question before the Sanhedrin: "Art thou the Christ, the son of the blessed God?" He says "I Am."[31] And at once He continues, "and ye shall see the son of man...." But everywhere else the title "Christ" is one that Jesus seems to *not want* people to give Him. He asks His disciples, "Who do people say I am?" They answer: John the Baptist, others say Elijah, others, one of the prophets.—"But you, who do you say I am?" Peter answers, "Thou art the Christ." *He strictly charges them not to say this to anyone.*[32] Why? Because He is not the Messiah of the apocryphal books and popular belief. If Jesus was able to say one day, "There is a greater than Jonah here," a greater than Solomon, as He said, "There is one greater than the Temple here," a fortiori He could say that the notion simple people had of the Messiah (and likewise the scribes) did not measure up to Him. This explains the enigmatic answer Jesus gave to the envoys of John the Baptist. They came asking, "Art thou he that is to come, or do we wait for another?" He answered, "Tell John what ye have seen: the blind see ... the poor have the gospel preached to them, and blessed is he for whom I shall not be an occasion of scandal."[33] Why speak of scandal? Because the Messiah expected by everybody is so different from Jesus, that Jesus can only shock, can only scandalize, everybody's faith.

So Jesus did not wish to be called the son of David, nor the Christ. Rather, "the Son of man" is the title He claimed. [It was less famous and enjoyed a useful ambiguity.] In itself, the title might seem to designate Jesus merely (or humbly) as "a man." But as recent critical studies have brought

29. Lk 19:40.
30. Mk 12:35; Mt 22:45; Lk 20:44.
31. Mk 14:62; Mt 26:64.
32. Mk 8:30; Lk 9:21.
33. Mt 11:2–6; Lk 7:20–23.

to light, it had another use; in the book of Enoch, it referred exclusively to the Messiah—the avenging Messiah, who will affright kings and mighty ones, loose the reins of tyrants, break the teeth of sinners, cast down kings from their thrones.[34] What is the difference between the "son of man" whose ferocious glory Enoch predicts and the "Son of man" who discloses Himself to us in the Gospel? "For the son of man is not come to be served, but to serve, and to give his life as a ransom for many."[35] To the great scandal of Peter, Jesus announces that the son of man must suffer much, that he must be rejected by the elders, the high priests, and the scribes, that he must be put to death, only to rise on the third day.[36] Jesus keeps turning his disciples away from the apocalyptic image of an avenging and triumphant Messiah so as to bring them gently to the idea of a suffering Messiah, the "servant of the Lord" described by Isaiah.

What a contrast between popular faith and the message of Jesus! What a disillusionment for the disciples who did not understand the new meaning Jesus was giving to Messianism! And how gently but tirelessly Jesus had to correct them, if he was to get them to understand. Such is the significance of the lesson given by the Emmaus episode. Two disciples are heading there disillusioned and sad; they expected something else of the prophet "powerful in deed and word"; they expected what the popular faith expected, the redemption *of Israel*. Jesus corrects them with a word addressed also to their whole generation of resistant Jews: *O stulti et tardi corde ad credendum!* ["O foolish men and slow of heart to believe!"]

V

For the themes of the Kingdom and the Messiah, we have verified the duality that structures the message of Jesus; we have noted the divine dawning that is the Gospel. We have also noted how its newness comes across incompletely in the synoptics and how it is not understood at all (sometimes) by the crowds to which Jesus' speech is addressed directly. Nevertheless, the whole of Judaism "after the flesh," from which the thought of Jesus disengaged itself as from a thick bark, was burst open. And thus the human

34. Enoch 46:3–4; Johannes Flemming and Ludwig Radermacher, *Das Buch Enoch* (Liepzig: 1901), 68. [In Charles, *Pseudepigrapha*, Enoch 46 is on 214–15.]

35. Mk 10:45; Mt 20:28.

36. Mk 8:31; Mt 16:21; Lk 9:22.

race inherited the words of eternal life, the Father who is in heaven, the Kingdom of God, Jesus Himself.

But then if Jesus so sovereignly liberated religious souls, how would all this novelty get spoiled in the implacable eschatology that certain scholars think they find at every turn of the Gospel?

Rev. Fr. Lagrange has pointed out very well in what direction one should look for an answer to this question. "For a long time," he wrote, "generations of exegetes have been succeeding one another without reaching a definitive clarification of the eschatological problem, *because in fact different perspectives are strangely mixed together in the Gospel.* This was the legacy of the Old Testament, where the perspectives are still more confused. The wisest thing to do in such a case is not to *reconstruct everything according to certain isolated texts* while forcing the meaning of others, but to accept them all while trying to distinguish what is traditional in them"—I would add: and popular in them—"as to ideas and images, from what is new leaven in them, which can only be attributed to Jesus. This is what Herr von Harnack tried to do, but with all-too-obvious a project to reduce everything to a quintessence."[37]

In the eschatology of the New Testament, then, we have to deal first off with a part from the past, from the extrabiblical past, from folklore. It was formed in popular credence like a whirlwind of images and terrors, older than Christianity; it continued to exist alongside nascent Christianity, not without having some effect upon it, and it was slow to disperse; the figure of the Anti-Christ (so complex, so enigmatic, but which scholars have resolved into its constituent elements) is supposedly a part of this apocalyptic folklore.[38]

Did the teaching of Jesus go beyond the popular belief? What allows us to answer is an analogy. Is there not a flat-out contradiction between

—the way Jesus freed souls from the carnal Messianism of His time and

—the way He is supposed to have oppressed them under the weight of the quick-doom eschatology the critics want to attribute to Him, which is an aspect of the carnal Messianism?

If Jesus' doctrine had been subordinate to belief in the imminent end

37. Lagrange, Review of Alfred Loisy, *L'Évangile et l'Église,* 309.

38. Permit me to refer the reader to an analysis I made of a book by Wilhelm Bousset (*Der Antichrist* [Gottingen: Vandenhoek and Ruprecht,] 1895), in the *Revue biblique* 6 (1897): 145–47.

of the world, wouldn't it have gotten a striking refutation from the facts? Would it have outlasted the generation that saw it arise? The critics tell us, "primitive Christianity perished so that the Gospel could be preserved."[39] But in this case, wouldn't the deadly error have been at the very heart of the gospel? The duality of letter and spirit, of the passé and the living, would no longer be verified here, because we would be face to face with an all-controlling error that the Savior's thought neither dissipated nor even survived, an error that would have imposed itself upon Him and wrapped all His good news in an atmosphere of death.

Far from judging the whole message of Jesus in light of the eschatological data in the gospel, is it not more prudent to judge these particular data in light of the message itself as a whole?

Let us go a step further. Jesus can hardly fail to have been questioned about the "day of the Lord," just as He was questioned on the coming of the Kingdom. But on the question of when the "day of the Lord" would come, the first Christian generation (on the testimony of St. Paul) knew nothing.[40] Ergo, Jesus said nothing about it. "For yourselves know perfectly," said Paul, "that the day of the Lord so cometh as a thief in the night"—a striking echo of a saying by the Master: "But of that day and that hour knoweth no man, no, not the angels which are in heaven, neither the Son, but the Father; take ye heed, watch and pray, for ye know not when the time is."[41] Thus the "day of the Lord" was left by Jesus in the future, an unknowable future; one could not doubt that it would occur, however, or that it would be an epiphany of righteousness and holiness. Hence the wise virgins kept vigil; but they did not fail to go on living.

There is no doubt that Jesus foretold His passion to the disciples, His death, His Resurrection, His return in glory. "Whosoever shall be ashamed of me and of my words, of him shall the Son of man be ashamed, when He shall come in his glory, and in that of the Father and the holy angels."[42] This glory will blaze forth at the time of the judgment, when sinners will be judged by the saints: "Verily I say unto you that ye which have followed Me, in the regeneration when the Son of man shall sit in the throne of His

39. So says Herr Harnack, *Dogmengeschichte,* 1:73, where no one has remarked the page's similarity to the key idea of Loisy's *L'Évangile et l'Église.*

40. 1 Thess 5:1.

41. Mk 13:32ff; see Mt 24:36–51; Lk 21:34–36.

42. Lk 9:26; Mk 8:38; Mt 16:27.

glory, ye also shall sit upon twelve thrones, judging the twelve tribes of Israel."[43] The queen of Sheba, "The queen of the south shall dispute in the judgment with this generation, and shall condemn it."[44] In His own eyes, the glorious return of Jesus blends into the inauguration of joy and righteousness in paradise. The eschatology is not a different perspective from that of the transcendent Kingdom.

The glorious return of the Son of man is not the commencement of His mission as Messiah, because His mission on earth is closed by His death—or better said, it is "finished"—it is finished as Jesus' plan conceived it. The glorious return is equally distinct from the resurrection. As Wendt saw it, it is like a way of expressing the fact that, in the transcendent Kingdom of Heaven, the Son of man will continue the unique, incommunicable role that the will of the Father assigned Him.

But that Jesus' audiences had trouble reaching such a lofty view, that they materialized His coming as they materialized the Kingdom, that they attached to the circumstances of His coming traits that they borrowed from Jesus' predictions about the chastisement of Jerusalem, that they overloaded this scenario with such terrifying signs as the Jewish apocalypses suggested to them, that they represented this end as imminent, and that this troubled view of things disturbed the tradition that redacted Jesus' *logia* about the future, confused their perspectives and exaggerated their application—this is what cannot be denied by anyone who examines these eschatological *logia*. It is up to the exegetes to analyze them one by one. But a *historian* will not accept the idea that these bits (the most problematic of all the pericopes) should be precisely the ones he should take as his scale for weighing the treasure of the Gospel. A historian does not want to make the doctrine of Jesus "of a piece" with the impercipience of a generation that Jesus himself reproached again and again for not understanding. A historian will keep it in mind continually that Jesus did not like to appeal to "signs in the heavens" and that He made the following answer to the scribes and Pharisees: "An evil and adulterous generation seeketh after a sign, and there shall no sign be given to it but the sign of the prophet Jonah."[45] A historian will stand by this sign above all.

43. Mt 19:28.

44. Mt 12:42.

45. Mt 12:38–41.

VI

If the Savior had addressed only a world doomed to imminent obliteration, the very idea of the Church would have been foreign to His message. By contrast, the ideas of a "Kingdom of God" and the role of a "Son of man," which we have found in Jesus' message, open up a lengthened perspective into the future; and in this perspective, the Church is going to appear.

At this point, however, even critics with whom I have been in broad agreement part company with me.—No, they say, Jesus never spoke of the Church; and if you want to see the organized Church of the second century, with her bishops and dogmas, as a realization of the thought-world we find in the Gospel, as an actualization of the Kingdom foretold by Jesus, you do so at the cost of huge misunderstandings.

All right, identifying the Church with the Kingdom (which has become the classic position since Augustine) is far from being a *literal* interpretation of the New Testament. I have no intention of defending it. But I simply do not see that the Jesuanic institution of the Church *rests* on this identification. Jesus announced the Kingdom—both the transcendent Kingdom that is in Heaven and the immanent Kingdom that is in Christian souls—and the Church that appeared is a different thing from either. Take the saying, "Fear not, little flock, for it is your Father's good pleasure to give you the Kingdom."[46] No one will claim that the flock and the Kingdom are one and the same reality.

But what is this "little flock"? The disciples, of course, taking "disciples" in a broad sense of the word, not just the twelve Apostles. Jesus could have said of the twelve tribes of Israel what He said of Jerusalem: "How often would I have gathered the children together, even as a hen gathereth her chickens under her wings, and ye would not!"[47] If He so vividly rejects the title of king, it is because [a "king" is such in relation to a people, and] in His eyes, Israel is not really His people, because He has found in it only a small flock of disciples to follow Him. But a flock is formed, and Jesus fully intends to be the shepherd of it.[48] How familiar to us this image of the "flock" has become! Yet we do not see clearly enough that it is quite different from the image of "the people" and that the flock-image is the very idea of the Church.

46. Lk 12:32.

47. Mt 23:37; Lk 13:34.

48. Mt 18:12–14; Mk 14:27; Lk 15:4–7.

I have forbidden myself to appeal to the fourth Gospel, so as not to complicate the present discussion. But on any hypothesis [about its date, authorship, and historicity], the fourth Gospel remains full of echoes of the synoptics; so, one can hardly fail to think of the saying reported by John: "Simon son of John [Σίμων Ἰωάνου] ... feed my lambs ... feed my sheep."[49] Loisy has said that use of the full name, "Simon son of John," marks the solemnity of the scene and recalls the apostrophe, "Blessed art thou, Simon son of Jona [Σίμων Βαριωνᾶ]" in Matthew's Gospel. He has said further that in both form and content this passage is parallel to Matthew's "Thou art Peter" and to Luke's "Confirm thy brethren." "They are three echoes of the same tradition," Loisy says, "equally faithful in their substance."[50] One could hardly say better, provided one sticks to it. But if the fourth Gospel was able to attribute his language to the Savior at the very end of the first century, is that fact not a reason to believe that the underlying text, "Thou art Peter," is *earlier* than the fourth Gospel and takes its place in the synoptic tradition just as legitimately as the texts that [report post-resurrectional sayings and are used by the critics to make the Church post-resurrectional but] really have nothing to do with the founding of the Church?

"Thou art Peter...." The critics want this pair of verses,

[18] And I say also unto thee that thou art Peter, and upon this rock I will build my Church; and the gates of Hell shall not prevail against it;

[19] And I will give unto thee the keys of the kingdom of heaven; and whatsoever thou shalt bind on earth shall be bound in heaven; and whatsoever thou shalt loose on earth shall be loosed in heaven,to be an insertion foreign to Matthew's Gospel, on the pretext that neither Mark nor Luke has a parallel text. But if it is a tendentious interpolation, shouldn't one rather be surprised that neither Mark's text nor Luke's suffered the same insertion?

The critics want this solemn affirmation to be foreign to the "thought-

49. Jn 21:15–17.

50. Loisy, *Le Quatrième Évangile* (Paris: 1903), 941. We should note, however, that Loisy does not accept the authenticity of John 21. He sees it as an appendix in which an editor has imitated the style of the fourth Gospel, and he is surprised that this editor was obliged "to complete the fourth Gospel with stories in which Peter holds so large a place. Mightn't the reason be that he had to reckon with the Roman tradition, and that sentiment in favor of Peter's primacy, abiding in the Church of Rome, constrained him to crown the gospel of love with a supplement that would safeguard the legal right of apostolic tradition?"; ibid., 943.—On the authenticity of John 21, see the *Theologische Revue* (1903): 569–70, where our colleague Prof. Belser of Tübingen reviews a very recent study of this subject by K. Horn.

world" of the gospel. But we have seen how the saying of Thou-art-Peter has echoes in Luke and John; so it is *not* very erratic.

Take the theory that this pair of verses is a late gloss. Perhaps one imagines (like Resch) that the interpolator is someone favorable to the development of Roman hegemony. Then [this development must have been older than the critics like to think, because] the alleged interpolation is older than Tertullian and Origen [both of whom quote the text with the "interpolation" in it]. And what an odd duck the interpolator must have been! He writes as if he knew Aramaic: "Simon bar-Jonah," when the fourth Gospel will translate it into Greek and say, "Simon, son of John." He even handles Aramaic well enough to make a wordplay that does not quite work in Greek (nor in Latin), a wordplay that is natural only if the word in question is the Aramaic "*Kepha*."[51]

More subtly, the critics ask us what meaning Jesus could have attached to the word 'ἐκκλησία.' This word, so frequent in the Epistles and in Acts, occurs only two times in the Gospels, and they are both in Matthew. The passage containing its first occurrence reads as follows:

> If thy brother shall trespass against thee, go and tell him his fault between thee and him alone.... If he will not hear thee, then take with thee one or two more, that in the mouth of two or three witnesses every word may be established; if he shall neglect to hear them, tell it to the Church; and if he neglect to hear the Church, let him be unto thee as an heathen man and a publican.[52]

The progression indicated in this instruction—one, three, all—implies that it is just a question of numbers. The Church as it will be (an organized authority) is not in the Savior's perspective (if I may, I will say that the instruction is purely rabbinic in form), and the word 'ἐκκλησία' denotes the people of a place assembled, in the sense we find in the Psalms.[53]

Things are not quite the same in the other text: "Thou art Peter, and upon this rock I shall build my Church." The critics tell us that the idea of a "Church of God" was introduced by Paul and that Jesus had only proclaimed a "kingdom of God," so that these words could not have been

51. [The problem with Greek and Latin is that they require a change in gender between the word for "rock" as a title of Peter and the same word as a common noun. Not so in Aramaic: ʾat hû kephā, wᵊʿal hadeh kephā ʾebneh lᵊʿedtî.—Tr.]

52. Mt 18:15–17.

53. Ps. 21:23–26; Ps. 25:5; Ps. 34:18; Ps. 106:32; Ps. 149:1.

said by the Savior.—To this we respond that the idea expressed by Jesus in Matthew's text is not exactly the idea (I don't say introduced, but) expressed so often by Paul. Here Jesus is still using 'ἐκκλησία' in the sense of the people assembled and as a synonym of the familiar 'flock.'[54] Jesus says, "My Church" as He says, "My lambs, my sheep." He sees around Him His Apostles and disciples, but beyond them a nameless set of crowds who had no shepherd but who nevertheless listened to the voice of Him who had come. It is this set of people whom He calls "My Church." He wills it to be something stable; hence the bold image of an assembly that is "built." Isaiah had already said, "Behold, I lay in Zion for a foundation a stone, a tried stone, a precious corner stone, a sure foundation; he that believeth shall not make haste [to flee in fear]."[55] As Isaiah said, "Zion," so Jesus said, "My Church." All these analogies fix the meaning of 'ἐκκλησία' as the Savior uses it here, as it differs from the more technical sense that we shall see it acquire gradually in Acts and in the Epistles.

That Jesus never spoke of His ἐκκλησία *thus* conceived—that is what one cannot maintain without incurring the charge of bias. "In fact," said Mr. Hort, "the apostles' making use of the word 'ἐκκλησία' is easier to understand if the word is based on a striking saying of our Lord."[56]

Thus, at one of the most decisive moments of Jesus' public life, when He is about to set out for Jerusalem, where the cross awaits Him, when He begins to disclose to His disciples the mystery of the Messiah suffering and dying—this is the moment when the scene in Caesarea of Philippi is made to occur: "Thou art Peter...." This scene

> is above all the occasion Jesus took to put the seal upon the essential constitution of his Church, by designating the one who would be its leader, and by proclaiming solemnly the powers which this role would confer upon him.

These are the older words of none other than Mr. Loisy.[57]

Jesus did not have to wait for His resurrected life, then, to announce either His passion or His Church. But this announcement of His Church was only a charter! The real founding of the Church had to be the work

54. The same meaning appears in Heb12:23, "Church of the first born."

55. Is 28:16; see also Eph 2:20.

56. [F. J. A.] Hort, *The Christian Ecclesia* (London: [Macmillan], 1897), 9. Permit me to refer to Batiffol, "The Idea of the Church in the New Testament," *Revue biblique* 5 (1896): 360–80.

57. Loisy, *Évangiles synoptiques* (1893–94), 2:120, quoted by Bruneau, *Synopse* (Paris: 1901), 82.

of the Apostles, who had received the mission to do it. In his *L'Évangile et l'Église*, Loisy knew quite well how to show that the Church gestated and thrived "through the development of an organization whose outlines had been drawn in the gospel." Jesus was not a sower who took no pains to know where His seed was falling. He called the poor to Himself and whoever was close to the Kingdom. But He made the Apostles come after Him. Around His person there appeared a group of disciples, to whom He said, "Go," and they went. It was not an anonymous group but a "flock" that followed. It was a solid group, and within it was a smaller and closed group, the Twelve. Those whom He took from their boats and nets were destined not to return to them; Jesus *intended*, then, to make them fishers of men.

Mr. Jean Réville wrote somewhere that there is no room for examining the words at the end of Matthew, "Go, teach all nations, baptizing them," on the grounds that "instructions given in Galilee after the resurrection cannot be an object of scientific study." I should not care to deny that, between the believer and the unbeliever, a preliminary question has to be cleared away (the question of the supernatural) before one can make a focal issue out of statements like the one just cited from Matthew. But suppose (*dato non concesso*) that Mr. Réville is right, and [a scientific historian has to think that] these statements of the first Gospel are not what made the Apostles set out to teach all nations. Who or what, then, gave them the signal to set out? You assume that Jesus proclaimed only the imminent demise of everything, and they set out to teach? You assume that Jesus' predictions fizzled sadly, and they set out to teach? Wouldn't that have been the occasion to go back to their boats?

We are in the presence of a fact more striking than all the objections that can be made to the texts: the fact that those very men who had eaten and drunk with Jesus got going on their mission, the fact that a society established by them existed in Jerusalem, in Judea, in the Roman Empire, the fact that a primacy was acknowledged for Peter in preference to those who were called the "brothers of the Lord" and in preference even to John or Paul. [Liberal critics like to compare the allegedly apostolic status of the Creed with that of the Church.] The critics play a good game when they take the text we call the Apostles' Creed and establish that it [was not written by the Apostles but] took form in the Church of Rome in the course of the second century. But the formation of the Church is quite different, because, having been announced and named by Jesus Himself, it became *a reality* soon after the Resurrection, thanks to the Apostles themselves.

VII

The message of Jesus, thus conceived, presents itself as an essentially organic thought, a unique flower appearing on a stem with deep roots, but a flower that is about to go into fruit; the Church will be that fruit. However, we are not finished with the difficulties that contemporary criticism poses to us. Mr. Harnack, so determined in his *Essence of Christianity* to repudiate the eschatological theory of Johannes Weiss, has undertaken to show in a more recent book that Jesus' horizon never went beyond the circle of the old Israel and did not foresee the call of the gentiles. The message of the Savior was thus nationalist in its terms and was only universalist in its spirit. The message contained so vivacious a love for God and man that the spirit of Jesus led the Apostles to conquer the world, but the Master Himself had told them nothing about doing so. Such is the thesis.[58]

To back it up, one is obliged to set aside the testimony of the evangelists as such. For the evangelists certainly bear witness that they believed the gospel to be destined for all nations. The fourth Gospel is as suffused with universalism as one could wish. It sees in Jesus the Lamb of God who takes away the sins of the world. God so loved the *world* that He gave His only begotten Son, so that whoever believes in Him should not perish. Jesus says that when He shall have been lifted up from the earth, He will draw all men to Himself. Same horizon for Luke and Matthew. The risen Christ sends His Apostles to preach the Gospel "throughout the whole world to every creature," as Matthew puts it, "throughout all nations beginning with Jerusalem," as Luke puts it. In these two evangelists, the infancy narratives are suffused with the idea that Jesus is "a light to enlighten the gentiles." And wasn't it magi from the East who came to His crib, as a symbol of the calling of the gentiles? Finally, Mark has Jesus saying to His disciples, "The gospel must be preached to all nations," in the same discourse in which Matthew has Him saying, "this gospel of the kingdom will be preached throughout the whole world, as a witness to all nations."[59]

58. Harnack, *Mission und Ausbreitung des Christentums* (Leipzig: [Hinrichs'sche Buchhandlung], 1902), 25ff.

59. Mk 13:10; Mt 24:14.

The personal conviction of the evangelists is thus beyond doubt; and to establish Harnack's intended thesis, one must put the personal thought of Jesus into contradiction with that of His evangelists. We know the scene that Mark and Matthew place in the house of Simon, at Bethany. A woman with an alabaster vase comes to pour the perfume it contains on the Savior's head; the disciples cry out against this prodigality, and Jesus answers them, "Verily I say unto you, wheresoever this gospel shall be preached throughout the whole world, this also that she hath done shall be spoken of, for a memorial of her."[60] Mark gives the original account; Matthew had only to reproduce Mark, as he did so many times. The genuineness of this saying of Jesus, though firmly guaranteed by the critics, is nevertheless not accepted by Herr Harnack. But his whole argument consists in saying that Matthew, instead of writing "the gospel" (τὸ εὐαγγέλιον), wrote "this gospel" (τὸ εὐαγγέλιον τοῦτο), and that consequently the saying attributed here to Jesus was "colored" by the later fact of Christianity's propagation throughout the world; the redactional tradition will have committed an anachronism.[61] To this I respond: no, for the original here is the text of Mark, and this text is without restriction. Matthew embellished the text with the demonstrative τοῦτο, but this demonstrative is a familiar form of language for him in a parallel occurrence and does not imply a sense of the word for "gospel" different from the sense Jesus Himself gave it.[62] Thus it was for a purely aprioristic reason that Harnack and company eliminated this saying from the debate.

Now let us say something about the parable of the vinedressers.[63] The vineyard that was planted, that was surrounded by a ditch, that was furnished with a press and a tower, and finally rented out to vinedressers, is an allegory of the people of Israel. The servants who are sent to the vinedressers are the prophets; they are assaulted, outraged, wounded, put to death. Finally the only son comes, who is killed by the vinedressers and cast outside the vineyard. What will the owner do? He will come; he will do away with those vinedressers, and he will give the vineyard to others. This parable has been given rough handling these days; the critics say it is an allegory containing a sort of philosophy of the history of Israel "insofar as this history has its decisive and climactic point in the apparition and death

60. Mk 14:9; Mt 26:13.

61. Harnack, *Mission*,, 26.

62. Mt 24:14.

63. Mk 12:1–12; Lk 20:9–19; Mt 21:33–46.

of Jesus." It is nothing more, then, than "a product of the allegorizing tradition that was exercised on the parables." But Jülicher's rule, to the effect that the genuine parables are not to be allegories, is hardly secure; Loisy admits it, Harnack has reservations, Bugge declares it unacceptable! We could reasonably wait before we tear this page out of the Gospel. Shall we say with Harnack that, on any hypothesis, the parable of the vinedressers has no bearing on the call of the gentiles? Say what? Here is a parable that proclaims the reprobation of Israel, that speaks of a transfer "to others" of the privilege Israel had of being God's people; and these "others," who are not Israel, are still Israel?

The case of this parable, then, is like that of Matthew's "Thou art Peter" text. It announces a new Israel, a new people, the flock of which Paul will speak when he tells the elders of Miletus about the mission they have "to shepherd the Church of the Lord which was acquired by His own blood."[64] The Gospel's images do not have the same firmness of the Pauline formulas, but the images foretell the formulas, and together they affirm the same thought, which is that Israel will not inherit the Kingdom of God and that this Kingdom will be given to "others." Such is the meaning of this other saying of the Lord in Matthew: "I tell you that the Kingdom of God shall be taken from you and shall be given to a nation which will bear its fruits,"[65] as Jesus turns His back on the sterile fig tree.

In the parable of the wedding feast,[66] the Savior's teaching is directed toward the same conclusion. The king, who is God, has prepared a wedding feast for his son. The king's servants go to summon the invitees, who excuse themselves, who rebel. Hence the king will exterminate them. "Then He said to His servants: the wedding feast is prepared, but those invited were not worthy: go therefore into the streets and alleys to summon those whom ye find." The invitees who excused themselves or rebelled are the same as the wicked vinedressers; God repudiates them in parallel fashion. The kingdom is given to those whom God substitutes for the unworthy but invited children of Israel. Matthew collected elsewhere a saying of Jesus that expresses exactly the same thought: "I tell you that many shall come from the East and the West, and will sit at banquet with Abraham, Isaac, and Jacob, in the Kingdom of heaven."[67]

64. Acts 20:28.
65. Mt 21:43.
66. Mt 22:1–14.
67. Mt 8:11.

One must conclude that, in a given moment in His preaching of the Kingdom of God, Jesus witnessed that the stubborn resistance of Israel was henceforth a settled fact. How many times did He want to gather the children of Jerusalem as a hen gathers its chicks? Jerusalem repulsed Him, Galilee repulsed Him, the scribes and Pharisees repulsed Him, the rich repulsed Him. The gospel of the Beatitudes and of the Kingdom was welcomed only by the poor; the poor at least have the gospel preached to them. And that is what the Master meant in the saying that comes so often to His lips and by which He seems to cast His lot with "the lost sheep of the house of Israel." These "lost sheep," these poor people, are the ones to whom the disciples will go first.

Jesus sends the Twelve and gives them this rule: "go not unto the gentiles, and enter not the villages of the Samaritans, but go to the lost sheep of the house of Israel."[68] And He says in the same discourse, "when they shall persecute you in one village, flee into another. Verily, I say unto you, ye will not finish the villages of Israel, before the son of man cometh."[69] At bottom, these two texts are the only ones on which Harnack relies to justify his theory.

For our part, we think that the Gospel is an organic thought and that the *logia* that clash with this organic thought should be interpreted as *logia* whose force the redactional tradition has gotten wrong by not putting them on their level or in their real context. "No one is ignorant of how little the Synoptic evangelists took pains to group the Savior's deeds and sayings according to an objective and real plan, taking them in overview."[70] They collected the Master's sayings in the existing tradition, grouping them as best they could, sometimes on the basis of merely verbal affinities. In such a case, the context of the saying, far from clarifying its meaning, denatures it, and this is what we call getting their force wrong. Here, Jesus forewarns His Apostles that the Jews will not give them a better welcome than they gave Him; the disciple is not greater than the Master, and certainly not more persuasive. The age will come to an end without your getting to the bottom of Israel's resistance. One thus sees that a saying like the one Luke quotes, "When the son of man shall come, think ye that He will find faith on the earth?"[71] probably has the same content as the obscure saying, "ye will not

68. Mt 10:5–6.

69. Mt 10:23.

70. Rose, *Études sur les Évangiles*, 173.

71. Lk 18:8.

finish the villages of Israel before the son of man cometh." And this view dispenses us from decrying this text like Holtzmann: "where is St. Paul? Where are the missions to the gentiles? How can one reconcile this with Matthew 24:14 and 28:19–20?"

We shall say the same about the text, "Go not unto the gentiles...." If we suppose with Maldonat that the Savior is giving instructions there for the apostolate after Pentecost and not for a temporary mission concurrent with His own preaching; if the *logion* just quoted has the absolute sense that its placement seems to give it, if Jesus strictly forbade the Twelve to go into the towns of the Samaritans, then how did it come about that, after Jerusalem, Samaria was the first place that "received the word of God" and that the Apostles in Jerusalem sent Peter and John there?[72] In this case, the historical facts are the context for the texts; the facts correct the absoluteness that the texts got from their redaction; the facts show us how the redactional tradition got their force wrong and how a prudent exegesis is to rectify their force by referring them to the organic thought of the gospel as well as to history.

Jesus, Mr. Harnack has written, did not give His disciples the commandment to go to the gentiles; his spirit is what carried them there! We say, on the contrary, that Jesus showed His disciples that something greater had appeared than John the Baptist, something greater than Jonah, something greater than Solomon and the temple, and it was He. He showed that, between Israel and Himself, a misapprehension was arising that was going to make the scribes, the Pharisees, and all of Israel a sinful and disinherited nation; the kingdom would go to others, and these others would be the flock dear to Jesus and confided to Peter.

It is time to conclude.

A critic of rare understanding, very discriminating, with whom I am happy to be in agreement on many points, has written that what has struck Catholics in *L'Évangile et l'Église* is "only the rather narrow and willfully small-minded way in which Loisy has interpreted the lofty figure of Christ and the far too one-sided idea he has formed of Jesus; with good reason, no doubt, they are scandalized by it. They might be willing to say that Harnack had a higher and more truly divine perception. But they were wrong to see only this much, where there was nothing but a purely individual conception, personal to Loisy, whose shortcomings it would be easy to show. The

72. Acts 7:14 and 25.

historical and dogmatic thesis about the role and necessity of the Church had quite a different bearing. People seem not to have noticed it."[73] On this precise point, I am not entirely of Mr. Saleilles's opinion. I think on the contrary that the Catholics who were initially (and a bit surprisingly) favorable to the first red book, were seduced above all by the historical role Loisy attributed to the Church, making her indispensable in preserving the Christian religion.

What they did not see clearly is that, in the biological evolutionism described by Loisy, the Church is an organism born of necessity. "For an historian," he writes,

> the Church followed upon the gospel of Jesus; she was not formally in the gospel. She proceeded from it by a *necessary evolution*, and one only needs to verify its conditions.[74]

A bit later Loisy says:

> The Church was really instituted by Christ, because in a very true sense she is nothing but the gospel continued and the Kingdom of Heaven realized.[75]

But doesn't this explanation create another equivocation? No institutions can be "really" attributed to Christ but those for which we can establish an intention on His part. If Christ never even foresaw the Church, how can we say He "instituted" her?

In the preceding pages, I think I have shown

—that Jesus did not identify His disciples either with the Kingdom or with Israel;

—that He viewed them as a certain number of people, a flock, whom He had to shepherd and whom the Apostles, with Peter at their head, would have the job of shepherding one day;

—that He called this flock the Church.

This view of the matter and this intention were expressed by Jesus as the culminating point of His Galilean ministry.

Pierre Batiffol,
Toulouse, November 30, 1903

73. R. Saleilles, *La Méthode historique et la Bible* (Geneva: Imprimerie Schautz et Cie, 1903), 23.
74. Loisy, *Autour d'un petit livre*, 26.
75. Ibid. 27.

Bulletin de littérature ecclésiastique 6 (January 1904): 62–90; (March 1904): 91–143

5

"DOGMA AND HISTORY"

Part 3 of "Autour des fondements de la foi"

Eugène Portalié

To Rev. Fr. von Hummelauer
Member of the Biblical Commission

Dear Reverend Father,

Last August, your gracious welcome made possible for us a happy conversation in your scholarly retreat at Valkenburg. I hope you haven't forgotten it. How many views we exchanged—on how things are going in biblical studies, on the work of the Biblical Commission, and on the hue and cry about *L'Évangile et l'Église*!

Absorbed in questions of interpretation, we asked each other whether, just possibly, Loisy's philosophy of religion had gone all the way to naturalism (accusations of it were already being whispered in no uncertain terms). I quoted to you, as I recall, the criticisms expressed in the *Bulletin de littérature ecclésiastique* [given as selection 1 in this anthology]—the journal that had the good fortune to be applauded in the wisely progressive pages of your article in the *Civiltà cattolica* for February 1903.[1] I told you that, if one examined Loisy's system at its base and not on its surface, the *Bulletin* of January 1903 seemed to have analyzed it perfectly and had come to understand it not as an exegetical theory but as a venture in Spencerian agnosticism.

Then I used the *Bulletin* of July 1903 to convey to you the exact words of Loisy, which made it clear to the point of being obvious that he rejected all revelation and all miracles.

I added finally that the danger at this moment would be to fail to distinguish the exegetical problems in his works (several of which may still be up in the air) from the fundamental questions of religious philosophy (which he takes in an absolutely rationalist direction).

Leaving aside his intentions, I told you that between Sabatier's *Esquisse* and Loisy's theological system as set forth in *L'Évangile et l'Église* (especially if one clarifies and supplements it with his articles in the *Revue du clergé* from 1899 to 1901), I look for a difference, and I do not find any, except perhaps that the recluse of Bellevue [Loisy] pretends to remain a Catholic. Even the plea that he opposes Sabatier's individualism in favor of a Church (whose origin he claims to have been purely human) would not have been enough to upset the Protestant philosopher, if he were still alive; and quite certainly he would have recognized a friend, perhaps even a disciple, in his colleague at the École des Hautes Études.

Little did we think at the time that these thoughts of ours would get such a quick and striking confirmation. Just a few weeks later, two books appeared at the same time; one was *Les religions d'autorité et la religion de l'esprit* [Religions] of Authority and The Religion of the Spirit], a cold, didactic study by the deceased professor Sabatier, and the other was *Autour d'un petit livre*, the partisan self-defense of a master of irony [Loisy], unveiling his inner thoughts in irritation. Now, these two writers were treating at bottom the same subject, the problem of authority in religion. Yes or no, does there exist in the world a doctrine, a single dogma, that has the right to claim divine authority for itself and to impose itself upon the human intellect as an external and immutable norm for our thought and belief? For both writers, the answer is the same: no, definitively not; historical criti-

1. Rev. Fr. von Hummelauer, "Bibbia ed alta critica," *La civiltà cattolica* 9 (February 24, 1903) 397–413; see also *Bulletin de littérature ecclésiastique* 5 (March 1903).

cism has torn off the veil that had hidden (they tell us) the all-too-human origin of these dogmas, their successive transformations, and their breakdown from internal contradictions—these dogmas that, up until then, people had surrounded with a divine nimbus and endowed with sacred immobility. Now that the veil has fallen, it is apparent to the eyes of "the people who think" that all pretended divine authority (that of the Church personified in the papacy for Catholics, or that of the holy Bible for Protestants) is the result either of a sacrilegious usurpation or a superstitious illusion.

Such is the thesis common to the two writers. If you ask me what is peculiar to each, the former doyen of the Paris faculty of Protestant theology, more of a philosopher than an exegete, gives us a study that is very methodical and sometimes more profound; he tries at least to prove his assertions, and one will find in his pages an almost complete arsenal of the objections against the immutability of dogmas.

By contrast, his Catholic colleague at the École des Hautes Études, a very learned exegete but a stranger to philosophy (he says so himself, and his admitting it was superfluous), who has been obliged at last to unveil the real bases for his doctrine (which at the end of the day rests entirely upon the a priori claims of a metaphysical theory), has proved that genuine erudition plus an infinitely spirited exercise of the art of irony are not enough to build a coherent system, or even throw one together, much less attract serious support for it. In the philosophical part of his book, he leaves the impression of a penniless traveler in an unknown country. Perhaps also, despite his promise to have no further recourse to the prudent reservations he used to use in his previous writings (since he now renounces that wisdom in order to show that he is not utterly a madman),[2] his long habit of writing in a complicated and evasive style is still exercising its influence. The thought is wandering, awkward, cloudy; the expression is often imprecise; and, usually, a definite idea can only be extracted with great effort. What gives the worst impression of all is the contrast between the cutting tone of his (often shocking) affirmations and the complete absence of proof or logic. Nothing like orderly procedure in philosophy is even admitted.

But if we switch to the field of history, how is he? Would you believe

2. Loisy, *Autour d'un petit livre*, 63.

it? The really personal and original idea in his book (perhaps the only one) is his claim to reconcile Catholicism with the negation of all immutable dogma and (on top of that) to make this negation our essential trait—yea, the hallmark that differentiates Catholicism from Protestantism. Yes, according to Loisy, it is Protestantism that has immutability of dogma as its hallmark; Catholicism, on the contrary, has as its fundamental principle the evolution and constant change of dogma. When you read these things, you think you are dreaming. People will certainly accuse me of calumny if I do not quote the passage:

> If you call yourself a Protestant, you implicitly affirm the absolute sufficiency and immutability of the evangelical revelation. If you call yourself a Catholic, you implicitly deny this absolute sufficiency and immutability.[3]

And note this well: it's not just a question of fact but one of law. He concludes triumphantly, "I need hardly add that, on this point at least, my little book is very Catholic." Look at what the man dares to affirm in the wake of Vatican I—the Council that defined the immutability of dogma with energetic expressions admitting of no evasion![4]

Up until now, not a single writer, no matter what school he belonged to, has made this discovery. People gladly mock the Catholic Church *for* her claim to immutability and infallibility; her enemies try to prove these missing from her history; but no one has doubted that this claim was the distinctive hallmark of Catholicism.

Even so, these categorical assertions of Mr. Loisy have troubled some minds. Is it true, they ask, that evolution is the law of every dogma and every doctrine? Our Christian truths—must they disappear and be replaced by creeds quite opposed to them?

To answer this question, I have decided to critique [the portion of *Autour* that is] Loisy's "Letter VI," addressed to a young scholar on the subject of the origin and *authority of dogmas*. But it will be necessary more than once to go back to his earlier writings, especially to the articles published in the *Revue du clergé français* under the pseudonym "Firmin." Loisy himself

3. Ibid., 206. [Observe that the issue is not just sufficiency, as it would have been in a clash over *sola Scriptura*, but also immutability—i.e., the permanent truth of the message as originally stated.—Tr.]

4. Constitutio *Dei filius* c. iv, §5; Denzinger, *Enchiridion*, no. 1647. [In later editions, this became no. 1800 and now stands at no. 3020 in the 36th edition: Denzinger. For the same doctrine as repeated at Vatican II, see the Dogmatic Constitution *Dei verbum* §§ 5–11.—Tr.]

refers us back to them, as an expression of his intimate thought. One finds in them his theory of religion (January 1899), his theory of revelation and the proofs for it (January and March 1900), and his theory of religious history in the Old Testament (October 1900). There remained his theory of Christianity, which, when it was denied publication in the *Revue*, appeared in *L'Évangile et l'Église*.

I

I cannot give even an outline here of Loisy's whole system; perhaps I shall have occasion to do so elsewhere. Let it suffice for me to note that the point of departure, for Loisy, is the following fundamental affirmation: in the conflict between science and faith, one can no longer hide the bankruptcy of the old Christian conception of truth, of God, of the world, of revelation, of the destiny of dogmas.

> The current crisis (1) was born of the opposition which young minds perceive between the theological mindset and the scientific one, between what is presented [by whom? the Church?] as the Catholic truth and what is presented more and more as the truth of science; (2) it was born in the field of philosophy thanks to the insufficiency of the old dogmatism in light of our current knowledge of the universe; (3) it was born in the field of religious history by the stubbornness with which the present dogmatism [that of the Church, no doubt?] ignores the evidence of the facts and the legitimacy [read: the absolute independence] of the critical method.[5]

In the name of his critical history of the gospel, the Church, and dogmas, he proclaims that the traditional conception of dogma has failed and must disappear forever.

For Catholics, indeed—it is Loisy who says so, without noticing the contradiction with his previously cited principle that Catholicism is essentially evolutionistic—the word "dogma" awakens an idea of great precision, the idea "of a revealed truth, immutable, divinely authorized." First off, this truth comes from God: "revelation is a communication of truth made directly by God to human beings." Next, this divine origin carries the consequences of immutability and absolute authority: "a truth spoken by God cannot change; it must be as immutable as God Himself; and it cannot be questioned; it is to be taken as it is given, since it comes from God,

5. Loisy, *Autour d'un petit livre*, 217; see also xxiiiff.

and man cannot flatter himself that he can correct the lessons of such a Teacher."[6]

Against these two assertions, Loisy launches a system diametrically opposed to them. Dogma is of human origin, not divine:

> the conceptions which the Church presents as revealed dogmas are not truths that fell from heaven and were then preserved by religious tradition in the precise form in which they first appeared.

Dogma changes and evolves:

> Traditional formulas are subject to a perpetual work of interpretation, in which the letter that kills is effectively controlled by the spirit that gives life.... The ceaseless evolution of doctrine comes about through the labor of individuals, as their activity reacts upon the collective effort of the whole.[7]

Let us study the two parts of the problem separately. (1) The origin of dogma: does it come from God? Does it come from man? (2) The evolution of dogma: in law, must dogmas change? In fact, have dogmas changed?

The question of the origin of dogma blends into the problem of revelation. Has God ever spoken to man? Has He communicated any truths to man?

Well, on this point, when rationalists and unbelievers deny all communication of truth from God to man, they are acting in character. But for a Catholic writer to join in this refusal to admit any statements by God, any guarantee of truth by God—is it possible? This gross naturalism—is it believable? The defenders of Loisy have protested against the accusation: "Has not Mr. Loisy said that the substance of Catholic dogmatics was revealed, truly revealed?"[8]

But Loisy's thought on this point is beyond debate. No, he has not said that the substance of the faith is *truly revealed*—not if you mean 'revealed' in the Catholic sense of the word.

Oh, if the issue is just the *word* 'revelation,' even 'supernatural revelation,' he has a great deal to say; and for one who reads his expatiations, there are few sadder things than seeing old words, clearly defined in meaning by the Church, being used today by some Catholics to convey the very opposite of what they were designed for. They want to fool us by leaving us with words

6. Ibid., 188.

7. Ibid., 189; see Loisy, *L'Évangile et l'Église*, 158, 174.

8. *Revue du clergé* français (November 1, 1903): 555; (November 15, 1903): 654.

emptied of meaning but still in use, to hide the loss of truths we love. This is the annoying equivocation (found even on the lips of priests) against which a just protest was raised by Mr. Brunetière not long ago.[9]

But if the issue is the unique *thing* that the word 'revelation' conveys in Christian language—that is, if the issue is God's teaching and a guarantee of truth by affirmation from God—then Loisy casts it aside in the most categorical fashion and with the disdain of a superior man who pities the credulity of ignorant folk and old women. (As we know, the opponents of the new school are people "of inferior mentality," products of a defective education.)[10] Since people make bold to dispute this, I must resign myself to putting Mr. Loisy's real thought about revelation under the spotlight.

To begin with, let us take up an open avowal. Loisy is honestly convinced that if a truth were affirmed by God, it would be absolutely immutable, as God is immutable. "A human being cannot flatter himself that he can correct the lessons of such a Teacher." Therefore, if our dogma has never been immutable, the reason is that it was not taught by God. Such is his thought so exactly that he dares to add the following: if one assumes the conception some Catholics have of revelation, that it communicates and guarantees a truth to our minds, "The assertions of my little book are worse than temerarious; they are absurd and impious."[11] So, his theory escapes absurdity and impiety only by sacrificing the dogma about revelation laid out by Vatican I.

His insistence on ridiculing this "vulgar" conception is nothing but another avowal. He means the Catholic conception of God's teaching and guaranteeing a truth. "Even *learned theology* [it would have been more honest to say: even the Church in general Councils] retains an extremely anthropomorphic idea of revelation, quite disconcerting for contemporary science and philosophy."[12] And he proposes to correct "the obvious puerility of this conception."

Yet another open avowal is his outright negation of *two orders of religious knowledge*:

> knowledge which is natural or gained by reason, and knowledge which is supernatural or given by revelation.... This distinction has no application at all in the reality of history.[13]

9. Ferdinand Brunetière, *Revue des Deux-Mondes*, November 15, 1903.

10. Loisy, *Autour d'un petit livre*, xxxv.

11. Ibid., 190.

12. Ibid., 192, 193.

13. Ibid., 194. This whole page has to be read.

For Mr. Loisy, then, there is but one religious knowledge (even though Vatican I explicitly distinguished two); and if he gives this one kind of knowledge the name 'supernatural revelation' and the name 'divine faith,' the reason is that he is going to interpret these names to mean natural perception of God.

In effect, what we have here is Loisy's explicit theory of revelation. With Schleiermacher, Ritschl, and Sabatier, he keeps the word 'revelation' but applies it to knowledge that man acquires about God, without any divine teaching, but with the providential concurrence or spontaneous evolution of man's religious sense.

> What people call revelation [says Loisy] can only be *the consciousness acquired by the soul* of its relation to God.[14]

Already in 1900 he was correcting a pantheistic formula of Sabatier's. He said revelation is "the consciousness which man acquires of God, not the consciousness which God acquires of Himself in man." But if he modifies the formula, he takes care to keep its sense by adding: "revelation is realized in man, and it is, *like God Himself, immanent* in man."[15] So God is *immanent* in man! It is quite clear that Sabatier didn't mean to say anything else, as Loisy remarked.

This purely psychological and naturalistic notion of revelation—Loisy supports it by a principle that excludes any special intervention by God.

> *All* reflective knowledge is born from previous notions, and progress results from newly combining ideas already acquired, a combining which brings the bearing of things to light more satisfactorily.[16]

Thus it is by a natural evolution of our mind that the treasury of revelation is amassed.

> The truths … which constitute (in theological style) the substance of revelation *were formed by combining ideas or images* which preexisted these truths in the minds of those who first conceived them.

The history of revelation is nothing but the history of the different phases, tentative positions, and progressive strides taken by the human

14. Loisy, *Autour d'un petit livre*, 195.

15. Loisy [Firmin], L'Idée de la Révélation, *Revue du clergé* 21 (January 1900): 251.

16. Loisy, *Autour d'un petit livre*, 196; see also Loisy [Firmin], "L'Idée de la Révélation," *Revue du clergé* 21 (January 1900): 265.

mind as it examined the mystery of God. Imagining that at the origin of the human race the Eternal made Himself Adam's "school teacher" is a ridiculous conception and a gross anthropomorphism.

> That which was, at a given moment, the beginning of revelation was the perception, *as rudimentary as you please*, of the relation which must exist between man (conscious of himself) and God (present behind the phenomenal world).
>
> The development of revealed religion was brought about by *the perception of new bearings*, or rather by a more precise and more distinct determination of the one essential bearing glimpsed from the beginning, with man thus learning to know better and better both the grandeur of God and the character of his duty.[17]

Christian revelation itself, in its source and point of departure, is nothing but "*the perception, in the soul of Christ*, of the relation which united him to God and of the relation which binds all men to their heavenly Father."

To revelation thus understood, there corresponds not doctrine and dogma (as one might wrongly suppose Loisy to think) but purely the *assertion of faith*. In fact, although he calls revelation the perception of a relation, it is not the fruit of intellect alone; "it is a work of the intellect carried out, so to speak, under the pressure of the heart, of the religious and moral sense, of a real will for the good."[18] Faith, or as Loisy says, the *assertion of faith*, is not properly speaking the affirmation of a truth; it is not the assertion of definite relations between God and man; it is a stirring, a vital striving toward the good, an *experience* of religious truths, not "an abstract consideration or systematic definition of their object."[19] The truths of the faith, he says again, "are *living* in the assertions of the faith, before being analyzed in doctrinal theorizing."[20] This is the real sense of his famous formulas:

> Religion is a reality before it is a theory; it is a spirit before it is an idea; it is a life before it is a formula.[21]

Dogma begins with intellectual interpretation of this vague and pious "stirring" that constitutes assertion of faith; dogma is the theory of this stirring, based upon a reflective analysis; dogma is a scientific commentary

17. Loisy, *Autour d'un petit livre*, 196.

18. Ibid., 197.

19. Loisy [Firmin], "L'Idée de la Révélation," *Revue du clergé* 21 (January 1900): 254. Loisy himself refers us to this article in *Autour d'un petit livre*, 199–200.

20. Loisy, *Autour d'un petit livre*, 200.

21. Loisy [Firmin], "L'Idée de la Révélation," *Revue du clergé* 21 (January 1900): 270.

on this stirring, expressed in formulas and symbols that are always conditioned by the current state of knowledge.

This distinction between a dogma and an assertion-of-faith is fundamental to Loisy's system. Faith is let in by a spontaneous stirring, without arguments or inquiries; it does not express any precise and definite judgment about God the totally Unknowable; and so, since it is not a theory of the scientific/abstract/analytical order, but rather a real and synthetic act of the intuitive order,[22] faith remains intact under all the changing symbols with which the human mind tries to translate it. A dogma, by contrast, is a doctrine, a work of reason and metaphysical reflection, and so (in Loisy's system) is an essentially relative doctrine without even a shadow of absolute truth.

The assertion of faith is immutable, then, *on the condition that it affirms nothing* of that divine Ground "impossible to express in human language."[23] Dogma is subject to perpetual evolution because it expresses the unknowable and because it borrows for this purpose, from the science of each age, symbols whose imperfections, and even falsities, philosophical progress will eventually discover.

But assertions of faith, like dogmas, are not revealed teachings—that is, are not guaranteed by God. We are left in a position of flat-out naturalism.

It remains to determine God's part in revelation and faith, according to Loisy. His defenders appeal to God's part to deny the naturalistic character of his theory. "It seems beyond doubt to us," we read in the *Revue du clergé*,[24] "that revelation for him is something other than a spontaneous and necessary product of human consciousness. It is God, the true God, the real God [the *Revue* could have added: the immanent God!] who enlightens the prophet and makes him see."

Yes, God acts. God enlightens (?) the prophet (he uses at least analogous terms),[25] but this divine action does not unveil anything, does not manifest anything; above all, it does not guarantee anything with the authority of divine speech. If God's action enlightens, it is not through a higher knowledge coming down from God, but only through our reason, through our natural

22. Ibid., 255.
23. Loisy, *Autour d'un petit livre*, 201.
24. *Revue du clergé* (November 15, 1903): 654; see also (November 1, 1903): 555.
25. Loisy, *Autour d'un petit livre*, 197–98; *Revue du clergé* (January 1903): 257.

perceptions; the entire material "has been furnished by the previous experiences of the seer and by the natural conditions of his existence."[26]—God acts, but He allows man's action, the movement of his thought, to take place under the ordinary and natural conditions of any other thought.[27]—God acts, but this action is nothing but providential concursus with the vague and indefinite striving of the soul toward the "better" in the moral order, the striving that constitutes, according to Loisy, the religious sense.

> It is not possible to understand this continual striving-to-be-better in one's knowledge and moral life, a striving always crowned with success though ever combated and ever seeming defeated, if one fails to include God's action in both the striving and the success.[28]

—God acts, but this divine influence has nothing to do with doctrine and dogma, which are posterior to faith; His influence concerns only religion, the believing that is "a life before it is a formula." Never is a judgment or religious doctrine affirmed by God or guaranteed by God. Every doctrine, every dogma, is only an

> intellectual expression, a reflexive consciousness, which religion gets of itself in man, with the positive concursus and assistance of God who creates him. *This consciousness is such that a human being can acquire it.* It does not surpass in clarity the consciousness a person can have of his own nature.[29]

—Yes, this divine action is called supernatural, but by the same glaring abuse that calls any knowledge of God supernatural. "The efficient cause of revelation is supernatural like its object, because *this cause* and this object are God Himself."[30] But he does not hide from us the fact that "even in the order of supernatural religion, it is *nature* that furnishes the subject and the matter, because the subject is man, and *the matter is a fruit of human activity*."[31]

Finally and above all, this divine action that "enlightens the prophets" is not unique to the prophets; it is exactly the same in everybody, in you, in me, in Confucius, in Buddha, in Christ, and in the savage worshiping

26. Loisy, "L'Idée de la Révélation," *Revue du clergé* 21 (January 1900): 264.
27. Ibid., 265.
28. Loisy, *Autour d'un petit livre*, 197.
29. Loisy [Firmin], "L'Idée de la Révélation," *Revue du clergé* 21 (January 1900): 270.
30. Loisy, *Autour d'un petit livre*, 198.
31. Loisy [Firmin], "L'Idée de la Révélation," *Revue du clergé* 21 (January 1900): 265.

his Manitou. Maybe there are differences of degree, but the divine action is essentially of the same order in all, and everywhere it gives the same guarantee of truth—that is, none. It is unbelievable, I admit, but this is by no means a mere deduction from Loisy's system. Even in the days when prudence prevented him from voicing his whole thought (as he now informs us), he was proclaiming boldly the universality of divine revelation: every show of confidence in a supreme power, every prayer, is a permanent witness to God's action in souls.

> One should conceive this divine action on the mass of humanity *as being of the same order as the revelatory action in inspired people. Between the poor savage whom God enlightens so that he may find life in his paltry cult and the prophet who serves as an organ of the most perfect revelation of religious truth, the difference is only in the degree of supernatural light and the extent of the object which is thus illuminated by faith—the quality of the light and the substance of the object remain identical.*

And lest there be any misunderstanding, Loisy attempts a proof. He says,

> Otherwise there would be many economies of revelation and salvation for the human race.[32]

So, to head off there being multiple economies, it has to be the case that the savage and the unbeliever not only *can arrive* at faith and salvation (which Catholic doctrine willingly says) but already *possess* revelation, true faith, and salvation, *in* their very unbelief.

The *Revue du clergé* would admit, wouldn't it, that allowing revelation to be essentially identical in all peoples and in all religions, on behalf of Jupiter, Wotan, Buddha, or fetishes, is denying "revelation" in the one sense it really carries, that of divine teaching? In any case, such is the thought of the new school on the all-too-human origin of dogma, and it remains for us to reach a judgment on it.

II

People will hardly expect me to make the whole case against naturalism again in this article. It will be enough to accentuate the special traits of the theory that (already old on the other side of the Rhine) Loisy has been wanting to import into the Church.

32. Ibid., 259f. [Note a parallel between Loisy and Rahner: revelation is made coextensive with grace, and grace with morally good action.—Tr.]

Let us observe first that biblical criticism is not involved here; the question is one of philosophy, of pure metaphysics a priori. And it is certainly a rather sorry sight to see a writer trumpeting so loudly his title as a critical historian (in order to escape the need to answer philosophers and theologians) and even damning people so backward as to still believe in logical deductions, who then sets up his entire system on the rickety basis of a rationalist metaphysics, especially one that is pretty much out of date and even ridiculous. *His entire system*, I said. One is really frightened by the number of a priori theories—on the relativity of our cognitions, on the immanence of God, on the impossibility of miracles, etc., etc.—in which he imprisons his thought, his criticism, and tries even to imprison the facts and the texts. One has to recognize, after all, that once a starting point has been laid down, Loisy is an intrepid logician: everything has to bend, even the best attested facts, before the inflexible deductions of this terrible Scholastic. Does a text, even an undebated and undebatable text, have the effrontery not to square with the a prioris of the system? It is quickly relegated to the *spuria*. Loisy reserves for those cases a most ingenious formula:

all the troublesome texts *might have been* interpolated,

and nothing more needs to be said. This is the lickety-split criticism by which he gets rid of Jesus' two sayings about the Church. With this system, it is easy to be right.

Let us give just one example. Loisy the philosopher does not admit the possibility of prophecy (any more than that of miracles). So what will Loisy the critic make of Jesus' discourse predicting so clearly the fall of Jerusalem? It's very simple: Jesus never said these words; and Luke, who was a witness to the fall of the city and the temple, thought it would be a nice touch to make Jesus predict it; so he attributed these sayings to Him.—But, people object, some respected critics have established that the text was written earlier than the siege of Jerusalem;[33] Luke wrote his Gospel before he wrote Acts, and Acts was written before the death of Paul.—Why bother with criticism? rejoins Loisy: the impossibility of prophecy trumps everything, and so Luke's Gospel has to be later than the year 70.

Yes, but at the end of the day, you may say, doesn't Loisy have the right

33. [For scholars holding the same today, see John A. T. Robinson, *Redating the New Testament* (Philadelphia: Westminster, 1976), c. 2.—Tr.]

to base his work on the metaphysics of his choice?—Well, no. He does not have that right, if he is really doing the work of a *historian*, as he keeps assuring us with solemnity and even with a bit of bad temper. A historian owes us the facts, nothing but the facts, taken from good sources. If he wants to go further and support his interpretation of documents with a priori principles, he may certainly do so as a serious and deep fellow, but on certain conditions: that he own up to it when he puts history-writing aside, in order to do the work of a philosopher or even (despite what he says) a theologian; that he admit that what he is putting at the basis of his historico-critical conclusions is not witnesses and documents, but a system of religious philosophy and metaphysical prejudices into which all the facts will have to fit, willy-nilly, even if this means mutilating the documents; that he condescend to give us some good reasons for his philosophy (which Loisy has always neglected to do); finally and above all, that he cease ridiculing theologians who have dared to install Aristotelianism in the study of religion, when he himself has installed at the very foundation of his religious theory (with edifying abnegation of his own judgment) all the commonplaces of Spencerianism and Ritschlianism.

These reflections apply quite particularly to Loisy's doctrine on the human origin of dogma and on revelation. He avoids all discussion of facts and texts. The sacred writers aver in a thousand different places that God *has spoken* to human beings, that He has sent them to publish His word. Isn't there an interesting fact to study here, in this insistence of theirs on attributing the origin of their statements to God? And even if one were to admit the impossibility of any divine speech, wouldn't the following acute problem remain:

> when the evangelists present Jesus as a wonder-worker, confirming His mission by miracles, are they ultimately deceivers or deceived?

The dilemma may be old, but it is nonetheless formidable: if they are deceiving us, please let us speak no more of these imposters; and if they are victims of hallucination, which made them import an interpretation of their faith (let us say: of their credulity) into the domain of history, let us rank them among the mystic dreamers to whom we would never think of committing the direction of our lives.

Loisy barely examines the problem; and, on the heels of Renan, he insinuates now the one and now the other hypothesis. By transforming Jesus' life and teaching in this way, *they were doing the work of the apostolate*; without these changes, Christianity would have perished, drowned in the shipwreck of eschatological hopes; they saved it by the pious fibs they used in "interpreting" things—that is, in altering and falsifying the words of Jesus and the events of His life.[34]

After this, one understands why he gives them very limited historical credence and why dogmas, having their source in the fibs of the apostles, no longer look immutable to him. But one is less able to conceive how he harmonizes these claims with his Catholic faith.

Now, what are the metaphysical principles on which Loisy relies, to banish from history any speech of God to man? They are, alas, as "paltry" in content as the point-to-be-established is vast in consequences.

He appeals first to the divine dignity: it is a gross anthropomorphism and unworthy of the Infinite to make Him humanity's "school teacher." This is a strange complaint in an era that pretends to divinize science and the teaching of science! And the Creator who deigned to share being with creatures—what would be so unworthy of Him to share secrets with them, as well? Loisy has never said. It is true that [Gotthold E. von] Lessing, the real father of the new school,[35] once upon a time wrote this:

> if God offered me in one hand immutable truth and in His other hand the pursuit of the truth, I would say in all candor: Eternal one, keep the absolute truth, it doesn't suit anyone but You. Allow me only the ability and desire to seek, even if I never attain it wholly and finally.[36]

But this—refusing the light on the pretext that it doesn't befit God to give it—is a paroxysm of pride.

Next comes the autonomy of human reason, which would be violated, they say, by any rule imposed from outside, even from God. (This pretended autonomy is what dictated the phrasing in Loisy's claim "never to have had in his small store of knowledge the idea of science approved by his superiors.") This is an ambitious myth, which daily experience proves false. When

34. Loisy, "Avant-propos," in *Études évangéliques*, 13–14.

35. This paternity was established by Prof. Sabatier in *Les religions d'autorité et la religion de l'esprit* (Paris: Fischbacher, 1903), 336 and 339, and independently by Fr. Fonck in the *Zeitschrift für katholische Theologie* (1903): 3:492–96.

36. See Sabatier, *Les religions d'autorité*, 337.

Mr. Loisy cannot visit all the Assyrian monuments himself but believes the facsimiles people show him to be authentic, on the word of scholars, does he not bow to a rule external to his mind? Does he think his autonomy has been violated?

Loisy will reply, no doubt, that he yields to authenticated testimony.—But I answer: that's precisely what our reason does in yielding to the word of God; it submits to this word after having carefully authenticated the existence of divine testimony and its incomparable value.

There remains for Loisy a fallback position. In the name of psychology, he rejects all divine manifestation of truth because this totally pagan, mythological conception results in "a violent and unforeseen insertion of ready-made ideas into human understanding and into a human brain."—But now he has too mechanical an idea of revelation. He would make revelation "a divine contraption or the fruit of an artificial mechanism [like the Delphic oracle's smoke pot? like the Mormon "translating" eyeglasses?], whose very notion is philosophically inconceivable."[37] But isn't this making a caricature of revelation, so as to give oneself the right to call it unintelligible? In what way is it more difficult to conceive of God speaking to us (even interiorly but) at least exteriorly without troubling the working of our faculties, than it is to conceive of Mr. Loisy teaching his audience? Does the latter present an artificial mechanism and violent operation? If a person can understand what another person confides—what a traveler describes of the countries he has visited, what a scholar tells of his discoveries—can one doubt that God could have something to say, and that if He had something unknown to us to impart, He would have the means to make His voice heard?

Theologians have examined in detail the different manners of divine communication with man: intellectual and imaginative visions, internal and external words, always guaranteed by signs attesting divine action. Take the simplest and clearest case: an audible voice catches our attention; it calls itself a divine voice and by multiple miracles attests divine intervention. It could use notions already acquired by the hearer—just as any speaker uses the ideas of his hearers—to reveal new judgments to them, which reason alone could not have discovered, for example: "Go, tell my captive people that I will soon free them from exile." How is the psychological economy of thought being troubled or violated?

37. Loisy [Firmin], "L'Idée de la Révélation," *Revue du clergé* 21 (January 1900): 261–65.

The subtle mind of Loisy cannot have been content with such miserable reasons. At the back of his mind he has a secret motive, latent, one that today he no longer dares to express openly, but that he frankly disclosed to us under the name "Firmin." Revelation in the Catholic sense would be a miracle, since by speaking to man God would become "a character in human history." Inevitably, He would influence the course of human thought and even give proofs of the divine origin of His message.

Well, Mr. Loisy believes and teaches quite clearly that a miracle is one of those infantile relics that modern science has banished from history forever. Not only has a miracle never been authenticated, not only is a miracle unauthenticatable (since any activity of God in the world is unknowable for us—supernatural), but also a miracle in the Catholic sense of a divine intervention producing an effect not forthcoming from the natural elements of the world alone is not even conceivable by our reason.

The author of a very penetrating criticism of Loisy's ideas noticed his silence on the subject of miracles and said with finesse:

> It remains for him to write a third "bad little book," in which he will tell us (clearly this time) that he does not admit the historical reality of miracles and gospel prophecies, that he rejects the probative value which the Church gives them.... If Mr. Loisy writes this, it will not be something new, assuredly, but it doesn't matter; we'll wait for it.

Well, the bad book exists. It was published on March 15, 1900, in the *Revue du clergé*, under the title "*Les preuves et l'économie de la révélation*."

Here again, one must avoid the jingle of words. Of course Loisy does not reject the *word* "miracle." He is all too prodigal with it. But there are two ways to deny miracles: one is not to acknowledge them anywhere; the other is to put them everywhere. Loisy chooses the latter. Oh, I expect protests from the *Revue du clergé*: Him deny miracles! He proclaims them everywhere in nature, in a stone that falls, in a plant that sprouts, in an animal that grows, in human thought; this divine action is everywhere, "the great force hidden behind all phenomena,"[38] an action totally unknown and unknowable to reason.

Precisely because this pantheistic conception of "God immanent in things" puts a miracle into every natural activity, it absolutely denies that

38. Loisy [Firmin], "Les preuves et l'économie de la Révélation," *Revue du clergé* 22 (March 1900): 128.

any miracle is a supernatural intervention by God. Here is the formula for this theory, attributed by Loisy to Mr. [Maurice] Blondel:

> At bottom, there is *nothing more* in a miracle than in the least fact of everyday life; but also there is *no less* in the most ordinary fact than there is in a miracle.[39]

This claim, already so categorical, gets further meaning from the explanation Loisy gives of it. Everything is equally natural and at the same time equally miraculous, because everything is equally the result of universal determinism and everything *can* be envisioned as divine action by faith (for no reason). One of the "conquests" of science claims that no fact can be introduced (even by God) into the world's network of phenomena but what is required and conditioned by preceding phenomena. A special intervention by God to heal a paralytic, to raise up Lazarus, or Jesus, would be a *coup d'état* [against the laws of nature,] absolutely unintelligible to science.

"For a philosopher and a scholar as such," says Loisy, "*everything that happens* is what could happen, *what must happen under the conditions of the given fact*; hence it follows that a miracle is an extraordinary fact whose divine meaning can be appreciated only by one who believes in the action of Providence in the facts of every day." To conclude, Loisy formulates the doctrine this way:

> Just as a miracle among primitive peoples and *from the viewpoint of faith* is nothing but a divine action which is a little more striking than the rest, so also *from the viewpoint of science and rationality, the best attested miracle is just a fact less common than the rest, but one which must fit into the same order as the rest, since it is really contained there; a miracle rightly conceived is the process of the world and of life* contemplated by faith, which alone penetrates its enigma; the same process of the world and of life observed somehow from the outside, by reason, is the order of nature, the domain of science and philosophy.[40]

So the illumination of the earth by the sun, observed by an astronomer, is a scientific and natural fact; but it is a miracle if I consider by faith (what reason can know nothing about) the great noumenal force, God, who acts in the sun as in all of nature.

The spectacle of this slick exegesis, keeping the word 'miracle' after emptying it of all its traditional meaning, would be curious if it were not

39. Loisy, *Autour d'un petit livre*, 10.
40. "Les preuves et l'économie de la Révélation," *Revue du clergé* 22 (March 1900): 128.

so profoundly sad. More curious yet is the assertion that "this doctrine can be authorized to a certain extent from St. Augustine," made at the very moment when Loisy is obliged to admit that "this conception of a miracle is not the one commonly accepted by modern theologians."[41]

It gets better. With a hermeneutical virtuosity that is truly stupefying, Loisy pretends to make Vatican I *deny* that miracles are special interventions by God and *reject* their probative value, precisely in the passages promulgated by the Council to establish those points solemnly against the very doctrine he is trying to advance today. For my part, I know of no theologian who has ever submitted a text to such torture. The Council declares that

> [1] to make our faith reasonable, it has pleased God to join to His interior graces *external* proofs of His revelation, [2] especially the miracles and prophecies which manifest clearly God's omnipotence and limitless knowledge, and which [3] are most certain indicators that a revelation is divine, well adapted to the minds of everyone.[42]

Well, Loisy interprets these three points as follows: (1) there is no real reason to believe but inner feeling and *experience* of divine life; (2) miracles are divine facts of the same order as other, natural facts and do not show a special intervention of God; (3) far from being a sure proof of revelation, "a miracle as such is only evident to faith." To see a miracle, one has to believe first. "The divine fact, insofar as it is divine, is not absolute evidence for reason, before reason contemplates it in the light of faith."[43]

After that, one will find Loisy having a fine time speaking of *probabilities* drawn from the divine facts; but this only accentuates his opposition to the Council, which does not speak of *probabilities* in connection with miracles but of "most certain indicators," *signa certissima*—the Council that even in Loisy's translation anathematizes anyone who says that "miracles can never be known with *certitude*." And reaching even this result cost Loisy the pain of putting himself in contradiction with his entire system. After all, speaking of rational probability in favor of a divine fact *qua* divine is an unpardonable lapse of logic, when one proclaims so loudly that every divine fact *qua* divine, even the existence of God, is absolutely outside the sphere of reason and is

41. Loisy [Firmin], "Les preuves et l'économie de la Révélation," *Revue du clergé* 22 (March 1900): 128–29.

42. Constitution *Dei filius*, c. 3, § 2; cf. Denzinger, *Enchiridion*, no. 1638. [In later editions, this became no. 1790 and now stands at Denzinger, no. 3009.—Tr.]

43. Loisy [Firmin], "Les preuves et l'économie de la Révélation," *Revue du clergé* 22 (March 1900): 130–31.

essentially an object of faith. How, then, can our reason, forever confined by Loisy to the realm of phenomena, get out of it, even for an instant, to enter into the domain reserved for the divine, the unknowable, which belongs only to faith? How will our reason conclude with any probability whatsoever to the divine character of events, when this character remains totally and forever outside reason's sphere? No, no. There is no more probability than there is certitude. Only absolute agnosticism is logical, and Loisy has to embrace it.

In the new school, then, naturalism is not the bottom line on revelation and the origin of dogma. One is forced, strange as it seems, to find agnosticism at the bottom, agnosticism in the most irrational form.

There is no sure and immutable dogma for Loisy because, at bottom, there is no truth.

> Truth in our case is something necessarily conditioned, relative, always open to expansion and always *vulnerable to diminution*.[44]

No one will deny that our true judgments about things can always get more clarity and new additions, and we shall have occasion to say as much. But that such judgments are always vulnerable to *diminution*—that is, that every truth about God (that He exists, for example) can become deniable someday and disappear—this is absolute skepticism. To support it, Loisy appeals to our powerlessness to know anything about an object.

> Our perceptions do not get to the depth of a reality. Our ideas exhaust it even less. They are faded images of *subjective impressions*.[45]

In the religious order above all,

> our most consistent ideas are never anything but metaphors and symbols, a sort of *algebraic notation* representing ineffable quantities.[46]

But algebraic notation doesn't just fail to represent things adequately; it fails to represent them at all. It is not even a provisional image or outline of an object. It is just an arbitrary sign with no resemblance [to what it stands for].

And there it is: the perpetual fallacy on which Loisy plays, as do his defenders, down to and including Mr. Fonsegrive.[47]

44. Loisy, *Autour d'un petit livre*, 171.

45. Ibid., 191.

46. Loisy [Firmin], "L'Idée de la Révélation," *Revue du clergé* 21 (January 1900): 267.

47. Georges Fonsegrive, "À propos de l'exégèse," *La Quinzaine*, December 15, 1903.

> We do not know the depth of things adequately; we do not know an object exhaustively; therefore, we do not know it at all; our ideas are not images or representations—no way—but mere algebraic notations.

With a more sane philosophy, one would have to have reasoned this way:

> Our reason does not exhaust a thing and does not give an "adequate" representation of it, but attains it partially. Therefore, our knowledge will always be perfectible, open to progress; but in what it does attain and does represent, it is truly a portrait or (if you will) an outline of the thing—or rather, not of the whole thing, but of the special element it attains in the thing.

When I say, "God is good," I do not exhaust the divine, since I express only one attribute of it, but this statement (incomplete as it may be) is true, with a truth that is absolute and irreformable. It will eternally be true that God is good.

By failing to distinguish incomplete cognition from false cognition, Loisy has thrown himself headlong into the utter relativism on which he builds his theory of dogmas evolving. In his very bitter defense of Loisy, Mr. Fonsegrive was not wrong about this point: right here is the first source of our disagreements. But I hope the learned director of the *Quinzaine* will permit me to tell him that he has not gotten to the bottom of Loisy's real thinking (any more than he has grasped Scholasticism). Mr. Fonsegrive's relativism, for all its allure of trenchancy, is too timid. At the very point where he means to defend Loisy against the "backward" Scholastics, he himself smites him with a blow made the more terrible by coming from a friendly hand:

> One must also recognize [he writes on page 450] that truth has its laws; . . . it must never come to contradict itself. The law of non-contradiction is the firewall of thought. A mental process that ends up contradicting itself destroys itself.

Perfect! But there is a bit of intellectualism in that, of the purest sort; the Scholastics never asked for more.

I am really afraid that Loisy will complain to Fonsegrive and send him back an amended version of what Royer Collard said about skepticism: "One does not give *intellectualism* a toehold; once it gets into one's understanding, it takes over completely." It is certain that Loisy admits "development" of dogmas up to and including the point of contradiction; he means to ask the Church to repudiate as "false for modern thought" dogmas she proclaimed to be true in the Middle Ages.

But what is in fact right is the intellectualism of Mr. Fonsegrive, which destroys all his previous claims in favor of relativism. It is not easy to take seriously a metaphysical doctrine or a religious dogma that does not pay attention to the law of contradiction. There is nothing intelligible in a Hegelian 'synthesis' of *yes* and *no*. This is what a serious Protestant, Mr. Henri Bois, said years ago to Prof. Sabatier. People were complaining about logical intolerance, and he replied, "Logical intolerance! So be it! But fighting the "intolerance" that consists of ruling out an affirmative by stating a negative, and ruling out a negative by stating an affirmative, is fighting against thought itself and making a vacuum in the mind."[48] No need to say more.

The logical consequence of Loisy's theory is that it saps the foundation of every Christian (or even just religious) conviction. What becomes of a dogma or "intellectual statement" of one's faith, when one asserts that "reason and science can say nothing about the basis of religion, which does not belong to their order"; that the very object one means to discuss is "outside reason's jurisdiction"?[49] A dogma will be a metaphysical reverie with no shadow of resemblance to reality. It will be condemned by definition to be nothing but a "formula" devoid of meaning, and in all the vicissitudes through which the evolution of philosophy makes it pass (because it is subject to the law of philosophy's evolution), it will never amount to anything but an algebraic *notation*, the *x* of an unknown.

And what do the first assertions of the Christian faith rest upon? It is all very well to repeat that they are a life, a striving toward the good. It should still be the case that, before we live that life, we know whether it really conduces to the good. It should be the case that, before we give our heart and soul to Christianity, our intelligence has been able to verify its titles and base its conviction on the sure indicators that distinguish Christian faith from the superstitious beliefs of India or China.—Oh, well, no! Away with proofs! Away with reasoning and argument! People tell us—and they make bold to put this among the advances of modern thought—that a man believes because he wants to believe, prior to any proof.

The true religion is made to be recognized *experientially*, *lived*, and this *inward experience* has always been the real proof, variable in its logical expression over times

48. Henri Bois, *Le dogme grec* (Paris: Fischbacher, 1893), 199.

49. Loisy [Firmin], "Les preuves et l'économie de la Révélation," *Revue du clergé* 22 (March 1900): 142.

and between persons, *but certain for all those who believe*—that is, for all those who see religion closely enough to know it for what it is in itself and in its relation to themselves, and who have the courage to adhere to it voluntarily.[50]

And a little further up he had said,

thanks to being a higher act of reason, faith does not need to be based on a collection of logical deductions.

Poor logic, how they despise her! And how cruelly she takes her revenge! Look at her despisers, reduced to "the apologetic adapted to the progress of the century," giving us nothing better than this: believe first, then you will see why.

Let us envision Loisy, as the apologist for modern times, addressing the freethinkers of the present day:

I have no proofs to give you for the truth of Christianity. I cannot even tell you whether there is a God, or whether evolution suffices for everything. But believe! Give yourselves to the Catholic Church! She is an all-too-human society that Jesus never dreamed of, and she even now is compromising her future terribly by her dogmatic stubbornness and her insatiable thirst for autocracy; she made up her dogmas all by herself, while attributing them always to Jesus in order to save Christianity from ruin; she transforms these dogmas in every generation, while proclaiming her immutable infallibility. No matter! Just believe, and you will experience "the astonishing power across the centuries of the *idea* of the Kingdom of God and the current effectiveness, the personal experience, of this ever lively *idea*, notwithstanding the limitations of its origin and the modifications it never stops undergoing."[51]

One doesn't need to be a prophet to foresee the result of this exhortation. No doubt we are too intellectualist. But the human race is intellectualist, too. Human reason wants *to see* some guarantees *before* believing, and simple moral uprightness (never mind reason) obliges one to judge any form of life, even the Christian life, before accepting it and living it.

Genuine facts, moreover, are speaking loudly. This apologetic, though new among us, has been dominating liberal Protestant books for a hundred years, from Schleiermacher in Germany down to Professor Sabatier, and (to speak only of France) passing through E. Scherer, Astié, Bouvier, Léopold

50. Ibid.
51. Loisy, *Autour d'un petit livre*, 116.

Monod, and Mr. Ménégoz. And its result is the same for the Catholics who have gotten into it: a profound humiliation. Yet they dare serve up to us, as the supreme remedy for unbelief, this wan rhapsody of old formulas, thoroughly obsolesced by polemics already forgotten. How in the world! Not a single new idea! Always this never-ending "consciousness of the divine," which inspires the Mormons to polygamy, inspires seers in New York or Philadelphia to climb the next hill to see the city of God descend from heaven, and inspires more "intellectual" types to a cloudy religiosity made up of pantheism and a morality stripped of the Gospel. But just look at the fruits of this new apologetics among our Protestant brethren! Let Mr. Loisy read the sad complaints of Mr. Doumergue, professor on the Protestant theological faculty of Montauban, and the letter that gave occasion to it, a letter from a mother:

> Since we have replaced external proofs with inward experience, she writes, we no longer know what to say to our children when they become young adults. When we try to dissuade them from doubt, from unbelief, the ground shakes under our feet. We have nothing left but our tears.[52]

This is the inevitable result of a theory that denies the divine origin of revelation and dogmas, and it is not the only result, as it remains for us to show.

III

A human origin for dogma must entail the ruin of its immutability. Loisy has been logical on this point. Naturalism at the origin turns development into Spencerian evolution. To get to the bottom of Loisy's evolution of dogmas, let us determine its foundations, its history, its extent, and its symbolic explication.

A radical evolution of dogma is not just possible in Mr. Loisy's system; it is strictly mandatory. By rights, it is inevitable. First of all, it is a metaphysical necessity based on the essentially relative character of all our cognitions. Only the absolute does not change. And once our knowledge of

52. Émile Doumergue, in *Le Christianisme au XIX siècle* (January 10, 1896); see Doumergue, *L'Autorité en matière de foi et la nouvelle école* (Paris: Fischbacher, 1892). [*Le Christianisme au XIX siècle* was a weekly that Doumergue had founded in 1872 and edited for some years thereafter. By the end of the century, he was the most prominent theological conservative in French Protestantism.—Tr.]

the absolute has been proclaimed relative, one does not see how we could dare call any output of our reason immutable.

> Such immutability is not compatible with the nature of the human mind. Our most certain cognitions in the fields of nature and science are always in motion, always relative, always perfectible. One cannot use the bricks of human thought to build an eternal edifice. *Truth alone is immutable* [here Loisy is using "truth" to mean the *object* known, as opposed to the knowledge of it], but not its image in our mind. Faith addresses itself to the immutable truth [that is, the *object*, according to Loisy, not the statement that expresses it], through the medium of a necessarily inadequate statement, open to improvement and hence subject to change.[53]

So evolution is a psychological necessity. Every human being, at least everyone who thinks, must put a certain unity into his or her cognitions, willy-nilly. Every believer must harmonize his faith with his philosophical convictions:

> once one has believed the Gospel, it is impossible not to think through what one has believed, impossible not to work on this thought and not to produce a theology of one's faith.[54]

This is basically true. But is there a reason to conclude from this alone (1) that this theology will be essentially modified and transformed by the ambient philosophy (that is, confused with it), and (2) that this philosophy will necessarily entrap the faith into the vicissitudes of its own successive evolutions and mistakes?

*

According to Loisy, the history of dogma justifies these expectations of continual evolution. History recounts the necessary victories of novelty over tradition, of philosophy over dogma. One can even reduce the historical odyssey of Christian thought to four phases.

The first phase embraces only the preaching of Jesus; it closes at His death because the resurrection is unknown to history. But, Loisy and his school tell us, no dogma comes to us from Jesus that would deserve to be called, strictly speaking, a Christian dogma. This is the standard thesis of German rationalism since Lessing, now joined by Loisy. No doubt, he did not come to this conclusion at one bound. In his little commentary on the synoptics (to

53. Loisy, *L'Évangile et l'Église*, 166.
54. Ibid., 171.

which he still refers us),[55] he had said that during the last months of the Savior's career He devoted Himself entirely to forming the Twelve who were to continue His work after Him and that such a plan was the germ of the idea of the Church. But, he adds, "I would not write this today."

For him today, after all, Jesus never dreamed of preaching a doctrine that would be transmitted by the apostles, nor did He give them "a program to follow after He left them." Jesus could not even imagine such a hypothesis (any more than He could imagine founding the Church), because "up to the end, His preaching had as its object the arrival of the messianic kingdom" upon this earth and quite soon. He preached at bottom only one article of faith, and this article soon received a complete refutation from events. So nothing remains of Him but a movement, a religious and moral "push," which has been perpetuated from century to century while also being diversified and evolving in a thousand ways, like every human movement.

Herr von Harnack wanted to safeguard one doctrine as coming from Jesus, just one: the sense in Jesus of God's fatherhood. He made this the essence of Christianity; whoever admits this article of faith is a Christian. All the rest (dogma, sacraments, the Church) is a creation of the "orthodoxies." So he conceived of Christianity "as a ripe fruit, or rather as a rotting fruit, which needed to be peeled away to arrive at the incorruptible kernel. And Herr von Harnack peels away with so much persistence that one can wonder whether in the end anything is left."[56] There does remain nevertheless a faith, or if you prefer, a sentiment: "filial confidence in God, the merciful Father." This is how Loisy describes Harnack's system. Now what reproach does Loisy direct at the Berlin professor? You would think, no doubt, that he restricted primitive Christianity and the preaching of Jesus too much. But no; Loisy's sole complaint against the Protestant critic is that he still tried to preserve "a kernel" of Christian doctrine coming from Christ. In fact there is no dogma whose origin goes back to Jesus—not a single truth, not even a single sentiment of definite form or object can be dated to Jesus. Everything changes, everything evolves in the history of Christianity; Jesus gave only a *push* to this dynamic movement that continues in the thousand dogmatic varieties that the centuries elicit, every one of which was considered essential to Christianity in its day, only to disappear in its turn to make room for a new form.[57]

55. Loisy, *Revue d'histoire et de littérature religieuses* 8 (July–August 1903): 410.

56. Loisy, *L'Évangile et l'Église*, xxx; compare xxiv.

57. Ibid., xxiv–xxv.

Admitting a permanent and immutable dogma, even if it is just "faith in the Father-God whom Jesus revealed,"[58] is contrary to the law of history, which brings in evolution everywhere. If Jesus had formulated a doctrine, His thought would have undergone more or less notable changes in being transmitted from generation to generation. Besides, Jesus never claimed the title of Teacher, and because Herr von Harnack wanted to save *the fatherhood of God* from the shipwreck, he is treated as a "theologian" (which, as we know, is the most derogatory title a "historian" can give anybody).[59] *L'Évangile et l'Église* is devoted to establishing this thesis, and on the last page of it we read this: "if we have succeeded in showing that Christianity has lived in the Church and through the Church, and that it is useless to try to save it by looking for a quintessence, this little book has done enough."

If we object (reasonably enough) that the Gospels attribute to Jesus many of our dogmas about the Church, the redemption, etc., in formally set terms, Mr. Loisy responds that all of this is not from Jesus but was retrojected into His life by the apostles handing on their own sentiments after the formation of the Church—as teachers, they corrected the eschatological doctrine of the Master and transformed it by importing their own thoughts into the discourses of Jesus—as historians, they transfigured "the Christ" by expressing the enthusiasm of their faith in marvelous stories. The apostles have deceived us, but they were doing the work of the apostolate; they were saving the Gospel, which would otherwise have perished.

There you see what Mr. Loisy dared to write on a page to which I have already alluded, but that I must now quote in its entirety, because, having been published at the same time as *L'Évangile et l'Église*, it gives the true key to its interpretation, and it also seems to have been too little remarked.

As depositaries and preachers of a living religion, the first disciples of the Gospel never dreamed for an instant that their teaching had to be tied down either *by the letter of the formulations* Christ may have used, *or by the material reality of the facts that occurred; they did not consider themselves guardians of a doctrinal essence which*

58. Ibid., viii and xii.

59. Ibid., ix: "Is Harnack's definition of Christianity that of an historian, or only that of a theologian who picks from history what suits his theology?" We know what this cruelest of epithets, 'theologian', means in Loisy's school. To see it hurled at the famous historian Harnack is a consolation to the rest of us who contradict Loisy and who are all treated the same. We hardly need to add that Harnack did not recognize his work in Loisy's analysis. "Was it the Latin who did not understand the German, or the Catholic who could not grasp the Protestant?" (*Theologische Literaturzeitung*, January 23, 1904, 59). We don't have to decide which.

Jesus had always intended to preach; in accordance with the *higher instinct of their faith (or, to use their language, as the Spirit who was in them* suggested), and *as the circumstances demanded*, they took the instructions, promises, hopes, that came to them from the Master and invested them as capital—capital which would have remained sterile (or would even have *perished promptly in their hands), if they had had the scientific or pseudo-theological worry of maintaining it at all costs in the exact terms of its original form.*

Jesus had been far less the representative of a doctrine than the initiator of a religious movement. The movement He inaugurated has been perpetuated *in the normal conditions of every fecund movement in human history*; and, if it is still possible today to feel its influence and spread it, *it was impossible in the apostolic period to relive its point of departure.*

By interpreting the Gospel that they professed to recount, the evangelists were acting in character and doing the work of the apostolate. No doubt they have caused us to lose something, but not much, of what they could have taught us if they had wanted to be sheer historians; and without being conscious of it, they have instructed us on the manner in which the religion of Christ was able to form itself in the Jewish world, then expand in the gentile world. *All we need to do is understand them well.*[60]

There it is, neat and clear. In a host of points too important to have missed, we are struck:

—by the illusion "of a doctrinal essence which Jesus always intended to preach"

—by the moral psychology of the apostles and evangelists, the state of mind that strangely dispensed them:

—as preachers, from all concern about reproducing the teachings of Christ. (After all, and keep this in mind, what they are supposed to have "transformed" in order to save the faith was not just *the letter of formulations* but the whole eschatological teaching from top to bottom.); and

—as historians and witnesses, from any vulgar scruples about telling the truth! "They never dreamed for an instant that they could be tied down by the reality of the events that occurred." They recounted the birth of Jesus, His life, His miracles, His resurrection, not in their reality but as it suited them for "doing the work of the apostolate."

From this we get a whole program of hermeneutics: to understand the

60. Loisy, "Avant-propos," in *Études évangéliques*, xiii–xiv. All italics have been added by me. The same holds for all the other quotations I shall give.

evangelists "well" is to remove from Christ's life and discourses everything they added of their own. Only he forgets to tell us what touchstone will serve for discerning this.

This same page shows us the real meaning Loisy attaches to "*the Spirit*," whose role is so exceptional in his theory of the Church. It is "the permanent action of the Spirit which animates the faith and makes real *for it* everything it believes . . .; it is *the Spirit of the resurrected Christ* that gave meaning and life to the rites; *it is the Spirit* who taught all truth to the Church, as the author of the fourth Gospel saw and said so well."[61] I know honest readers who have been sent into ecstasy over this exaltation of the role of the Spirit and of the resurrection of Christ, in the name of the fourth Gospel. What a magnificent apologia for the *charism of infallibility*! Alas! For Loisy, "the Spirit" is just a word to indicate *the higher instinct of the faith*, and nothing more. This higher instinct makes us *attribute* to Christ and His Spirit all the decisions of the Church; it has no further efficacy. "*For the faith*, whatever the community has ruled, the immortal Christ and the Spirit have willed."[62] As far as infallibility is concerned, we are told again and again that it is not an inhabitant of this earth. Once a person has become familiar with this evasive language, the meaning is not in doubt. But it would have been nice of Mr. Loisy to give us the interpretive key. We regret that he reserved it for the readers of his *Études évangéliques* alone.

✳

In the second phase, *Pauline or Judeo-Hellenic* dogma takes the place of the eschatological doctrine, which dies and gradually disappears. It owes its formation to the apostles and first disciples [not as they originally spoke, but] as they all came to be dominated by Paul, and later as they were deeply penetrated by the still more Hellenic Johaninism of the fourth Gospel.

According to Harnack, if Paul did not himself formulate dogmas, he laid the foundations for them and oriented the Church on the path of dogmatic development.[63] Loisy puts it this way:

61. Loisy, *Autour d'un petit livre*, 257–58; one really has to read this whole chapter, especially pages 230 and 233.

62. Ibid., 234.

63. See the French translation, Harnack, *L'Essence du christianisme* (Paris: Fischbacher, 1902), 115; Loisy, *L'Évangile et l'Église*, 128 f.

The first, the most decisive, the most important change that the gospel underwent, and perhaps also the most rapid, is the one that turned a Jewish movement (based on the messianic-Kingdom idea) into a religion acceptable to the Graeco-Roman world and to humanity as a whole. Prompt as it was, this change was gradual: St. Paul, the fourth Gospel, St. Justin, St. Irenaeus—these mark the stages of the progression, for purposes of the evolution of ideas and the adaptation of beliefs to the conditions posed by the intellectual culture in the first centuries of our era.[64]

It was Paul, with his theory about abrogation of the old Law (the law of servitude) and about the Gospel of freedom, who prepared the way for the conversion of the Gentile world. Also, his dominant idea of Christ as our Redeemer by His *death* for our sins wholly transformed the role of Jesus, completed it by "faith" in the resurrection and the Eucharist, and opened the way to movement in Christology. Finally, in the realm of practice, he corrected the excesses of inaction and passivity to which waiting for the Parousia gave rise, as did too much fidelity to Jesus' original lessons about the "lilies of the field" that toil not.[65]

This all amounted to innovations in utter contradiction to the preaching of Christ. Yes, we find traces of this in the [synoptic] Gospels, but this is because Paulinism influenced their redactors, who modified Jesus' discourses in this direction. Even in Mark's version, which represents "on the whole a fairly historical tradition," one has to distinguish "different layers of redaction"; the last redactor is "more or less soaked in Paul's doctrines."[66] This is how Loisy eliminates the "naïve thesis" of Catholics who believe in a logical development of doctrine, working within a constant meaning, under the influence of Jesus' intactly preserved teaching.

Loisy goes so far as to formulate the following principles. In that first era, heresy was not a doctrinal innovation at all, but just a too hasty innovation, one not yet ripe in people's minds. Thus, one was a heretic and condemned as such

—either because one innovated too much, before souls were prepared by the ambient ideas (the heresy of today being often the truth of tomorrow)

—or, on the contrary, because one was too conservative with the old doctrine. One had to know how to yield at the right time. "In the first days

64. Loisy, *L'Évangile et l'Église*, 134.

65. Anonymous, "Chronique biblique," *Revue d'histoire et de littérature religieuses* 8 (July–August 1903): 411.

66. Ibid. (May–June (1903): 294, 297; (July–August): 408–11.

of Christianity (as later), one could be a heretic for wanting to innovate inappropriately, and one could also be a heretic for wanting to preserve what could no longer be kept";[67] such were the pious do-nothings, or the Judaizers, or the millenarians;

—or finally, one was a heretic because one developed the old dogma in too logical a direction; the heresiarchs were progressives who were too conservative, while orthodoxy bent smoothly and always yielded to innovations (even contradictory ones), all the while protesting that it never yielded. "Each forward step in doctrine took place despite a resistance and finished in a certain accommodation with what had preceded it."[68]

Paul in particular was the boldest innovator of Christianity, and "*if the Apostle was not the first and greatest of heretics*, it is because he innovated while remaining faithful to the spirit of Jesus"[69]—don't think of the "spirit" of His doctrine, but that of His morality and religious sentiment. And since this rather mystical explanation might not seem convincing, Loisy has another one in reserve, and this one is peremptory. "*The pretensions of Paul were justified above all by their success.*"[70] At long last! Now it is clear! Every idea that succeeds is a true idea ... to the extent it succeeds.

✳

The third historical stage corresponds to Greek or Graeco-Roman dogma, which reached its apogee in the fourth century and extended down to the beginnings of Scholasticism. The principal characteristic of Patristic theology is an infiltration of Graeco-Roman philosophy into the gospel of Paul.

This Hellenization of the gospel "dates back to the apologetical Fathers." It intensified with the mass entrance of pagans into the Church and the necessary development of Christology. After all, "to the extent these converts were imbued with Greek culture, they needed to interpret their new faith in their own way." Thus,

> there arose the Greek interpretation of Christian messianism, and the Christ (son of God and son of man, predestined Savior) became the Word made flesh.

67. Ibid. (July–August 1903): 411.

68. Loisy, *L'Évangile et l'Église*, 135.

69. Anonymous, "Chronique biblique," *Revue d'histoire et de littérature religieuse* 8 (July–August 1903): 412.

70. Ibid., 408.

People adapted the metaphysics of Plato and of Philo, and soon

> the divinity of Christ, the incarnation of the Word, was the only suitable way to convey the idea of the Messiah to the Greek mind.[71]

Nothing exposes Loisy's thought about our dogmas so well as this account of the formation of Trinitarian/Christological doctrine, as he has just described it. On the one hand, with Harnack and Sabatier, he maintains that "from the point of view of history, the Trinity and the Incarnation are Greek dogmas, since they were unknown to Judaism and to Judeo-Christianity."[72] (One gets the feeling also that Loisy is among the critics for whom "the Trinitarian/Christological dogma *weighed too heavily upon all the Christian orthodoxies*, binding them to an obsolete doctrine, to the science of Plato and Aristotle, long since outstripped by modern science.") On the other hand, instead of criticizing and rejecting this introduction of philosophy into dogma, here is where Loisy takes up the defense of these two dogmas, even speaking of the Trinity and Incarnation with enthusiasm.

> This was at its origin a show of life, a great effort of faith and understanding.[73]

Isn't there a contradiction? Not at all. Loisy is faithful to his criterion: every formula useful for putting harmony between faith and the state of people's minds at a given time is good, but *for that time*. Upon his praises for the Trinitarian/Christological formula, he also puts this little restriction: it was good, excellent ... for the fourth century. He praises these dogmas on the condition that we let him interpret them in a different sense today.

This is what you have to keep in mind when you ask yourself if Loisy affirms the divinity of Christ (I do not say *if he believes it*; that is God's secret). Alas! Even in his latest book, he takes back nothing of what he had said before. Rather, at the very moment when he writes:

> what has been gained is gained. Christ is God *for the faith*,

he takes care to explain that this statement no longer has meaning today; "a translation is necessary"; hanging onto the divinity of Jesus is "handing over many souls to doubt or unbelief."[74] The status, then, of

> Christ is God for the faith

71. Loisy, *L'Évangile et l'Église*, 135–40.
72. Ibid., 141.
73. Ibid., 136–37.
74. Loisy, *Autour d'un petit livre*, 155.

is this: it is not a revealed dogma; it is an explication of faith, imagined at a time now remote from us. Today this statement should disappear.

The fourth stage covers the whole Scholastic period down to our day. It has been dominated by Augustine's influence and Aristotle's philosophy. Loisy speaks very little about this period, but one sees that the Council of Trent (which synthesized the progress of the period) seems to him to have innovated a great deal, especially on sacramental topics. Likewise, he does not hesitate to say that people became used to putting into the Bible dogmas that are not found there. He protests against the tyranny that theology has exercised over scholars to the detriment of science.[75]

As for *modern dogma*, if one wants to make it acceptable for the philosophy and science of the present day, one must first of all proclaim the principle of unlimited doctrinal evolution; then, one must emancipate scholars and critics completely, a step that is called "a change of mind and attitude toward the intellectual movement of our century";[76] finally, by interpreting the main dogmas of antiquity anew, one must put them into harmony with today's science—that is to say, wipe them out. These dogmas are [1] the inerrancy of scripture, [2] the immutability of [divino-apostolic] tradition, [3] Christ's divinity and infallible knowledge, [4] the redemption, [5] the resurrection of Jesus, [6] the real presence in the Eucharist, [7] the divine origin of the papacy and even of the episcopate[77]—not to mention the problem of God, "posed in new terms" by the progress of science.

*

It is now easy to nail down the scope of the "dogmatic evolution" affirmed by Loisy. It has an absolute universality: it extends to every dogma without exception and extends in each to every element constituting it.

And it is not just a matter of "progressive" evolution, forming entirely new dogmas or deducing new truths from old dogmas; it is a matter of changes that alter the prior statement, up to the point of adopting a contradictory statement. A peremptory proof of this is the ultimatum he hands to the Church: she has to clear away seven impossibilities of agreement with science, created by seven dogmas of yesteryear.

There is more: for Loisy, even simultaneous contradiction is one of the

75. Ibid., 210f.

76. Ibid.; see also 208 and following.

77. Loisy, "Avant-propos," in *Études évangéliques*, xxiii, xxxviii.

great laws of dogmatic development in Catholicism. Look at how Loisy explains the origin of our Christian mysteries.

From the very first centuries, he says, theology found itself caught in two diametrically opposite currents, first by the very complexity of the questions. For example, theology had to safeguard liberty and at the same time affirm man's total dependency vis-à-vis God. Above all, theology was pulled two ways by the duality of its origins: on one side, Judaism lived on at the root of Christianity and animated it with the monotheistic spirit; on the other side, Greek philosophy infiltrated bit by bit into its bosom and infused trinitarian speculations, from whence there would arise bit by bit the dogma of three distinct persons.

Now, caught between these contrary currents, what attitude will the Church adopt? How will she reconcile the development of her dogmatic thought with reason?

The answer given by yesteryear's theology was simple: from the beginning, the Church had proclaimed (though in less clear terms) both the oneness of God's nature and the threeness of persons, as witness the ancient formula of Baptism: *In nomine Patris, et Filii, et Spiritus Sancti*. Philosophy furnished only an accessory to the dogma, we would say, and a way of formulating it.

According to Loisy, however, the real process was quite different. At the beginning, the oneness of Jewish monotheism predominated; the Father alone was the true God, the Creator. The *Logos* and the Spirit appeared only on a secondary basis as modalities of the one God. Contradiction had not yet arisen; but the more one accentuated these two modalities or aspects of the divine, [the more] contradiction sprang up. Well, the special character of Catholic development, we are told, is never to sacrifice (either to reason or to good sense) either of the two opposed principles that the Church finds in her heritage from the past; let reason perish, if it must, but the Church will develop her thought in the direction of both the opposed currents; she will sharpen the contrasts to the point of formulating the most obvious contradiction, as she did according to Loisy, in the dogmas of *one* God, and *three* persons, of *one person* in Christ and *two natures*. Only, once the contradiction looms into sight and begins to trouble people's minds, the Church has a supreme resource: she proclaims it *a mystery*. The contradictions are not suppressed, but they no longer shock.

All we have done is summarize Loisy. But we should quote his words, while being content to underscore the course of his thinking. (1) Contradiction in theology is a source of success. In speaking of the formation of the Christological dogma, Loisy writes:

it is not surprising that the result of such a peculiar labor seems to *lack logic and rational consistency*. Nevertheless it turns out that this defect, which would be fatal to a system of philosophy, is in theology a source of duration and solidity.[78]

(2) The difference between heresy and orthodoxy lies in the fact that heresy wants to avoid the contradiction and, to do so, develops logically just one of the two opposed principles:

Don't people say that all the heresies are born from deductions pursued one-sidedly, starting from a point of tradition or science isolated from all the rest and erected into an absolute truth, to which one attaches by reasoning conclusions incompatible with the general harmony of traditional religion and teaching?—Orthodoxy seems to follow a sort of political line, straddling the fence and obstinately conciliating the extreme conclusions one can draw from the data in her deposit. *When she ceases to perceive logical accord between the assertions she seems to advance against one another, she proclaims a mystery and declines to secure unity of theory by sacrificing an important element of her tradition.*

(3) Such is the origin of all the mysteries:

This is what the Church did for the Trinity, when the consubstantiality of the three divine persons had triumphed definitively, and *it was no longer possible to oscillate between modalism* (which admitted only one person manifested in three works: creation, redemption, sanctification) *and subordinationism* (which attributed the three works to three unequal powers). This is what she did for the Incarnation, when duality of natures was affirmed decisively in the oneness of the person, and one had to fight against Nestorianism and monophysitism at once.

More or less consciously, the Christian tradition refused to enclose the real order of religious things in the rational order of our conceptions; she thought to render to eternal truth the only fitting homage by always supposing it to be higher than our intelligence, as if seemingly contradictory assertions ought to be held compatible at the limit of infinity.

(4) The issue is complete logical contradiction, not just apparent contradiction, because the mere appearance of a contradiction is not fatal to philosophy. Loisy believes he has confirmed this

78. Loisy, *L'Évangile et l'Église*, 143.

—in the dogma about God: there is only one eternal God, and Jesus is God;
—in the dogma about grace: a man's salvation is entirely in the hands of God, and the man is free to get saved or not;
—in the dogma on the Church: the Church has authority over people, and a Christian bows to God alone. Then he concludes:

> *An abstract logic would demand in each case that one suppress one or the other of the propositions so strangely coupled.* But close observation shows that one could not do so without compromising the living equilibrium of religion.[79]

Which is to say that Christianity lives on contradictions.

✳

It is true that the *Revue du clergé* is still trying to defend Loisy and restrict the evolution to within certain limits, where it would be compatible with Catholicism: "According to Mr. Loisy's explicit declarations, this evolution does not affect *the substance of the dogma*, the assertion of faith contained in and expressed by the dogma."[80]

But if his declarations are so explicit, why don't they quote any? Don't they think it important to refute the many critics, Catholic and Protestant, who have understood Loisy-style dogmatic evolution as I have done? The *Revue du clergé* thinks its say-so should suffice, without any text to back it up. The truth is that if the *Revue* had quoted Loisy's actual words, its readership would have seen all too clearly that it has been taken in by ambiguous sentences, whose real meaning downright confirms a *universal* evolution of dogmas.

The logic of the system should have made this obvious. Where are you going to find an immutable "substance of dogma" in a theory whose very foundation is the denial of *all* absolute truth in man?

> The truth as a good of man is no more immutable than man himself. *It evolves with him, in him, and through him, and this does not stop it from being the truth* FOR HIM. It is his truth only on this condition.[81]

There is a truth, then, for *this man*, in *this century*, and in *this environment*. But *the truth* for everyone is a pure fantasy! Again, how is evolution supposed to spare a single statement in Christian dogma, when one of Loisy's

79. Ibid., 144.
80. *Revue du clergé français* (November 15, 1903): 654.
81. Loisy, *Autour d'un petit livre*, 192.

dearest principles is precisely that there is no *essence of Christianity*, no immutable Christian kernel, no truth that is untouchable, not one, not even the fatherhood of God that Harnack wanted to keep?

Nevertheless, Loisy does speak of an immutable element in revelation; quite certainly he does. But it is just a decoy, to console the naïve, and the *Revue du clergé* would agree with us if it reread Mr. Dubois's article, which it published on December 1, 1903. According to Loisy (interpreted by Dubois in the same sense as we do), the "substance" that cannot change is not our knowledge, nor any element of it (hence is not a dogma, not even reduced to its simplest and most primitive terms, because anything amounting to a judgment is subject to evolution), but is solely the *object* we know, considered *in itself* and *apart from us*. Thus God and Christ, the ground of things, taken in themselves and in their reality, are absolutely immutable—that is, they are as they are and not otherwise. Only the absolute does not change *in itself*. But as this absolute is outside the sphere of our intellect, everything we can think or say about it (about God, about Christ, etc.) is subject to complete evolution and, over the course of the ages, is transformed in its entirety.

Such is the theory explicitly formulated by Loisy: *only the object of knowledge is eternal and immutable in itself, not the form that knowledge has taken in human history*.[82] Thus no form of knowledge, no dogmatic statement, is immutable; *only the object* does not change.

Further along, the theory is not only expounded but applied:

> The meaning which does not change is not precisely the one resulting from the letter, i.e., is not the particular form which the truth [the object] took in the minds of those who worded the sentence; nor does it lie in the particular form of the interpretations that have succeeded one another as needed; it lies in *their common basis*, impossible to express by a definition that would be adequate to the object and sufficient for the ages.[83]

These last words repeat the ever-present sophism: no sentence expresses the whole of the divinity, and so none is true forever. Applying his theory right

82. Ibid., 190. The phraseology has been changed but not the meaning. Here is Loisy's exact text: "If one supposes that the truth *qua* accessible to human understanding is something absolute, that revelation has this absoluteness and that dogma shares it, that what is *eternal and absolute is not just the object of knowledge in itself* but the form which knowledge of it has taken in human history, then the assertions of the little book are worse than temerarious; they are absurd and impious."

83. Ibid., 201.

away to the main articles of the Creed, Loisy asserts that "they do not have entirely the same meaning for today's Christians as they had for those of the earliest times." Today we see *three divine persons*, whereas, for the first Christians, "God the Creator" was identified as just the heavenly Father, the title "son of God" characterized the providential mission of Jesus, and "the Spirit" stood for the action of God and Christ in the Church.

Furthermore, even faith in God, that fundamental truth of religion, has an "infinitely complex history," according to Loisy, "and the idea of divinity has never ceased to change." He gives a proof that will put a smile on the faces of those who keep up with contemporary theology. Recalling the energetic declarations of an Augustine or a Bossuet on the incomprehensibility of God, Loisy thinks we will find an *agnostic* aroma in them nowadays.[84] We can assure Mr. Loisy: modern theologians borrow the same formulas from their predecessors and use them in the same sense.

The formulas he declares obsolete come all the way down to recent Vatican definitions:

> I venture to bring up a case much closer to us. Take the *idea of the Bible, the inspired* book, which the definitions of Trent and Vatican I assume, and which Pope Leo XIII's encyclical *Providentissimus Deus* has commented on—is this idea not palpably different from the one that historical study of the Bible is suggesting to Christian scholars?[85]

So now the pope has to reject the idea of inspiration formulated at the Vatican Council.

"The truth *alone* is immutable, not its image in our minds."[86] With this stroke (as Mr. Dubois remarks quite well), Loisy relegates immutability to the transcendent world, to the *noumenon*—that is, to a region with which we have no rational communication.[87] But *every* conception reached by our mind, *every* dogmatic formula, is essentially subject to transformations.

Consider, for example, our faith in God. Only one thing is immutable; it is (considered in itself and in its objective reality) "*the great force* hidden behind all phenomena," which in fact constitutes the ultimate explanation.[88] But this mysterious "ground" is totally beyond the scope of our science; we

84. Ibid.

85. Ibid.

86. Loisy, *L'Évangile et l'Église*, 166.

87. Dubois *Revue du clergé* (December 1, 1903): 90.

88. Loisy, *Autour d'un petit livre*, 10.

cannot even know if it exists. Yet faith (that is, a spontaneous stirring not based on reason) heads toward it blindly, affirms its existence, and makes us try out representations of the unrepresentable and formulations of the ineffable.[89] Not a single one of these formulations is irreformable, because all of them are pure *symbols*, whose resemblance to the transcendent reality is absolutely null or, at least, absolutely unknown to us. Thus when we say, "God is personal," it is a symbol, an *algebraic notation*, by which we designate "His absolute perfection and the essential distinction that exists between a real God and the real world."[90] Loisy *believes* we must still keep using this symbol, but on the understanding that it is purely a symbol. A day may come when a better understood pantheistic symbol will deserve to replace the personhood of God. Even the affirmation "God exists" is only a symbol by which we try to represent the ground of being. Does it correspond to reality? We know nothing about it; absolutely nothing! A day may come, perhaps—and aren't we seeing its dawn already?—when the formula of atheism will be preferable and will correspond better to the philosophy of the time.

In the dogma of the incarnation, expressed by the Nicene formula, "Christ is the true Son of God, consubstantial with the Father," where is the immutable element, or, for that matter, the variable element? Here again there is nothing immutable but the relation between God and Christ, a relation considered in its objective reality, which is totally unknown to us. We do not even *know* whether there is a relation; we *believe* it by *faith*, independently of any reason. All our formulations are reformable, having been imagined by *faith* alone, without a rational foundation, to represent this mysterious reality. So it is not just the affirmation of consubstantiality that can change (as Mr. Dubois seems to suppose in his otherwise very penetrating and judicious pages on this subject, which I have cited); it is also the very formula "Christ is God," or "Christ is the Son of God," or even this one: "Between Christ and God there are special relations." All those claims, as expressions of the absolute, are pure conjectures of faith and hence subject to being replaced by a different conjecture more in harmony with updated science.

*

89. That faith does not and cannot have a rational basis is one of the fundamental points of Loisy's system, and the reader should have it in mind constantly. Hence, the witness of faith carries weight only for faith; see *Bulletin de littérature ecclésiastique* 6 (January 1904): 84, 87–88.

90. [In the text of the *Bulletin* for February 1904 footnote 5 is missing from the bottom of page 109.]

But, people object, doesn't Loisy recognize even in us (outside the object) an element that remains invariable? "Revelation," he says,

> is not immutable in the sense that its symbols, once given, escape all transformation, but because it always remains *for the faith substantially identical to itself*, and because the changes that take place in its external determination and in its formulas are something secondary compared to the oneness of its spirit and the continuity of its development. In this order, also one may speak of permanent orientations whose truth is no less incontestable than their moral effectiveness, and whose form is no more immutable than the human condition.[91]

So evolution is not absolute, or universal, for him; it respects a bottom line of immutable truth that suffices to assure the self-identity of Christianity over the centuries.

I regret to say it, but this conclusion goes far beyond what Loisy says. He admits a stable element, but this element is far from being an affirmation of a *truth*, however simple. On this capital point, it is essential to understand Loisy's exact thought, especially since it is often hidden behind confused formulas. Sometimes what abides in Christianity is (as he was saying just now) an *orientation* that ensures unity of spirit and continuity of development. Sometimes *the assertions of faith* are represented to us as equally living and efficacious under all formulations, even the most opposed.[92] At still other times (and this is the formula that seems most orthodox), he speaks of *a seed* that grows and produces the great Christian tree. He even describes with satisfaction the components of this seed: "it contains in germ the tree that we see:

1. it had *charity* as its sap;
2. its vital thrust was in the hope of the Kingdom;
3. its force of expansion was in the apostolate;
4. its gauge of success was in sacrifice;
5. as its general form, this embryonic religion had faith in the oneness and absolute sovereignty of God;
6. and as its particular and distinctive form, it had faith in the divine mission of Jesus, which got it the name "Christianity."

All this was the *real essence* of the Christian religion."[93]

91. Loisy, *Autour d'un petit livre*, 198–99.

92. Ibid., 200.

93. Loisy, *L'Évangile et l'Église*, xxvii f. The whole passage has to be read. The numbers have been added by me.

Has Mr. Loisy then constructed—he also—an *essence of Christianity*, an immutable dogmatic teaching with six basic dogmas? A superficial reader would think so. In reality, he has done no such thing.

Let us remark first that if Loisy had limited essential Christianity to these six dogmas, it would have been a Christianity of shocking poverty. Who among us would dare to claim that, to be an authentic Christian, it suffices to accept these vague and indefinite sentiments, saying nothing of the redemption, or of the Church?

Second, how could Loisy set up a series of immutable truths at the very moment when he was reproaching Harnack so severely for having preserved a single immutable truth? "To set up such an essence in Christianity," he said a few pages earlier, "one has to transform it into a metaphysical entity, a logical essence."[94] And then he said that any dogmatic minimum, however small,

> would be an obstacle to the free and legitimate movement of thought ... an obstacle the more serious to the exercise of thought the more indispensable it was in what concerned the Church, if by chance it was not found in the Gospel or was not in the meaning people understood. Those who oblige themselves to see an essence here also force themselves not to take the Gospel as it is.[95]

If one rereads the pages quoted from Loisy with attention, one will recognize that the "permanent essence" he talks about is not a doctrine-essence, not a truth taken as central to the Christian faith. It is quite simply the initial *impetus* given by Jesus, the *orientation* toward the good, the *movement* received from Him and transmitted by the generations, even when they modify all the ideas and hence the form of all the sentiments born of those ideas.[96] For then "the sentiment remains the same by *its orientation*, one might say by the *spirit* which sustains it." And "this identity of orientation and impetus that come from Christ make up what people call the immutability of Christianity."

Thus the essence of Christianity is "in the fullness and totality of its life, which, by the very fact that it is a life, is movement and variety."[97] The six sentiments previously mentioned are only the initial *physical* essence of Christianity. They, too, take on various forms in each epoch; but, "if the figure changes, its type does not vary, nor the law which governs its evolution."[98]

94. Ibid., xxiii.
95. Ibid., xiii.
96. Ibid., xxv.
97. Ibid., xxvi.
98. Ibid., xxviii.

Everything is new, no doubt, in today's Catholicism, with its Church, its rituals, its dogmas created of whole cloth; but however different it may be from the religion of the apostles, it is nevertheless essential Christianity, because it *has succeeded* primitive Christianity by natural evolution of the movement impressed by Jesus. This is not to say that dogmatic development derives new dogmas from old as flowing from them or as normal consequences. It suffices for Loisy that the present is no stranger to the past.[99]

But—as Father Tyrrell has very rightly pointed out in a remarkable article in *The Month*—right here is precisely the essential trait that distinguishes the liberal theology (of Caird, of Gardener, of A. Sabatier) from Catholic theology. According to the liberals, there is a succession of doctrines, and not a transmission of the same doctrine in different phases of development.

> The religious doctrine of today is never identical to that of the past, any more than the science of today is identical to the science of our ancestors;

the one has just succeeded the other. Likewise, the current theories about God and the world

> are not strictly speaking the same; they are doctrines *about the same object*, but they are not the *same doctrines*.

The theology of one century has to be *supplanted* by that of the following century, as the chemistry, physiology, biology, of our day have supplanted the dark fumblings of yesterday. Things go quite differently in Catholic theology; for it, *custodire depositum* (that is, to remain unshakably attached to the primitive records, if not to their very words, then at least to the ideas, the symbols, the categories in which revelation has been confided to us) is a question of life or death.

These ideas, these categories, these symbols, which make up the revealed presentation of reality, belong to the *very substance* of the *depositum fidei*; the accidental and contingent element resides only in the formulas or verbal signs expressing these ideas. By contrast, for liberal theology, the constant element, the *semper idem* is solely the *reality* and not a doctrine, not a representation of this reality.[100]

This liberal theology is the one to which Loisy's thought belongs. Also,

99. See *L'Ami du clergé* (November 26, 1903).
100. George Tyrrell, "Semper eadem," in The *Month*, January 1904, 5–8.

when he seems to say that the *assertions of faith* persist through all the changes of formula, it would be naïve to believe that he is admitting the permanent affirmation of a truth. If these "assertions of faith" are immutable, it is because, in his system, they affirm nothing—absolutely nothing in a definite manner.[101] They are by definition a vague and confused sentiment without any definite judgment. The *substance* that remains immutable is always, under one formula or another, *the object*, and uniquely *the object in itself.*

In sum, every religious formula, however simple, however primitive, by the very fact that it expresses an inexpressible object, is provisional, destined to disappear as soon as another formula will harmonize better with the thought of the day.

And if you conclude that this system gives free reign to individualism, that each believer will carry the formula he pleases, Loisy answers that the choice of good formulas must be left to the Church, which is to say, "the general consciousness of the community." Not, of course, because she was founded by Jesus Christ, with a divine mission and *infallibility*. That is the dream of an infantile theology. "With the bricks of human thought, one cannot build an eternal edifice."[102] But since religion should be social, an authority must maintain uniformity of the creeds that are the visible bond between the members of the religious society. Thus the Church can err, and she is erring even now when she rejects the theory of evolution and the doctrine of Mr. Loisy. But she enjoys a practical infallibility,—that is, she pronounces at the last resort, and one must give her decisions respectful silence. Isn't it the job of every supreme tribunal to impose its sentence, even if erroneous?[103]

Need one add that, in this system, the first duty of the Church is to adapt her dogmatic formulary to the philosophy of the day and to reform (or at least interpret in a new way) her previous decisions, in accord with the new conditions of times and places?[104]

✳

101. See above, 130.

102. See above, 145.

103. In the *Revue du clergé* 22 (March 1900): 152, Firmin [Loisy] writes, "infallible Church, i.e., *one having full power to regulate the creeds*"; see also 148, and Loisy, *L'Évangile et l'Église*, 173.

104. *Revue du clergé* 22 (March, 1900): 152: "The relativity of creeds . . . obliges those empowered to teach in the believing society to explain the creeds and symbols *always* according to the lights of the time, lest these creeds and symbols become unintelligible and fall into the status of a dead letter." In *L'Évangile et l'Église*, 175, Loisy insinuates very clearly that "the tendency of modern Catholicism has been too much a matter of playing safe." *Autour d'un petit livre* is a summons to Church authority to modify the meaning of seven or eight fundamental dogmas; xxiii, xxxviii, and in passing.

It remains to show how Loisy pretends to reconcile this evolution of dogmas with the unalterable truth of the faith; this is the last part of his system, and not the least subtle.

Since rationalists and liberal Protestants have admitted that our dogmas formed and evolved under the influence of purely human forces, they have concluded logically enough that orthodoxy has had its day and that the funeral bell for dogmas has tolled. Such is not the thought of Loisy. He deduces on the contrary that this evolution is the very law of Catholicism, that one must shout it from the house tops, and that thus the truth of Catholicism (strange paradox) will be salvaged.

You see, his agnosticism about creeds and symbols is going to immunize the Church from all error and contradiction:—(1) from all error by his theory of *relative truth*, and (2) from all contradiction by his theory of *the intention* involved in an act of faith.

The basic principle that he is hiding under these big words is the following: since the divine ground of things is unknown to us, the truth of dogmatic formulas does not consist in their more or less close resemblance to their object, but solely in their greater or lesser effectiveness in promoting religious sentiment, the vague and moral sentiment that is (in Loisy's system) the only serious and somewhat immutable component in all of religion. In choosing among dogmatic formulas, taking as one's criterion their truth or resemblance to the transcendent object is intellectualism. The great law that presides over the evolution of formulas is not truth but utility—or rather, every conclusion that is useful and that acts upon the heart will be, by that very fact, true.

This is how Loisy justifies all the changes introduced by the Church.

> If all this development is animated by the spirit of the Gospel [note that this spirit has no dogma to it], if it is *necessary for the Gospel's preservation and diffusion*, if it *serves to promote the religion of Jesus, what is the objection*? Blaming the Catholic Church for all these things is just blaming her for having lived and living still, isn't it? And if the Church had not lived, where would the Gospel be today?[105]

What is the objection? Well, just this little detail: you should never lie, even to save the gospel; you should not make a travesty of the facts in order

105. Firmin [Loisy], "La religion," in *Revue du clergé* 18 (January 1899): 212;—Loisy, *L'Évangile et l'Église*, 160–61. This thesis, borrowed from Ritschl's *value judgments*, has been developed with approval in the brochure by "Engels," which Mr. Franon has subjected to such an interesting analysis (*Bulletin de littérature ecclésiastique* [June 1903]: 163f) [translated in this volume as selection 6].

to have miracles, nor should you read into texts what is not there, as (according to you) the Church has always done. You say the Gospel would have disappeared? All right, it was not worthy to live, if it could only be saved by such falsifications as the apostles and their successors committed.

But once the rule "Choose the most effective formulas" has been adopted, psychological experience shows that the effectiveness of a formula depends essentially upon the state of souls in each epoch, the dominant ideas—in a word, the ever-so-changing mentality of the generations. Hence we get the necessity to make successive changes and transformations. For the recently converted pagans of the fourth century, the formula "Christ is God" was in perfect harmony with their mental habit of divinizing great men. Today the same formula repels our contemporaries by its metaphysical or anthropomorphic flavor. Evidently it will be necessary to change it and proclaim (at least by way of equivalent interpretations) that Jesus Christ is not God.

But then, we say, you are admitting that the ancient Church erred!—Not at all, Loisy will answer. Just as there is no absolute truth, neither is there absolute error. Confronted with the unknowable divine, our mind (condemned as it is to knowing nothing) is also thereby preserved from all error. Insofar as a formula does the Church good, excites religious sentiments, it is *true* with a *relative truth*—that is to say, *true for her* and *true for that era*. The day it ceases to act upon the soul (because science has modified the general mind and is now preventing it from getting a grip on our intellect), it ceases to be true for us, after having been true for others. Also, Loisy does not say that obsolete, ineffective formulas are *false*: no, in view of the progress of philosophical thought, they are *unsatisfying*.

Thus agnosticism about the absolute preserves the Church from all error. Next, the *intention* involved in faith is going to preserve the believer from all contradiction.

It is true that the Church may adopt (successively) two contradictory formulas; "the Word became flesh," she used to say; "the Word did not become flesh," she will say tomorrow. But, for Loisy, the contradiction is merely apparent. After all, when the believer adheres to a dogmatic formula, he should know quite certainly that he cannot know anything of the *object* in which he believes, nothing of that *Ground* hidden in impenetrable mystery. So when the believer imagines a symbol to express his faith, such as "The Word became flesh," his *intention* is not to affirm the dogmatic formula itself but only the unknown ground of reality, whatever it is. So one must convey this intention as follows:

> *I speak* the symbol, "The Word became flesh in Christ," but I do not affirm in any degree an intimate union of the Word with Christ's humanity, nor in consequence the divinity of Christ, because I do not know if this symbol corresponds to reality. I want to affirm only the objective relations of Christ to God, whatever they are; but I do not even know whether there are relations between Christ and God, since the divine never falls into history.

So implausible is this theory that people will accuse me of being unfair and defamatory, will they not? Nevertheless, this *is* Loisy's explicit contention:

> *An ecclesiastical formula is not true absolutely, because it does not define the full reality of the object it represents*; yet it is the symbol of an absolute truth.[106] Until the Church judges it opportune to modify it by explaining it, it is the best and surest expression of the truth with which it deals. *The believer adheres by intention to the full and absolute truth that the formula symbolizes imperfectly and relatively. Adhering to the formula as such with an assent of divine faith would be adhering to its inevitable imperfections*, would be proclaiming it unimprovable and adequate, even though it is inadequate and imperfect. *In this way, a Catholic can believe* in the authority of the Church and *in that which the Church teaches.*[107]

Let us understand this well: a Catholic man can adhere to the dogmas defined by the Church, even when interiorly he believes them false and outmoded; a Catholic priest can sign all the formularies, provided that he knows how to direct his *intention*. A Catholic woman can affirm that Jesus is the Son of God, even though she believes this creed-statement to be absolutely in opposition to the modern philosophy she holds, because what her inward thought adheres to in this formula is not the divine filiation that offends her philosophy but only *Jesus as He really is*. There you have the real and undeniable meaning of this rather enigmatic statement:

> faith addresses itself to the immutable truth [i.e., to the object] *via* the necessarily inadequate formula.[108]

106. This means that the formula is the symbolic expression of an *object* that in itself, and not in our knowledge of it, is a reality, *an absolute*, a noumenon.

107. Loisy, *Autour d'un petit livre*, 206.

108. Loisy, *L'Évangile et l'Église*, 166.

This intention to believe in the object (of which one knows nothing) is what the Church demands, according to Loisy, in her definitions:

> *The Church does not require faith in her formulas as adequate expressions of the absolute truth*, but presents them as the least imperfect expression that is morally possible; *she demands that one respect them according to their quality*, that one seek the faith in them, that one use them to transmit it; the ecclesiastical formulary is the auxiliary of faith, the plumb line of religious thought; it cannot be the integral object of religious thought, given that this object is *God Himself, Christ and His work*; each believer appropriates the object as best he can with the help of the formulary.[109]

How many mistakes lie in these words! The Church demands a good deal less and a great deal more than Mr. Loisy thinks. She demands a good deal less, because she has never claimed that her formulas are "the least imperfect possible"; she teaches that her definitions are exact and represent a part of the truth, but not that this truth cannot be presented by another formula with equal or greater success. Even when she affirms the rightness of the word "transubstantiation," for example, she does not say that no other expression could have the same precision.

The Church also demands a great deal more: for she affirms that what these formulas say about the object is true, eternally true. It is not enough to "respect" the formulas; one must affirm in so many words what they express about their object. When the Church defines the consubstantiality of the Son (and the virginal birth of Christ), she obliges the believer to affirm quite vocally and with interior mental assent not just vaguely some relation or other between the Word and the Father (and between Jesus and His Mother), but the sameness-in-substance of the two distinct Persons (and the virginal conception of Jesus in the womb of Mary).

It is quite true that these formulas do not express the reality in its totality, and when the Church gives us the *Credo* to recite, she never dreams of asking us to believe that every truth about God and His plan of providence is contained in it. Whereas Loisy, playing on words, goes from

> the Church does not require faith in her formulas *as the adequate expression of the truth*

109. Ibid., 174.

to conclude that

> the Church does not require faith in her formulas at all, and asks only "that one respect them," while one's *intention* is directed *solely* towards the object, so as to avoid the ever-present possibility of error in the formulas,

the truth is that the Church demands a sincere and convinced adherence to all the judgments expressed in the formula of the *Credo*. She anathematizes not only one who refuses to pronounce the formula, but also one who does not adhere to the judgments thus expressed.

These truths are so elementary that one is flustered to find oneself obliged to explain and defend them against sophisms like this: "adhering to the formula as such would be adhering to its inevitable imperfections, would be proclaiming it adequate."—Nonsense! When I affirm the Trinity of persons in God, I make no pretense that I am exhausting the divine nature, nor that I am using an unimprovable formula. Rather, I have the certainty that I am expressing a true judgment, an image of the divine reality—a very imperfect image, very incomplete—but a faithful image in all that it affirms.

Such is the system of a writer who blames the Scholastics for their logical subtleties. At the price of abdicating our reason, we purchase the ability to change dogmas without changing the faith, because, thanks to our *intention*, we never adhere (for fear of going wrong) to the *Credo* we recite but only to the unknown and unknowable object that this *Credo* pretends to be about. Thus, when we change a formula, we affirm the new version no more than the old; we recite them materially without believing the one or the other. This is attributing laughable antics (contrary to the most elementary sincerity) to the Church as well as to the faithful:

- to the Church, which makes fun of her faithful by imposing on them formulas that they must take care not to believe
- to the faithful, who are supposed to be proclaiming unto death their unshakable faith, in formulas that they know will have to be denied tomorrow with the progress of science.

Loisy demands *respect* for the formulas, but at bottom he is introducing among us the equivocation practiced by liberal Protestants. He is setting up in the Catholic Church, and as a universal law, the practice of the all-too-notorious Pastor von Sydow of Berlin, who tore up the Creed in front of the liberal "Protestant Association" and pronounced it piously in front of his congregation in Church. To anyone who was surprised at this, he replied, "I am not professing these articles; I am reading them."[110] The same should be done among us: we will read the formulas without believing them. Thus we shall be at ease. And if anyone experiences a bit of discomfort over the creed, it will surely be just a wave of disappointment.

At the cost of the same equivocation, we shall be able to keep even today the old formulas that no longer meet the intellectual situation of our time, provided we void them of their intellectual content and infuse a new meaning into them, more in harmony with science. Thus we shall keep the formula "born of the Virgin Mary" not to affirm a miraculous birth, of course, but as a symbol of our faith conveying the greatness of Jesus, of Mary, and of virginity.

✳

We shall also say that Jesus "rose again," not to claim that his body really came back to life, but to express the *life of Jesus in the memory* we keep of Him, the memory that makes us live.

We shall believe finally in "everlasting life," not by affirming Heaven and Hell, but by symbolizing the triumph of justice, which will one day commence its reign on this earth.[111]

Loisy says, thus Catholicism will be saved! We say, thus the ruin of all faith, all Christianity, and all religion would be accomplished!

IV

This exposition of dogmatic evolution suffices, no doubt, to inspire an instinctive revulsion in every Catholic who understands it. Nevertheless, people have piled so many obscurities on top of elementary notions that it will not be amiss to expound the *Catholic* doctrine on the historical progress of dogma, without "evolution," or (what amounts to the same thing) without change of meaning.

We set down against Loisy these three fundamental truths:

110. Georges Goyau, *L'Allemagne religieuse* (Paris: Librairie Académique Didiet Perrin, 1901), 1:642.

111. These examples, whose relevance will not be lost on anyone, are taken from the previously cited pamphlet by "Engels," which was warmly recommended in Loisy's journal by one of his close friends, Mr. Jules Dalbret, the ancestor (we think) of Mr. "Jean de la Rochelle" and surely also of Mr. "Firmin." Mr. Dalbret wrote the following: "In this interesting little work, one will find a delicious exposition of the psychological conditions that will permit Christian religion and mysticism to enter one's individual and living soul as an element of moral life"; *Revue d'histoire et de littérature religieuses* (July–August 1903): 414.

1. From Adam to the death of the Apostles, dogma advanced substantially through successive promulgation of new revealed truths.

2. At all times, the Church herself proclaims a subjective development of dogmas through progressive cognition of the revelation already closed.

3. An evolution of dogmas by change of meaning, like an appearance of dogmas that are substantially new, is a contradiction with the Church's fundamental principle and with the record of history itself.

From the primitive revelation to the end of Christian revelation through the Apostles the Church admits augmentation of the revealed deposit—this is a trivial truth that no one, prior to Loisy, had dared to deny. I would never have dreamed of bringing it up, if the author of "the little books" had not sharpened his lance to ridicule theologians by attributing to them the stupid mistake that everything, absolutely everything, had been said to Adam, and that God allegedly "gave to humanity from its first hour the fund of truth whence we were to draw until the end of time, with no need to renew it unless most people had allowed it to fall by the wayside over the course of the ages."[112] Thus traditional exegesis, according to Loisy, is supposed to have overlooked the forward march that God followed in revealing things from Adam down to the last of the prophets, and especially the sublime crowning that Christian revelation added to the Old Testament.

Such is today's mania for bad-mouthing theologians that even people who ought to know them and defend them are letting such remarks pass. Is all-around ill-will toward theologians worth a diploma in critical studies? Mr. Ermoni has not been able to resist the temptation: "Go get a hard-core theologian to admit that literary and historical criticism has established a religious development within the Old Testament; and go get an intrepid critic to admit that this development is explained by the data of theology."[113] I do not know if the critics are this ignorant of the history of theology, but I assert that you will never find a serious theologian who ever denied the progress in question. St. Thomas proclaims it like all the others,[114] and Father La-

112. Loisy, *Autour d'un petit livre*, 193; see Loisy [Firmin], "L'Idée de la révélation," *Revue du clergé* 21 (January 1900): 259–60. [The idea that God had taught everything to Adam was part of the misnamed "Traditionalist" ideology introduced by the Viscount de Bonald in the 1820s and condemned by the Church in the 1830s. Is it possible Loisy was confused about this by some early teacher of his?—Tr.]

113. Vincent Ermoni, "La méthode historique à propos de l'Ancien Testament," *Annales de philosophie chrétienne* (July 1903): 427.

114. Thomas Aquinas, *Summa theologiae*, II-II, q. 1, a. 7.

grange puts his assertion of it under the patronage of Cardinal Franzelin.[115] Quite recently, a young future critic, Mr. Venard, wrote this: "no one denies that the deposit of revelation grew bit by bit over the course of the ages."[116] There you have the truth.

Really, it is time to put an end to this procedure of making caricatures of theology, the more easily to triumph over it and display one's powers of irony in the same breath.

✳

The Church also recognizes and encourages the progress of dogma in people's minds by a deeper and broader knowledge of revelation.

Loisy says dogma cannot be fixed and petrified; hence it must change and evolve.[117] Loisy has never thought it appropriate to inform his readers of the answer given by theologians: dogma is not petrified, and so it is studied, deepened, fecundated, enriched with new truths grafted onto it, but *without change of meaning*, without "evolution" understood in Loisy's sense, *without loss or diminution*. When, then, did conserving truths already gained "petrify" a science?

It is true in Catholic doctrine that revealed dogmas have a genuine "life" in the bosom of the Church. They are fertile like all truths, even more fertile than other, purely human truths. They contain a whole world of lofty conceptions that will expand under the sun of reason clarified by the faith. Need one recall the magnificent invitation to doctrinal progress that Vatican I borrowed from Vincent of Lerins, with the classic comparison of grain that sprouts, grows, expands in flowers and fruits?

I am well aware of Loisy's abuse of this comparison: on the ground that one does not find the trunk, the branches, the leaves of the oak tree in an acorn, he concludes that there is no identity between the primitive dogma and the development accomplished by the work of centuries, but only a continuity and succession of quite different symbols. But lest we be fooled, I should say with Father de la Barre, "There exists in the seminal species something constant and unchanging which must always be recognized in these exuberant plants. The same is true of an idea."[118] In the acorn you *do*

115. Lagrange, *La méthode historique*, 51.

116. L. Venard, *Revue du clergé* (November 1, 1903): 520.

117. Loisy [Firmin], "La definition de la religion," *Revue du clergé* 18 (January 1899): 213; Loisy, *L'Évangile et l'Église*, 166f.

118. André de la Barre, *La vie du dogme catholique*, 109.

not see what constitutes the identity between the tree and the seed—it's too early! But it is still there: a secret force *that controls in a constant fashion the direction of the plant's development.*

This is how Vincent of Lerins understood it. There has to be progress in the faith, not change. If you say progress, you say development; if you say change, you say corruption. So there is to be progress . . . but within perpetual sameness of doctrine and interpretation, "*in eodem scilicet dogmate, eodem sensu, eademque sententia.*"[119]

This progress has to occur in every scientific activity that reason puts at the service of revelation:

- progress in the defense of the faith. Not only will apologetics use the contributions of philosophy, psychology, and history to establish the general premises for a rational proof of the historical fact of revelation, but its first duty is to analyze the state of mind of the contemporaries, to penetrate their souls, not in order to share their intellectual weaknesses, but to heal them by a current application of traditional truths. Who does not feel that, in today's disarray of moral ideas and poignant preoccupations, the great test of an evangelist will be to show in Christianity the unique and inexhaustible source of sanctity?
- Progress in the critical study of biblical texts, so as to nail down the revealed doctrine. To determine the literal sense of the entire Bible, what an immense work still remains to be done, if one thinks of the small number of texts that have received an authentic interpretation from the Church, and if one thinks of the spectrum of opinions that appear in each century! The creation narrative alone is far from exhausted. After twenty-four-hour days, the day-periods begin to yield to the Augustinian system of simultaneous creation. What a vast field for exegetical and theological researches is opened up by archeological discoveries!
- Progress in dogmatic definition by the Church of truths contained in the deposit of revelation but long left in the background of Christian preaching. The history of the dogma of the Immaculate Conception (from the angel's *gratia plena*, understood by the Fathers as a grace preserving Mary from all taint of sin, down to the definition by Pius IX) would be a striking example of Christian thought appropriating and developing further and further a truth sown by God in the fertile field of revelation.

119. Vincent of Lerins, *Commonitorium*, c. xiii.

▪ Progress in the rational explication of the faith. Theology scrutinizes the meaning of each revealed truth deeply and deduces (so to speak) the whole philosophy of them, their various harmonies and consequences; then, by forming a vast synthesis of all the dogmas scattered in revelation, where each dogma has its place and where all shed light on each other by being connected, theology constructs the incomparable edifice of Catholic doctrine (before which every other philosophy pales) and retraces the vast history of the humanity in the world: the creation and the fall, at the center the coming of Christ, the redemption, grace, and the mission of the Church up to her triumphant rest in the bosom of God.

After that, how vain are the fears of doctrinal stagnation and of "petrifaction" of dogmas voiced by Loisy! "If one had to attribute [to formulas] a constant immobility, one would have a book containing the definitions by councils and popes, and strictly speaking one could pass beyond the pope and the councils. One would thus be applying the old Protestant idea to the documents of tradition, which would be completing the text of the Bible as an absolute rule of faith."[120]

How could Loisy have failed to see that he is refuting himself? If the revealed book does not halt the flow of thought and needs a living rule, why would the book of past definitions have a more pernicious or more powerful effect? In the sciences, does one place achieved certitudes in doubt again, under the pretext that they are an obstacle to progress and are a "petrifaction" of the truth? Is it not rather the whole set of already established truths that facilitates new conquests of science? Even though she determines certain fixed points as a salutary barrier to preserve us from error, does not the Church herself proclaim that every formula is incomplete and susceptible to new progress? Does she not invite her doctors to seek new explications or new justifications or new applications? Doesn't the collection of conciliar decisions prove that while preceding definitions calmed mental worries on some points, they have stimulated people's minds to undertake new investigations? It does not bother us, anymore than it bothers Mr. Dubois, to admit that dogmatic development, once finished on one point, continues on other points of doctrine still in an implicit or virtual state in the revealed deposit.[121] Let Mr. Loisy rest assured that the fertil-

120. Loisy, *Autour d'un petit livre*, 207–8.
121. *Revue du clergé* (December 1, 1903): 95.

ity of Catholic efforts in the past is a guarantee for their future and that the stagnation of the Greek Church (with which he threatens us) is due to other causes foreign to this debate.

*

As for progress by changing old dogmas or hatching new ones—it would be the negation of Catholicism. In principle, it contradicts the very idea of revelation as well as the fundamental law of tradition. In fact, it falsifies the history of dogma and the real role of philosophy in the development of the faith.

In principle, the divine origin of dogma excludes all change and all absolute innovation. If, indeed, dogma is the very speech of God, how could man ever dare to correct the thought expressed by such a Teacher? And if God has declared that henceforth His revelation is forever closed and His confidential messages to humanity terminated, where could a new dogma come from? However wise the commentaries by disciples upon their master, they will never add a line to his authentic speech. The proclamation of a new dogma then, can only be an authentic declaration by the Church of a truth contained really (though perhaps rather obscurely) in the traditional deposit of faith.

That this immutability of dogma has always been proclaimed by the Church as the foundational principle of her faith—that is a fact so luminous that no one until Loisy has ever dared to put it in doubt. From the earliest period of her life, the Church proclaimed as the unique source of her doctrine the *teaching of Christ through the apostles*, the immutable *rule of faith, tradition*.[122] Later, in each definition, she affirmed that she is maintaining the traditional faith and is condemning every heterodoxy as contrary to antiquity. In our century [the nineteenth], when Günther tried to introduce the theory adopted by Loisy to the effect that, *thanks to the progress of science, dogmas proposed by the Church take on another meaning from what she understood and now understands*, Pius IX reproved it, and Vatican I struck it with an anathema.[123] The facts are decisive, it would seem. Even genuine critical scholars do not hesitate. Herr von Harnack accuses

122. See the innumerable proofs of this fact gathered by Harnack in the supplement to [August] Hahn's *Bibliothek der Symbole und Glaubensregeln der alten Kirche*, 3rd ed. (Breslau: Morgenstern, 1897), 366f.

123. Vatican I, Constitution *Dei filius*, c. iv, n. 5, and canon 3 (Denzinger, no. 3043).

the Church of "conjuring tricks" by which she has continually changed her doctrine even while proclaiming it immutable, but he does not contest that she so proclaims it. Rev. Fr. Semeria (whose testimony Loisy can hardly refuse, after the praise he gave to his lectures on *Dogma, the Hierarchy, and the Cultus*) affirms energetically the unshakable insistence with which Catholicism, more than any other Christian denomination, affirms her dogmatic immutability.[124]

Loisy's criticism makes other daring statements. Would you believe, he proclaims quite solemnly that the Church has decided nothing about this matter?

> One may want to say that the Catholic Church has not even recognized the existence of this development, and that she has condemned the very idea of it.[125]

But those who do say this are naïve or ignorant:

> perhaps it would be more true to say that she has not become conscious of it, and that *she has no official theory* on the philosophy of her own history.

Crisply said: the Church has never spoken on the subject. And yet the *Revue du clergé* informs us that Mr. Loisy does not ignore the decrees of Vatican I and that he even tried at one time to put himself into agreement with them. The attempt must have been unfruitful, since he dares to say today, after the Council's proclamation of this dogma of immutability, "the Church has no official theory." As I have already said, he goes still further by claiming that the immutability of dogma is a Protestant theory, whereas evolution is essentially Catholic.

> In effect, Catholicism consists in receiving, as coming from a divinely established authority, the interpretation which the Church gives *currently* to the Gospel.[126]

This adverb "*currently*" is a superb touch. Would Mr. Loisy deign to tell us in what Church document he has found it? It deserves to be printed in golden letters on the frontispiece of every theology book, because it would transform all of theology from top to bottom. Well, we do not doubt that

124. Giovanni Semeria, *Dogma, gerarchia e culto nella Chiesa primitiva* (Rome: 1902), 343. For the same point, see the abbé Félix Klein, *Le fait religieux et la manière de l'observer* (Paris: Lethielleux, 1903), 21–22.

125. Loisy, *L'Évangile et l'Église*, 161.

126. Loisy, *Autour d'un petit livre*, 206.

a critic as informed as Mr. Loisy has found this word in some unpublished council. We, poor theologians, are obliged to be content with a definition in which, instead of the word "*currently*," we finds its opposite, "*perpetuo*."

In the interpretation of sacred dogmas, one must *perpetually* retain the meaning which holy mother Church has once declared, *and never, under the pretext of a deeper understanding, is it permitted to discard this meaning*."[127]

And to cut short all subterfuge, the Fathers of Vatican I affirmed this immutability of dogma three times, and the third time is in a solemn canon:

If anyone says it can come about because of the progress of science that one should some day attribute to the dogmas proposed by the Church a different meaning from the one which the Church has understood and now understands, let him be anathema.[128]

And it is in the aftermath of these decisions, so neat, so striking, that Mr. Loisy, a historian and critic, does not fear to answer the capital objection that crushes his entire system by saying, "the Church has no official theory" on the development of dogma.

One would never imagine the exegetical *tour de force* to which Loisy resorts to escape texts this clear. According to him, Vatican I either

- attributes immutability to the truth *in itself—that is, to the object*, and not to the definition the Church gives of that truth;
- or else imposes the formula (as the Church has a right to do) but not an interior adherence to it, as the believer's intention ought to turn to the mysterious object.

Mr. Dubois has shown quite well that the Council Fathers sanction the immutability of the Church's authentic interpretation.[129] Forgive me for not harping on this, since the definition is so clear. But one must show how far prejudice can go. I fear that the reader may raise the following problem: If one can deal so off-handedly with contemporary documents under everyone's eyes, what is one *not* permitted to do with documents that are inaccessible and date back thousands of years?

✳

127. Vatican I, Constitution *Dei filius*, c. iv, n. 5; Denzinger, no. 1647 [currently no. 3020—Tr.]
128. Ibid., Canon 3; Denzinger, no. 1665 [currently, no. 3043—Tr.].
129. *Revue du clergé français* 36 (December 1, 1903): 91.

Study of the history of dogma, when done without preconceived ideas, deposes in favor of the *essential* immutability of Christian dogmas.

People have said smugly, if St. Peter came back to Rome in the midst of this maze of dogmas, canonical procedures, or solemn ceremonies, he would no longer recognize where he was.—This is just a fallacy, in which people confuse the accidental development of a vast society with essential changes in its purpose and its beliefs. Of course St. Peter didn't know Pius X and didn't have a college of cardinals; of course the Vatican basilica is rather different from the rooms in Jewish or Roman houses where the first believers met. And of course Church rulings did not yet have the complications of our canon law. But read the *credo* today, and imagine St. Peter there to hear you; must you not admit in all honesty that he would recognize the identity of our beliefs with his preaching?

Within the bounds of this essay, it is not possible to retrace the history of our faith's development or to refute Loisy's groundless assertions in detail. Moreover, as regards the earliest era, the job has already been done in the studies published by Msgr. Batiffol and Rev. Fr. Lagrange. It has been well established that the Church was willed and announced by Jesus Christ as an organized society, even before His death. Mr. Bricout has recognized the authenticity of the famous "Thou art Peter" text (Mt 16:18), so arbitrarily rejected by Loisy.[130] And this mistake in the foundation of Loisy's system makes the whole thing come tumbling down.

The universal [rather than exclusively Jewish] character of Christianity was not an invention of St. Paul's ardent genius—so clearly not, that his own traveling companion and historian, Luke, says God revealed the plan to save the Gentiles to Peter (in a marvelous vision of kosher and non-kosher animals).

The theory of redemptive expiation, far from being a Pauline creation, predates the Apostle, according to Harnack, who has found it in the faith of the earliest Christian community *as a fundamental dogma*. This testimony—all the more remarkable for the fact that Harnack himself believes neither in the divinity of Christ nor in the value of the redemption—is must-reading.

130. Joseph Bricout, *Revue du clergé* (February 1, 1904): 479. The author concludes as follows: "Soundly practiced criticism, here as everywhere else, is in agreement with history: in agreement with the historical fact of a society founded by the apostles, in agreement with the historical fact of a recognized primacy for Peter." At issue is the text of Mt 16:18–19, and not Mt 13:18–19, as is misprinted twice on page 479.

It is an absolutely certain historical fact that the Apostle Paul was not the first to put Christ's death and resurrection front and center; rather, the Christian Church already had this emphasis before his time. "For I delivered unto you," he wrote to the Corinthians, "that which I also received as tradition, how that *Christ died for our sins* and rose again on the third day."

Paul did make Christ's death and resurrection the center of an entire theory, and he did (so to speak) recast the whole Gospel in terms of these events; *nevertheless, the earliest circle of Jesus disciples and the primitive congregation held them as fundamental.* One can affirm that these were the point of departure for the idea they had of Jesus and for the adoration they paid to Him …

And it was precisely *His death "for our sins"* and His resurrection that would strengthen the impression His person had made on them and would give the faith this starting point: *He offered Himself up as a sacrifice for us*; he died and yet is alive.

After establishing that these facts have lost much of their interest for many of our contemporaries, Harnack adds:

It is not our place to confirm this idea and its value; but it is an historian's duty to recognize both, so as to understand the significance they had and still have. *There is no doubt that the death and resurrection seemed essential to the primitive Church*; even Strauss did not question them, and the great critic, F. Christian Baur, recognized that *the oldest Christianity was based on them.*

Finally, he calls Jesus' death on the cross "an expiatory sacrifice" that rules out other victims:

In the times that followed, in all the places where Christianity was preached, altars for expiation were abandoned.… The death of Christ—undeniably—put an end to bloody sacrifices in the history of religion.[131]

The dogma of redemption by Jesus' expiatory sacrifice is, then, like the resurrection, anterior to Paul. But now questions crowd in upon us. Where did the dogma come from? How can one continue to deny the authenticity of the Jesuanic sayings that announce the shedding of His blood for many, under the pretext that they were influenced by Pauline theology? And if one does not deny their authenticity, how can one refuse to attribute at least this dogma to Jesus Himself? From the beginning, where was the Church's faith in the resurrection born, if it was not a historical event? Likewise, how could apostles who had witnessed the failure of Jesus' doc-

131. Harnack, *Das Wesen des Christentums*, lecture 9, 97–99; in the French translation, *L'Essence du christianisme*, the pages are 164–67.

trine (when His sole dogma, the imminent end of the world, was absolutely falsified by events) keep a faith so deep in this discredited prophet? What fanaticism made them keep preaching points that were henceforth baseless, and how did they make the whole Christian Church accept their change of viewpoint on a doctrine that (according to Loisy) had been so precise?

*

But let us leave these more special problems aside. Our task is just to show, in the history of dogmas as outlined by Loisy, his failure to recognize the laws that really presided over their development.

At bottom, Loisy and his admirers set against us three series of "facts":

- the perpetual introduction of the reigning philosophy into dogma;
- the formation and proclamation of new dogmas hitherto unknown; and finally
- modification of old dogmas (like Jesus' descent into hell and His ascension into heaven) to fit the progress of science.

Their first objection is that proclaiming the immutability of old dogmas is proclaiming not just the immutability of the Gospel but also the infallibility of Aristotle's logic and Plato's philosophy, since our Doctors [of the Church] were inspired by this long-obsolete metaphysics.

No, we reply, the Church does not proclaim the infallibility of Aristotle or of Plato; in her treasury of doctrine, she does not recognize a Platonic dogma or an Aristotelian dogma. The rightness of this assertion would seem evident to anyone who reflected on the fundamental law that regulates the role of philosophy in the Church. The alliance of philosophy with the faith is not a fusion (of two sources of truth in more or less equal doses). It is just the use of philosophy by a Christian thinker to the exact extent philosophy can serve revelation without transforming or modifying it in its depths. Thus philosophy will not absorb dogma and will not change it to suit the taste of fashionable systems; rather, Christian thought will use philosophical thought as a light to show new rays.

Such is the fact that the history of Christian speculation verifies in every century. It borrows from philosophy some formulas, some images, some principles, in harmony with the revealed doctrine; but it prunes away without pity the principles of any philosophy if they are incompatible with the faith. Christian thought, living and spirited, refuses to assimilate any philosophical maxim alien to the faith. St. Thomas corrects Aristotle, as St. Augustine corrects the Platonists. About all the Doctors of the Church, one can say what Mr. Grandgeorge said recently about the bishop of Hippo: "everything in neo-Platonism that could accord with the Christian mysteries or that found an explanation in these mysteries, St. Augustine kept and would always keep; but what was exclusively neo-Platonic he rejected more and more. So, insofar as his philosophy agreed with his religious doctrines, St. Augustine was openly neo-Platonic; but when a contradiction appeared, St. Augustine never hesitated to subordinate philosophy to religion, reason to faith.... In his mind, philosophical questions were relegated to the background (and ever more so)."[132]

Thence derive the three particular laws that regulate the influence of philosophy upon dogma.

(1) The faith does not borrow from philosophy either particular systems or theories more or less based on the nature of things. The faith takes only the primordial truths and essential principles that constitute mankind's *philosophia perennis*. In this sense, it is quite correct to say that a believer is not free to embrace just any philosophy, even absolute skepticism. Ages ago our Doctors remarked that one cannot deny the principle of noncontradiction without renouncing the faith, unless (these theologians said carefully) a special state of mind prevents one from observing the inability of one and the same mind to assert two formulas simultaneously:

> the existence of God is an eternal truth,

and on the other hand:

> it is perhaps also true that God does not exist.

Such minds are less rare than one might think, and the fourteenth century gives us the example of Nicolas de Ultricuria, a Hegelian before Hegel, who (fortunately) was forced to retract assertions that, in their barbarous Latin, have a strange kinship with the agnosticism of some modern thinkers.[133]

(2) Likewise, when the Church borrows from philosophy images, metaphors, expressions, or even theories, she does not thereby define the sys-

132. L. Grandgeorge, *St. Augustin et le néo-platonisme* (Paris: Ernest Leroux, 1896), 155–56.

133. See Heinrich Denifle and Émile Chatelain, *Chartularium universitatis Parisiensis*, 2:576fn1124. [More accessible is the list of his propositions in the recent editions of Denzinger, nos.1028ff. In most respects, Nicholas was more like an anticipation of Hume.—Tr.]

tem itself from which these formulations were borrowed. In those cases, great circumspection is needed to sort out the dogmatic idea wrapped in a philosophical envelope without the philosophy that furnished the formula or the image being sanctioned by the faith. Who is unaware of the fact that the distinction drawn by Church teaching between two components in a sacrament, matter and form, is taken from Aristotle but *does not oblige us to adopt the hylomorphic analysis of bodies*? The distinction just means that, in baptism, for example, one of the components (the word) plays toward the more material one (the water) the determining role that form plays toward matter in Aristotelianism. In the same way, when the Church adopts the dogmatic expressions "nature," "person," "transubstantiation," she defines in general the distinct idea that each term expresses, but she makes no pretense of settling all the systematic questions philosophers raise about the inner nature of the realities involved. Hence the great number of points freely discussed and debated among theologians.

But, you may say, the Fathers who introduced the terms "matter" and "form" into conciliar language were firmly committed to the Aristotelian analysis of bodies.—They probably were, we answer. But they adhered to it in their capacity as philosophers, not as believers and teachers of the faith. For her part, the Church retains only the dogmatic idea that interests her.

She authorizes comparison between the components of a sacrament and the Aristotelian components of bodies, and beyond that she allows her children to speculate to their hearts' content on matters of a purely philosophical nature. No doubt, and I do not deny it, a thinker runs the risk of identifying his philosophy with his faith. But the Church is ever at hand, and the day a Christian thinker wants to muddle up his personal metaphysical opinions with her dogmas, the Church will know how to separate the metaphysician from the believer. This is how she could be inspired by St. Augustine and yet allow amendment of those notions of his that came from his exaggerated admiration for the Platonists.

(3) A final law governing philosophy's influence in doctrinal development obliges us to distinguish *dogma*, which is strictly delimited by revelation (that is, by the divine say-so), from theology, which embraces the conclusions we can draw with the help of philosophy. Despite what some doctors may have thought in the past, *theological conclusions never* compose the Christian dogma, even when the Church guarantees their truth by an

act of her sovereign authority. The field in which her doctrinal infallibility can act extends beyond Revelation, in effect, to cover all the truths without which a dogma itself cannot be guaranteed sufficiently. This is what Loisy failed completely to take into account.

*

History also does not confirm any case of proclaiming new dogmas. And since Loisy has followed other writers in alleging the "recent" character of sacramental theology, it is easy for us to apply the laws just mentioned. Yes, the *theology* of the sacraments is relatively modern, but the sacramental *dogmas*—that is, the practice of the rites that we call sacraments— and the faith attributing to these rites a power to sanctify, thanks to their being divinely instituted by Jesus Christ (and we do not have to decide here whether He did so mediately or immediately)—go back to the very origins of Christianity.

The role played by theology in this branch of Catholic doctrine was determined perfectly just a few days ago, in the defense of a doctoral thesis at Toulouse. It was the Scholastics who took the term "sacrament," previously applied to various rites and mysteries symbolizing grace, especially the mystery of the Incarnation, and restricted the term in a precise way to these sanctifying rites. It was they who separated the seven sanctifying rites from other, accessory ceremonies; it was they who added them up and consecrated the number seven. But their systematizing work rested always upon the traditional practice of each and the traditional faith in each.

As for the transformation of aboriginal dogmas, Loisy goes back constantly to an example he thinks decisive: the phrases in the apostle's creed, "descended into Hell," "ascended into Heaven," have to have changed their meaning since science revised the ancient world-picture. But as Mr. Dubois has shown very well, this is a strange confusion between the *truth* the Church has meant to express and the *sensory image* in which that truth is clothed.[134] The truth that we believe is the presence of Jesus' soul in the place of the dead and the triumphant entry of the risen Christ into Heaven. The image of Heaven "above," Hades "below," was borrowed from the cosmological beliefs of the time without the Church's taking the trouble to ei-

134. Dubois, *Revue du clergé* (December 1, 1903): 92; see also de la Barre, *La vie du dogme catholique*, part 2, chap. iii, "Images symboliques," 189. See also the very interesting articles by Rev. Fr. Léonce de Grandmaison on "L'élasticité des formules dogmatiques" in *Études* 76 (August 5 and 10, 1898).

ther affirm them or correct them. What has changed as a result of scientific progress is solely the image; the truth held by the faithful of yore is still the truth we embrace today.

V

It is time to conclude. The purpose of these pages has just been to expose in its broad traits the *basis* for the doctrinal evolutionism that Loisy has been trying to introduce into the Church. One of his disciples in Rome expresses surprise that "his adversaries have fallen gleefully upon two books (one historico-apologetical and one historico-philosophical) and have said nothing about his *L'Évangile de saint Jean*." The reproach is unjust. Aside from the fact that the fourth Gospel has not been forgotten, the book deals only with a specialized question. What matters most, as we have said, is getting to know the foundations of the whole system and leaving aside the particular problems of biblical exegesis (each of which requires a study of its own).

It has been as a historian and a critic that I have analyzed Loisy's works. What is one supposed to do about it if a thoroughly objective study of the texts hands us a *philosophy of religion,* borrowed from theories of evolution and utter agnosticism?

The *Revue du clergé* accuses me of "violence." Fortunately, the documents of the case are under the reader's eyes, and I am confident he or she will judge such language severely. This is how the debate gets impassioned, and I do not see what calmness of discussion, or the authority of the *Revue*, which is already compromised on this matter, has to gain from that. These days, with a censure from Rome in effect, the *Revue* proclaims at last that there are "*very serious errors*" in Loisy's books, after more than four years of refusing to see them, and without sparing the time even yet to refute them. Yet nothing would seem more urgent. The editors prefer to attack those who, with sincerity and good faith, point the errors out, and they abstain from saying a word about the "violence" (this time quite real) in *Autour d'un petit livre*—violence in its address to bishops, who are seen as "sticking out their crosiers, not to guide the hard-working exegete, but to smite him down with solemnity" or, as it says a bit later, "to bludgeon" him with blows that do not kill an idea; those who disapprove of Mr. Loisy are people "who wish to learn nothing outside their pretended tradition, who wish to *understand nothing that does not flatter their insatiable appetite for domination*." They have gotten "*from a specialized and defective formation, a particular and inferior mentality*, which brings with it a *partisan spirit*, a defiance towards anything that is light and progress."[135] And the whole volume carries this tone of persiflage, mocking Church authority and our most venerable dogmas. But all of that, for the *Revue du clergé*, counts as serene, courteous discussion; it never has a word to say to its readers about this new kind of charity. But as soon as a writer leaves all personal issues aside and tries to dissolve the "deplorable equivocations" of which Mr. Brunetière has spoken, as soon as he comes texts-in-hand to show Catholics where Loisy wants to lead them, a call-to-order is given right away and he is denounced as "violent" because he has spoken the truth too clearly.

The same *Revue* complains that the citations I have made are incomplete. Alas, I have reason to believe that its bad mood is motivated, rather, by certain texts of which I have reminded them *too completely*, whereas they had thought them forgotten. So long as these texts stand, it will be impossible for the *Revue du clergé* to show that Loisy admits *a single truth* guaranteed to man by God, *a single dogma* that cannot be replaced someday by a contrary one. And since Mr. Loisy's friends are surprised to see utter skepticism attributed to him, I remind them that this is nevertheless the main foundation on which he rests his systematic distinction between rational science (restricted to phenomena) and faith, which alone gets to the bottom of things. He is the one who wrote, "Reason and science can say NOTHING about the basis for religion, which *does not belong to their order*."[136]

Also, the agreement which we ventured to affirm, between Loisy's all-dissolving criticism and that of Prof. Sabatier, is now incontestable, after the studies published on all sides by Protestant writers. All of them have observed this fundamental likeness: unrestricted evolution of all dogma and the ruin of all divine authority. The moderates and the orthodox are saddened by it; Mr. Sanday published his reservations in *The Pilot* of January 23, 1904. Prof. Sabatier's friends and disciples have exulted loudly.[137] Suffice it for now to just mention this highly important fact; I shall come back to it elsewhere.

135. Loisy, *Autour d'un petit livre*, introduction, xx–xxi, xviii, xxxv.

136. See Battifol, *Bulletin de Littérature Ecclésiastique* (January 1903) [translated earlier in this selection].

137. See the articles in the *Revue chrétienne* by Mr. Paul Sabatier (January 1904) and Mr. Ménégoz (February 1904).

Our duty as Catholics at the present moment is to dissipate the fog of confusion that certain publications are trying to spread; they are trying to identify Loisy's works with science itself, and they say over and over that the pope, by condemning them, has condemned all criticism, every historical method. Nothing could be worse for the cause of truth than to let this misunderstanding remain undisturbed in people's minds.

No, it is not at all true that the Roman verdict condemns historical criticism. It reproves the "serious errors" that Loisy derived from a false application of criticism or even from the a priori of an agnostic metaphysics. Equally, the verdict repudiates the total independence claimed by Loisy for criticism and history, just as the Church condemned the same claim when Frohschammer advanced it for philosophy. She will never admit that the same mind can assent *qua* believer to what it denies *qua* historian or philosopher.

At the same time, the Church always proclaims for criticism and history, as for all the human sciences, the just independence that suits them and the right to conduct their researches in their own fields according to their own principles and their own method, provided they respect the faith.[138] She encourages Catholic labors in this direction, and by his encyclical *Providentissimus Deus,* Leo XIII wanted to give a new spur to biblical studies.

It would be an immense evil, then, if some Catholics, shocked by the excesses of false criticism, should cast the blame on criticism itself, on history studied by the most exact methods. Let no one say, "Better to shield the faith of the coal miner than to raise troublesome questions."—The coal miner's faith does not suffice for those who should teach coal miners. The day when the clergy have only the naïve faith of the people, the people will soon fall into unbelief. The troubling of souls does not come from the Catholic solution to problems but from problems raised outside the Church and left unanswered.

May the Church of France draw from Rome's verdict a unity of mind in submission and, along with that, a new striving for scientific defense of the truth!

E. Portalié
February 16, 1903

138. Vatican I, Constitution *Dei filius*, c. iv; Denzinger, no. 1646 [now no. 3019—Tr].

part 3

critical responses to george tyrrell

Bulletin de littérature ecclésiastique 5 (June 1903): 157–66

6

"A NEW CATHOLIC MANIFESTO OF AGNOSTICISM"

Eugène Franon

An English Catholic recently published a brochure of a little less than a hundred pages, entitled *Religion as a Factor of Life*.[1] It is a sort of very brief compendium of agnostic and symbolist theology. The author signs himself "Doctor Ernest Engels." For this pseudonym, under which he judged it prudent to disguise himself, we could substitute the real name. But we shall abstain from doing so. We shall not even say if he is in the diocesan clergy or a religious order—but he is a priest. The details about his person matter little in any case. But there is a great deal of importance in making known the theories of religion and Christianity expounded in his study. The second of these theories builds on the first. So we must begin with it.

I

There are two viewpoints that one can take up to determine the nature of religion: the objective or historical viewpoint and the subjective or

1. "Doctor Ernest Engels," *Religion as a Factor of Life* (Exeter and London: William Pollard).

psychological one. Until just the last few years, Catholic theologians have preferred to adopt the former. The Abbé de Broglie in particular never departed from it. Hence his definition of religion: "The essence of religion consists in belief in a higher world in which the supreme object of the heart's legitimate aspirations and also of human consciousness is found, and [in belief] that it is possible here below to have communications with this higher world."[2] Since the partial triumph of [Maurice Blondel's] philosophy of action and the apologetics of immanence, the psychological point of view has tended to predominate. This is the one chosen by "Mr. Engels."

Thus he does not make the essence of religion consist in dogmas, precepts, and rituals, but in particular modifications of the "Me," a special state of soul, a "sense" that is neither the aesthetic sense, nor the moral sense, nor anything analogous, but a *sui generis* sense specified by the element of our interior experience to which it corresponds and that he ascribes to it.

The "sense" that is "religion" in its primordial form has indeed a proper object. But this object is not a distinct entity. Rather, it is that which constitutes the common ground of all beings and binds their diversity into a unity. Grasped in all the realities we perceive, and grasped simultaneously with them, all it does at first is stir up in the mind an impression, a conviction—the impression or conviction that our personality is not independent but subordinate, and that the True, the Good, the Beautiful, have of themselves a sovereign and unconditioned value—in other words, that there exists an Absolute.

Thus the Absolute is sensed before it is thought. But then, thanks to our reason, whose function is to classify the data of experience and transform them into intelligible notions, the Absolute becomes the most important object of knowledge and the central point of our scheme of things. It is thereupon conceived as a person and a will: an infinitely free and intelligent person; a supreme will upon which all other wills depend.

So long as a man is not in possession of this conception of the Absolute or, if you prefer (they are equivalent), this perception of God, he is not religious and cannot be. For being religious consists essentially in putting one's will into accord with the divine will and with human wills to the extent that these latter are themselves in accord with the divine. But in order to es-

2. August-Théodore-Paul de Broglie, *Religion et Critique* (Paris: [Lecoffre,] 1896), 29.

tablish this accord, at least in an explicit fashion, one must have a complete view of the world of the will, and hence one must know not only that (as St. Augustine said) we are nothing but wills (*nihil alius quam voluntates*) but also that there exists, at once transcendent and immanent to all finite wills, an infinite will, whose domain we must recognize and that we must also love, not as one loves an abstraction, but as one loves a living person.

Thus one sees how it is legitimate to affirm that religion organizes the life of the will; and since this life once ordered implies adherence to all the divine desires, one sees how it is legitimate to conclude that the love of God forms the very substance of religion. Thus also it becomes apparent that the end of religion is to direct the will and regulate action, not to enlighten the mind and augment knowledge. From there, finally, there follows this consequence of capital importance: that the truth of religion should not be defined by the conformity of its metaphysical doctrines to the supra-empirical realities that those doctrines claim to represent, but by its influence upon conduct and its aptitude to render the union of the human will with the divine will more extensive and more intimate. This amounts to saying that one must distinguish the practical or moral truth of religion from its theoretical or logical truth.

Of these two truths, the first is the effective one, not the second. And the reason for this is that all our conceptions of the Absolute have only the value of analogies and symbols. Does this mean that one should pay no attention to them? Not at all. For even though one has but an inadequate and even false idea of God, when one imagines Him as a being endowed with activity and power, with whom one can enter into communication, or as a plexus of attributes and properties, this idea is nevertheless useful. It plays in the moral order the role that scientific theories play in the physical order, by systematizing the results of experience; the theories open up for us reliable routes through the world of phenomena; and hence in practical terms they are true. But in speculative terms, they are false; the notions upon which they rest are not exhaustive, and our experience remains necessarily limited to a moment of time and a portion of space. The idea of God is similar: despite its lack of objective value, it is a rule of action such that following it has certain advantages; nothing more is needed to assure its practical truth.

Such is Mr. Engels's theory of religion in its main outlines. Having been deduced a priori from a systematic psychology and metaphysics, it has no more value than the said psychology and metaphysics have.

Well, Mr. Engel's psychology, to start with it, hardly seems incontestable. Isn't it a mutilation of human nature, in effect, to reduce it to the voluntary element? As if man were not also an intelligence and a reason, and thus more than a sensibility and a will. As if man did not need to know prior to loving, and as if in order for him to act, especially to act for the sake of an order of things that is universal and surpasses him infinitely, man did not have an indispensable need for motives—and not just any motives, but rationally justifiable motives. This preeminence of reason over the will and this subordination of the need to love and act to the need to know and understand are affirmed in the clearest possible way in the higher types of humanity. What were Plato, Aristotle, St. Thomas, Descartes, Voltaire, Goethe, Leibniz, Kant, if not intelligences—that is to say, men in whom intelligence absorbed the other faculties and dominated their entire being?—To this one needs to add that even if religion were to be resolved finally into a "sense," it would still remain the case that religion starts by being a cognition, since nowhere is religion born of the soul's spontaneous activity, but everywhere is a product, in one way or another, of education and the result of an external teacher.

The metaphysics of Engels is no more acceptable than his psychology. The Absolute, he declares, is an object of experience for us. A proposition as big as that is not one that can be allowed to pass without proof. Does Mr. Engels prove it? Not in the least. Besides, even if he did prove it, the possibility of basing religion upon it would not follow. For—and this is what he maintains—if when we try to think the Absolute, the representations at which we arrive are all false and unreal, we are certainly deceiving ourselves when we conceive the Absolute as a free will and a living person. In vain would one allege that this conception, through the mere fact that it gives us a way to regulate our voluntary activity and make a coherent whole out of the multitude of our acts, is the practical equivalent of a true conception. For rather than direct their conduct in accord with ideas that they know to be fanciful, minds that preserve some concern for logic will prefer to base their actions upon verifiable data of experience like pleasure, personal interest, or social utility or will prefer to live without any rule at all, at the whim of impulses from without and passions from within. Will they be wrong?

Assuredly not. For one cannot imagine anything less reasonable and more upsetting than the religion of the Unknowable, unless it is perhaps Christianity in the theory of it that Mr. Engels proposes.

II

Since religion is essentially a "sense" and has as its primordial purpose not to communicate new cognitions to the intellect but to guide the will, Christianity likewise addresses itself to the heart more than to the mind and has as its purpose not to make us penetrate further into the realm of truth but to make us grow in our love of God and our love of our fellows for the sake of God, so that among all the beings composing the world of the will, the harmony might be more complete and the accord more durable. And all the Christian dogmas—dogmas of the divine paternity, the Trinity, the incarnation of the Word, grace, the communion of saints, the resurrection of bodies—are marvelously adapted to produce this increase and diffusion of charity in the spiritual universe. The sacraments also contribute, especially the one that *is par excellence* the sign of incorporation into Christ and the attestation of Christian solidarity: the sacrament of the Eucharist.

If no other religion offers the soul (which wants to develop in itself love of God and man) such abundant resources and such efficacious means, it is because the Christian Church gives us in its doctrine the highest conception of the world of the will that has ever been elaborated by humanity's collective reason under the influence of revelation and inspiration. For the divine is not discovered all at once, but bit by bit. The work of mind and will by which this progressive discovery is accomplished is precisely "revelation," just as the desire consequent on the part of each partial revelation for a new revelation, conjoined to the effort used to reach the new revelation, is "inspiration." Revelation and inspiration, then, are not exceptional phenomena. In every human being at one time or another and in one degree or another, revelations take place and inspiration makes itself felt. However, the prophets, through whom the great religious steps forward have been accomplished, are more inspired than other people. By living in sympathy of mind and sentiment with the general mind and sentiment, and by concentrating in their souls as in a focal point the rays of light and warmth that radiate from the souls around them, they arrived at a more comprehensive intuition of the world of the will and found new formulae to express the divine, superior to the formulae that mankind had used hitherto. The Church has collected the formulae thus inspired in the prophets of the ages prior to Christ. Once completed by those that Christ offered, and those that the Church herself has created, these formulae constitute Catholic doctrine.

Is this doctrine true? That is the question that inevitably comes up. And we must answer it as we did the one about the conception of the Absolute: the doctrine is true with a practical truth, not with a theoretical truth. And the legitimacy of the distinction comes directly from the fact that charity is the substance and the unique goal of Christianity. This fact imposes itself with so much obviousness that its statement can rightly pass as a mere truism. But it is a truism from which two consequences follow, which have the highest importance, even though people do not generally pay attention to them.

The first is that one must interpret dogmas in function of charity, and hence one must hold as inspired (and thus true) only those elements of each dogma that result in manifesting the love of God toward people and augmenting the love of each person toward God and all members of the human family. Applied to the dogmas of the incarnation, the resurrection, and the ascension, this rule leads one to reject the virginal conception of Jesus Christ by the working of the Holy Spirit as unhistorical and to see in His resurrection and ascension only symbols that express His victory over sin and His spiritual survival.

There can be no conflict between faith and reason—such is the second consequence. The impossibility of such conflict is recognized, no doubt, by all Catholics. But they maintain that it arises from the fact that faith and reason are two complementary and mutually adapted parts of one and the same intelligible world—which is incorrect. It really arises from the fact that faith and reason belong to two totally separate worlds; and since the faith refers exclusively to the domain of the will and is by definition independent of what we call positive knowledge, faith and reason can no more contradict each other than history and poetry.

If we have not mistaken its genuine meaning, these are the basic points to which Mr. Engels's theory of Christianity boils down. How gravely it departs from traditional doctrine, no one will fail to perceive, even at first glance.

To begin with, it implies the negation of Christianity's supernatural character. Yes, Mr. Engels admits revelation and inspiration. He even speaks to them as two capital factors in theological development. But what sort of notion of them does he give us? A purely naturalistic notion. According to him, revelation and inspiration are not the results of a particular and extraordinary intervention by God; they derive quite entirely from the spontaneous tendency of reason to translate the religious sentiment at the bottom of the soul's life into higher and higher concepts of moral beauty. Why does Engels thus strip away from Christian reality the transcendent character that the Church has always attributed to it? Nowhere does Engels say. But one will probably not be going wrong if one supposes that he does this because the historical reality of miracles, if not their metaphysical possibility, appears inadmissible to him.

One who no longer believes in miracles should not remain a Christian, it would seem. Mr. Engels judges otherwise. His opinion will not be understood unless one recalls that he sees in Christianity much less a doctrine than a sentiment, a spirit, (to say it best) a life. Given this conception, it goes without saying that only the practical truth matters in the Church's teaching, and that all dogmas or aspects of the dogmas that, taken in their literal sense, do not contribute to directing action conformably to the supreme law of charity can and should be interpreted (almost always) symbolically.

Because this is the depth of the debate—the reality of the supernatural and the objectivity of metaphysics—it is obvious that interpreting Catholicism symbolically amounts to destroying it. At the outset, it is denying the Church's infallibility, since the miraculous conception of Jesus Christ, His resurrection, and His ascension are not freely debated questions but are points of faith irrevocably defined. Next, it is to despoil Catholic doctrine of all its moral efficacity. The day when not just a few elite intellectuals (upon whom the Christian and ecclesiastical disciplines, loyally accepted for perhaps half their lives, have left an indestructible imprint) but all Catholics without exception (who take from their realistic faith their reasons to act) are persuaded that the divinity of Jesus Christ, the virginity of Mary, the redemption, grace, and the sacraments are nothing but very noble metaphors and incomparable symbols, you may be sure that you will find no one practicing—I won't say the evangelical counsels, but just the Ten Commandments—for the sake of Christ.

Also, and this will be our conclusion, the symbolistic Catholicism for which Mr. Engels (along with some other pious agnostics) has hopes for tomorrow has no chance of having a tomorrow. For the issue is not to know whether people will transform the dogmas of the Church, but whether people will continue to accept them as they are or reject them *en bloc*. People of logical intelligence and frank character, to whom sentimental equivocations and hypocritical compromises are repugnant, will not hesitate. When they are no longer able to believe in a personal God and a Word made flesh, they will go straight to absolute irreligion. Fully disabused, and henceforth on their guard against the music of words, they will have no further thought of embracing symbolistic Christianity, but will devote themselves to the strictly lay cultus of Truth, Justice, and Solidarity. And while they wait for death to deliver them from the woes of sensing and thinking, they will try to live as best they can, if they still think it worth the trouble in this vale of tears.

E. Franon

Bulletin de littérature ecclésiastique 8
(February 1906): 33–49

7

"THE RELIGIOUS PHILOSOPHY OF FR. TYRRELL"

Eugène Franon

"He would give twenty syllogisms for one tear." With this picturesque trait, Ernest Dimnet describes Fr. George Tyrrell on one of the pages of the suggestive and rather disquieting study that he has devoted to him.[1] Irish by birth, a convert from Protestantism, and a Jesuit to boot, Fr. Tyrrell, of all the Catholic writers in modern England, is the one who has the most admirers in France today, hands down. This is because there exists among us a certain school of philosophy and theology (not very numerous, to tell the truth—because its most notable members would dissimulate—but active, united) working hard over the last three or four years to give Tyrrell a reputation as an apologist without equal.

Recently, one of his books, a book of meditations, *Nova et Vetera*, has been translated into our language. Already in 1903 some of his sermons had received the same honor, and a collection of these, *La religion extérieure*, was

1. Ernest Dimnet, *La pensée catholique dans l'Angleterre contemporaine* (Paris: Lecoffre, 1906), 170.

right away proclaimed in some quarters a "powerful work."[2] Latest of all, the *Annales de philosophie chrétienne* published an article by him under a title full of promise: "Notre attitude en face du pragmatisme."[3] I do not propose to speak about any of these works of Fr. Tyrrell, nor of his two-volume tract *The Faith of the Millions*, but rather about his book *Lex Orandi*, or *Prayer and Creed*.[4]

For a Frenchman who has preserved the taste, or the mania if you prefer, for logical distinctions and classifications, this work is rather disorienting. Is it a series of "uplifting thoughts" modern style "on the mysteries of the Christian religion," a collection of "considerations" on the dogmas of the Creed, a summary of Catholicism's "harmonies"? Would one be misrepresenting its author substantially if one thought of him as continuing the work of Bossuet, Garbet, Gratry, or at least as a sort of Bernardin de Saint-Pierre of the supernatural? Is the book on the contrary an apology, a work of dogmatics, or even a criteriology, a methodology for the particular use of theologians? On first inspection it would seem difficult to say. Upon reflection, however, the conviction becomes overpowering that one should see in this book nothing less than a theory of religious knowledge, a philosophy of Christianity "in terms of psychology and history," an essay on the genesis and value of Catholic doctrine.

To expound this essay and criticize it with the exactitude, impartiality, and deference that it deserves—that is what I shall undertake.

As Mr. Dimnet bears witness, Fr. Tyrrell "is not a clear man," and "one needs an education to read him."[5] I hope you will not find me too presumptuous if I hope that the study I made of the brochure *Religion as a Factor of Life* has helped me acquire this needed "education."[6]

I

What the dogmas of the faith are in the Catholic system is far from being obscure and uncertain, whatever people have said to the contrary in a

2. *Bulletin critique* (February 15, 1903).

3. Tyrrell, "Notre attitude en face du pragmatism," *Annales de philosophie chrétienne* (December 1905).

4. George Tyrrell, *Lex Orandi or Prayer and Creed*. London: Longmans Green, 1904.

5. Dimnet, *La pensée catholique*, 137.

6. See Franon, "Un nouveau manifeste catholique d'agnosticisme," *Bulletin de littérature ecclésiastique* 5 (1903): 157 [translated as selection 6 of this volume].

now closed controversy. Truths, some accessible to reason, others inaccessible, that God has revealed supernaturally—that is, manifested and affirmed to man through processes that, whatever their nature, fall outside the series of causes flowing from the ordinary order of providence; truths that, with all due note of the imperfection inherent in all presentations of the real in human language, are objectively and immutably true; truths, finally, that we discern by the sign that the Church, in virtue of her infallible authority, has in one fashion or other defined them and obliged all the faithful to accept them—there, if I am not mistaken, is what dogmas represent for the Catholic tradition.

For Fr. Tyrrell, on the contrary, they are the immediate data of religious consciousness progressively transformed (under the influence of reflection and action) into ideas and into systems of ideas, which, as soon as Christian society establishes always and everywhere their spiritual fecundity, have an absolute value from the practical point of view, but are not true from the intellectual point of view except relatively and for a time. How he arrived at this conception may be seen by expounding the three master theses into which his thinking resolves itself.

Dogmas are, in their origin and their results, creations of religious experience—such is his first master thesis.

According to Fr. Tyrrell, there exists in man a religious sense, which is not the moral sense, or the scientific sense, or the aesthetic sense, or a combination of all three. This special sense is the sense of the Absolute or of the Infinite; by it we are put into immediate contact with God, and we acquire consciousness of its existence as we do of our own.[7]

In fact, it is not "right away" or "always" that God is sensed and known. Immersed as we are in the world of matter, we first need to convince ourselves that this world is composed only of appearances and that above it, and incomparably more real than it, there is another world, the world of the spirit, the world of the will. Next we have to establish that a will, which each of us primarily and essentially is, stands related to a society of similar wills; and then we have to discover, through the joy and the power as also through the suffering and the weakness that come to us from our accord or disaccord with other people, that love is the supreme law of the spiri-

7. Tyrrell, *Lex Orandi*, xi–xxiii.

tual world. Finally we have to understand that, above all the finite personal wills, there exists an infinite personal will from which proceeds all that there is of good in the realm of souls, and with which one must live in the closest possible union, loving what it loves, hating what it hates. Rising in this way from vague knowledge of God to clear knowledge of Him and from implicit love for Him to explicit love is the essential act of religion.[8]

At the same time as it perceives the Absolute, the soul yearns toward Christianity. By all the faculties and all the needs of its being, the soul aspires to it, desires it, seeks it, postulates it. Hence the soul in fact, if not in law, is naturally Christian, in the sense that the soul's life, such as it was ordained to be from the beginning, requires for its expansion not just natural religion but the Christian religion, with its beliefs, its *cultus*, its sacraments, its hopes. Christianity then is not a mode of thinking and acting that is foreign to the soul and introduced into it from outside, under the pressure of a logical or juridical constraint. It is positively and literally an immanent manner of being. For "Christianity is nothing but theism developed." But theism, of which one should say correlatively that it is in substance "Christianity in embryo," certainly offers nothing but what is proportionate to the faculties of man.[9] In order to evolve, so as to rise from intuition of the Absolute through the sense of the divine up to being the Christian faith, the knowledge and love of God have undergone a double action: that of God continually present through all consciousnesses, and that of seers, inspired persons, apostles, saints, privileged human beings of whom Christ is the chief and the model—Christ in whom the realities of the invisible world were revealed more clearly than to others, and who found the most comprehensive or most stirring formulae to express them.

✳

These formulae—and this is Fr. Tyrrell's second master thesis—into which the results of humanity's religious experience have been condensed and, so to speak, crystallized, have a double truth or, what amounts to the same thing, a double value: an intellectual truth and value, a religious truth and value. The former is relative and variable; the latter is absolute and immutable.

Fr. Tyrrell was led to establish this distinction by combining what he

8. Ibid., 6–26.
9. Ibid., xxvii–xxxii.

calls the "sacramental principle" with the theory of analogical knowledge of supra-empirical realities and the idea that religious beliefs have mainly a practical bearing.[10]

According to the sacramental principle, just as we distinguish in rituals their material from their spiritual aspect, we must distinguish in beliefs their literal value from their religious value. The literal value of dogmas corresponds to the world of appearances, while their religious value relates to the world of the will. The literal value, bound up with a historical fact, a scientific conceptualization, or a philosophical theory, is of the intellectual order; the religious value is independent of fact, of conceptualization, or of the theory from which the conceptualization is inseparable and is of the practical order.[11]

Thus faith in God, the doctrine of the freedom and the immortality of the soul, the dogmas of the Trinity, the incarnation, the miraculous conception of Jesus Christ, the resurrection, the ascension—all these beliefs have an intellectual truth or value and a religious truth or value. It belongs to the intellectual truth of the theistic dogma to represent God to us under the concepts of a first Cause, a pure Act, an eternal and infinite Thought; it belongs to its religious truth to make us adore in this sovereign Being an all good and all merciful Father, who knows us, loves us, protects us, and wants to make us happy forever.[12] A physical and substantial union of divine nature and human nature in the sole person of the Word—that is what the incarnation is from the intellectual point of view, and the truth of this point of view is measured by the truth of the philosophical-theological notions of nature, of substance, of person, and of union. God is the Father of human beings, human beings are the children of God, and in Jesus Christ all humanity is deified—that is the religious significance of the mystery of the word made flesh.[13] If, in your belief in Jesus Christ's resurrection, you consider the material fact of the revivification of the Savior's body, you have the literal truth of this belief. If you wish to see in that belief only a symbol of the Master's glorification and of the permanence of His action upon the Church until the end of the ages, you have the spiritual truth of it.[14] And so on for the other articles of the creed.

10. Ibid., 1–5.
11. Ibid., 51–58.
12. Ibid., 70–80 and 106–7.
13. Ibid., 47–153.
14. Ibid., 182–86.

What led Father Tyrrell to distinguish in this way two elements in each dogma (the one intellectual, whose objective truth is not obligatory, the other a religious element, whose value as a principle of the spiritual life is absolute) was above all the interpretation he thought we had to give to the analogical knowledge of metaphysical reality, an interpretation according to which this knowledge is not just inadequate and indirect but erroneous and imaginary. If one presumes that he was equally driven by the conviction that many dogmas are irreconcilable with the certified conclusions of history or the sciences, one will not be making a risky judgment.

Moreover he has not just split in two the truth of Christian beliefs but has also altered them or weakened them. He is persuaded in effect that they have no other purpose than to guide action and that they can and do obtain this purpose independently of the truth or falsity of the philosophical or historical notions to which they have been joined. This is why, in his opinion, for each dogma the Church has written into her credo, she is not concerned to know whether it contains anything contrary to reason or to the facts, but has only asked if it accords with the spirit of the Gospels, if it has been of a nature to increase the piety of the faithful, and if it can contribute to strengthening the bonds between creature and Creator.[15]

*

By what test, by what sign, is one to recognize among the different dogmatic formulae the ones that will favor progress of the Christian life—that is the question that Fr. Tyrrell has undertaken to resolve in the last of his three main theses. The thesis is summarized in the maxim *lex orandi, lex credendi*, and it consists in setting up the universal experience of the Church as the supreme criterion of the religious value of doctrine.

> This proposition—the rule of prayer is the rule of belief, *lex orandi, lex credendi*—does not mean [Fr. Tyrrell explains] that every popular devotion rests upon a solid dogmatic foundation. Neither does it mean that a relic, by the mere fact that it has been venerated greatly and from time immemorial, is authentic. Even less does it imply that we must believe *de fide* in the relocation of the Holy House because there is a Mass in honor of this relocation. The maxim *lex orandi, lex credendi* bears exclusively upon the prayer and belief of the universal Church, i.e., the prayer and belief of the whole body of the faithful,

15. Ibid., 55.

in whom Christ lives and to whom He gives, so to speak, a common soul through His spirit shed upon all.

> The word "prayer" [Fr. Tyrrell continues] must be taken here in the sense of life inspired by charity, life filled with divine love, life based on union *via* the will with God and His saints; the word "belief" must be understood in terms of how one conceives those natures and laws of the other world that are presupposed by Charity and that give the divine love its distinctive character and its distinctive qualities.[16]

From thence it follows that one must hold the dogmas of the faith to be absolutely true—that is, true with a practical truth, not a theoretical truth—which is to say, more precisely, that the dogmas have a religious value that is certain and unconditional. Dogmas are "the experience, not of this or that man, however wise or perfect he may have been, but of the whole Christian people, of the total Church of the Saints, in all centuries and among all nations."[17] This is proved by the moral benefit and influence of the dogmas upon souls.

Let there be no mistake, then: Catholic doctrine is much more a creation of piety than it is of dialectic. To be sure, theologians have done a useful and even necessary work, because it is of great importance that the formulae destined to express the results of religious experience should be worded conformably to the rules of logic and should be put into harmony with the philosophical, scientific, and historical knowledge of each epoch. Nevertheless, in the end, the saints, the true friends of God and the perfect imitators of God, have been the ones who, under the continuing compulsion of the Spirit, have suggested or chosen now one belief and now another, and who by purifying, rectifying, refining, combining the ideas and sentiments on which Christian society has lived over time, have gradually fixed the articles of the creed. As for the teaching Church, its function in this work of elaboration has not been so much to direct the movement of minds, or to propose new doctrines, as to collect, classify, prepare, and harmonize the data (revelatory data of the natural order) furnished to the elite among Christians by their integral practice of adherence to the Gospel.[18]

Reduced to what I call its bare bones, such is Fr. Tyrrell's theory on the genesis and value of the creed. The eminent Jesuit's superiors certainly

16. Ibid., 59.

17. Ibid., 58.

18. Ibid., 207–9.

thought his theory to be philosophically and theologically irreproachable, because his book appeared with the approbation of Fr. Charnley, SJ, and it has the imprimatur of the bishop of Southwark. Alas, there is no shortage of reasons not to share the opinion of these venerable guardians of orthodoxy.

II

The first reason is that religious experience, in which Father Tyrrell wants to see the initial, general cause of dogmas, is nothing but one of those imaginary conceptions that, because of the irresistible "power of obscure ideas over human minds,"[19] always have some success but leave nothing behind upon analysis. This experience, according to Fr. Tyrrell's own doctrine, assumes in effect that there exists a sense of God and that the human soul postulates Christianity.

Well, in the first place, the sense of God (whose reality had been defended by [Auguste] Gratry [1805–72][20] and [Louis] Thomassin [1619–95],[21] not to speak of Jacobi, long before Fr. Tyrrell) is nothing but a thought-up entity. Of course, the immediate action of God upon the soul cannot be denied. For since it is in God, with God, and through God that we will, it is also in Him, with Him, and through Him that we know, since by reason of our contingency we depend upon him necessarily in everything we are and everything we do. But we have no awareness of this relation to God. Only through arguments that are very complex and that imply a prior solution to the two problems of the soul's nature and the value of metaphysics do we conclude that God exists. But as far as grasping Him intuitively and having a consciousness of Him is concerned, no.

Besides, to verify the emptiness of Father Tyrrell's hypothesis, it suffices to cast the most superficial glance at the ego. Physical sensations, agreeable or disagreeable emotions, desires, sentiments, volitions, mental images, concepts, judgments—that is all that we discover within ourselves. And for

19. Ferdinand Brunetière, *Sur les chemins de la croyance* (Paris: Perrin, 1905), 71.

20. See Auguste Joseph Alphonse Gratry, *Logique* (Paris: Douniol, 1855), 1:98, 2:193; *De la connaissance de Dieu* (Paris: Douniol, 1854) 1:379, 2:263; *De la connaissance de l'âme* (Paris: Douniol, 1857), 1:233; see also Amédée Chauvin, *Le Père Gratry* (Paris: Bloud et Barral, 1901), 221.

21. See Louis Thomassin, *Dogmata theologica* (Paris: Vivès, 1865), 1:50; compare Louis Lescoeur, *La théodicée chrétienne d'après les pères de l'église, ou essai philosophique sur le traité de Deo du P. Thomassin* (Paris: Remquet, 1861), 72.

these states of the soul, strictly subjective in themselves, we assign an internal or external cause only after we have made an inference based upon the principle of causality. So to maintain that we have directly a consciousness of the Absolute and of the Infinite is to contradict the most indisputable results of psychological analysis. What is worse, it is to make an assertion that is literally unintelligible. Each mind, after all, isolated and enclosed within the impenetrable precinct of its individuality, does not know anything "immediately" except itself. Thus we cannot have "immediate" consciousness of God any more than of the external world and of the souls of our fellows.

In the second place, it is by no means clear that the human soul demands or postulates Christianity, as Fr. Tyrrell claims on cues he takes from Maurice Blondel. No doubt, the people—and this is the case with the philosophers who defend the apologetics of immanence with such lovely ardor—the people, I say, who received a Christian education and who have not let their minds or their hearts be detached even for a moment from Jesus Christ, find between their faith and the aspirations of their soul a proportion that looks rigorous and a harmony that seems preestablished. But for those who have never believed, or who no longer believe, Christianity runs the strong risk of seeming, as Pascal says, "a religion against nature" and "against common sense."[22]

For, as Mr. S. Prudhomme comments on these words from the *Pensées*, Christianity is a religion that

> offends all the human faculties: the intelligence by its mysteries, which are as disconcerting in the order of ideas as miracles are in the order of facts; the senses by the mortifications which it inflicts upon them or the illusions to which it leads them in the Eucharist, where the body and blood of Christ are supposed to appear under the species of bread and wine; the heart by its repression of all movements of passion and even inward yearnings; the will by the abdication which it imposes upon it in the practice of obedience and humility; and finally the conscience by the consequences of original sin, which are incompatible with the sense of personal responsibility.[23]

These words go too far, no doubt, but they express with accuracy a state of mind that is very frequent these days, and they contain a partial truth that the facts confirm. After all, the failure, or rather the limited success of

22. Blaise Pascal, *Pensées et opuscules*, édition Brunschveig (Paris: 1900), 599.
23. René Sully Prudhomme, *La vraie religion selon Pascal* (Paris: Alcan, 1905), 154.

Christianity, and the extreme difficulty with which it is propagated when it finds itself up against a powerful religion like Mohammedanism or Buddhism—if they prove anything, do they not prove that man feels as much repulsion toward Christianity as attraction?

But suppose we grant that the soul requires Christianity; it will still remain the case that Christianity has been supernaturally revealed. Well, what becomes of revelation in the system of Fr. Tyrrell? One does not see it, or rather one sees too much of it. As a natural phenomenon—that is, conformed to the normal order of providence, immanent to the mind and not brought to it from outside, and submitted to a perpetual evolution—revelation does not keep any of the characteristics it has been defined to have *de fide* by the Vatican Council.

*

The distinction that Fr. Tyrrell sets up between the intellectual truth of dogmas and their religious truth or value calls for just as many reservations as his theory of revelation does.

If the issue is the metaphysical notions presupposed for dogmatics (or incorporated into it), let us recall that Fr. Tyrrell demands that the theoretical point of view not be confused with the practical point of view because of the imperfections, he says, of analogical knowledge.—On this point let me just observe that, for Fr. Tyrrell as well as for anyone else, analogical knowledge has to amount either to true cognition (although inadequate and indirect) or else to erroneous cognition. If he admits the first, one cannot see where his theory differs from that of the Scholastics. Should we therefore interpret his thought in the second direction? If so, we land at once in pure agnosticism, whereupon, how can *trusting* the intuitions of the heart and the conscience fail to be inconsistent, when the realities they imply turn out to be by definition unintelligible and nonexistent entities?

If the issue is the facts that the Church has always demanded we take as real—for example, the virginal maternity of Mary, the healings done by Jesus Christ, His resurrection, the supernatural conversion of St. Paul, how exactly does Fr. Tyrrell apply his distinction between the historical truth and the religious truth of the New Testament accounts? Does he mean to insinuate that the miracles reported in the synoptics and Acts are just pious lies or, if you prefer, unconscious idealizations, just like the prodigies that Buddhist legends attribute to Sakya-Mouni? But in that case Tyrrell puts himself into formal opposition with Catholic teaching.—Does he recognize on the contrary the historicity of the miraculous events that accompany the birth of Christianity, and does he propose just to put the mystical significance of these facts into a more vivid light? But in that case, Tyrrell is not introducing anything new into theology. For, after all the meditations of the Fathers and St. Ignatius, St. Francis de Sales, [Fr. Charles de] Condren, [Fr. Jean-Jacques] Olier, [Bp. Jacques-Bénigne] Bossuet, [Fr. Louis] Bourdaloue, Fr. Faber, and Msgr. Gay et al. on the moral symbolism of the Gospel miracles and the "mysteries" of our Lord, there is not much more to say. Besides, if the distinction between the historical truth and the religious truth of the facts affirmed in the credo amounts to no more than this, it would be more than a little naïve to present this distinction to apologists as the most efficacious means to put a permanent end to the difficulties raised against the Christian supernatural in the name of higher criticism. But according to the opinion of its inventor, this distinction will offer the priceless advantage of resolving the conflicts between religion and science. What can one conclude but that, in reality, the purpose of this distinction is to give a decent burial to the miracles that encumber the Gospels and give them an air of kinship with mythological stories?

*

Without dwelling further, I come at last to the rule of faith preached by Fr. Tyrrell: *lex orandi, lex credendi*. Is this rule, which replaces the judgment of the Church with the religious experience of the whole Christian world, so as to make this experience the proof that Christianity acquires experimentally of the spiritual fecundity of certain doctrines, an acceptable rule? I think not. It runs into two objections: a historical objection and a philosophical one.

History—this is the first objection—does not show that the Church ever resorted to the criterion of moral utility to define doctrines as "of the faith." Popes and councils, when they had to fix a point of Catholic belief, asked themselves just one question: is this proposition contained in scripture, and if not, was it continually taught at least implicitly by the universal Church as a revealed truth, or does it at least follow logically from a proposition already defined? If you will study, for example, the history of the dogmas of transubstantiation and papal infallibility, you will easily convince yourself that the dialectical work of theology, which the definitions of Trent and Vatican I brought to these terms, bears no resemblance whatever to the operation of experimental asceticism that Fr. Tyrrell imagines to have been conducted by the saints. After all, unless the saints were theologians of genius, like St. Augustine and St. Thomas, their influence upon the doctrine reduces to zero. Far from its being the case that the Church judges her faith by their opinions, it is rather the case that she judges their sainthood by the conformity of their opinions with her faith.

If you object that Fr. Tyrrell does not mean to speak of the individual actions of officially canonized saints but of the collective action of all the Christians who live the life of Christ, or, if you prefer, the action of "the Church's soul" and of "Christian consciousness," I would answer that one should attribute no more reality to the "soul of the Church" and to the "Christian consciousness," at least as these expressions are used in the *Lex Orandi*, than one attributes to "the soul of the mob" and "democratic consciousness." Even when currents of popular opinion arise that make people desire the definition of a belief not previously obligatory, the definition always comes either from papal initiative, as happened with the immaculate conception, or (more ordinarily) from the efforts of theologians, preachers, and Catholic writers, as one sees in the case of papal infallibility. All the rest (setting aside, of course, the influence of the Holy Spirit, which I have no dream of denying) is explained by the general laws of group psychology and especially the laws of imitation.

The philosophical objection with which the criterion of religious utility collides is this: there is nothing more imprecise, more variable, less objective, and more dependent upon the mood, the environment, and the moment than such a criterion. A Buddhist can evoke it to justify his faith. Ditto for a Muslim.

It does not cease to have a certain force.

The diffusion of Buddhism, for example, and its vitality become inexplicable if one does not admit that for the five hundred million or so Asians who profess it, it is a religion marvelously adapted to their aspirations and to their mentality. The same holds for Mohammedanism and the populations in which it has subsisted for so many centuries, or among which it has recently been implanted.

With nothing in hand but the criterion of utility, spiritual utility, then, there is no way to give a cogent reason to convert to a non-Christian or a heretic who finds in the religion with which he was raised these three things: "interior illumination, logical satisfaction, practical fecundity." These are the three things that, in the eyes of William James—a theoretician of religious experience whom Fr. Tyrrell has certainly read—are sufficient of themselves to legitimate any religion.[24]

If the Church had no ambition but to *present herself* as a spiritual society that it is advantageous to join, but that there is never an obligation to join, the theologians who reject the psychological ideas of the American author and the English Jesuit would be committing a signal mistake, beyond any doubt. For as Mr. [Émile] Boutroux has written,

> by deliberately reducing the question of value to the question of utility, and by locating utility in what gives people moral force and joy, [these writers] make the value of religion palpable and tangible to every one of us. This value itself becomes a matter of experience. As for the objections people draw from the deadness of dogmas or their conflict with science, these objections fade away before a psychology which wants to see in dogmas nothing but an epiphenomenon and not the essence of religion, and before a philosophy of science which makes science itself a mere way of organizing our representations, one which tends, like religion itself, towards the realization of our personal goals and practices.[25]

The Church, however, has always claimed, and today claims more than ever, the right to *impose herself* with incontestable authority as the sole religious society which teaches the truth infallibly and in which people can "work out their salvation." The Church is therefore forbidden, under pain of condemning her entire past, from entering the path onto which Fr. Tyrrell and other "agnostics with religious needs" dream of hurrying her along.[26]

✳

At this point it is up to each reader to put a classifying description on Fr. Tyrrell's religious philosophy. Will a reader who chooses to treat the work as something even more fragile than it is ingenious and brilliant, and who doesn't want to see in its author anything but a meditative man of poetic and mystical temperament—will such a reader be lacking in insight or fairness? Perhaps. In any case, let no one be too hostile to the poor theologians who,

24. William James, *L'expérience religieuse*, French trans. Frank Abauzit (Paris: Alcan, 1906), 17.

25. Ibid., preface by Émile Boutroux, xvii.

26. This expression is from Mr. Henri Lichtenberger; see the *Revue universitaire* (January 15, 1906): 56.

after reading Fr. Tyrrell's book, decide not to abandon the Catholic conception of dogma but propose to adhere to it with even more force and security. For in believing that by maintaining her traditional doctrine the Church is staying in accord not only with herself but also with reason and the facts, with logic and psychology, with metaphysics and history, these theologians seem excusable enough. And they have far from negligible reasons to think that "if there exists an interpretation of the faith whose spiritual fecundity Christian man has verified," it is the interpretation that has helped so many great, pure, valiant, and religious souls to sanctify themselves already, from St. Paul down to the Curé of Ars.

E. Franon

part 4

critical responses to édouard le roy's *"qu'est-ce qu'un dogme?"*

Bulletin de littérature ecclésiastique 7 (October 1905), 187–221

8

"WHAT IS A DOGMA?"

Léonce de Grandmaison

Within the strict limits of this article, there can be no pretense of answering all the complicated and delicate questions raised recently by Mr. Édouard Le Roy, under the title, "What Is a Dogma?"[1] It would take a whole book. But in compliance with a desire expressed by the eminent rector of the Institut Catholique in Toulouse, I hope to do a little bit to clear up the traditional notions about Christian dogma and to show that they have nothing about them but what is compatible with the legitimate needs of contemporary thought.

My jottings get some currency from the text of Mr. Le Roy, I suppose, but it has seemed to me that the supreme weight of the issues at stake should make one forget personalities, even if it is a question of so qualified a scholar and so sincere a believer as the distinguished contributor to the *Quinzaine*. Why embitter the debate? Why focus, for example, on the disconnect we see in these disclosures of his, where a seemingly limitless confidence in "the new philosophy" is joined to so ardent a contempt for "intellectual" cognition? Beyond doubt, it will be more valuable to try to show what Christian

1. Édouard Le Roy, "Qu'est-ce qu'un dogme," *La Quinzaine* (April 16, 1905): 495–527. [Hereafter in this selection, references to this article will be shortened to *QD* and the page number.—Tr.]

dogma has been historically and what relations it has to the human mind and to a believer's action. "An effort towards the light, in the bosom of Catholic truth faithfully accepted in its fullness and in its rigor"—the explanations that follow have no aim to be anything else, and I could hardly hope to formulate the ambition better.[2]

Dogma and History

The life story of words is a useful thing to know when they deal with capital notions. So let us take more than a passing interest in watching two nouns, δόξα and δόγμα, coming from the same verb, at first almost synonyms, as they become more and more differentiated in classical usage. The first, although yielding widely to secondary uses, keeps the modest and moderately approved sense of *opinion*; the other, with a firmer and denser meaning, becomes fixed in juridical language. At this stage it enters into the terminology of the first Christian writers, and everywhere in the New Testament δόγμα means a decree, an ordinance coming down from an uncontested authority: the edict of Caesar Augustus (Lk 2:1), prescriptions of the Mosaic Torah (Eph 2:15; Col 2:14), a commandment coming from on high and binding every human being. In the Apostolic Fathers, "dogma" keeps this value, even while enlarging it a bit; the accent is put on the authoritative character of the decision. Then the usage evolves under the influence of philosophical vocabulary, especially Stoic, and by a remarkable return to its root sense, δόγμα is restricted to rules that are addressed above all to reason, *to the truths that command an intellectual adherence*. This development, already visible in the Alexandrians, is finished at the outset of the fifth century; and for Vincent of Lerins, the *caelestis philosophiae dogmata* are religious truths that are irreformable because they are revealed.[3] After having fallen into near complete obsolescence in the Middle Ages—St. Thomas does not use it in his theological works[4]—the word subsequently regained a growing favor, a new lease on life. In current church usage, people sometimes distinguish a "dogma of divine faith" (a revealed truth imposing itself

2. Ibid.,496.

3. Vincent of Lerins, *Commonitorium* 22; Jacques-Paul Migne, Patrologia latina (Paris: Vrayet, 1841ff.), v. 50, col. 668. [This immense series will be cited hereafter with the abbreviation PL plus a volume and column number.

4. Heinrich Josef Wetzer and Benedikt Welte, *Kirchenlexicon*, vol. 3, 2nd ed. (Freiburg im Breisgau: Herder, 1881) even says that the word is not found at all in St. Thomas, but there is the line "dogma datur Christianis" in the *Lauda Sion*.

prior to any formal definition) and a "dogma of defined faith" (*a revealed truth proposed by the infallible magisterium of the church*). This last meaning, the one most commonly received in the sense of Cardinal Franzelin,[5] is also the one that best accords with the declarations of Vatican I. These have affirmed above all the objective value of dogma and have determined the limits on the development it can have.[6] In what follows we shall be speaking of "dogma" thus understood.

But before seeing whether this obviously intellectualist meaning (which finally prevailed) is justified, and in what measure, it will serve some purpose to cast an eye upon the collection of doctrinal propositions, which we also designate with the name "dogma" (as in "exposition of Catholic dogma," "introduction to the study of dogma"). From the very beginning it was demanded of those who sought to join the Christian community that they make a profession of faith, an explicit declaration of attitude toward the Gospel, toward the apostolic κήρυγμα: "if thou shalt confess with thy mouth that Jesus is Lord, and shalt believe in thine heart that God hath raised him from the dead, thou shalt be saved" (Rom 10:9)—an abridged and pregnant formula, which very quickly developed into an apostolic baptismal creed. Not only in each of its articles but also as a whole (apart from short, later additions that I cannot go into here), this creed goes back to the first Christian generations: it is an authentic echo of the original preaching.[7] For several hundred years, it was around this text, by way of clarifications, additions, precisions, that the work of doctrinal elaboration crystallized (so to speak) under the stimulus of the growing needs of the faithful, the perversions of heresies, the influence of ancient philosophies, the uncertainties of the then-current terminology. But these enrichments of the Apostolic Creed obviously did not exhaust the fruits of theological effort. Above and beyond the points

5. Johannes Baptista Franzelin, SJ, *Tractatus de divina traditione* (Rome: Ex Typographia Polyglotta, 1882), 308.

6. Vatican I, Dogmatic Constitution *Dei filius,* session III, c. 4 (Denzinger, no. 1315–20).— On the sense of the word δόγμα, one may consult, among others: Heinrich, *Kirchenlexicon*, vol. 3, col. 1979ff.; Joseph Tixeront, *Histoire des Dogmes* (Paris: Lecoffre, 1905), 1:1–2; J. Koestlin, at the beginning of the article "Dogmatik," in the *Realencyklopaedie für Prot. Theologie* (Leipzig: Hinrich'sche Buchhandlung, 1877), 4:733ff.

7. Alfred Seeberg, *Der Katechismus der Urchristenheit* (Leibzig: Deichert,) 1903. If the author does not prove his whole thesis, he proves at least what I am stating here.—The French reader who wishes to get oriented in the immense literature produced by the study of the apostolic creed will be well served by the article "Apôtres (Symbole des)," by Pierre Batiffol and Alfred Vacant, in *Dictionnaire de théologie catholique*, ed. Émile Amann et al. (Paris: Letouzey, 1906ff.), vol. 1, col. 1660–80.

that were imposed definitively upon the obligatory belief of the faithful, many other points emerged bit by bit and found their place in the common teaching. One must also distinguish within these doctrinal advances—more than Mr. Le Roy seems to have done, and more consciously than the ancient Fathers themselves were able to do—that which is dogma from that which is theology properly so-called. St. Augustine explains the matter excellently at the beginning of book XIV of *De Trinitate*; he marks within the knowledge of divine things the split between *wisdom* and *science*: the first is a matter of faith necessary for all, "*quid homo credere debeat propter adipiscendam vitam aternam*"; the second is a matter of knowledge limited to a few, "*illud tantummodo quo fides saluberrima … gignitur, nutritur, defenditur, roburatur.*"[8] These two knowledges differ

- by their object: on one side, conclusions deduced by human discourse from the revealed truths; on the other side just those revealed truths;
- by what motivates their acceptance: on one side, rational demonstration; on the other, the divine authority of the Revealer;
- by their value: on one side, a sovereign certitude that admits of no degrees; on the other, variable certitude proportioned to the evidence of the argument.

An example will make this brief description clearer. God is incomprehensible: there is the defined dogma. "*Firmiter credimus et simpliciter confitemur quod unus solus est verus Deus … incomprehensibilis.*"[9] Thereupon theology intervenes, shows without difficulty that this dogma was contained in scriptural and patristic tradition; but theology's role is not limited to that. *Why* is God incomprehensible? On this we debate, and along with the traditional data, systematic ideas about knowledge in general enter extensively into the solutions that the different schools present as probable. For some, the fundamental reason is that there is not and cannot be an image, a created *species*, capable of expressing the divine essence; others do not accept this idea and look for the distinctive reason God is incomprehensible in the impossibility of representing the "possibles"; and here again opinions divide according to the relations people judge to exist between the possibles and God's essence.

The conduct of the church's magisterium is quite different depending

8. Augustine, *De Trinitate* XIV.1; PL 42, 1037.

9. Lateran Council IV, c. 1 (Denzinger, no. 355) [currently no. 800].

on whether one is dealing with dogma or with theology properly so-called. In the second case the magisterium does not depart from a wait-and-see attitude, most often permissive, at most approbative. In the first case, authority intervenes and clearly takes sides. Even there, reserving judgment is the church's characteristic, and to budge her out of that reserve takes a spread of errors that have to be exterminated or prevented; and her aim has always been to safeguard a deposit that she does not think she has the right to augment.—Thence arise the ups and downs of dogmatic formulae, disconcerting at first sight. The same phraseology (ὁμοούσιος τῷ Πατρί; *unus de Trinitate passus est*) will be at first reproved or suspected, only to become in the end the watchword of orthodoxy. This is because the words only matter here to the extent that their meaning, as actually received, sufficiently expresses a truth that precedes them, goes beyond them, and will always surpass them.[10]—From thence again comes the usually (but not always) exclusive form given to dogmatic decisions; these decisions only determine in order to conserve.—From thence finally comes the concern not to press the technical sense of expressions that encapsulate a good deal of philosophical speculation: λόγος, *forma, etc.* The church only accepts them, or only imposes them, in their general sense, and purified of the systematic conceptions with which they have been, as it were, encrusted. To confess that Jesus is the Word is, for a Christian, not at all to accept the infinitely complicated and sometimes contradictory notions that the Stoics or Philo understood by this term. In adopting this term, the church indicates only that the first idea suggested by it, and made clear in the prologue to the fourth Gospel, expresses with a sufficient approximation the origin, the transcendent dignity, the universal role of the person of Jesus.[11] Thereupon the theologian is free to build upon this foundation a systematic construction: he should know that everything that goes beyond the traditional and so-to-speak vulgar meaning of the word is not covered by the formal proposition of the dogma. On the other hand, every conception that preserves faithfully this first sense can be proposed and defended freely.

It remains the case that adoption of this technical terminology by the church's magisterium is a mark of the aptitude (partial aptitude, greater or

10. I have explained myself at length on this point in a work that is still very imperfect: Grandmaison, "L'Élasticité des formules de foi," 520.

11. Jn 1:1–14; and for the sense, 1 Cor 8:6; Col 1:14ff; Heb 1:2ff.

lesser, but always relative aptitude) of a human philosophy to express the mysterious realities of our faith. To adhere to dogmatic truths thus stated, the believer is in no way bound to form himself into an Alexandrian mentality or even a Scholastic mentality; he must only recognize that this conception, Stoic or Peripatetic in origin, is apt to give the revealed truths a no doubt precarious but sufficiently correct translation, and sometimes the best translation. Many of the difficulties brought up by Mr. Le Roy collapse, it seems to me, under these remarks.

But one would be going to the opposite extreme if one were to conclude from this strictly conservative and often minimalistic attitude of the church's magisterium that dogmatic definitions have only a negative or prescriptive bearing. It is not true to say that doctrinal formulations, beginning with the first of them all, the Apostle's Creed, "affirm realities of which they give no intellectual representation, not even a rudimentary one,"[12] and that as a result their "only role in relation to abstract and reflective knowledge is the following: to pose objects and hence problems."[13] It would be easy to pick out the intellectual element of later and more elaborate formulae—such as the Athanasian Creed—but let us keep to the example proposed by Mr. Le Roy. When a catechumen undergoing the rite of "receiving the creed," in the course of the ceremonies of solemn baptism, recited the formula of the Apostle's credo, he was no doubt doing an act of Christian loyalty and manifesting his union with the community of believers. He was separating himself cleanly from all those who did not belong to this community: pagan idolaters or agnostics, non-Christian Jews, heretics.... But did this attitude exhaust the meaning of his act, and must one think the intellectual representations were incidental things, or things left up to the liberty of each person—intellectual representations that necessarily accompany the attentive recitation of these sentences? If so, we should not be far from Sabatier's "religion of the Spirit"; but this is surely not how people understood it in Christian antiquity!

In the course of the catechumenate, there used to be a day of special importance, on which the candidate "was officially initiated into the Gospel, the Creed, and the Lord's Prayer. In other lands (outside Rome) this ceremony was limited to the Creed and was called the handing over of the

12. *QD* 514.
13. Ibid.

Creed."[14] But in all of the churches, this handing over was accompanied by instructions meant to explain the meaning of the articles of faith. We happen to have several catecheses done by St. Augustine in this circumstance.[15] The theological tone is clearly emphasized, and the effort goes less toward inculcating the point that one *must believe* than toward aiding the minds of the catechumens to form a correct and definite representation of the realities to be believed in. The end is charity, but "one reaches it through the faith contained in this Creed," in such a way that one believes (I am going to let Augustine himself explain the first article):

> in God the Father Almighty, invisible, immortal, king of the ages, creator of the visible and the invisible, and anything else worthy of Him stated by sincere reasoning or by the authority of Holy Scripture.[16]

The brief indications that accompanied the *traditio symboli* in the ancient liturgical books display the same character.[17]

But let's go even further back, all the way to the writings of the New Testament, limiting ourselves for brevity's sake to the Pauline letters. Whatever the import of his teachings on the moral life, can one seriously doubt that Paul had in view above all a credence that was positive, formal, and "took the intellect captive" (2 Cor 10:5) when he spoke in these great letters about the "typical teaching," hence irreformable teaching, which the faithful have "received by tradition" (Rom 6:17)? When he exalts the mysterious Wisdom of God, unknown to the princes of the age, but revealed to believers by the very Spirit of God, who searches and knows and *makes known* the depths of God (1 Cor 2:4–13)? When he multiplies doctrinal formulae to support practical decisions (1 Cor 8:6, 12:3, 15:1ff.)? In this last example the dogmatic conception is proposed first to the mind, and the conclusion drawn is aimed at action; but other times the order is reversed (Phil 2:1–12), but in such a way that the value of the moral exhortation presupposes and is based upon

14. Louis Duchesne, *Origines du culte chrétien: Étude sur la liturgie latine avant Charlemagne* (Paris: Ernest Thorin, 1903), 301.

15. Augustine, *Sermones* 212–16, PL 38, 1058–76.

16. *Sermo* 212, PL 38, 1058: in Deum Patrem omnipotentem, invisibilem, immortalem, regem saeculorum, visibilium et invisibilium creatorem; et quidcquid aliud digne de illo vel ratio sincera, vel scripturae sanctae auctoritas loquitur.

17. One may look, for example, at the exhortation that appears in the Gelasian Sacramentary: Dom Pierre de Puniet, *Les trois homélies catéchétiques du Sacramentaire Gélasien* (Louvain: Peeters, 1905), 23–30.

the distinct and positively known truth of the divine reality at stake. Will one say that there is "no intellectual representation, not even a rudimentary one" imposed upon a person who must believe that Jesus Christ, "being in the form of God, did not judge it usurpation to be equal to God but emptied himself, taking the form of a servant, having become like unto men"? Or will one say that this high theology goes simply to affirm "that reality contains (*in one form or another*) something to justify as reasonable and salutary" the counsel of humility given by St. Paul!?[18] If we go on to look at other epistles, the (I don't say exclusively but clearly) intellectualist character of the faith demanded by the Apostle becomes even more clear. It is not too much to say that the Letter to the Colossians is saturated with technical expressions borrowed from the religious philosophy of the time (*pleroma, elements, eons, epignosis, energia*), full of doctrinal precisions remote from the primitive Gospel, to which one must adhere firmly and faithfully. I am well aware that this theological terminology introduced admirable developments in Christian action, but who will be persuaded that its first aim was not to perfect (and if need be reestablish) in the *minds* of these believers the *representations* necessary for orthodox faith? Perhaps the most penetrating of modern commentators on this epistle, Lightfoot, a man otherwise little disposed to emphasize the Faith's intellectual element, has rightly discerned in St. Paul's exposition of this Christology "a firmness, a precision, which leaves no doubt about the master conception present in the mind of the writer." And after making a comparison between "the vigor and clarity of conception" present here and "the above-all *practical* appreciation of the person of Christ in the Apostolic fathers," he shows that the doctors of the fourth century were the legitimate heirs of St. Paul's complete thought.[19]

18. *QD* 517. I have italicized "*in one form or another*," because it optimally summarizes the point in debate. If the "duty [of the believer] concerning the action of thought" reduces to believing *that humility is proper*, then all formulae are equally good for us because none of them bears a *sure* relation of resemblance, or even a nonlogical resemblance, to the objects that the formula symbolizes. All we have to affirm is that the practice commanded has in its unknowable reality *something or other* to justify it. We have landed in flat-out agnosticism; and in that case one asks oneself what good the "negative or prohibitive" sense of a dogma is, the sense admitted by Mr. Le Roy. Imposing upon me the duty to affirm "God is personal" rather than "God is impersonal," when I am otherwise ready to believe there is a God in one form *or another*, to justify my religious attitude, is trying to make me say "God = X" rather than "God = Y," where the hypothesis is that X and Y are entirely arbitrary symbols.—But maybe this is pushing a parenthetical remark too far.

19. Joseph Barber Lightfoot, *Colossians* (London: Macmillan, 1875), 190–91. [The volume is part of the International Critical Commentary (ICC).—Tr.]

One may say: suppose these declarations are just barriers against the false representations advanced by the Judaizing gnostics of Colossae; the doctrinal teaching of the Apostle, purely negative, is limited to closing off dead ends.—But besides the fact that false representations *presuppose a true one*, call for it, and *determine it to some extent*, who can fail to recognize the existence of a set of positive beliefs, intellectually nailed down, (even though inadequate to their object and leaving the mystery largely intact) in passages like the following?

He [the well-beloved Son of God] is the image of the invisible God, the firstborn of every creature; for in Him were all things created in heaven and on earth, visible and invisible, thrones or dominations, principalities or powers—all were created through Him and for Him; and He Himself is before all things, and all things have their subsistence in Him; and He is the head of the body, the Church; He is the beginning and the firstborn of the dead, that He might hold the first place in everything; for it has pleased [God] that all the fullness should dwell in Him.... See that no one seduces you with philosophy or vain subtlety according to the tradition of men, according to the elements of the world and not according to Christ: for in Him dwells the fullness of Divinity incarnate.[20]

So those who want to keep giving dogma a proper and positive intellectual value are the ones who are maintaining the most authentic Christian tradition. Wherein this value consists, exactly, we shall try to define by speaking of dogma in its relations to the life of the mind.

Dogma and the Mind

A dogmatic proposition is a judgment that expresses in (that translates into, if you will) human language the reality of (or one of the aspects of) a mysterious object. But this object is not always (or entirely) inexpressible through proper concepts. This does not permit one to define the dogma as the mystery pure and simple, and it justifies the role attributed to revelation by Vatican I in the conservation of rational truths. Of the two terms that are joined or separated by the doctrinal proposition, it either happens that at least one of them is well known in its concrete nature ("the canoni-

20. Apart from one or two details of punctuations, I am using the text of Eberhard Nestle, *Novum Testamentum graece*, 5th ed. (Stuttgart: Wittembergische Bibelanstalt, 1904). The interpretation of the last word, σωματικῶς, is supported by the usage of the word, by the context, and—what is decisive for me—by the parallel contexts in the Johannine Prologue. But it is not our job here to make a detailed exegesis of these texts: Col 1:16–19, 2:8–9.

cal Gospels are inspired")—or else both escape our immediate and proper knowledge ("the Son is begotten not made"). But in both cases, and this is the main point, the dogma proposes a truth that informs us to some degree about the nature of the reality that it translates. That this reality remains largely unknown to us, that it may even be in a true sense "unknowable," everyone will agree who wants to avoid merely verbal disputes. (In the terminology of many of our contemporaries, the word "know" is reserved in effect for objects of which we can form an adequate, comprehensive conception, or at least a proper and direct conception. In *this way of talking*, which changes the traditional and theological use of the word "know" without much foundation, it seems to me, God and supernatural realities, the primary objects of dogmas, are and will remain "unknowable.") But in that case, Le Roy objects insistently, we have no choice where these objects are concerned but the choice between an avowed agnosticism and the doomed effort of a naive anthropomorphism. Take for example the proposition "God is personal." Le Roy says,

> Either one defines the word "personal," and then one falls fatally into anthropomorphism; or else one does not define it, and then one will turn no less fatally to agnosticism. We are caught in a cleft stick.[21]

Happily there is a way out; and perhaps one can indicate it even in the terminology I was just mentioning, by distinguishing the "unknowable" from the "unthinkable." Be that as it may, one can know something of an object, surely and positively, even though partially and by analogical concepts: whether this inadequate and indirect grasp merits the name "knowledge" is a question of vocabulary. What matters here is to appreciate the difference that exists between an analogical grasp and a pure symbol. The latter *holds the place* of an object without at all disclosing its nature (for instance, the letters by which one designates the different parts of a geometrical figure); and so it is entirely conventional. An analogical notion on the contrary *represents* the object and thus supposes a resemblance founded on reality, between that object and our concept. It is a "symbol," if you will, but not a purely verbal and conventional one; it is rather an appropriated symbol and in some measure revelatory of a distinct reality. Thus the notion of "life" designates (for the unlearned as well as for the learned) a property that shows its presence by definite effects. And no doubt this term awakens

21. *QD* 510.

in us imprecise images, often mistaken or too compromised with anthropomorphism; but this does not prevent the concept of life from being significant and positive. Is affirming an object as living the same as saying nothing about it? The same goes, proportionately, for dogmatic propositions.

Let's go back to the example put forward by Mr. Le Roy, even though his choice of it may seem less than fortunate.[22]

> Let the dogma be "God is personal" ... I see quite well that it is telling me "God is not impersonal"—that is, God is not a simple law, a formal category, an ideal principle, an abstract entity, not to mention a universal substance or I-know-not-what cosmic force diffused in all things. In short the dogma "God is personal" does not give me any new positive conception, and it does not guarantee for me the truth of a particular system among those that (as the history of philosophy shows) have been proposed one after another,[23] but it does make me aware that such and such forms of pantheism are false and should be rejected.[24]

And that is already quite a lot, I would add, especially if one notices that in its ecclesiastical tenor the formula that comes closest to "God is personal" excludes not only "such and such forms" but every form of pantheism.[25]

A negative result, you may reply; dead ends closed off!

But no; for the dogmatic proposition that forces me to take sides, taking the place of the work of discursive thought for those who do not have the talent or the leisure to pursue it that far, and giving to others a new assurance, from another order, that their conclusions are well-founded—this proposition does not just affirm that God *is not* this or that; it also gives the reason, which is that *God is more than all that*. It gives the reason that "He is a spiritual substance, unique, absolutely simple and immutable," "infinite in every perfection," that He must be proclaimed (*qui cum sit ... praedicandus est*) "distinct from the world in fact and essentially, and ineffably exalted above all that exists or is conceivable outside of Him."[26]

22. It is *de fide* that there are three persons in God; but one cannot say that "God is personal" is in that form the statement of a defined dogma. It is rather the necessary rational foundation for several dogmas. Still, one must recognize that Vatican I expressed this truth in more or less equivalent terms in an incidental statement of the Constitution *De fide catholica*, "Holy ... Church believes and confesses that there is one true and living God ... who, since He is a unique ... spiritual substance, should be called really and essentially distinct from the world"; (Denzinger, no. 3001).

23. These last words are quite true if what one means by "system" is the further rational explication of a primary conception that is positive and obligatory.

24. *QD* 512.

25. See footnote 22.

26. Vatican I, session 3, c. 1 (Denzinger, no. 1631) (currently no. 3001).

All right, let us proclaim Him such, you may say; but let us not flatter ourselves that we know anything by that—know anything positively and definitely about the realities we are affirming; otherwise we shall fall fatally into anthropomorphism.

I remark in passing that this response implies a ruinous postulate of agnosticism—namely, that a *totally inaccessible* object can and sometimes should be affirmed by us as real and even necessary.[27] But once again, a direct examination of our formula allows us to see a clear path between the anthropomorphic and agnostic dead ends.[28] The notion we have of *God*, as it results from the successive employment of the different classical procedures[29]—the way of exclusion, called the negative way, having its value only by purifying a concept already formed and that remains after the purification more positive than ever[30]—this notion of God is no doubt analogical, imperfect, deficient. Nevertheless it conveys something about God; thanks to it we affirm the existence of a first Being, absolutely independent, pure of all imperfection, incomprehensible, and such finally that we must distinguish Him essentially from every other being in which we observe any vestige of contingency, of impotence, and of vicissitude. The second term, God is *personal*, offers more difficulty if, as it seems, anthropomorphism is inevitable here, and if to stamp it out one runs the risk of removing all precise meaning from what we are affirming. And it is true that we naturally model our distinct concept of a person upon the ever-present reality that

27. On this point the remarks of Mr. Lucien Lévy-Bruhl, *The Philosophy of Jacobi* (Paris: Alcan, 1894), preface, xiv, seem to be absolutely well-founded: "Nothing is strictly unknowable but that which is in fact completely unknown, and whose existence (even if real) is in no way revealed to us, and which finally just absolutely does not exist at all for us. But then this is no longer "a negative idea." This is a meaningless expression, a pure nothing. If, on the other hand, while declaring a reality unknowable, we affirm its existence, we are thinking it. Since we are thinking it, we are comparing it (at least to the knowable, by contrast);— it all ends up going forward as if we had some idea of it … the idea of a reality forever inaccessible to thought is thus deceptive. It is a way for the mind to give itself an illusion."

28. One will do well to remind oneself that the task here is not to *justify holding* this truth but to *define* it within the limits possible.

29. These are called the ways of affirmation, exclusion, and eminence.

30. "And besides, the understanding of a negation is always based on some affirmation … so unless the human intellect knew something about God affirmatively, it could not deny anything about Him. But it would not know anything about Him, if nothing it said about God were affirmatively verified by Him," says St. Thomas in *De potentia*, q. 7, a. 5. On the *completive* employment of the different procedures, affirmative and negative, in the church fathers, one may consult Thomassin, *Dogmata theologica*, vol. 4, chap. 8.

we are. But a more attentive reflection discovers (underneath this anthropomorphic image that habitually overlays them) traits that do not necessarily imply a manner of existing and hence do not imply human limitations. A subsisting ego, spiritual and incommunicable—an ego that abides, which devotes itself to a purpose for activities otherwise scattered, which possesses itself and governs itself—an ego that is living, cognitive, exercising volition and love, which one cannot treat as a "thing" without injustice, which cannot consider itself such without self-betrayal—this is what all people perceive with more or less clarity, what they all affirm with a more or less distinct consciousness, when they speak of a person. And such is the notion that, when purified of the limitations of our human personhood, serves us in representing, in symbolizing (if you will) the incommunicable, spiritual, and loving perfection of the divine Being. A negative "way," but a positive and "thinkable" result. And this is what, far from weakening, strengthens the practical rule of action to which Le Roy thinks he can reduce all the affirmative meaning of the dogma that "God is personal"—that is, "in your relations with God, behave as you would in your relations with a *human* person."[31] For either the word "human" is too much—and positively falsifies our relations with God by rendering adoration impossible—or else one must explain that word by the preceding remarks and say, "in your relations with God behave as in your relations with a Person conceived by analogy with the human person but possessing personal attributes in such a degree of eminence and purity that this recognized transcendence confers a new character on your acts," a character which participates to its finite extent in the infinity of their object.

The other example suggested by Mr. Le Roy (the dogmas of the Resurrection of Jesus Christ and of his real presence) would support analogous conclusions. But we need to hasten on to a second mark of dogma: its pretension to impose itself categorically, absolutely. On this point, Catholic teaching is clear, and its intransigence does not need to be shown; one must believe, without hesitation or misgiving, everything which is presented to us with certitude as a matter of faith.[32] But if the prescribed attitude is clear, one still has to explain it a bit. For one sees clearly enough that this

31. *QD* 517.

32. This intransigence—need one even say it?—is a necessary consequence of the infallible character of the revealed truth.

point poses a difficulty for Mr. Le Roy and for all those who share his conception of immanence.

I shall not discuss the awfully haughty assertions with which this usually more reserved thinker accuses everybody of philosophical incomprehension if they refuse to interpret "immanence" as he does.[33] The history of philosophy teaches us to take these integrist declarations with a grain of salt. "Reality," he tells us,

> is not made up of distinct, adjacent pieces; everything is interior to everything else; analysis discovers all of science and all of nature in the least detail of nature or of science; each of our states and each of our acts envelops our entire soul and all of its powers; thought, in a word, implies the whole totality of thought at each of its moments or in each of its degrees.[34]

If you wish to say by this that really and formally "everything is *in* everything else," that in the nervous system of a bug, analysis will reveal to me the laws of celestial mechanics, or that my religious convictions are implicit in a reflection on the properties of the triangle, I have to ask if you are being serious.... If you just mean to say (and this is no doubt what Mr. Le Roy intended) that

> all things are caused and causing, helped and helping, mediate and immediate, so that all things are bound together by a natural and insensible bond which links even the most remote things and the most diverse things, and it is held impossible to know the parts [with an adequate and comprehensive knowledge] without knowing the whole[35]

with the result that our cognitions, even when incomplete and fragmentary, must take this universal linkage into account, under pain of error—if you mean to say again that "truths are not logically fertile unless they are linked one to another,"[36] so that a notion that is *entirely* isolated, like an adventitious bloc, does not enrich and does not nourish our mental life—if you mean to say that our operations are in solidarity with one another, so that we should not and, in a sense, cannot "reach the truth except with our

33. "He who refuses to admit [the principle of immanence] no longer counts as a philosopher; he who does not manage to understand it shows thereby that he does not have a philosophical mind"; *QD* 502.

34. *QD* 503.

35. Pascal, *Pensées*, section 2, §72 (Brunschvicg, 355–56).

36. Henri Poincaré, *La valeur de la science* (Paris: Flammarion, 1905), 138.

whole soul," and that in the end a truth, in order to become *ours*, has to be submitted *in some way* to the control of our reason,[37] and has to correspond to a need or at least to a "possibility" of our mind[38]—then a thinking person can hardly fail to reach agreement with Mr. Le Roy.

But it is also the case that the requirements of Catholic dogma do not contradict this conception. The conflict would come either from the dogma itself or from the way in which it comes to us: as an incomprehensible proposition, it would load our mind with a dead weight, having no value for religious life; as imposed from without, it would do violence to our intellectual autonomy. On the second point, I fear there has been a misunderstanding: every truth known with certainty "imposes itself upon us" as such, and no matter what part the knowing subject's faculties may play in the fertile union whence the knowledge results, one must admit (under pain of absolute idealism) that this truth comes in large measure from without. To know is to be informed—that is, moved to an assent. Willingly or unwillingly, one must yield to the evidence, and the "autonomy" of our thought, at the end of the day, is no less affected by the case of direct evidence than it is by the case where the evidence comes to us by transmission through a certain witness. The result in both cases is not an abdication but rather a conquest and an honor; our cognitive faculties are means to enrich our mental life, and everything that comes to them, far from violating them, does them credit.[39] It is just that when direct evidence is absent, what substitutes for it leaves a bigger place for good will, for freedom, for merit. Is one going to say that this is a "fall"? That assent given to what is otherwise assuredly true, because it is *good* to believe it, humiliates the mind? One should recognize at least that this "humiliation" is necessary in our present condition and that our moral and social life is predominantly based upon certitudes that are not "evident."

As for the result of an assent thus given, even in the particular case of dogma, it is not a matter of accepting sterile formulae passively. Granted,

37. On the nature of this control in the particular case of dogma, I shall be explaining my meaning shortly.

38. This word "possibility," as abstract as it may be and as little used as it is in French, seems to me less vulnerable to misinterpretation than "virtuality." It is well known that, in the case of a mystery, this "possibility" is much reduced; but it does exist.

39. I am not going to dwell on this point, which has recently been put in a good light in this very journal: Franon, "An Anti-Intellectualist Scholastic," *Bulletin de littérature ecclésiastique* 7 (1905): 137–38. Translated as selection 9 in this volume.

the sentence "The Word was made flesh," presented in isolation from any context, to a mind deprived of even an elementary understanding of the Christian faith, would remain uncomprehended and hence void of immediate usefulness for a person who accepted it by way of simple authority. But this is not how the dogmatic truth comes to us. With its way prepared by the teachings that precede it in our fourth Gospel and accompanied by the notions that these teachings presuppose, the formula truly enters into our religious life: it reveals to us the "great mystery of piety," of which St. Paul spoke. To be sure, a veil remains over the *how* of this immense fact; and, of the terms joined by the dogmatic affirmation, the first remains almost impenetrable to us. Nevertheless we know—and what knowledge is more useful, what glimpse of infinite Goodness is deeper than the knowledge that the one who "was in the beginning with God" and even was God has taken flesh like our own and "pitched his tent" on our desolate earth, to make us adoptive children of the Father whose eternal fecundity He exhausts in His person?[40] Far from remaining isolated, then, and unattached to the rest of our religious life, this central notion brings unity to it and at the same time corresponds to the deepest desires, to the seemingly most unrealizable aspirations, of our soul.[41]

From a psychological point of view, I doubt that anyone could dispute the truth of these observations, nor the point that even the most mysterious dogmas are apt to become in fact, for the believer, spirit and life, light and nourishment. But it still needs to be shown that in the manner in which they are imposed upon us, in the preparations that lead us toward believing, there is no intrusion, no violence, nothing like a "coup d'état" forcing our adherence without regard for our legitimate requirements.

Set aside, please, the most common and normal transmission of the faith. A Christian child receives (from those who have the natural mission to teach him, and receives with a no less natural and no less reasonable docility) teachings whose meaning at first escapes him almost completely.[42] But

40. Ac ratio quidem, fide illustrata, cum sedulo, pie et sobrie quaerit, aliquam, Deo dante, mysteriorum intelligentiam, eamque fructuosissimam assequitur, tum ex eorum quae naturaliter cognosci, analogia, tum e mysteriorum ipsorum nexu inter se et cum fine hominis ultimo; Vatican I, Constitution *De fide*, c. 4 (Denzinger, no. 3016).

41. Do I have to remind Mr. LeRoy's readers that this point was developed by Mr. Maurice Blondel in his book *L'Action*?

42. I am speaking only of what falls under psychological consciousness; I am thus abstracting here from the virtue of faith infused at baptism.

the light grows with the years, the reasons to believe multiply with the growing needs of the child's intelligence; the moral fertility of the principles received, their aptitude to resolve the problems posed by the world and by life, their inner harmony, authorizes them, confirms them; in this way without any need to resort to a formal examination, without damage, without any sharp crisis (at least most frequently), by a peaceable and continuous work of personal appropriation, the naive believer of the early years becomes the experienced member of the faithful, conscious of his faith, and "wisdom is justified in her children." Things go quite differently when this normal development has been interrupted abruptly by influences from outside, or when the normal development never took place. It then happens that a man in full possession of his faculties is dominated by a philosophical conception in which Christian truth has not had its place (and sometimes cannot make a place without excluding opinions previously accepted without contest). Then it happens that a mind formed by the methods of empirical science, excessively jealous of its rational autonomy, finds itself confronted by a dogma. There is an impression of deep shock, often accompanied by disdain or anger, which wells up first in the unbeliever's soul in the face of these new demands. They seem to him outdated, exorbitant, hostile to the dignity of his person, incompatible with the needed independence of his thought. What repugnance then arises, what objections come to light, what intentions to "not buy it" get formulated—Mr. Le Roy tells us with the emotion of a man who has met them all around him. And right there (I fully agree)—on the preliminary question, prior to the point where the moves of classical apologetics begin—is where the decisive battle is most often waged in our day. Of the many difficulties that tend to make people reject the faith as unacceptable, prior to examining the idea of dogma in any detail, just one (but it is the main one) holds people back, according to what was said above: it is the difficulty that bears upon the weakness of the alleged reasons to believe, bears upon the impossibility of the indirect demonstration without which there is no room for an assent except one that is more or less fideistic.

After all (we are told), either the reasons that authorize the faith are certain, and then how does the act of faith remain free? Or else they are not certain, and then how is one obliged to believe?—Theologians answer this classical dilemma after the manner of St. Thomas, by saying that the judgment by which we see that we must believe is one thing, and the act by which we do believe is another. The former is a human judgment, and although moral dispositions play a necessary part in it because of the practical consequences of this adhesion,[43] the ultimate basis for the assent is rational evidence, and the assent remains proportionate to the perceived force of the grounds for it. Thus, primacy of place remains with the intellect in this first motion, and the will only cooperates to set aside possible obstacles and to assure the normal play of a mind in pursuit of the truth. Things go quite differently in the very act of faith: here the proper ground is the authority of the one who reveals; and the signs through which God authorizes this revelation (though fully sufficient in themselves) are still only *signs*. Interpreting them

> depends essentially upon the clarity, the vivacity, the force of our moral dispositions, especially of our love for the truth, of the felt need that we have for the truth, of our respect for the authority of God, of our confidence in His goodness and His provident wisdom.... If these moral dispositions are not there, if the mind fears or mistrusts the truth ... one tries to break the living bond that connects the signs to God's authority and to His veracity; one does not allow oneself to be persuaded either that these signs come from Him, or that He used them as witnesses to revelation.[44]

With this first reason for an intervention of the will there joins a second and even more basic reason—namely, the obscurity of revelation's content. The supernatural realities upon which we ought to pronounce are and will remain mysterious; dogmatic propositions do not cast upon them the light of direct, intrinsic evidentness, which alone can settle the mind irresistibly, forcing the mind's adherence. It's like a sealed letter. Yes, it bears the divine seal; but we will never read its content in this life; one must believe it on the authority of the One who communicates its essential content to us through

43. Licet enim in demonstrationibus necessarius non sit affectus voluntatis et bona illius dispositio, ut apprehensis propositionibus statim homo ... assensum praebeat iis rebus quae notissimae sunt et nullo modo ad pietatem pertinent; in iis tamen quae ad pietatem spectant quales ... sunt de unitate Dei, de illius scientia et providentia, etiamsi demonstrationes intra propriam mensuram habeantur, necessarius est pius affectus.... In iis ergo plurimum confert affectus bonus, non quidem ut visa extremorum conformitate assentiatur intellectus, sed ut illam propositionem tali modo interius apprehendat et formet, ut faciat apparare eam extremorum conformitatem; Gabriel Vasquez, *Commentariorum et Disputationum in S. Thomae Summam Theologiae Tomus I* (Alcala: 1598), *Disputatio* I, c. 2. The great scholastic theologian applies this theory to the very "Demonstration" of God's existence; ibid., *Disputatio* 19, c. 3.

44. Mattias Josef Scheeben, *Handbuch der katholischen Dogmatik* (Freiburg im Breisgau: Herder, 1873); in French *La Dogmatique,* trans. Abbé Paul Bélet (Paris: Victor Palmé, 1882), 1:491. The whole context should be read.

His duly accredited envoys. You may say: can't the evidence of divine attestation force my assent, like the evidence of the witnesses who tell me for example that the city of Berlin exists, which I have never seen?—Given what was said previously about the interpretation of the signs of credibility, this difficulty will appear rather theoretical. If one admits the practical possibility of the supposition in an exceptional case, one will answer that the assent thus *imposed* will not be an act of faith properly so-called and that it will not render impossible *another* assent, free and meritorious, given on the simple authority of the *Revealer*.[45] However that may be, we see clearly enough how the free act of a good will takes predominance in the act of faith.[46] This is how to explain the meritorious character of our adherence, its moral nobility, as well as the psychological unrest that accompanies it, as St. Augustine long ago remarked and explained.[47]

But if the judgment of credibility does not imply the act of faith as a necessary consequence, it still provides a basis for it in reason. It has to be the case, then, that the proofs on which this preliminary judgment is based, taken together and in the concrete, are *certain* in the sense that, after sufficient examination, they leave no place for *justified* doubt. The language used to describe this certitude—"moral, practical, equivalent, as good as proved, relatively valid"—varies with the terminology of the logic-theories of the theologians; but on the point of fact they are all agreed. And one does not have to have read the *Grammar of Assent* to see that the "probability" assigned by Newman to the reasons for believing is such that those who refuse to adhere after having *realized* them at their best (which is again a duty) are without excuse.

Where does the force of this indirect demonstration lie?—Above all, I think, in the overall sufficiency and the practical conclusiveness of these reasons;[48] and these marks apply no less to the preliminaries postulated by the theses of classical apologetics than they do to these theses themselves. One needs to take note of this because, in our day, as in the time when

45. Jean Vincent Bainvel, *La foi et l'acte de foi* (Paris: Lethielleux, 1898), 21ff; 123ff.

46. "in cognitine autem fidei principalitatem habet voluntas. Intellectus autem assentit per fidem his quae sibi proponuntur quia vult, non autem ex ipsa veritatis evidentia necessario tractus," says Aquinas in *Contra Gentiles* III, c. 40, 2.

47. One may see his words with the profound commentary of St. Thomas in *De veritate*, q. 14, a.1.

48. I mean by that not only that the reasons to believe hold good above all by their convergence, and taken together, but also that they suffice for the legitimate and very diverse requirements of different minds.

Clement of Alexandria wrote his *Protrepticos*, there are often two stages to get through before reaching the life of faith: the stage of remote preparations, especially moral and philosophical, and the stage of properly Christian apologetics, which is above all historical and positive. Of the fact that the church does not neglect the former we have a striking proof in the dogmatic constitutions of Vatican I. There one finds in few but substantial words the theses necessary for an orthodox and reasonable faith: the existence of a unique and all-powerful God, distinct from the world that He freely created and that He governs by His Providence, which is infallible and yet respectful of human liberty.[49]

Logically speaking, it is necessary to be convinced of these truths before even starting to examine the problem of revelation; but practically speaking, the two inquiries often go hand in hand. It is not unheard of, especially in Protestant countries, to see people reach certitude of God's existence through the evidence for the divine that has appeared to them in the person of Jesus Christ. But this backwards progression, though not impossible to justify in reason, perhaps, is obviously not the best or the most common. What poses itself first for a sincere nonbeliever is the religious question in general, the "question of God," in relation to the world or the moral life. The necessary directive to look (beyond the mutually conditioned phenomena that form the framework for a positive or empirical science of real causes) for a first cause, an ultimate end, leads the mind toward solutions that render adherence to Christianity possible. Other times the first issue to come up is the felt need for a firm foundation for moral action, action in which no one can be disinterested, and whose directive is revealed to us continually by conscience. I do not have the time to dwell on these facts, which have been described often and excellently elsewhere; one can sum them up without going too far wrong, perhaps, by saying that the need to believe is first stimulated by the felt necessity of giving thought and action a stable and hence absolute foundation. Anyone who means to preserve or reestablish in his life something like a firm foundation tends to end up believing in God. The experience of agnostics (who at the price of an initial contradiction transpose the attributes of divinity to the Unknowable) is quite instructive on this point.

Once this first stage has been gotten through, or its conclusion has at

49. Vatican I, Constitution *De fide*, c. 1 (Denzinger, nos. 3001–3).

least been anticipated by an intuition of the mind or a secret appeal of the heart, the question of Christian revelation is open—I mean for a person living in a society like ours, still impregnated with Christianity and profoundly affected by its leaven. In fact, it is only in the Christian community that one can find God, the true God "living and all-seeing."[50] This is where the inevitable problems have received an answer that is less precarious, that does away with the scandal without denying the mystery: this is where the moral virtues are germinated from the seeds of heroism, made fruitful in selfless, humble, and brotherly devotion. How many stained souls have been purified here, rejuvenated; how many conflicted minds have been brought back to inner peace; how many weak wills have found a gentle rule and efficacious helps! This is where doctrinal rigidity has been reconciled at least in part with the ceaseless progress of peoples' minds; where moral austerity has been reconciled with human needs; where the unity of all in faith and love has been reconciled with the virtually endless differences of heredity, education, intelligence, and interests; where the rights of the person have been reconciled with the good of the social body; where the spirit that "makes free" has been reconciled with the practical letter that preserves the spirit by incarnating it.

Under many forms that it is impossible to delineate one by one or altogether, these reasons to believe act silently upon the upright soul and incline it to accept an Authority that shows itself strong by many titles. Jesus then presents Himself and is worthy of being believed. His miracles of goodness and power, His lessons and appeals, His holiness so unapproachable and yet human, the divine simplicity of a teaching drawn originally from the bosom of the Father—all that speaks to anyone who has a human heart. And if His words, at the distance of twenty centuries, seem less persuasive to some people, His work in our midst continues and authorizes His witness: "Turn your attention to me," the church is telling you.

50. "The God of the Christians is not just a God who authored the truths of geometry and the order of the elements; that is for pagans and epicureans. He is not just a God who exercises providence over peoples' lives and goods, so as to give a happy train of years to those who adore Him; that is for the Jews. But the God of Abraham, the God of Isaac, the God of Jacob, the God of the Christians, is a God of love and consolation, a God who fills the heart and soul of those whom He possesses, a God who makes them feel inwardly their own misery and His infinite mercy; who unites Himself to the depth of their soul; who fills them with humility, joy, confidence, love; who makes them incapable of any other end but Himself"; Pascal, *Pensées*, 13:556 (Brunschvicg, 581).

> Turn your attention to me, whom you see, even if you would rather not. There were believers in the land of Judea in those days who learned the wonderful birth from a virgin and the passion, the resurrection and ascension of Christ, all His divine words and deeds as present-day facts—learned them by their very presentness. These facts you do not see, and hence you refuse to believe. So turn your eyes to the things which you do see; pay attention to these things; think about these things, which are not told to you as stories from the past nor foretold to you as future events, but shown to you by their presentness.[51]

Like her Master and through Him, Christianity, with what it promises and what it gives, what it commands and what it makes possible,

> makes visible to people an authority and a gentleness which have never appeared before … it announces high mysteries but confirms them with great miracles; it commands great virtues but gives at the same time great lights, great examples, and great graces.[52]

Thus it ends up by imposing itself as *the* solution to the problems of life.[53]

The conviction that thus prevails, with the help of God's grace, in an upright soul—is it entirely and in every detail translatable into intellectual formulae? It certainly is not for most people. But who will deny that it is reasonable, or who will hold that an indirect demonstration thus supported does not do justice to the mind's legitimate requirements? Is it not reason itself that has discovered, at first unconsciously but then with growing desire and in an ever purer light, a liberating submission, where previously reason had only seen a scandal and a bondage?

If one wishes to reduce this assent of the soul in its intellectual aspect to the common types of human knowing, and if one asks, for example,

51. "Me attendite, vobis dicit ecclesia, me attendite, quam videtis, etiamsi videre nolitis. Qui enim temporibus illis in judaea terra fideles fuerunt, ex virgine nativitatem mirabilem ac passionem, resurrectionem, ascensionem Christi, omnia divina dicta eius et facta praesentes praesentia didicerunt. Haec vos non vidistis, properea credere recusatis. Ergo haec aspicite, in haec intendite, haec, quae cernitis, cogitate, quae vobis non praeterita narrantur, nec futura praenuntiantur, sed praesentia demonstrantur"; St. Augustine, *De fide rerum quae non videntur*, IV.7; PL 40, 176.

52. Jacques-Bénigne Bossuet, *Discours sur l'histoire universelle* (Paris: Librairie Firmin Didot, 1871), 2:19. These words were said about Jesus Christ. If I follow Vatican I and apply them to this proof of our faith *by the present*, it is certainly not to take anything away from the force of the historical argument drawn from the very person of Jesus Christ. On the contrary, I am persuaded that the historical argument holds first place in effectiveness as well as in dignity; but looking at the *present* fruits of Christianity is a good way to open people's eyes to this admirable light.

53. Of course I am only speaking here about intellectual preparation for the faith; one knows quite well that this is not enough, even if it is the most important.

like Mr. Le Roy, if these "arguments" are comparable to the ones we use in mathematics, in physics, in history, it seems that one must utterly put aside the first kind of "demonstration"—the mathematical kind. One could not even speak of "demonstration," if one reserved this term for the mental procedure that employs only elements entirely "given"—that is, adequately known and defined. One will far more rightly compare the unbeliever on the road to faith "to a physician accepting a fact that corresponds for him to precise experiences."[54] For even though they belong to the moral order, the religious experiences occurring within us and observed outside of us still have enough precision to make us able to assign to them with assurance a quality and a cause. One who examines in good faith the transformation worked in souls by the Christian idea cannot refrain from according to this idea a value capable of inclining the mind to accept it as divine. Historical knowledge also has its place in the apologetical procedure. It is not in fact awkward, and it conforms to good methods to consider historically certain, prior to all discussion of the inspiration of the New Testament books, the broad outlines at least of the Savior's life, His teaching, and the beneficial influence exercised by His Person. The "fifth Gospel" appealed to by Harnack in a famous phrase would suffice for this task and would almost dispense one from consulting the four others, if it did not otherwise confirm them by bringing to them a precious extra light.[55] Well, it is upon this first and incontestable foundation that Christian apologetics bases its major arguments.

To tell the truth, however—and this is perhaps the nub of the difficulty—the procedures used by the mind in examining the reasons to believe are not rigorously comparable to the procedures nowadays called "scientific." The nature of the objects to be attained goes against the comparison; the certitude for which one strives is of another order. It is a question of transcendent realities, going beyond not only empirical knowledge, but often proper and distinct knowledge. It is a question of a "certitude" that leaves

54. *QD* 502.

55. "Besides the four written Gospels, we have a fifth, not written, clearer and more striking in many regards than the four others: I mean the collective witness of the primitive Christian community. It is this fifth Gospel which shows us what a victorious impression Jesus gave of his person, and in what sense his disciples understood his words and the testimony which he bore to himself … historical criticism will not change any of that"; Adolf von Harnack, *Das Christentum und die Geschichte* (Leipzig: Hinrich'sche Buchhandlung, 1904), 17.; Msgr. Batiffol, *Jesus et l'histoire* (Paris: Lecoffre, 1904).

a place for free will and settles the mind without forcing it. So let us call this certitude "moral," if you like, or "vital," but let us not try to assimilate it to direct and necessitating insight; let us look for terms of comparison among the convictions on which we base our moral life, family life, social life. Although these convictions have less rigor than certain scientific determinations, they outweigh the latter through the diversity, harmonious complexity, and final bearing of the motives that give rise to them. To reject them ever so little, or disdain them, or hold them suspect, would be to confine oneself within a sterile intellectualism, within an untenable rationalism, and this should be clear above all to philosophers of action. Granted, traditional apologetics does try, and rightly tries, to sharpen its arguments, to group them, to put them in proper series, to give them all the scientific rigor they can sustain, and to translate them finally into intellectual and hence more communicable formulae. But in so doing the traditional apologetics limits itself to providing each person with seeds that only a good will aided by grace can cause to ripen into practical judgments and efficacious resolutions.[56] The very nature of faith is opposed to a mechanical transfusion of certitudes, to an *opus operatum* infallibly provoking the saving assent. This observation moves us to end this essay by speaking briefly about the relations that obtain between dogma and action.

Dogma and Action

Dogma directs the moral life and inspires it; it is a rule; it is a revelation. The primary duties of man—respect for parents, purity of life, submission to legitimate authority, worship toward God—are effectively specified by our dogma and become religious affairs, venerable by a new title. Nowhere is this trait better marked than in the writings of the apostolic period. In them, one looks in vain for the exhortations of common morality, for the development of natural philosophy, which have had such remarkable success in the Christian preaching of the eighteenth century and later. Timeless duties that would have bound human nature, no matter what, are presented by the Apostles in a concrete framework, inserted and engaged, as it were, in the positive data of apostolic doctrine: one must act thus-and-so because it is the will of God the Father, revealed and realized in the exem-

56. "A certain woman by the name of Lydia, a dealer in purple stuffs . . . was in the audience, and the Lord opened her heart to pay heed to the things Paul was saying"; Acts 16:14.

plary life of the Lord Jesus, rendered accessible by the ineffable gifts of the Spirit. Everything is life, light, and grace; and the abstract words of Alexandrian vocabulary take on a direct and warm accent in John's Gospel, which helps them to convey personal feelings, thoughts, and desires. An attentive analysis has no trouble disengaging from the apostolic letters—and it has often been done—the elements of a natural morality that is almost complete: duties toward God, duties toward others, duties toward oneself are prescribed with specificity. Also, the law of nature promulgated in man's heart is recalled in explicit terms, and the pagans are said to be without excuse for not having followed it (Rom 1:18–32, 2:1–17). But the requirements of this law are repromulgated for Christians by the explicit revelation made by God in Jesus Christ. Exhortations, examples, threats, even solutions to cases of conscience are attributed to the positive teachings of Jesus' gospel. To put the Corinthians on guard against the sin of fornication, what reasons does St. Paul give?—Three in all: the bodies of the believers are members of Christ; they are temples of the Holy Spirit; the baptized have been bought [upon the Cross] at a great price (1Cor 6:15–20). The liar is inexcusable because he acts as if all believers were not members of the same body. Woe to the one who engages in bad talk: he grieves God's Holy Spirit (Eph 4:25, 29–30)! Let women be subject to their husbands: the church is submitted to Christ as to her head; and for their part let the husbands cherish their wives: Christ has loved the church and given himself up for her (Eph 5:22–26).

Above and beyond these necessary duties, there is a new attitude to assume in consequence of the preaching of Jesus' Gospel. After dogma has nailed down the obligations of the moral life in the concrete and shed upon them a superior light and made them easier by its assurances,[57] dogma opens yet a new path. Born as servants of God, we owe Him submission, adoration, and respect, but now we have also become sons by a freely given adoption; and this filiation (whose effective cause is Jesus and whose pledge is the divine Spirit residing in our hearts) imposes upon us stricter duties toward our heavenly Father and toward those who have become, by a new title, our "brothers." A Wisdom that is not of this world (and compared to which all

57. One needs to say it again: after dogma has *conserved* and *proclaimed* moral truths of the natural order, which would have been obscured or neglected without the dogma, Vatican I recalls this a supreme usefulness of revelation: Constitution *De fide catholica*, c. 2 (Denzinger, no. 3005).

human prudence is folly) will henceforth inspire our conduct. Even believers can rise only slowly and by stages to this Wisdom (1Cor 3; Heb 5). It will teach the Apostle, for example, an absolute selflessness in a case where he could rightly have demanded a compensation for his pains. It will discern among the gifts of the Spirit those that have a primarily exterior and auxiliary value for Christian expansion, though they can be abused, from the eminent and excellent charism that sanctifies the soul itself (1Cor 9–12). It will reveal to the persecuted the conditions and the bearing of evangelical blessedness, incomprehensible to the carnal man (1 Pt 2). It will unveil to the believer the infinite value of the death and resurrection of Christ Jesus and how baptism gives one a real participation in this divine economy. Everything follows from there: liberation from legal servitude, and a hope that does not disappoint, and death to sin, and new life in peace, patience, and a love that is stronger than death.

This is not the place to dwell upon this beautiful theology of human action; what needs to be noted is just the strict dependence it has upon the data of the faith. Far from being an ulterior construction or a mere point of departure, dogma is the foundation of Christian morality and remains its objective rule. Action helps one to understand it, to realize the depths of the truths that dogma teaches, but the direct role belongs to the teaching. No doubt it will happen that this doctrine remains in part unexpressed and implicit, as it were, in the liturgy, in pious practices, in the general "sense" of the faithful. In that case the *lex orandi* will serve to determine more explicitly the *lex credendi*, and (to take no more recent example) we know the role that traditional doxologies played for the Fathers of the fourth century in the trinitarian controversies. But even then dogma did nothing but "take back its own," if I may be so bold, because it was the dogma, under the helpful influence of the Holy Spirit, which first gave to rituals and to prayers of the liturgy their full meaning. And in the "sense" of the faithful, it was dogma that provided the analogies that guided the people's doctrinal anticipations.

Take, for example, the liturgy of baptism: one cannot contest the fact that the trinitarian formula was for many minds the vehicle of the dogmatic truth: *lex orandi statuit legem credendi*.... Nevertheless, when one looks closer, one has no trouble seeing which side had the primacy. The baptismal ablution was indicative of the purification worked in the soul by the Sacrament. Death to sin, resurrection to new life on the model of Jesus Christ and by his grace—all that was sufficiently expressed by a baptism given *in nomine Jesu*. Why was the trinitarian invocation imposed, if it was not as a formulation of people's dogmatic belief?

Between dogma and action, then, there is a continual exchange of mutual influences; but in this exchange doctrine gives more than it receives. This is why one should hesitate quite a bit, it seems, or rather explain oneself very clearly, before one accepts the conception according to which "the value of a truth is measured above all by the services it renders."[58] This conception is very much in favor, I am aware, not only among independent psychologists like William James,[59] but also among many Catholics, who Mr. Le Roy thinks are right. And judiciously applied, the conception is quite useful. When the issue is *discerning* where the truth is found, what teaching agency is qualified to teach it, what religious denomination merits our joining it, the evangelical rule that *a fructibus eorum cognoscetis eos* ["by their fruits ye shall know them"] has always had an incontestable and often decisive value—and now more than ever. To a primarily practical problem, the solution is also practical. But if you want to use this rule to determine the content of revelation, and if you want to say that dogmatic truths impose themselves upon us primarily through their usefulness, then I think you are taking the wrong road. You will be brought to a choice, to a triage in the set of dogmas that the church proposes for our faith. The dogma of the Holy Spirit's procession *ab utroque*—what "services" does it presently render to many souls? What "new results" does it suggest? Will you therefore declare it outdated, or say that it is permissible not to believe it?

This theory will come to nothing less than changing the primary motive for adhering to the faith; it will replace divine authority with a private, circumstance-dependent appreciation mired in subjective contingencies. That there is a certain utility to the revelation of dogmas, and of such and such dogma in particular—we believe it, we know it, sometimes we see it—but are we the judges of it? Are we to measure by our human lights the depth of the ways of God? At the end of the day I am afraid (and I am speaking as a theologian, because Mr. Le Roy is asking for pointed advice from theologians)—I am afraid that the sense of our dogmas, which is

58. *QD* 504.

59. One sees it developed by William James in *The Varieties of Religious Experience*, lecture 18, 441ff.

supposed to remain the same despite enrichments and precisions,[60] will be altered by this doctrinal utilitarianism. Easy solutions, attenuations, even perversions could appear (and certainly have appeared) useful at certain moments—such as Sabellianism, which took away from the dogma of the Trinity its paradoxical appearance and almost suppressed the mystery. One should not give private judgment a role to play in a matter that does not belong to it. Excellent as it may be in the domain of apologetics, the criterion of utility, when employed exclusively or principally, will thus be seen to be dangerous in the properly dogmatic domain.[61]

*

At this point, I must bring an end to these reflections, of whose insufficiency I am more aware than anyone. If I have been able to shed a little light upon the Catholic position on any of the problems raised by Mr. Le Roy, my effort will not have been entirely in vain. More competent theologians will do more and better.

What I should like to combat in concluding is the impression of disquiet that arises for many people, I fear, when they read the pages that have been the occasion for these jottings of mine [that is, the pages written by Le Roy and his supporters]. People say to us that contemporary philosophy poses irrefutable objections to the "common" notion of dogma such as it exists among Catholics; they say that we must change the traditional methods, even the traditional positions profoundly; they say that the church is in the process of losing all intellectual influence … that closing one's mind to this cry of alarm, refusing to examine the reasons people bring forward to support these complaints, treating all progress a priori as temerity and all development as perversion would be a mistake and a fault. The history of theology does not authorize such an attitude, and concern for souls does not permit it.

60. Si quis dixerit, fieri posse, ut dogmatibus ab Ecclesia propositis, aliquando secundum progressum scientiae, sensus tribuendus sit alius ab eo, quem intellexit et intellegit Ecclesia, A.S.; Vatican I, Constitution *De fide*, c. 4, canon 3 (Denzinger, no. 3043).

61. "Assuredly, God can have his reasons to reveal to us doctrines which do not tend naturally or directly—at least as far as we can see—to influence the formation of our character … aren't people always asking us—alas, have we not asked ourselves—what can be so bad about a Sabellian—as if we could be ungrateful enough to cast into the bottomless pit one of these jewels which God has been good enough to give us"; John Henry Newman, *Tract on the Introduction of Rationalistic Principles into Revealed Religion*. I am borrowing the quotation from a recent book of Henri Bremond, *Newman, psychologue de la foi* (Paris: Bloud 1905), 232–34.

But history is also what puts us on guard against radical solutions, and concern for souls forbids brusque innovations and excessive confidence in systems made by the hand of man. It is no less dangerous to swallow them whole than to ignore them wholesale. Whatever truths they contain will see the light of day eventually, and then it will emerge that far from contradicting the revealed truth, they harmonize with it. The experience of the past shows us beyond any doubt that this result is the fruit of long patience and that good minds have opposed necessary progress for too long, as other good minds have been caught and compromised by reckless novelties. Experience also teaches us that useful steps forward eventually take place and that God is always there for His church. We shall not hasten this hour by restless hankering for new ideas, any more than by the stubborn resistance of an uninformed zeal.

Let us work rather to understand each other, to come to understand each other; let us never lose from view the defined truths. In the development of philosophical ideas and the ever so exacting study of facts, let us try to distinguish what is lasting and of good alloy; let us search in the Christian tradition for what meets the particular needs of souls in our time, so as to bring it into the light. The infinite fertility of dogmatic truths leads in many directions, and the church's magisterium is a living one.

Need I add that we shall try to mix as little passion as possible into our defense of a Cause that can only lose from such human weakness? "For the good of a man [in controversy] is not to overcome another man; rather it is good for a man that the truth should overcome him willingly, because it is bad for a man that the truth should conquer him unwillingly. For that the truth will conquer must be the case."[62]

62. "Non enim bonum hominis est hominem vincere; sed bonum est homini ut eum veritas vincat volentem, quia malum est homini ut eum veritas vincat invitum. Nam ipsa vincat necesse est," says Augustine, Epistle 238; PL 33, 1049.

Bulletin de littérature ecclésiastique 7 (June 1905), 137–138

9

"AN ANTI-INTELLECTUALIST SCHOLASTIC"

Eugène Franon

Mr. Le Roy, the mathematician-philosopher whose scientific nominalism and rabid anti-intellectualism has been attacked forcefully by Henri Poincaré in his latest book, *The Value of Science*, has now put out an article in the *Quinzaine* of April 16, under the title "What Is a Dogma?" This article has caused a stronger reaction than surprise in various quarters generally recognized as competent. Very soon this *Bulletin* will publish a thorough study of Le Roy's theological essay. What I am going to be talking about here is rather a letter *about* the essay, written by Fr. [Antonin Gilbert] Sertillanges[, OP] to the editor of the *Quinzaine*.[1]

✳

That Fr. Sertillanges, the eloquent professor at the Institut Catholique of Paris, who got his philosophical formation among the Dominicans in the environment of methods quite certainly impenetrable by "Kantian infiltrations," and who has gotten by his collaboration with the *Revue Thomiste* a

1. You will find the letter in the *Quinzaine* (June 1, 1905): 412–19.

spotless reputation for orthodoxy, which he has lately enhanced by the exemplary vigor with which he defended knock-down demonstration of the immortality of the soul against Fr. Piat—that this man should be separated from the author of "What Is a Dogma?" by nothing but "verbal equivocations" and "a few nuances of thought"—that is something that surely seems impossible. Well, the impossible has come to pass; the improbable has turned out true. For, given the proviso that the proofs of credibility for Christianity shall be recognized "each in its own order" as valid in themselves and as valid scientifically insofar as they appeal to science, Fr. Sertillanges declares that he accepts the conception of dogma proposed by Mr. Le Roy. And the acceptance thus given is not a mere matter of words or a case of mere politeness of some sort. It is effective, as effective as possible.

Fr. Sertillanges affirms that a dogma is essentially a "practical direction," an "article of life," a "rule of action," a "declaration of attitude." Hence he attributes nothing to Catholic dogmas "from the strictly intellectual point of view" but a "negative value," "in the sense that their formulae do not intend to consecrate a scientific interpretation of the facts which they state, but to maintain their practical value and defend it in case of need against alleged interpretations which would be their negation."

It is hardly necessary to remark that by making this anti-intellectualist notion of dogma his own, Fr. Sertillanges is agreeing not only with Mr. Le Roy but also with Fr. Tyrrell and with the author of *Religion as a Factor of Life*, that priceless handbook of agnostic and symbolist theology.[2]

In support of his opinion, Fr. Sertillanges observes first that dogma is a "practical light" and that revelation is "a lantern and not the sun," "having as its purpose not to fashion us a science but to make us attend to our end."—On this point we will permit ourselves to observe that adopting this language could well come down (unconsciously, no doubt) to playing with the word "science." If it is quite true, indeed, that revelation does not have as its object to teach us geology and astronomy, obviously theoretical sciences, it is nevertheless quite false to say that, on a question like the nature of God (a question whose relevance to human destiny should make us consider it practical), revelation does not have the purpose of furnishing us with objectively correct ideas.

2. See Franon, "A New Catholic Manifesto of Agnosticism," *Bulletin de littérature ecclésiastique* 5 (June 1903): 157ff [translated in this volume as selection 6].

To tell the truth, Fr. Sertillanges pretends that furnishing us with such notions is something that revelation, the supernatural, or the divine (I am not the one lumping these together) cannot do, since such ideas are inexpressible. "The supernatural," he says,

> cannot be expressed correctly.... *Omnis determinatio est negatio.* This dictum of Spinoza's is exactly correct here. From an *absolute* point of view—and here the Catholic doctors agree unanimously—everything that we can say about God is false. Well, if all that is false, one falsehood is as good as another, and the better falsehood will be the one that brings us closer to the divine and makes the divine play its only role in our regard: to make us live.

From the pen of a theologian who published a few months back *Les sources de la croyance en dieu*, these lines (unless they have no precise meaning, which it would be a mistake to suppose) constitute (despite the restrictive words "from an absolute point of view") a profession of agnostic faith so explicit as to disconcert the most indulgent critics. For at the end of the day, make all the reservations you please about the essential incomprehensibility of the divine nature, and hold with certitude (against the Cartesians and the ontologists) that our idea of God, as the fruit of reasoning and not of intuition, is analogous, inadequate, approximate, and indirect; it nevertheless remains the case that when we affirm the personhood of God, His liberty, His justice, His immutability, these affirmations (albeit conceived and posed *humano modo*) are true in themselves and absolutely, with a metaphysical truth that imposes itself upon every mind.

To buttress his thesis, Fr. Sertillanges appeals to the Gospel and to the language of Jesus Christ:

> We are not going to give dogma lessons to Jesus! When He speaks to us of our God, He does not *define* Him; He names Him. He is the *heavenly Father*, not *Thought Thinking Itself*, or the *Father of the Ideas*, or the *Prime Mover*. These theoretical ideas are of little use for the moral life.

This argument, if it is one, puzzles me. Would Fr. Sertillanges be thinking like the Abbé Loisy that "the Gospel contains no theoretical teaching at all"?[3] After all, he might. For our part we agree with an Anglican theologian of penetrating mind, Mr. Arthur C. Headlam, Professor of Dogmatics at London University, that if one keeps from traditional Christianity noth-

3. Loisy, *L'Évangile et l'Église*, 16.

ing but the Our Father, one would still be keeping with that alone a whole theodicy that is quite complex and well defined.[4] After all, to pray to the Father who is in heaven, who sees our most intimate thoughts, who knows all our needs, who rewards even our least good actions and who forgives us if we forgive one another, unquestionably amounts to professing that the cause of the universe is neither an abstract law, nor an unconscious force, nor matter in perpetual and necessary evolution, but a being sovereignly intelligent, free, powerful, just, and merciful. Hence many people will probably conclude, and rightly in my opinion, that by limiting Himself to "naming" God the "Heavenly Father," Jesus may well have summed up and concentrated in this expression (so disdainfully dismissed as anthropomorphic) a theodicy that is on the whole far deeper and more comprehensive than He would have conveyed if He had "defined" God as the Father of Ideas and the immovable Prime Mover.

✳

From the reduction of dogma to the status of a simple recipe, relative and provisional, which it is advantageous to use to direct our action but which it would be wrong to consider as meant to put us in possession of incontestable truths, there flow a certain number of consequences that Fr. Sertillanges has not listed methodically (as I shall do here for clarity of exposition) but all of which one does find in his letter, and all of which he admires and approves.

The first is that all conflict between science and dogma becomes quite impossible, there being no longer any point of contact between them or any common measure. "Dogma," he says in summarizing the thought of Mr. Le Roy and making it his own,

> is above all a practical direction, and one advances towards it and adheres to it according to the laws of praxis, so that accusations made against it in the name of our modern conception of science have no validity.

Well, *there* is an elegant solution for you—to all those conflicts between science and faith, which for over half a century have fully occupied the apologists and have made them write so many pages. Do Mr. Ferdinand Buisson or Mr. Gabriel Séailles raise difficulties against the miracles of the

4. Arthur C. Headlam, *The Sources and Authority of Dogmatic Theology* (London: Macmillan, 1903), 13.

Gospel in the name of universal determinism? It's useless to wear yourself out proving the contingency of the laws of nature. Tell these gentlemen that the resurrection of Christ and also His conception *de Spiritu sancto*, which are dogmas as well as miracles, imply no definite scientific interpretation, since they are only anthropomorphic expressions of moral ideas—and that will suffice.

No doubt people will reproach me for exaggerating, and I am indeed convinced that Fr. Sertillanges would reject the content of these deductions. But don't the deductions follow logically from the premises he accepts? That is the whole question.

Here is another consequence: each person is free to apply to dogmas the philosophical or scientific theories that he likes, on the sole condition that he not thereby deprive them of their value for life, their moral significance.

From the properly intellectual point of view, as Mr. Le Roy says quite well,

> [dogma] does nothing but pose problems, as does experience itself. In the first case no more than in the second is a particular *solution* or *theory* imposed from without upon science or upon philosophy. It is up to them in all liberty to state and translate *in terms of science* what has been put to them *in terms of life*, under the sole condition of not destroying it, preserving all its practical significance, all its value of life.

Thus Fr. Sertillanges expresses himself, and lest any doubt remain in the reader's mind on the sense of his thought, he continues as follows:

> For example: it is demanded of us that we treat God as a Father and Jesus as a God; fashion thereupon all the theories you please about the Incarnation and about the First Principle, provided that your theories do not render impossible, in the unity of a human being, the soul's act of honoring and loving God, the soul's act of honoring and loving Him in Jesus.

To find these words at least peculiar, and to confess that one does not see very clearly how they can be reconciled with the definitions of the councils of Ephesus and Chalcedon, or with such and such canons of the constitution *Dei filius*—does one have to be exhibiting an excessive critical severity or an ugliness of mind far above the authorized mean? After all, try proving that Nestorian Christology, for example, renders impossible "the soul's act of honoring and loving God in Jesus." It certainly does not look like an easy job. Moreover, it does not look as though the Fathers of the Council of Ephesus (any more than those of Vatican I), in order to discern the revealed truth and formulate their canons, made even an unconscious use of the criterion of "practical significance" and of the dogma's "value of life."

The third consequence of the new conception: the philosophical or scientific envelope of dogmas is neither untouchable nor eternal; one can, indeed, modify it at the pace and to the extent of the progress of philosophy and science.—This consequence, if I am not mistaken, is neither entirely false nor entirely true. To get things into perspective, would it not be advantageous to distinguish two cases:

- the case where the philosophical/scientific datum that one is calling the envelope of the dogma remains exterior to the dogma and independent of it;
- and the case where it makes an integral part of the dogma in one way or another?

Thus it is perfectly allowable for theologians to put the Leibnizian theory of monadism in place of the Aristotelian system of matter-and-form in their attempts to explain the Eucharist. This is because the doctrine of the Real Presence can be conceived and was in fact formulated independently of any philosophical theory about the constitution of bodies and the nature of space. Apologists on the other hand are not free, under the pretext of adapting Catholic teaching to the discoveries of modern thought, to replace the traditional notion of a person with the corresponding phenomenalist concept. For when the traditional notion is taken away, the dogma itself disappears, and, on the hypothesis I just mentioned, the real distinction of the Father from the Son and from the Holy Spirit, would become impossible; similarly in man, the soul's surviving the organism would become impossible.

A final consequence flows from the ideas that Fr. Sertillanges welcomes with so much warmth—namely, that dogma simply obliges the Catholic to observe certain rules of conduct and thus gets no grip upon his intelligence. "A doctrinal definition"—I am again quoting Fr. Sertillanges,

> [even in the form of an anathema] has only its first value, the value of a practical notion; it does not add anything to science, but neither does it impose anything

upon science beyond a fact to respect, which science may interpret in its own manner. As Mr. Le Roy remarks, this is why dogmas have been able to find expression over the course of the ages by borrowing their formulations from different philosophies; and it is very reasonable to conclude, where our own time is concerned, that a modern Catholic is not restricted by dogma in anything but the rules of conduct, provided that he understands thereby, as Mr. Le Roy says elsewhere, an attitude of mind as well as exterior attitudes. In any case, the believer does not find himself bound to any particular scientific conception which would come ready-made from the outside with no logical connection to his prior knowledge and hence with no possible assimilation, such as a stone in an organism.

—But, people will scream, you are denaturing Fr. Sertillanges's thought outrageously. You are making him say that, by the force of dogma, a Catholic is not bound to anything but rules of conduct! But in the lines you just finished quoting, he remarks explicitly that by "rules of conduct" one has to understand (and he understands) "attitudes of mind as well as exterior attitudes."

Here is my answer to that. Either the phrase "attitudes of mind" is a synonym for absolute intellectual assent to the dogmas of the creed considered as objective truths, or else the phrase has another meaning. In the first case, there's nothing to change in the classic notion of dogma; and then why use obscure and equivocal formulae in place of the ones consecrated by usage, which are clear? In the second case let people explain the phrase once and for all, down to the bottom. But please don't let loose upon the Catholic public the ruinous illusion that our dogmas require nothing but a sort of social conformism and I-know-not-what half-intellectual, half-sentimental consensus of all well-intentioned souls, if they are to use the beliefs of yesteryear morally—or the ruinous illusion that our dogmas do not impose upon the mind the acceptance of certain philosophical conceptions and certain historical theses, which the church is never going to abandon and is never going to "correct."

The reservations that Fr. Sertillanges expressed in the last part of his letter do not seem to me sufficient to head off this danger. Apologetics is one thing, and theology is another? So be it. Nevertheless, inevitable relations of dependency exist between them. If one rejects the theology, what good is it to preserve apologetics? A flight of steps, a vestibule, have no value in themselves. The apartments to which they lead have to be inhabitable. Besides, isn't it contradictory to affirm on the one hand that "from the absolute point of view everything we can say about God is false" and affirm on the other hand that "the proofs for God must have value as philosophy; the proofs for revelation must have value as history; the proofs for the necessity of the Church must have value as psychology and as social science"?

*

It would be indiscreet to insist further. Perhaps I have already said too much. Many people will suspect me, no doubt, of having the mentality of an inquisitor. They are free to think so. And if some go further and accuse me of doing nothing but engaging in an irritating polemic with the fixed aim (which is unintelligent, if not vicious) of discouraging opportune and generous initiatives, I shall be neither surprised nor troubled. In reality, my intention has been quite different. As much as anyone, I suffer the intellectual anxieties from which so many souls are suffering in the present crisis of Catholic thought. I have no more Scholastic prejudices than Fr. Sertillanges does. But I know what perils certain ways of speaking (by no means exempt from obscurity and imprecision) create for the faith, not only in lay people preoccupied with religious problems but also in theologians who are aren't alert enough (and that is most young priests). Besides, I am convinced that one must say of theology what Mr. Poincaré has said of science: "It will be intellectualist, or it will not exist."[5]

5. Henri Poincaré, *La valeur de la science*, 21. [Henri Poincaré, the foremost French mathematician of his day, is not to be confused with Raymond Poincaré, a prime minister of the Third Republic.]

Études 103 (July 20, 1905): 147–73;
(August 5, 1905): 315–42.

10

"ON THE MORAL EXPOSITION OF DOGMAS"

A Response to *La Quinzaine*

Eugène Portalié

The study written by Mr. Édouard Le Roy, which appeared in *La Quinzaine* of April 16 under the title "What Is a Dogma?" cannot pass unnoticed. The author, far from being an obscure person, is a very distinguished mathematician-philosopher and, at the same time, a convinced Catholic. He is the man of whom Mr. Henri Poincaré wrote recently, "This thinker is not just a philosopher and a writer of great merit, but one who has also acquired a deep knowledge of the exact and physical sciences and has even displayed rare faculties of mathematical invention."[1]

Scholars have strongly appreciated his various publications on math-

1. Poincaré, *La valeur de la science*, 213. *La Quinzaine* presents Mr. Le Roy to its readers in these words: "A graduate and doctor of science; he has published many *Mémoires de mathématiques*, some quite remarkable articles in the *Revue de métaphysique et de morale*, a study on 'La science positive et les philosophies de la liberté' (at the philosophy congress of 1900), and various communications to the Société française de philosophie."

ematics and philosophy. *La Quinzaine* has drawn attention to this article by opening up a sort of inquiry on the subject; it has invited, perhaps a bit pompously, "all the authorized specialists in Catholic theology, the professors at our three universities, major seminaries, members of religious orders, priests, etc." to offer the public clarifications (not at all on Mr. Le Roy's *thesis*; he declines to decide anything, but) on "the projected solutions which he has proposed to the criticism of those who have authority to draw conclusions on such a matter."[2]

Despite this invitation, it is with reluctance, we confess, that we take part in this debate. To defend the faith against the attacks of our declared enemies, whether they are named Voltaire, Renan, or Séaillès, is a relatively sweet and consoling duty. But to have to face minds that are eminently sympathetic thanks to their knowledge, their sincerity, their courage to be and call themselves Christians, even their sufferings for the faith, sufferings laid bare in these pages so vibrant with the poignant emotion of a doubt against which one struggles to fight; to be condemned to hear from the mouth of these friends accusations of the irremediable absurdity of all our dogmas; to hear of the absolute and radical opposition between these dogmatic affirmations (understood as everyone without exception, friends and enemies, have understood them for nineteen centuries) and everything that is good sense, reason, true and rational philosophy; to feel constrained to say flatly to these writers, for whom one has only feelings of sincere esteem and sympathy, that they are not only not defending the Christian faith, as they hope to do, but that they are destroying it *totally* and radically, from the ground up, so that not even a single fragment of it remains intact; what is more, to see oneself compelled to add that their system is not only destructive in itself of all Christian belief, but that its publication in magazines addressed to the general public, far from being a harmless discussion, is in fact a broadside against all dogma and all faith, whose immediate result is to cast into many souls a deep and sometimes irremediable trouble (for these souls, alas, will not read the refutations, not even those published in *La Quinzaine*)—this is a bitter and unhappy duty. But it is a duty.

Since the appearance of the regrettable red books of Mr. Loisy, the disarray in certain minds—or better said, in certain circles—is lamentable. Unhappily, some worse-than-overbold publications (greeted with an imprudent

2. Édouard Le Roy, "Qu'est-ce qu'un dogme," *La Quinzaine* (April 16, 1905): 441.

benevolence in certain open opinion columns, where anonymity along with the absence of responsibility favors the hatching of the most foolhardy ideas) are periodically stirring up agitation and trouble. In the great number of communications, signed or unsigned, received by *La Quinzaine* from April 16 to June 16, would you believe, only one dares to reject Le Roy's system clearly, and a goodly number salute it with enthusiasm as the dawn of the "theology needed for these new times." The boldness of these affirmations demands and justifies the frankness of our remarks.

I

Let us try first to analyze the system proposed by Mr. Le Roy. The task is easy in any case, thanks to the fact that, in his exposition, the philosophy he uses has been able to shed a great deal of clarity. Indeed, this is the salient characteristic of this study: that on the main points, the thought is presented with a neatness that can be frightening sometimes but that, at least, keeps the conclusions clear of the equivocations and shadows in which some other writers have enveloped them. For Mr. Le Roy does not pioneer a philosophy of his own invention; he invokes blatantly the school of "immanence." But what was veiled, obscure, blurry [in that school's] wavering and imprecise formulae, he puts into a harsh light, which leaves no further room for evasions. This is a merit so rare these days that one wants to congratulate him for it. Hereafter, will the philosophers of "immanence" acknowledge the legitimacy of Le Roy's deductions, and will they take responsibility for this system? It is not our place to answer. But it seems that unless they furnish some explications of their own, one will have good reason to attribute to them the inspiration of this theory, which professes to translate "moral dogmatics" [into clear thought].

The problem raised under the somewhat vague title "What Is a Dogma?" is not one of the subtleties that occupied the leisure time of the Schoolmen; it is rather a question of life and death for Christianity, especially when brought before the public. Yes or no, are all the dogmas forever condemned by the progress of modern philosophy? Yes or no, is there (as alleged) an absolute and irreducible conflict between the unquestionable advances of contemporary thought and the affirmations of the Catholic (or just plain Christian) credo? On another front, if one turns one's attention from the object of faith to the act through which we affirm it, must one admit that there is absolute incompatibility between true philosophizing and an act of faith that admits revealed affirmations in reliance on divine testimony?

And let us understand this well: the question is not about this or that dogma in particular. Mr. Le Roy has said it fair and square: the time for partial heresies is over. Today's negation does not especially attack the Incarnation, nor the Trinity. It opposes every dogmatic affirmation with "a blunt refusal, in advance and in every case." It is the very idea of dogma that disgusts, that gives scandal. What is at stake, then, is to decide once and for all "if it is necessary, in thinking as a Christian, *to no longer think at all*?"[3] and if to remain a Christian it is necessary to renounce all reason, all intellectual life, except to console oneself by repeating "*Credo quia absurdum*" or (following the advice of Pascal) "*turn yourself into a moron.*"

Now before he answers, Mr. Le Roy observes quite frankly that up to now believers and unbelievers have been at one in accepting a flatly *intellectualist* conception of dogma. Both groups envision dogma as the doctrine revealed by God and rendered obligatory by the definitions of the Church. This conception

> takes as secondary and derived the practical and moral sense of the dogma and puts in first place its intellectual sense, thinking that the latter *constitutes* the dogma, while the former is a mere consequence. In a word, a dogma is made to be something like the statement of a theorem: an unalterable statement of an indemonstrable theorem, but a statement having nevertheless a speculative and theoretical character, addressing one's understanding most of all. Such is the common postulate which one uncovers by analysis at the bottom of both the conflicting doctrines, I mean, the one which accepts the idea of dogma and the one which rejects it.

And indeed, doubt about this point would too openly flout the obvious facts. Who will dare deny that the Apostles' Creed, the Nicene Creed, that of St. Athanasius, and the profession of faith of Pius IV, which are the most authentic formulae of the Christian faith, express directly and essentially theoretical truths, which the mind affirms by basing itself on the authority of divine teaching and not precepts imposed upon the will as rules of practical life? Mr. Le Roy's avowal has, nevertheless, its merit, when one compares it to the hemming and hawing of other writers, who must have

3. Ibid., 499, 507.

been more familiar than a layman with the sense of ecclesiastical formulae and who seemed to contest the unanimous agreement (up to now, at least) on the intellectualist conception of dogmas and of the faith.

With the question thus clearly posed, Le Roy answers with great frankness with two assertions that very accurately sum up his study: (1) yes, the dogmas understood in the ancient manner, as intellectual affirmations, are dead forever, in that their essentially anti-philosophical character is evident today; (2) so if one wishes to preserve the formulae, one must transform them integrally by giving them solely the moral character of precepts directing human conduct. On these conditions (or so one pretends at least) "*a doctrine of the primacy of action allows one to resolve the problem without abandoning any of the rights of thought nor any of the requirements of dogma.*"[4]

For anyone who is a bit familiar with the history of religious philosophy over the last hundred years, especially outside the Catholic Church, such a claim goes beyond the limit of the probable; and we are not forgetting that when we pointed out a radical evolutionism in the little red books of Mr. Loisy, certain writers (and they were not all naïve) appeared to be scandalized, protesting that such an error would be improbable, and appealing to our "good will" to interpret Mr. Loisy more favorably. Today is not the time to take up this question; its time will come. But it gives us the duty of insisting upon Mr. Le Roy's two claims and giving them, with all possible good will, an absolutely objective exposition. Good will should never veil the truth, especially when the thought in question belongs to a writer who includes among his characteristic traits, it seems, an absolute sincerity.

The irreducible opposition between dogma understood in its traditional sense as the intellectual affirmation of a revealed truth and what Mr. Le Roy regards as the most certain data of modern philosophy is affirmed with so much energy and conviction that more than one mind will have been upset by it. Not that the proofs for this opposition have in themselves anything new in them; they are the already old objections of ancient rationalism, as one of the writers to *La Quinzaine* has already remarked quite rightly.[5] But these commonplaces of antireligious polemic, harmless when

4. Ibid., 325.
5. *La Quinzaine* (May 16, 1905): 254.

they are formulated by enemies, are uniquely troubling to minds that are still weak, and especially to impressionable youth, when they are put forward and affirmed in the name of his personal experience by a scholar who presents himself as an apologist for Christianity.

Four characteristics of dogmas seem to Mr. Le Roy to legitimate true philosophy's rejection of them.

1. First of all, dogmas are *indemonstrable by an intrinsic demonstration.*

A dogma is a proposition that presents itself as neither proved nor provable. The very people who affirm its truth declare it impossible that one should ever succeed in grasping the deep reasons for its truth. But … isn't the first principle of method, uncontested since Descartes, that one must not take as true anything but what one clearly sees to be such? Where would one get the right to make an exception for exactly those propositions that present themselves as the most important, deepest, and most unique of all?[6]

2. Furthermore, dogma is unverifiable even by an *indirect demonstration.*

A certain apologetics that believes itself to be purely traditional pretends to establish that these propositions are true, even though it acknowledges that it is unable to show in a plain light the how and the why of their truth.

But in the name of modern agnosticism, one saps every such demonstration at its base; for, we are told:

> One must have proved *directly* that God exists, that He has spoken, that He has said this and that, that we possess even today His authentic teaching. This amounts to saying that one must have already resolved by a *direct* analysis the problem of God, the problem of revelation, the problem of biblical inspiration, the problem of the Church's authority; but these are questions of the same kind as the properly dogmatic ones—questions on which it is quite impossible to produce arguments comparable to those of a mathematician.[7]

So categorical a negation makes another objection seem feeble, based on the nature of dogmas, "these mysterious, singular, disconcerting facts to which there corresponds nothing analogous in our human experience." Mr. Le Roy concludes thus:

6. Le Roy, "Qu'est-ce qu'un dogme," 499.
7. Ibid., 501, 502.

It is easy enough to say: the pretended indirect demonstration has as its inevitable basis an appeal to the transcendence of pure authority. It pretends, or at least seems to pretend, to introduce the truth into us radically from the outside, in the manner of a ready-made "thing" which would enter into us by violence. *Any dogma thus appears as an enslavement, as a limit to the rights of thought, as a threat of intellectual tyranny, as a bound and limit imposed upon the freedom of research from the outside; these are all things radically contrary to the very life of the mind and to its need for autonomy and sincerity.*[8]

3. Dogmas are absolutely unintelligible and unthinkable. They are strictly bound to Aristotelian and Scholastic conceptions.

Well, these different philosophies are often dubious as to their foundations and obscure as to their expression; and in every case long since outdated, fallen into disuse among philosophers and scholars. So then, in order to be a Christian, is it necessary to begin by becoming a convert to these philosophies? That would be a rough undertaking, before which many believers would feel acutely embarrassed.[9]

One might think at first that Mr. Le Roy is only charging dogmas with an overly vague imprecision, from which one should conclude nothing. But further on, he tries to establish that the three dogmas of the divine personhood, the resurrection, and the real presence, have absolutely "nothing to them that is expressible through concepts."[10]

For example, we are told that if God's personhood does not resemble in any way what we in fact recognize in persons, then we should designate it with a new word, which will be radically indefinable.[11]

Imagine a set of syllables devoid of any positive meaning; let *A* be this set; "God is personal" has no other sense on our hypothesis than "God is *A*." Is that an idea?

The dilemma is insurmountable for one who seeks an intellectualist interpretation of the dogma "God is personal." Either one will define the word "person," and then one is fated to end in anthropomorphism; or else one will not define it, and then one is fated no less surely to end in agnosticism. We are caught in a cleft stick.[12]

Likewise, the resurrection or the new life of Christ is "a simple metaphor unconvertible into precise ideas." As far as His presence in the Eucharist is concerned:

8. Ibid., 502.

9. Ibid., 504.

10. Ibid., 511.

11. Does anyone fail to see that a thing can fail to resemble another thing perfectly, and yet one cannot deny all resemblance and all representation thanks to analogy?

12. Le Roy, "Qu'est-ce qu'un dogme," 510.

A being is said to be present when it is perceptible, or else when, though itself beyond perception, it shows itself through perceptible effects.[13] But according to the dogma itself, neither of these conditions is met in the present case. The presence in question is a mysterious presence, ineffable, singular, without analogy to anything that we usually understand by this word. In that case, I ask what idea is there for us? Something one can neither analyze nor define can only be called "an idea" by an abuse of the word.[14]

Further on, he adds that if these dogmas are viewed as intellectual affirmations, they reduce themselves to purely verbal formulas, to mere slogans whose repetition would constitute an unintelligible kind of deposit.

When all is said and done, the attempt to conceive dogmas as propositions, whose primary function will be to communicate certain theoretical understandings, collides everywhere, it seems, with impossibilities. It seems to end up by fatally turning dogmas into *pure nonsense*.

4. Finally, dogmas are incompatible with the unity of the human mind.

Neither by their content nor by their logical nature do they belong on the same level of knowledge as other propositions. Hence they cannot be put together with other propositions to build up a coherent system. The mildest reproach that one can raise against them is that they seem to be of no use, unemployable and infertile—a reproach that is quite serious in an age when we are seeing more and more clearly that the value of a truth is measured above all by the services it renders, by the new results that it suggests, by the consequences with which it is pregnant—in a word, by the vivifying influence it exercises upon the entire body of knowledge.[15]

Before we conclude this destructive part of his system, we need to add that (despite the reservations expressed at the beginning) Mr. Le Roy proclaims very loudly that, for him, these objections are irrefutable, and that in the century-long battle between dogma and philosophy, dogma has been routed decisively.

These reasons—and for my part, with my intellectual education, I cannot fail to recognize it—are perfectly valid. I do not see any legitimate way to refute the pre-

13. With this definition of presence, God will not be present anywhere; the soul will cease to be present to the body, since it will not show itself, for example, during a fainting spell; what is worse, even a body will no longer be present as soon as it ceases to produce perceptible effects, which is hardly rare. In a surprising mistake, Mr. Le Roy has confused presence with the perceptibility of this presence.

14. Le Roy, "Qu'est-ce qu'un dogme," 511.

15. Ibid., 505.

ceding argumentation. The premises that it invokes cannot be contested, it seems to me, any more than the deductions drawn. Indeed, *I do not see that people have ever answered this otherwise than with worthless subtleties or with the artifices of rhetoric.* But eloquence is not a proof, and neither is diplomacy.[16]

According to him it is even *an established fact* that no one (even among believers) who has truly understood the spirit and methods of science and contemporary philosophy can fail to give assent to these objections.

He proclaims without any restriction whatsoever the principle of the most radical rationalism:

No authority, in fact, can make me find (or prevent me from finding) an argument solid or fragile, and above all it cannot make such and such a notion have or fail to have meaning for me. I am not just saying that authority does not have the right; I am saying that the thing is radically impossible. For in the end, it is I who think and not authority who thinks for me. Against this fact nothing can prevail. I go back therefore to what I said a moment ago. And speaking as a philosopher, I declare myself incapable of thinking otherwise than our enemies do on the points previously mentioned.[17]

However, he is about to take the dogmas thus ruined from the intellectual angle and restore them, in the name of the moral philosophy of action, as rules of practical life.

*

Mr. Le Roy's first move is based on a new theory, alleging that all dogmas have a purely *negative* force, but this long development is a sidetrack; for if it were true, a dogma would still remain a truth of the intellectual order, and hence would always be in opposition to autonomy and subject to the refusals of free thought.

Then Mr. Le Roy proposes—but under the guise of a problem and without asserting anything—to make dogmas assimilable to modern minds by giving them not an intellectual sense but a *practical* sense.

A dogma has above all a *practical* sense. It states above all a prescription of the practical order. It is most of all *the formulation of a rule of practical conduct*. That is its principal value; that is its positive meaning.

This doctrine takes shelter under the authority of Fr. Laberthonnière:

16. Ibid., 506.
17. Ibid., 507.

Dogmas are not just dark and enigmatic formulas which God promulgated in the name of His omnipotence to crush our intellectual pride. They have a moral and practical sense; they have a vital sense more or less accessible to us, according to the level of spirituality we have reached.[18]

The same dogmas already highlighted as refractory to all intellectual representation are now used as examples of this moral transformation.

They also represent the different types of dogmas. "God is personal" means: *in your relations with God, comport yourself as in your relations with a human person.*

Likewise, "Jesus is risen" means: *in your relationship with Him, be as you would have been before His death, and as you are towards a contemporary.*

Likewise, again, the doctrine of the real presence means that when one is faced with the consecrated Host, one must have the same attitude as one would have when faced with Jesus appearing to you visibly.[19]

Thanks to this transformation, which (we are assured) will hardly be contested by anyone, we may boast of having cut the Gordian knot. The difficulties smooth themselves out.

The ordinary intellectualist conception worsens the conflict and makes the difficulty insoluble. Now, on the contrary, a possibility for a solution is becoming visible. Since one is no longer trying to get a theoretical proposition in conditions radically opposed to those which sound intellectual method demands, one no longer finds oneself faced with a logical scandal but only with a problem bearing on the relations between thought and action. The problem is difficult, no doubt, but it is approachable, and in any case it no longer appears absurd as soon as it is stated.

Mr. Le Roy freely admits that serious questions remain to be resolved, like that of furnishing a *proof* for a dogma. But "practical truths are established otherwise than speculative truths." Dogmas are no longer speculative truths, and despite the twenty centuries when the faithful based their faith on the authority of God and understood by this expression, not the right to command that the Creator has over the creature, but the right to be believed upon His word, when He who is all knowledge and all truth deigns to guarantee an affirmation, we are now advised to see in faith the authority of God as the sovereign power, the master of the world.

"Recourse to authority, totally unacceptable in the order of pure thought,

18. Lucien Laberthonnière, *Essais de philosophie religieuse* (Paris: Lethielleux, 1903), 272; see also Le Roy, "Qu'est-ce qu'un dogme," 517.

19. Le Roy, "Qu'est-ce qu'un dogme," 517, 518.

seems a priori less shocking in the order of action, because, if authority has legitimate rights somewhere, it is surely in the domain of practice."[20]

Dogmas cease, we are told, to be unintelligible, because they are acts imposed upon us.

> Dogmatic formulae, irremediably obscure and even inconceivable when one wants them to furnish positive determinations of the truth from a speculative and theoretical point of view, show themselves quite capable of clarity, by contrast, when one agrees to ask of them only instruction in practical conduct.[21]

But finally the reader will ask if there does not remain in Mr. Le Roy's thought an intellectual side of dogmas. Is the moral aspect the *only* one, or is it only the *main* one?

We answer that the capital vice of the system is precisely to pass alternately from the one to the other of these positions. At the outset, the formulations are moderated, and what is excluded is the idea that dogmas "are without relation to thought; for (1) there are also duties incumbent upon the action of thinking; (2) it is affirmed *implicitly* by the dogma itself that reality contains (under one form or another) something to justify the conduct prescribed as reasonable and salutary."[22]

At this point, then, there is agreement that one must affirm the existence in reality of that which justifies the practical attitude of the believer. To be sure, that is a point of capital importance. But if one were to persist in this affirmation, if the dogma continued to be envisioned, even partially, as a theoretical affirmation, however vague and indefinite it may be, all the difficulties will come to life again, and intellectualism will be the winner. Also, the inner logic of the system operates unconsciously to bring about a complete transformation of the dogmas. And soon one will suppress everything that resembles a theoretical affirmation, and the obligations that result from the dogmas will become exclusively moral and practical.

"The Catholic, obliged to admit them, is only bound by them to rules of conduct, not to any particular conceptions."[23]

20. Ibid., 519.

21. Ibid., 520, 521.

22. Who can fail to see here a change in the *sense of words*? Even if we admit that the dogma of the Resurrection, for example, has a practical sense, it is evident that this sense is not at all expressed, but assumed, and hence is all the more implicit. On the other hand, affirmation of the reality justifying the practical conduct is expressed very *explicitly* in the dogma that Jesus is risen, that God is personal, etc.—will anyone dare to deny truths as clear as these?

23. Le Roy, "Qu'est-ce qu'un dogme," 522.

"Of itself and in itself, the dogma has only a practical meaning. But a mysterious reality corresponds to it, and it puts before the mind a theoretical problem."[24]

Some time ago, in front of the French philosophy society at a meeting of January 30, 1902, in a discussion on *the Christian elements of contemporary consciousness*, Mr. Le Roy had already expounded his theory and had claimed for the educated Catholic the absolute liberty of the critical spirit.

If you like, let the dogma be, "God is personal." *A reflective Catholic who accepts this dogma will not see A POSITIVE AFFIRMATION in it and a determination of the divine personhood.* The dogma will have for him first off a *negative* character: "God is not a law, a category," &c. Thereupon, this will be a proposition having a *practical* character, looking to regulate practical conduct: "Conduct yourselves in your relations with God as you do in your relations with a human person." Given that much, the Catholic in question will have complete liberty to fashion for himself such a theory as he pleases, such an intellectual representation as he pleases, of the divine personhood.

We will indicate further along the limits that M. Le Roy imposes on this liberty.

II

There you have it, the system in its broad outlines, disengaged from sidetracks. If we compare it with other theories put into circulation in recent times, we discern quickly enough that the point of departure for these new schools of thought is always the same: the alleged impossibility of keeping our defined dogmas in their ancient sense. The destructive element, therefore, is always the same, even though Mr. Loisy is mainly struck by historical difficulties, while Mr. Le Roy is bothered by rational objections. The difference between the new schools is more marked, at least in appearance, in their elements of dogmatic reconstruction—some making appeal to *evolutionism*—that is, to the perpetual and integral change of religious conceptions over the course of the ages, others having recourse to *symbolism*, which allows one to preserve the formula while modifying radically its meaning—Mr. Le Roy emphasizing, under the patronage of the school of immanence, *moralism* or the purely practical character of our dogmas. But in reality these different systems are varying aspects of one

24. Ibid., 524.

and the same theory, and this fact is brought to light by the numerous letters of approval addressed to *La Quinzaine*, letters that promote by turns evolutionism, symbolism, and moralism.

A general criticism should be leveled at Mr. Le Roy—namely, that he has posed the question badly—or rather, that he has forgotten to examine beforehand a preliminary question, without which his problem can make no sense.

It was one of his admirers in *La Quinzaine* (issue of June 1) who put the point very neatly. Before looking into "what a dogma is," he should have asked himself "what is faith?" and "what is revelation?" For our part, before we answer Mr. Le Roy's questions, we have the right to make a demand of him: yes or no, do you admit that God has spoken to man; do you admit that God has stated, through the mouth of Jesus, man's origin—for example, his wretchedness through sin, his salvation through the cross, his destiny for eternity? If your answer is yes, then the discussion is closed, and dogma obviously includes theoretical truths that are to be believed as the foundation for our Christian morality. But if your answer is no, then this is the point that should be under discussion. It is superfluous to investigate *what* dogmas can be, if you deny *there are any* by denying revelation.

Well, on this point, M. Le Roy has not explained himself very clearly. "One freely imagines God in the act of revealing," he says,

> as a very learned professor whom one must believe at his word, when he communicates to his audience results whose proof the audience is not able to understand. *But this does not seem to me at all satisfying.*

The vagueness of these last words can rightly trouble one, and theologians have the right to expect a more precise answer.

We, however, are not going to pursue this as our reason to reject Le-Roy's position. We shall judge his system of moral explication as it has been presented to us.

Two problems are put before us:

1. Is the moral exposition of dogmas acceptable, and does it resolve the difficulties raised?

2. The incompatibility between dogma in its ancient sense and genuine philosophy—has it really been demonstrated?

To the first of these questions, our response will be quite categorical: far from salvaging the existence of dogmas, the moral exposition given by Mr. Le Roy, as proposed by its author and approved by the various correspondents of *La Quinzaine*, will spell the end of all Christian dogma. To repudiate this moralist theory of dogma is, for Catholicism, an elementary duty of sincerity. If there is an area where underhanded conduct inspires strong repulsion, it is the area of professing the faith. Well, whether Mr. Le Roy wishes it or not, he is asking the Church to play wretched word-games and try to save her empire over souls at the cost of a disgraceful equivocation.

There is in history a fact that is established, beyond discussion, evident to the point of being incontestable (and it is not at all contested by Mr. Le Roy): for nineteen centuries Christianity (or, if you prefer, the Church) has presented herself to the world as the custodian not merely of a sublime morality but also of a treasury of truths that is the basis for this morality (a basis at once necessary and indestructible); the Church has proclaimed as true and infallible forever a philosophy superior to all the transitory systems that our frail humanity has produced about the origin of the world, its providential history, and the final destiny of human beings; she has called all men, all peoples, and all social classes, scholars as well as janitors, and has imposed upon all of them an intellectual adherence by asking them: do you believe that there are three persons in God? that Jesus became man? If you do not admit intellectually that Mary is truly the mother of God, out with you.

This treasury of truth—the Church has always affirmed that it is not an invention of human intelligence, although several of these truths do not surpass the sphere of its activity; she affirms rather that they have been taught by God Himself, who revealed them to the prophets, and that He has Himself come down to earth in the person of Jesus, to be the source of *truth* as well as the source of life.

Over the course of nineteen centuries, she has continually defended this deposit of truths in its entirety, saying *anathema* to whoever would demolish a single one of these dogmas. And since several of her sons in these latter times, acting in the name of the progress of science but misled by a false philosophy, have wanted to change or modify the sense of these dogmatic affirmations—Hermes, Günther, and others—she has proclaimed solemnly the immutability of their meaning: *in eodem sensu eademque sententia*.

And now today you come to ask this same Church to tell her sons that she has never pretended to impose an intellectual *credo*, nor to set norms for the human mind;

- that she has no authority to regulate the intellect and that she never dreamed of claiming for herself an intellectual and theoretical infallibility;
- that she has no such thing as a deposit of immutable truths received from heaven, and that the ancient idea of a revelation by which God supposedly spoke to man is a gross anthropomorphism, unacceptable to our modern philosophy;
- that every dogma, if understood as an intellectual affirmation on the authority of any master at all, is "a bondage, a curb on the rights of thought, a threat of intellectual tyranny, a yoke and a restriction imposed from without upon the freedom of research; all things radically contrary to the very life of the mind, to its need for autonomy and sincerity";
- that "no authority can make a man find (or prevent him from finding) an argument weak or solid, and especially cannot make such and such a notion have or not have any meaning for him";
- that the Church has never wanted to impose upon her faithful any affirmation, any argument, or any notion;
- that when the Church defined in her councils the consubstantiality of the Son, the divine maternity of Mary, or a single divine person in Christ but two natures with two wills and two minds, she was not proposing to affirm anything, but only to give practical commands to the will;
- finally that one can be a Christian and a Catholic while declaring that to admit even a single dogma as a doctrinal assertion is to condemn oneself "to no longer think at all."

Well, this is asking of the Church not only an underhandedness toward her children but also a lie, against which all of her children who can read and understand texts will rise up in indignation. One should really think about this! Here is the dogma of the Eucharistic presence; the Church has defined in the most explicit way that there is contained in the Sacrament, in truth, in reality, in substance, the Body, the Blood, the Soul, and the Divinity of Christ; she has defined the miraculous manner in which this change occurs; she has defined the duration of this real presence. She imposes upon her teachers an intellectual adherence to each one of these definitions. And now today she will declare that she never wanted to impose upon the mind any intellectual conception! Is this serious?

Here is another example. Mr. Le Roy mentions the canon of Vatican I "attaching an anathema to anyone who says that revelation does not contain mysteries in the proper sense of the word and anyone who says that reason in its legitimate steps forward will come to understand and demonstrate all the dogmas of the faith." Then, by an a priori argument he tries to demonstrate that the Council can only have been speaking *of a practical submission to commandments bearing upon action*. For

> one cannot understand that assent to irreducible mysteries would ever be legitimate, nor what such consent could consist of, nor what sort of utility or value it could offer us, nor how such assent could constitute a virtue.[25]

But we ask him how people can be made to believe so enormous an absurdity—at least the people who know how to read and the people who by knowing history know that the Council intended precisely to answer German philosophers who objected to mysteries with the same contentions raised by Mr. Le Roy. We have here a question of straightforward conduct: yes or no, did the Fathers of the Council say and mean to say that by faith we must *affirm* some mysteries—the Trinity, the Incarnation, the Redemption, etc.?

But now you will say that, if these dogmas understood intellectually are in reality unacceptable, something must be done to save the situation. (We shall discuss further along how lightly people are rushing to proclaim the bankruptcy of our dogmas.) But in the end, when the thesis of Mr. Le Roy shall have been proven, no, there will be nothing to do to save the situation; no, there will be no place for a dishonorable about-face in which the Church, not daring to tell the faithful that all her dogmas are unthinkable, gives them this advice: "Act as if all that were true; these are precepts, not truths." The only position the Church could take would be to declare frankly that she is not what she believed she was for all those centuries, that she has not received the mission to conduct mankind infallibly to its end; thereupon, she should disappear by giving place to another school of philosophy (because, after all, the Church would be no more than that), a school less compromised by an ugly past of nineteen centuries of ridiculous faith.

25. Ibid., 519.

Thus, when you require the Catholic Church to renounce all intellectual meaning to her faith and require her to adopt along with the new doctrines of evolution the purely practical meaning of her dogmas, everything reduces to this dreadful dilemma:

- Either you are asking her to declare that she never believed in that theoretical meaning, even when she was anathematizing anyone who refused intellectual adherence; and then she will have to rip out the most striking pages of her history;
- Or else you are expecting her to proclaim her nineteen-hundred-year-old mistake, and the nineteen-hundred-year-long distraction of mind, in which she required an adherence of the mind to dogmas whose absolute inconsistency she recognized, all the while adding that she remains forever the *infallible* interpreter of true Christianity; and then you are asking her to proclaim with her own mouth her dethronement and her mental disorder.

In either case, it is the end of Catholicism.

✳

Let us recognize in any case that some of the friends of Mr. Le Roy think at bottom as we do, and that what they are asking of the Church is a complete abdication. One of the correspondents to *La Quinzaine* who felicitated the editor and Mr. Le Roy warmly "for their courage and their sincerity" asks for the conversion of theology to the philosophy of our time, a useful conversion "at a moment when *the problem of Christ risks being mostly cast from the domain of history (history-science) into the domain of thought, where the problem of God has been posed already and very sharply*."[26] And if you want to know the role that these people reserve for theology—that is, for the religious authority whose expression is theology—they tell us with as much ill humor as impertinence: "We are not condemned to repeat the theories of our ancestors; we have only to continue their 'action' and to fertilize what is still alive in what they have bequeathed to us; and *where shall we find this, if not in ourselves*? In order to know what we should believe and profess, our generation will try, *with the help of competent authority, to formulate its religious aspirations in function of its own thought*. In this work, the past can assist our generation with its lessons, but it cannot

26. F. P., "Some Views on the Nature of Dogma," *La Quinzaine* (June 16, 1905): 557.

do the work in our place." One must recall that Mr. F. P. has advised us that the idea of a revelation imparting to human beings truths of divine origin, and hence immutable, has long since fallen into bankruptcy. He continued at once:

The thing to believe is that, *in order to keep a place in bright contemporary minds, dogmatic theology should make itself the science of beliefs*, as morality is making itself "the science of customs" and as physics has made itself the science of nature: instead of pretending to deduce what ought to be and imposing it, theology will do better, no doubt, to pay more attention to what is.

Theology still has today, it is true, the airs of an old queen who has lost much of her power and charms, but who keeps (alongside her memory of what she was) an instinct for arrogance and the mannerisms of dominance. If theology cannot run the whole show, she still does not have to mix with the hoi polloi (that would be to fail); she prefers isolation in a sulk, a bit disdainful of the times which have withered her beauty and *of the freedom which has dethroned her*. But she begins to perceive that people are not paying much attention to her person and that often they look at her with a smile; she begins to perceive that she can no longer say seriously, "la science c'est moi" and that her servants of yesteryear are not about to return to their old docility.

You see there a roundabout way of telling the Church that her teaching is finished, and that she should limit herself henceforth to writing the history of her developments. The only thing this act of courage in *La Quinzaine* is lacking, to merit congratulations, is a frank signature. But at the end of the day, is this persiflage not preferable to the less-than-honest transformation that people are (ever so gently) asking the Church to make? We are very confident about the life of our dogmas; they have seen disappear quite a few philosophies that thought they had vanquished dogma forever. But if our faith must die, at least let us expect it to die without equivocation and underhandedness, even if it is "to keep a place in bright contemporary minds."

And—please allow us this digression, if it is one—this is what we should like to say to all the panegyrists of Mr. Loisy, in particular the last of them, Mr. Paul Desjardins. He at least makes no bones about the results of the evolution of dogmas, results that Mr. Loisy proposes as "a sample of the apologetical systems which free higher criticism, once admitted, will leave for the orthodox."

Oh, that is just one hypothesis; "one can well conceive another set of results, and perhaps one must. Mr. Marcel Hébert has made a critique of Loisy's 'sketch,' strongly grounded in logic."[27] Also, far from joining the new Church, the broad Church of Mr. Loisy, he recognizes that it can only be a transitory shelter for illogical souls. Once the thesis of the absolute evolution of dogmas is admitted, what is in question is the very transcendence of God; and this freethinker, who thinks he is already sure of the final victory of unbelief, finishes his book with this prediction: "One can also foresee that, in a generation or two, insertion of the absolute into the framework of facts will no longer be even intelligible."

Up to this point, for my part, I understand this attitude; it rests upon a mistake, but it is logical—indeed the only one that is logical.

But where the role of Mr. Desjardins and so many others is incomprehensible is where, being a logical thinker and therefore unbelieving by his own account, he congratulates Mr. Loisy for wanting to stay Catholic after having overthrown all the dogmas; it is when he blames the Church for not having gone along with this strange attitude people at once demand and exemplify, and that consists in hanging on to a *Credo* and preaching it to the people, while proclaiming that each article in it is in radical opposition with the only acceptable philosophy; it is when he addresses seminarians—he the unbelieving critic, as he calls himself, the convinced freethinker—and gives himself the mission of forming in the bosom of the Church a young clergy so trained in the double talk of symbolism that they can remain in the hierarchy even after having lost the Catholic faith, and therein continue the work of Mr. Loisy. He is afraid that the young clergy (whose minds are supposed to be seduced by these theories) will not see sufficiently the ultimate consequences; he fears that these young minds will be either terror-stricken by this complete incredulity and throw themselves back into the old faith or will find themselves out of place in a Church and among a clergy whose dogmas they repudiate and will then resign forthrightly from a society whose faith they have abandoned. And on and on he goes, through long pages, eager to put these young seminarians at ease, to sugar-coat what is too shocking in this intellectual evolution. He goes so far as to insinuate that it harmonizes quite well with the Catholic faith.

27. Paul Desjardins, *Catholicisme et critique: Réflexions d'un profane sur l'affaire Loisy* (Paris: Cahier de la Quinzaine, 1905).

Oh, he thoroughly highlights all the strangeness of the role he has played, and he steers clear of affirming anything; he proceeds by marvelous attenuations and interrogations:

> Let us suppose that indeed the thesis of their literalness and their exact historicity can no longer be maintained honestly for the creation story, the flood, the story of the patriarchs, or for miraculous events in general, or for the deeds of Jesus reported in the fourth Gospel. Is it inevitable that the Catholic faith be swept away, as well? Will a belief that is less based on history but more deeply experiential be less efficacious? Will there follow an impoverishment of spirituality, a loss of power and of joy? In the end, *is the point of view of pure symbolism flatly extra-Christian or even anti-Christian*?
>
> UnChurched critics have no authority to answer that. All that they can advance are the precedents furnished by history.[28]

And now our unChurched critic tortures himself to find in Church history admirable symbolists with Catholic fervor, and, furnished with the examples he seems to have found, he presses the young clergy to examine whether the alternative is as drastic as their superiors maintain.

The *Bulletin de littérature ecclésiastique* of Toulouse has already drawn attention to these sad pages and has quoted lines of sounder inspiration, with which the *Bulletin de l'union pour l'action morale* condemns symbolo-fideism. Then the reviewer adds, "Could Mr. Desjardins tell us what moral value there is to the attitude he is now advocating?"[29] We in turn pose the same question.

III

Does the practical conception of dogmas at least remove the difficulties that frightened Mr. Le Roy? Not in the least—and this, one must say, is what astonishes us the most in this study: how a thinker so reflective and penetrating can have failed to see that, in his system, all of the alleged antinomies of intellectualist dogma remain, and that the issue has not been advanced a single step. "Christianity," they tell us, "is not a system of speculative philosophy but a source and *rule of life*, a discipline of moral and religious action, in short *a set of practical means* to attain salvation. Why

28. Ibid., 111.

29. Franon, "An Anti-Intellectualist Scholastic," *Bulletin de littérature ecclésiastique* 7 of Toulouse (June 1905): 186.

should one be surprised, then, if dogmas concern primarily conduct rather than pure reflective knowledge?"[30]

But who can fail to see that this *rule of life* assumes a mass of theoretical truths, known and previously established, without which no precept is even conceivable?

To be precise, one would at least have to prove first of all the *existence of the precept*—that is to say, the origin of the law, the authority from which it emanates, and its efficacity. After all, if Christianity is a purely human invention, if the *salvation to be attained* is a pure fantasy, if everything ends up in death, what need do I have for the rules invented by Jesus, Paul, or Augustine?

Traditional Catholicism gives a clear answer by going back to divine revelation, whose reality it proves by history and by divine "signs." But how will Mr. Le Roy, who has so solemnly declared that any proof of the existence of God or of revelation is forbidden to our reason, establish that there is a salvation to be gotten and that the dogmatic rules really help one reach it? One can dare him to justify any one of these laws, other than by a fideism that is blind and contrary to plain good sense. Thus, after Le Roy has spoken well of "the requirements of morality, which cannot approve an action that is systematically unreflective,"[31] he imposes upon the believer, by virtue of his own system, not only an action but an entire life that is systematically unreflective—better said, systematically unreasonable.

The difficulty did not entirely escape the learned philosopher. "There are still large questions to be resolved. One must somehow *furnish a proof and a justification of dogma. And that is not an entirely easy thing*." Well, here is his answer: "nevertheless, one of the great obstacles has been leveled. Practical truths are established otherwise than speculative ones. Recourse to authority, totally unacceptable in the sphere of pure thought, seems a priori less shocking in the sphere of action, because, if authority has legitimate rights anywhere, it is surely in the domain of the practical."

On one condition, however—namely, that there is an authority having the right to command. This is the one point that Mr. Le Roy forgot. So where is this authority that dictates all the dogma-rules of life? On what ground does the Church's right repose, if she is the one to whom we are to have recourse, as it seems? So long as one has no answer, all the *rules of con-*

30. Le Roy, "Qu'est-ce qu'un dogme," 518.
31. Ibid., 522.

duct rest on a vacuum; and as soon as one tries to furnish an answer, what one has to build up is a theory that is perfectly intellectualist.

Mr. Fonsegrive also had no idea of how to avoid this roadblock. But with more subtlety, he tried to establish that, by the very fact that the issue here is practice and action, it is not necessary to have absolute and certain proofs.[32] The need to act forces one to decide rapidly, without having the time to examine everything. One makes a decision on the basis of probabilities: one ventures, one makes a leap, one must undergo the risks of error. One chooses a religion on trial, one experiments with it; and if one finds it good, one remains in it. This is the law of action.

Who can fail to see what grave consequences would flow from this mitigated fideism? Where would the certitude and the immutability of the faith be? What has deceived Mr. Fonsegrive is the fact that he has confused *practical certitude* (or probability), which suffices for the ordinary conduct of life or for the practice of virtues different from faith, with the *theoretical* certitude required by faith. For me to give alms prudently to a poor man, it is enough that I have serious reasons to think him poor; no doubt, I will be fooled sometimes, and a person who never wants to give charity until he has an absolute proof of the real needs of the unfortunate would be the worst of misers. But when the issue is my turning over my entire soul to the Christian faith, even if it is envisioned as a practical law, I have to have complete certitude that I am not deceiving myself and that the arguments for doing so are of a nature to exclude all possibility of error.

The reason for this difference is obvious, even though it has eluded Mr. Fonsegrive and many others before him. It rests on the honesty, the sincerity, and the firmness of the act of faith, whether one envisions it as an intellectual adhesion or as a consecration of one's whole soul as given to God (as modern thinkers prefer to view it, wrongly, by the way). In the first case, when I give alms to a poor man, I can be fooled, but I know it, and it has never entered my mind to pretend that I have absolute certitude of making no mistake. On the contrary, when I embrace the Christian faith, if I understand what it demands of me, I must be so deeply convinced that it is the true rule of salvation that I would banish any voluntary doubt on the subject,

32. George Fonsegrive, "Catholicisme et libre pensée," 2nd article (*La Quinzaine* [May 16, 1905], 226–30). See also the first article, *La Quinzaine* (May 1, 1905): 98–102. [During the era of these selections, Fonsegrive was the director of *La Quinzaine*—Tr.]

that I would be ready to shed my blood with the martyrs, rather than admit a hesitation in my deep conviction—conduct that would be unreasonable, senseless, and (let's use the word) fanatical, if I did not have sure proofs of the truth of Christianity, even viewed as a life. For me to admit the Christian faith and practice it "on trial" would be for me to lie to myself and lie to Christ, since I would be affirming an unshakeable conviction that I do not have. Putting this faith on the same level as human philosophies, which one successively adopts or rejects, would be an unheard-of novelty. We have always had a quite different idea of faith within Christianity, since the time of the apostles. *Si credis ex toto corde* [Rom 10:9; see also Acts 8:37]. One has to commit oneself with one's whole heart and without reservations as to "trying it," examining it, reflecting, and later pulling back. But I repeat, apart from gross fanaticism, this is only possible if the demonstration has been complete.

But, objects Mr. Fonsegrive, one has to decide, time is short, one must make do with probabilities. It is an insult to God's providence to think that it obliges people to embrace the Christian revelation without shedding a light powerful enough that souls who seek in good faith reach certitude. One who has been born outside the true faith has the duty to seek the truth, as soon as he suspects its existence; and he has the right to examine, to take the time that is morally necessary. One must go further: he is forbidden by the moral law to make a premature decision; without valid proofs, he may no more admit the Incarnation of the Word nor strike an attitude of worship toward the Incarnate Word or toward Jesus in the Eucharist than he may believe in the incarnations of Brahma or the revelations of Muhammad.

This is what the great theologians would have taught our modern philosophers, if the great theologians were any longer read by those who propose to reform theology (and religion itself). They would have taught them furthermore that these questions, far from being new, as people imagine, were lengthily and vividly discussed in the seventeenth century; that certain Christian thinkers were already struck by the difficulties that moved Mr. Fonsegrive. But the solutions were so clear that, since then, all the theologians have been unanimous in rejecting the proposition condemned by Innocent XI, which said that one may make an act of faith while knowing it merely probable that there has been revelation.[33]

33. "Assensus fidei supernaturalis et utilis ad salutem stat cum notitia solum probabili revelationis, una cum formidine qua quis formidet ne non sit locutus Deus"; Proposition 21, condemned

The moral system of Le Roy and Fonsegrive is thus powerless to legitimate the precept that they acknowledge in a dogma. Their system is equally powerless to determine its meaning and force.

Just here is where the inner contradictions of the system show themselves starkly. On the one hand, they tell us that believing in the resurrection of Jesus or the real presence assumes no theoretical conception but only a practical attitude of the soul. But on the other hand, they are forced to admit that this attitude has to be definite and has to have certain traits that exclude contrary dispositions. Thus believing in the resurrection of Jesus "is relating to Him as one would have done before His death, as you do toward a contemporary of yours."

However, if the dogmatic formula "Jesus is risen" has no definite intellectual meaning, where, I ask, does this precise attitude, analogous to the one we would have toward Jesus as our contemporary, come from? Is it not the case that the resurrection presents itself to your mind as a new life, an immortal life, that makes Jesus the contemporary of all the human generations of the future? If one adds that this life of Christ is a life *in His body* and in His soul, one adds enough to express in a formal way all that the most intellectualist of theologians have seen in this dogma.

But then Le Roy and Fonsegrive are faced with the inevitable and pressing and great question: by what right do you determine such and such an attitude, rather than such and such another, if it is really the case that the formula "Jesus is risen" does not correspond to any precise concept? You still have to choose. Either you maintain your thesis that dogmas have no theoretical meaning, and then you are forbidden to nail down this attitude rather than that one toward the Eucharist, the Incarnation, the personhood of God, etc. Or else you avow that Jesus present in the Eucharist excludes the disrespectful attitude of Calvin, and thereby you reestablish the most formal "intellectualism," verifying for theology, despite yourselves, what Mr. Poincaré said about science: "It will be intellectualist, or it will not be at all."

*

A final weakness of the theory and a new contradiction burst forth as soon as Mr. Le Roy wants to explain the intellectual duty that a dogma im-

by Innocent XI on March 2, 1678. ["An assent of faith that is supernatural and useful for salvation is consistent with a merely probable knowledge of revelation together with the hesitation by which one doubts whether God has spoken." See Denzinger, no. 2121.—Tr.]

poses and also wants to explain the veto power that he attributes to dogmatic formulae.

Wishing very sincerely to be a Catholic, he has understood quite well that if a dogma/rule-of-life seems to allow free rein for the human mind, this autonomy still has a limit.

> After having accepted the dogmas, a Catholic keeps full freedom to fashion objects corresponding to the divine personhood, to the real presence, or the resurrection, for example—to fashion such a theory or such an intellectual representation as he pleases.... The Catholic's situation in this regard is the same as his situation vis-à-vis any scientific or philosophical speculation, and he may allowably adopt the same attitude in either case. Just one thing is imposed upon him; a single obligation binds him: his theory has to justify the practical rules stated by the dogma; his intellectual representation has to provide an account of the practical prescriptions stated by the dogma. This prescription stands more or less, in a word, as the statement of fact stands, in that it is possible to construct plenty of different theories explaining the fact, but every theory must give an account of it.... Should a theory arise someday which damages the dogma in its own domain by altering its practical meaning, the dogma turns at once against it and condemns it, becoming in this way an intellectual proposition, but a negative one, superimposed upon the rule of conduct which is all it was originally.

No doubt about it: we have here an important proviso, and one that at bottom suffices, we dare say, to safeguard the dogma. We do not wish to examine at this point where one gets this "*fact* which every theory must take into account" or this "mysterious reality which corresponds to it." We shall not even investigate at this point whether it is true that the dogma becomes a *negative* intellectual proposition rather than a *positive* one. We merely observe that a dogma is acknowledged to have an intellectual value, at least a restrictive one, in virtue of which the dogma will turn against certain conceptions and condemn them.

However, if we are happy to congratulate Mr. Le Roy for this very Catholic account, we must add that his proviso is forbidden to him by his system. There is an obvious contradiction between the principles of absolute autonomy (which he has posited) and the limits within which he now imprisons it.

If it is true in fact, as we have been told in every way, that "recourse to authority is totally unacceptable in the order of pure thought," by what right are you going to stop Nestorius or Eutyches in their interpretation of the dogma of the Incarnation, or stop Berengarius or Calvin in their symbolic theory of the Eucharist?

No doubt you will say to them: your theory "alters the practical meaning of the dogma." For example, you Calvin, you Nestorius, you are destroying the cultus of adoration that the Church renders to Christ and to the Eucharist.

But then these thinkers will give you the answer, "It is precisely this cultus of adoration that we wish to destroy, as an immoral remnant of paganism, a veritable idolatry." Wasn't it you, Mr. Le Roy, who taught us that there is no "revealed logic," that no authority can make me find an argument weak or solid, and above all that no authority can dictate whether such and such a notion does or does not have meaning for me? Well, then, when you pretend that the dogma of the real presence means "that you must assume before the consecrated Host *an attitude identical to the one you would assume in front of Jesus appearing to you visibly*," I am telling you that this conception, from the practical point of view as much as in the order of pure thought, has no meaning for me, or rather I am telling you that it is absolutely contrary to sound reason! On your principles, it is forbidden for you to condemn me, since, after all, every affirmation coming from outside would be "an enslavement, a threat of intellectual tyranny, a yoke upon the freedom of research."[34]

It is evident that Mr. Le Roy has no answer to this. He will have a fine time saying that dogmatic definitions are "negative, do not limit knowledge, do not stop progress, that *all they do is close off dead ends*." And what if it seems to me that what he calls dead ends are in fact the only ways forward? How will they force me to believe that these ways are dead ends, "in virtue of such and such a proof which I judge unconvincing? One might as well demand that I no longer think at all." Thus did Mr. Le Roy speak against intellectualist dogma; and thus people will argue against his pretended intellectual duty to respect the law of practice. Mr. Le Roy has been given notice:

- either (so as to save the autonomy of the mind) withdraw all the restrictions you have put upon freedom of thought (and then all faith goes down);

34. Le Roy, "Qu'est-ce qu'un dogme," 502.

▪ or else (so as to preserve dogma, even understood in the sense of a precept) repudiate this absolute independence of the mind (and then down goes the whole superstructure of his system). Was it a waste of time to say so much against dogma as a doctrinal truth, under the pretext of rational antinomies, whose fictitious character will be shown below?

IV

The antinomies between intellectual dogma and genuine philosophy—are they as real and as formidable as Le Roy and Fonsegrive think?[35] It is time to examine them and to come to closer grips with the four objections displayed in *La Quinzaine*.

I. In the name of modern reason, which (we have been told since Descartes's day) requires direct proofs and clear insight into the truth, these gentlemen reject any dogma unverifiable in itself, and they declare that authority is totally unacceptable in the order of pure thought.

In that case, we admit, dogmas are indeed dead. And the winner is the old rationalism of the eighteenth and nineteenth centuries, slightly rejuvenated, and proposed with a naïveté that makes one smile. If they still hold that position, it was idle and almost childish to consult the theologians. Let me assure Mr. Le Roy that the old refutations have lost none of their force. When he pretends that his position has never been answered except by worthless subtleties or tricks of rhetoric, he shows that he has read little, or that his mind is made up. What good will it do to take up again a proof of revelation, which people will not read, no doubt, any more than they read the others?

Nevertheless, we should like to see Mr. Le Roy choose sides between these two alternatives, which sum up the whole problem: does he deny to God the power to communicate with human beings and give them secrets about Himself, His designs, their destiny?

Or, admitting that God can speak to us, is his mind not convinced of the truth of these disclosures from God? Inasmuch as he has made no choice, we theologians will be able to rest in peace; and since people dare to set Descartes against us, they will have the happiness of counting him in their ranks.

35. Henceforth the source is *Études* (August 5, 1905): 315ff.

On this point, we are happy to be able to set against Mr. Le Roy an authority that he will not decline—that of the director of *La Quinzaine*. In his first article, "Catholicisme et libre pensée," Mr. Fonsegrive, with his great penetration, has perfectly shown up the gross illusion of the free-thinker who proposes to make incumbent upon each mind a personal solution to every problem, a solution resulting from a direct examination without recourse to authority. In the order of practical life, this is a veritable madness:

Suppose we are sick; under the pretext of trusting no one but ourselves, shall we dispense ourselves from resorting to a doctor? Suppose we have a lawsuit; under the same pretext shall we refuse ourselves permission to consult a lawyer? Suppose we want to make a trip; shall we decide not to get on the train until we have learned the physics, the mechanics, and verified for ourselves the good condition of the machine? And to be completely consistent with the principles of free thought, must we learn the art of the engineer before we embark from Paris to Bordeaux, for example? Must we have verified for ourselves minutely the state of the rails, that is, must we first have gone to Bordeaux before having gotten the right to get on the train to go there? Must we eat nothing and drink nothing without having first—not *had* it analyzed, for that would be again a recourse to authority but—analyzing it ourselves? And what am I saying? That will not suffice, because it is never demonstratively certain that the portion tested resembles the rest of the food from which it was taken, so that the only steak, the only milk, the only wine, or the only water surely known scientifically to be harmless will be the steak, the milk, the water, the wine destroyed by the chemical analysis. We will only be sure we can eat or drink what will be no longer suitable for nourishment or refreshment.

A man who would act this way would not be a reasonable man, but demented. He would be acting exactly like the patients whom psychiatrists know all too well, who are sick with the madness of doubt.[36]

In the scientific order, recourse to authority and to the testimony of others, without personal verification, is a necessity acknowledged by Descartes himself:

He recognizes in science itself [says Mr. Fonsegrive] the legitimacy of admitting certain propositions, certain experiences, on the trust of another, without one's having verified them directly oneself.

And this is indeed what all scientists have done. How could the astronomers

36. Fonsegrive, "Catholicisme et libre pensée," 98.

get on, if they did not accept the observations made by their predecessors? How could Le Verrier have made his discoveries if he had not referred to the mathematicians whose work he directed and if these in turn had not relied on the logarithmic tables? Complete verification for each scientist is not possible in any of the experimental sciences, and it will become less and less possible as science progresses. There must come a moment when human life will be too short for the scientist to have the time to repeat for himself all the prior experiments before pushing on; thus the very progress of science, even in a scientific matter, requires that the scientist defer to the authority of others.[37]

Why, then, resist divine authority by entrenching oneself behind the autonomy of human reason, which yields so easily to human authority?

II. In the name of agnosticism, Mr. Le Roy declares impossible an *indirect* demonstration of dogmas. The existence of God, the fact of revelation, its preservation by the Church—all of that should be shown (and we agree), but all of that is also as indemonstrable as the revealed mysteries themselves.

None of our readers will have missed the confusion to which Mr. Le Roy has fallen victim here. No, the question of the existence of God, of revelation, to say nothing of the rest, is not of the same kind as the question of the revealed mysteries, the Trinity, the Incarnation, supernatural grace. To deny, without even attempting a proof, that God's existence and the fact of revelation can be demonstrated directly by reason, as all Catholic theologians teach, is a begging of the question, which is surprising in a philosopher so well informed.

It is true that he speaks at once of *arguments comparable to those of a mathematician*. But the begging of the question is only the more disconcerting in a scholar who is at the same time a philosopher. We do not even imagine that he has failed to observe that each branch of human knowing, to get at the truth, has a quite special method of demonstration. Would he dare to demand mathematical procedures in history? And, to stay inside philosophy, when he all of a sudden presents us with the *principle of immanence* as an incontestable truth, outside of which there is no philosophical salvation, will he believe that he has produced for his thesis *arguments comparable to those of a mathematician*? We cannot believe in such an illusion. But then, why be so demanding toward others?

37. Ibid., 101.

Having made this reservation about the kind of demonstration, we refer Mr. Le Roy to the answer given by Fr. Sertillanges about the need to prove *the preambles of the faith*. This learned professor has made (perhaps without assessing their scope) too many unhappy concessions [to Le Roy], which makes it all the more irresistible for us to quote him on the following happy formulation: "*The preambles of the faith have to be provable in every system under the penalty of that system's being declared unacceptable by the faith*, and this by proofs of the same order and of the same validity as any other proposition belonging to the same kind of research."[38]

And when people put to him the famous dilemma "*either* apologetical proofs are absolutely certain and rigorous (and then what becomes of the liberty of the act of faith), *or else*, to preserve this liberty, the proofs are insufficient and just more or less probable (and then the faith lacks its basis), because (in short) an insufficient proof is not an acceptable proof," Fr. Sertillanges rightly responds that the dilemma is not a strict one, and that its first member is at fault. Proofs can be sufficient and acceptable in themselves without constraining the mind absolutely. There is a difference between the *certitude* and the *necessity* of an affirmation. Even a modestly deep psychological reflection on the functioning of our mind and the influence it receives from the will makes this obvious. But the subject is too large and too delicate to be taken up here.

It is of more value to point out the hidden postulate on which rests Le Roy's flat negation of any proof of God's existence or of revelation. This thinker is not just agnostic in religious matters; he is a radical anti-intellectualist in the philosophy of science, to the point of having alarmed the least dogmatic among contemporary scientists. Mr. Poincaré devoted an entire chapter of his latest book to combating Le Roy's philosophy, which regards the intellect as incurably powerless.[39] For Mr. Le Roy, science is made of nothing but arbitrary conventions, and it is thanks to this circumstance alone that science owes its apparent certitude; the scientific facts themselves are an artifact of the scientist, and so a fortiori are the laws that the scientist deduces from these facts; thus science can teach us nothing about the truth; it can only give us a rule of action. Science is, one may say, a collection of *recipes*, often enough efficacious.

38. Letter of Fr. Sertillanges, *La Quinzaine* (June 1, 1905): 418.

39. Poincaré, *La valeur de la science*, 243–47.

This is the pure nominalism to which this philosophy joins another trait, due no doubt to the influence of Mr. Bergson. For Le Roy, the mind deforms everything it touches, and this is even more true of the mind's necessary instrument: "discourse," language. The only reality is in our fleeting and changing impressions, and even this reality vanishes the moment one touches it.

We can only refer the reader to the penetrating and irrefutable discussion that Mr. Poincaré has published on these assertions. With full justification, this scientist observes that an anti-intellectual philosophy, by rejecting analysis and "discourse," thereby condemns itself to being incommunicable... In this system, the thinker exhausts his strength in a negation and "a cry of enthusiasm," to which he can add nothing. "And then would it not have been more consistent to keep silent?"

The laws of science, you say, are rules of action, not knowledge. But, Mr. Poincaré responds, these rules of action have the peculiar trait that they succeed, at least generally, whereas the contrary rules will never succeed.

> If then these scientific "recipes" have a value as a rule of action, the value is that we know that they succeed, at least in general. But *to know that is already to know something, and then why do you come along telling us that we cannot know anything*?
>
> There is no way to escape this dilemma—either science does not permit one to predict, and then it is without value as a rule of action, or else it allows one to predict in a more or less imperfect way, and then it is not without value as a means of knowledge.[40]

The essential (and at the same time the most paradoxical) point in Le Roy's argument against intellectualism in science is a claim of his according to which *the scientist himself creates the scientific fact*—as if the scientific fact (as Poincaré shows in an extremely fine analysis) were something other than the *brute fact* given by experience and transmitted in a more technical and sometimes more precise language.

We shall be fully permitted to say, in the name of metaphysics, what Mr. Poincaré has said in the name of science. And we shall be allowed to make ourselves clear, once and for all, on the latent skepticism that people are trying to introduce into our minds under the pretext that we cannot *exhaust* reality.

Still, it is a strange spectacle to see intelligent people pleading in favor of absolute relativism without noticing the internal contradiction in their

40. Ibid., 220.

thesis. They put all metaphysics under suspicion and affirm not only that absolute truth does not exist for our mind, but also that it cannot exist. What they are saying, according to the sharp reflection of Mr. Fouillée against the neo-criticalists, is that they deny the absolute value of *all metaphysics*, in the name of *a new metaphysics* whose absolute value they proclaim. They deny *every immutable dogma* in the name of a new dogma that is untouchable and beyond discussion. For these moderns, this principle of relativity is indeed an immutable dogma, which they call the great philosophical breakthrough of this century. This is always the sorry outcome of Kantianism: in the name of a faculty of reason proclaimed powerless to give us anything but a *subjective* certitude, they proclaim their very objective certitude of this incurable subjectivism.

*

But then (they repeat constantly), we are not getting to the bottom of things. Every formulation is "necessarily inaccurate, susceptible of amelioration, and hence subject to change."—Subject to change for the better, by the addition of new truths; quite right.—But subject to *alteration*? No, certainly not.

People have criticized the Scholastics for having defined true knowledge as *adaequatio rei et intellectus*, "conformity of the mind to the thing," or the adequate representation of the object by the intellect, as if the intellect were supposed to make the object known in all its bearings and in its inner nature. The neo-Scholastics especially are supposed to have adopted this theory that "truth is a taking possession of the object by the subject, such that the mind possesses the thing fully in itself or in the absolute." It is supposed to be a breakthrough of contemporary philosophy that it has established that nothing exists but the concrete and the singular and that our intellectual knowledge, by contrast, attains only the abstract and the general, so that we cannot enclose the absolute concreteness of the thing in itself within our conceptions. Hence the condemnation of Scholastic intellectualism:

> Truth follows the laws of life, it evolves, it develops, and some even say that it changes. And if one talks to modern people about absolute scientific truth, immutable and nonprogressive truth, modern people do not stay to discuss the matter; they smile and leave.[41]

41. Fonsegrive, "À propos d'exégèse," *La Quinzaine* (December 16, 1903): 447.

Well, not to annoy the moderns, but their mistake is precisely to smile instead of reading the Scholastics and discussing things with them. For my part, I am persuaded that the upright, sincere, penetrating mind of the learned director of *La Quinzaine* would have agreed with the Scholastics. He would have seen in their works that the general and abstract character of our intellectual knowledge, far from being a recent discovery, is the most elementary principle of the Aristotelian and Thomistic theory and that the neo-Scholastics as well as their ancestors, far from pretending to have intellectual possession of the "integral truth," teach unanimously that *comprehensive* or complete knowledge even of a grain of sand is impossible for us. Also one is quite surprised to hear Mr. Fonsegrive, in a study that includes so many sound or profound views, give tongue to this reflection: "*At this hour* … no one is any longer a pure objectivist, and *one can no longer find a single person* to say that things are entirely as we think them to be, so as to say that the sun-in-thought is wholly like the one in the sky—which would be a bit much."[42] Could the learned thinker please tell us at what time and in what school of philosophy it was ever affirmed that the sun in our thought is *entirely* like the real sun? For us, the *modus repraesentandi* has always been distinguished from the *modus essendi*.

The Scholastics, with as much finesse as depth, said this about the things we do not know everything about; from there, is it legitimate to conclude with the relativists that we know nothing at all? Without falling into skepticism, dare we affirm that, with the progress of science, 2 + 2 will no longer equal 4? Photography does not exhaust the sensible and phenomenal reality: it does not give the shade, or the relief, or especially the life. Who then will have the madness to deny all resemblance between the image and the object represented? And, in line with the very sharp remark of Mr. Poincaré,

> from the fact that no painter can make a portrait that resembles me totally, should we conclude that the best painting is not to paint at all?[43]

Our senses also make an abstraction in their own fashion: in their object they grasp only the element corresponding to their nature. The eye grasps color. The ear grasps sound. From the fact that they do not represent the whole object, or even that they do not reveal to us the inner essences of

42. Fonsegrive, "À propos du centenaire de Kant," *La Quinzaine* (March 1, 1904): off-print, 19.
43. Poincaré, *La valeur de la science,* 216

the objects appearing, should we infer that they tell us nothing about reality, and that we wrongly make a distinction, whatever its nature, between colors and sounds?

By abstracting, our faculty puts something of itself into knowledge, and this is the meaning of the famous axiom that people quote against us, even though it is a witness to the depth of Scholastic theories: *quid quid recipitur, recipitur per modum recipientis*—every modification of a being (its coming to know, like all the rest) conforms to the nature of this being. But far from damaging a sound intellectualism, this axiom traces its limits. For if our reason separates by abstracting what is inseparable in the object—for example, general and essential traits from individual and accidental qualities—our reason itself makes us aware of this separation. It does not put the separation into the object, and it prevents the confusion that could otherwise arise in our minds. And when our reason defines man as a rational animal, by affirming that these two abstract notions really belong to every man, our reason takes care not to tell us that man exists thus abstracted and composed solely of two general notions.

"When a zoologist dissects an animal," writes Poincaré against Le Roy, "he certainly *alters* it by dissecting it and resigns himself *to never knowing everything*; but when he does not dissect, he condemns himself *to never knowing anything*, and hence to never saying anything."[44]

We therefore encourage Mr. Le Roy to renounce his agnosticism in science; by the same stroke he will be healed of his agnosticism in religion. Then, on the pretext that the risen life of Jesus is not of exactly the same nature as our life, he will no longer say to us that, in the dogmatic formula, the word "resurrection" is utterly devoid of meaning, an unknown *X* to which our mind can attach no concept. But this problem is about to resurface under a new aspect.

III. In the name of the clarity demanded by understanding, Mr. Le Roy rejects dogmas as absolutely indefinable and unrepresentable *via* concepts. They are "purely verbal formulae," to which he attaches the word "pharisaism" (523).

Let us observe first that clarity is a relative thing. We are surely allowed to be amazed at this strange insistence on clarity, from a philosophy that up

44. Ibid., 217

until now does not seem to show an excess of lucidity. It would be easy, but too cruel, to use Mr. Belot's remark to believers against the philosophers of this school: "What would most embarrass the majority of the *doctors of immanence* would be that, before even asking them for a *proof* of what they believe, we should order them to *define* with precision what they *affirm* and what they *deny*."[45] This, at least, is what one of their friends, Mr. O. Jousse de la Motte, thinks, writing to Le Roy: "Let's admit it, the essays which have appeared up to now have satisfied no one. Why? Because they have all lacked clarity and hence cannot be convincing .... *Immanentism has remained in a fog; this is why it gives more trouble than light*.... Let us clarify the ideas; let us give them not this off-putting algebraic form, nor this cloudy envelope which masks them and makes them impossible to grasp, but the precision in their contours that will make them intelligible and viable. Immanentism will not prevail until the man in the street can understand it." To go by what we see, the dawn of that day has not yet arrived. Until it does, it would behoove these philosophers to be less demanding.

Here is a second observation. If people only wanted to say that our mind will never exhaust the Absolute and will never represent its total reality, that our knowledge of God and our representations in the dogmas (divine personhood, resurrection, real presence) are not only obscure but incurably analogical, inadequate and purely approximate, because they do not come from an intuition of divine realities but from an abstraction of our mind working upon creatures infinitely remote from the greatness of God, we should be the first to applaud this doctrine, which was that of the Fathers and of the great Scholastic doctors. Fr. de la Taille has also established this, in these very pages, with an extensive and also sober erudition, in the place to which we refer the reader.[46]

But such is not the contention of the new school. For Mr. Le Roy, every dogma is "unthinkable," a nonsense—and what is most troubling is the fact that fear of seeming retrograde is pulling along even thinkers whose education and whose past would seem to put them most on guard against such excesses. Sad symptom of intellectual disarray! Nothing is more disconcerting than to see Fr. Sertillanges give his approval to Le Roy on this point and proclaim the following law of agnosticism:

45. Le Roy, "Qu'est-ce qu'un dogme," 505.
46. *Études* (May 5, 1905): 355–58.

The supernatural cannot be expressed correctly... *omnis determinatio est negatio*; this saying of Spinoza's is flatly true in this area. From an absolute point of view—and the Catholic doctors agree unanimously on this—*everything we can say of God is false. But if all that is false*, one falsehood is just as good as another, and the best falsehood will be the one that joins us to God and lets Him play His unique role towards us, that of making us alive.[47]

Well, no: all the Catholic doctors do not agree that these two formulae, "God exists" and "There is no God," are equally false. And while we recognize that his choice of expression has no doubt gone beyond the real thinking of the learned professor, we must regret the public approbation that he has given to these deplorable theories.

No, it is not at all true that the dogmas of God's personhood, the Resurrection, and the real presence represent nothing to our mind. Whoever reflects on what he thinks when hearing these words "sees very well that, if the *how* of these mysteries escapes him, the fact in itself is perfectly well understood." Even a child asked about the resurrection of Jesus will be able to express the naïve concept that he has formed of this life taken up again by the reunion of Christ's soul and body. And Le Roy will be forced to agree with this—after all, when he speaks of the resurrection, of the real presence, he knows what he means by these words, and he does not confuse the resurrection with the ascension, or with the virginal conception. It is therefore the case that he has a concept, and hence a definition, of these dogmas.

No, it is not at all true either that our representations of the divine are always false. The Fathers and the great theologians (we will be quoting them soon) have taught the *analogical* character of our conceptions of the Infinite; we apply to God ideas and terms that directly concern things created, temporal, and finite. Mr. Le Roy, following Loisy, concludes from this that our affirmations about the divinity are simple *algebraic notations*, having no resemblance to the divine Being and perpetually in need of amendment. Everything we say about God's personhood, for example, should be suspect, because divine personhood cannot be assimilated to human personhood.

But this deduction is illegitimate; our own reason itself tells us that there is a mere analogy between the divine perfections and those of creatures. When we say, "God is intelligent," "God is personal," we affirm abso-

47. Letter of Fr. Sertillanges, 412f.

lutely that He has in Himself the perfections that we call intelligence and personhood; but we add that He has these in an infinitely higher way than any creature can conceive. Is it "nothing" to know this, and to know it in such a way that no advance of science can ever diminish its certitude?

Also, as Mr. Franon wrote a little while ago on the remarks of Fr. Sertillanges, "make all the reservations you like about the incomprehensibility of the divine nature . . . , it will always remain the case that, when we affirm God's personhood, His freedom, His righteousness, His immutability, these affirmations, albeit conceived and posited *humano modo* are true in themselves and absolutely, with a metaphysical truth which imposes itself upon every mind."[48]

Mr. Le Roy is unfortunately still in the grips of an intransigent agnosticism in which (as Fr. de la Taille justly remarks) by a sorry confusion "one treats as synonymous the impossibility of being known *in its own nature* and the impossibility of being known *as having a nature of its own* different from all others and yet proclaimed by the others—or at least spelled out by all the others."[49]

Hence there arises, we are happy to say, the superiority of Mr. Fonsegrive's study over that of Mr. Le Roy. While Le Roy seems to exclude from dogma any kind of intellectual concept and representation, the learned director of *La Quinzaine* only criticizes dogmas for not being reducible to ideas that are entirely clear and precise. Here is a clearer avowal, which deserves notice and which negates in advance all of the unhappy concessions Fonsegrive made to the moral thesis of Le Roy:

> No doubt, [he says] *each of these propositions has a meaning*, and a meaning clear enough to exclude a great number of propositions, but if one sees that meaning as a luminous kernel, this kernel nevertheless remains surrounded by a penumbra and even a thick umbra whose contours get lost in the infinite—which amounts to saying that each dogmatic proposition includes a mysterious content.[50]

Mr. Fonsegrive's mistake is to then abandon the truth he has seen in order to rally to Le Roy's formulation: "Since the object of faith is marvelous, it cannot be expressed by concepts."[51] But since every dogma has *a*

48. Franon, "An Anti-Intellectualist Scholastic, 167.
49. *Études* (May 5, 1905): 354.
50. Fonsegrive, "Catholicisme et libre pensée," 2nd article, 222.
51. Ibid., 223.

meaning, how can one say that they cannot be expressed by concepts? One may say, and one must say, that our representations of God, of creation, of original sin's transmission, of redemption, are incomplete and affirm the mystery. But it is contradictory to maintain in the same breath that dogmas have a meaning and that they cannot be expressed by concepts.

In vain does Mr. Fonsegrive tell us,

> the realities signified by the formulae go infinitely beyond all that our mind can conceive. But it is to these realities that we adhere by faith; *hence our faith is not stopped or limited by concepts; it goes further than our ideas.*

Right there is the chief illusion of the system. It is not true at all that our faith goes further than our ideas, or that it attains the divine reality otherwise than through the operations of our mind or will. Well, our mind attains objects only through its concepts, and the will is attracted to these concepts only insofar as they are presented to it by the intellect. Such is the meaning of the ancient adage *ignoti nulla cupido*. For a mysterious divine reality that had no sort of representation in the mind or in the heart would get neither desire nor admiration. And if it is true to say that we love God even for these mysterious beauties that our concepts do not reach, it is no less correct to say that this love would be impossible if our concepts themselves had not revealed to us that there are unknown beauties in God that we cannot attain explicitly. There is, then, a contradiction in terms in the claim that our faith goes beyond our ideas, and we have a hard time grasping why Mr. Fonsegrive did not see it.

IV. Finally, in the name of the unity of the human mind, Mr. Le Roy rejects any dogmatic affirmation, because it does not form a coherent system with our other knowledge and would therefore be useless and logically infertile.

One is stupefied by these strange difficulties. No doubt chemistry, natural history, astronomy are foreign to the sphere of religious knowledge. But how is it a "rupture" in our mind, or any incoherence, to complete our knowledge of nature by knowledge of the Author of nature?

A useless knowledge, dare one say? How so? How dare one thus misdescribe the highest science of all, the science of God as first cause of the providential plan for humanity, of our redemption, of the ultimate destinies that await us! If this is useless, what science will be useful? Please give us the favor of a reply.

An *infertile* knowledge, they add. Yet it seems that for a long time experience has been showing what a sad end morality comes to, when it is separated from the intellectual affirmations of dogma. The history of all the pietisms, ancient and modern, is there to show us that the abandonment of dogma leads in short order to the ruin of morals.

Immutable dogmas are *foreign to progress*!, so they say. This is a strange illusion. These people have never compared the condensed and, as it were, embryonic dogmatics of the Apostolic writings with one of the great monuments of Catholic theology, whether it be called the *Enchiridion* of Augustine, the *Summa theologiae* of St. Thomas, or the *Exposition of Catholic Doctrine* by Bossuet!

We haven't the heart to go on—so shocking a contrast do Mr. Le Roy's arguments, by their weakness, make with the triumphal assurance with which he puts them forward as invincible.

V

As a conclusion to this debate, may we be permitted some reflections to clarify the origin of the divergences between the new schools and the traditional doctrine? No doubt the ultimate roots of the current crisis (and the current intellectual disarray) go back to fundamental problems in the philosophy of knowledge and (whatever people may say) to the influence that Kantianism has been exercising since 1780, even upon those who boast of having "gone beyond it." But without getting into the depths of this debate, which are too large and too important to be given an abridged rehearsal here, one may point out—in the method employed against traditional philosophy or theology—certain procedures, ordinarily unconscious, that unfortunately paralyze every discussion and make the misunderstanding incurable.

One of the first characteristics of the anti-intellectualist philosophy—and one has the right to be amazed at it—is a narrow and intransigent dogmatism that cuts short every discussion at the very moment when we seem to want it and to call for it. Oh, Mr. Le Roy protests a thousand times that he does not dogmatize and that he does not affirm; "he raises problems, he questions." And indeed he addresses his study to all the professors of theology. Yes, but at the same time, he takes pains to inform them that "the generative and fundamental principle which is the principle of immanence" has been put above all dispute.

The principle of imminence [he says] has not always been well understood. People have made a monster out of it, whereas *nothing is simpler and, in short, more obvious.*

Aren't these affirmations already, and a tad overblown? But let us hear the rest.

One may say that having acquired a clear consciousness of it is the essential upshot of modern philosophy; *one who refuses to admit it no longer counts as a philosopher; one who does not come to understand it shows thereby that he has no feel for philosophy.*

For one thing, this goes beyond all measure. This way of excommunicating people who do not think as you do, putting them outside the pale of philosophy, habitual as it may have become to the inflexible enemies of all "intellectualism," never ceases to be disturbing. We doubt that it facilitates inquiry at *La Quinzaine*. For us who have been invited to discuss a problem, it is hardly very encouraging (the minute we don't admire the system of those asking the questions) to hear ourselves awarded an instant certificate of philosophical incompetence. If only this philosophy had in its favor the sanction of the ages! But our own generation saw its cradle, and nothing guarantees that, before long, it will not join in the tomb the many, many systems that, for the last hundred years, have been coming into fashion and passing into oblivion.

This mentality of sovereign contempt for all those who have the unbelievable audacity not to admire the principle of immanence is expressed with embarrassing, child-like candor in the letter of one of Mr. Le Roy's admirers. "What gives?" said in substance a Mr. Jousse de la Motte, "You are asking theologians for their advice? You should not dream of it!"

We shall be very much surprised if Mr. Le Roy gets many responses. The older theologians will not understand him and will see in his article disturbing novelties.... The most sympathetic will take advantage of the occasion to denounce once again the dangers of "laicism." The deck is stacked. But Mr. Le Roy has no need to worry much. These theologians have their "siege mentality," and a new idea can only bother them. Do not expect too much of them. A person's knowledge cannot keep renewing itself forever. One soon reaches an age when the mind will only live upon its own past.... At the age of sixty, as an irreverent remark has it, people do not swallow anymore; they ruminate.... Today everyone admits that theology needs to be renewed; but the renewal can only be the work of young people. All one can ask of the old folks, if not good will for those who are doing the work and taking responsibility for the future, is at least the tolerant humility to admit that good can be done by other hands, and that God can use others to accomplish His work.[52]

This dogmatism is not just inflexible; it dispenses itself from proving anything; it replaces demonstration with gratuitous affirmations or a priori postulates. Does Mr. Le Roy want to convince us that his four objections to dogma are insuperable? He transforms his thesis *into a fact* whose obviousness is such that a demonstration would be superfluous.

It is a fact that anyone (even *among believers*) who has really understood the spirit and the methods of science and contemporary philosophy *can only give his assent to these objections.*[53]

Is the job at hand to establish that our faith in revealed doctrine on God's authority is an "*extrinsecism*" and so "in opposition to the spirit, the attitude, and the method of modern thought"? People are content to affirm without even attempting a proof that nothing *is simpler, nor, in short, more obvious* than the principle of immanence. But let the reader judge; here is what this principle amounts to:

Reality is not made up of distinct juxtaposed pieces; everything is internal to everything else; in the least detail of nature or of science, analysis rediscovers all of science and all of nature; each of our states and each of our acts envelops our entire soul and the totality of its powers; thought, in a word, implies itself as a whole at each of its moments or degrees. In short, there has never been for us a purely external datum resembling I-know-not-what brute matter; such a datum would remain absolutely inassimilable, unthinkable; it would be a "nothing" for us, for where would we get hold of it?

Experience itself is not at all an acquisition of "things" that are at first totally foreign to us; *no, but rather a passage from the implicit to the explicit, a movement in the deep revealing to us the latent demands and the virtual riches in the system of knowing that has already been clarified, an effort of organic development exploiting the reserves or awakening the needs which increase our action.* [And this is what they call "the clearest, the most obvious" of principles.]

Thus no truth ever enters into us unless postulated by what has preceded it under the title of a more or less necessary complement, like a food that, in order to become effective nourishment, presupposes in the one who receives it prior dispositions and preparations, such as the call of hunger and the ability to digest.

52. Le Roy, "Qu'est-ce qu'un dogme," 546–47.

53. Ibid., 506.

Even the establishment of a scientific fact exhibits this character; no fact has a meaning and hence an existence for us except through a theory within which it comes to birth and into which it fits.

I hope Mr. Le Roy will allow us to say that, after these promises of his, we have the right to expect more light. I want to leave discussions of the theories of immanence to others;[54] but even if I must be put under the ban of this philosophy, I continue to think that what we have here is not a clear and evident principle, but a mixed bag of confused affirmations closing off discussion of the most complex problems

- some quite unacceptable for us in their absolute and universal tenor (which nevertheless seems to be the deliberate and wanted tenor) "everything is internal to everything else"—only monism could use such a vague formula
- others true but rapt in clouds
- most of them so vague and imprecise that, depending on the sense one gives them, they can hide a truth or cloak an error—as the theory about the data of experience seems to cloak agnosticism in science.

All, however, are powerless to justify the opposition to dogma raised by modern philosophy. They tell us over and over in a thousand forms: a dogma would be a truth that we did not make and did not find within ourselves. And so? When you confide to me your thoughts so different from mine, or your plans for the future, don't the truths that I am learning from you come to me from outside? Am I the one who made them up or found them in myself? Why can't God's confidences to us about his thoughts, about the free designs of His providence, be learned "from without"? Could they possibly be known any other way? This is the question that theologians have been posing in vain, for a long time, to the philosophers of immanence. Mr. Le Roy pretends that we have never answered his objections except by worthless subtleties or by artifices of rhetoric. In our turn, we observe that Le Roy and Co. have given the theologians no answer except one word: "extrinse-

54. In "On the Nature of Dogma, *Revue biblique* of July 1905, Fr. Wehrlé is publishing a very sharp critique of Le Roy's theories [appearing in this volume as selection 11]; it is all the more remarkable that this learned theologian is himself quite sympathetic to M. Blondel and the school of immanence. He interprets its doctrines in a quite different direction from Mr. Le Roy's system. The *Bulletin de littérature ecclésiastique* of Toulouse is also set to publish a penetrating study of this problem by Fr. Léonce de Grandmaison [given as selection 8 in this volume].

cism"! Is this word supposed to be anything but a subtlety or artifice of rhetoric? Never mind. In no way can it take the place of a proof.

I am more embarrassed to point out another characteristic of these religious discussions. Have they been prepared with enough maturity? To instruct themselves about the doctrines they attack, have people taken the care they would before criticizing a philosophical theory? And yet who can fail to see the incalculable consequences of ill-considered attacks and of systems dreamed up in an hour's reverie? It is trouble cast into souls, perhaps forever. I already understand the protests: "you want to forbid lay people from reasoning out their faith and defending it; you want to make religious knowledge the specialty of a closed caste, closed off from all the currents of modern thought, a caste which mummifies religion and crystallizes it in dead formulas." Well, no; I just want to state a truth of common sense: the primordial law for any writer, be he priest or layman, is to study the problems he seeks to address. Is theological science supposed to be the only one that dispenses people from a serious preparation?

We advise anyone who dares to say so to meditate on the reflections of a judge who is certainly impartial in this matter, a Mr. B. Jacob, professor of philosophy at the university. The French philosophy society was discussing, at its meeting of February 23, 1905, the place to give to *the religious idea in education*. After a speaker named Appühn had concluded to [for? in favor of?] a very active role of the teacher in aiding the young person to become conscious of his religion, a letter by Mr. Jacob combated these conclusions, and here is one of the reasons brought forward:

> You want the teacher to study the dogmas less as an historian than as a philosopher; but it is still necessary that he know the dogmas historically, if his interpretation is not to go astray. So, what chances of error there are! The Catholic dogmatic system, to speak only of that one, is a construction of formidable complexity. How many teachers are there in France, even among historical philosophers or philosophical historians, who know this construction in detail?

And to give an example "of the risks we run when venturing into the theological underbrush," he tells the misadventure of a Mr. Lavisse, who, in a lecture to the students of Fontenay-aux-Roses, made the claim, on the authority of Bossuet, that in Catholic doctrine *faith precedes or rather excludes examination*. But, Mr. Jacob adds, this is an error often condemned by Catholicism in the nineteenth century.

The result is that Mr. Lavisse tried to define Catholicism on the authority of a formula of Bossuet's that, taken literally, is heretical. How many such mistakes will our philosophy teachers commit, the day they want to teach and interpret the principal Christian dogmas?[55]

People can talk if they want to about the "underbrush" of theology; people can regret the complexity and even the subtlety of dogmas; this complexity is a fact that one must not forget, and this fact imposes great hesitancy (and detailed studies) upon anyone who gives himself the mission of reforming the Catholic faith. The writers of recent days—have they taken sufficient account of this law? Alas, the answer is only too clear. What unheard-of confusions are multiplying, even on the most essential and most elementary points of Christianity! With disarming candor, they present to you as the genuine Catholic faith who-knows-what pretended *intuitions*, which have nothing in common with *the testimony of God* (that is, the infantile *extrinsecism* with which all Christians up until now have been so naïve as to content themselves). Or again, they confuse the dogmas with the systems of explanation thought up by the theologians of various epochs. At other times, they attribute to St. Thomas or to Augustine opinions that are utterly contrary to their explicit teaching. People think they are free not to read and not to understand the doctors of Hippo or Aquino. It is a misfortune, I agree; but I can do nothing about it. When one sees a friend of Mr. Le Roy's, for example, a writer as distinguished as he is sincere, affirming and maintaining against all evidence that St. Thomas taught new articles of the faith could be revealed after the death of the apostles—and this in the very article where the great doctor proclaimed the law of the substantial progress of revelation up until Christ, and not thereafter[56]—how can one not deplore a carelessness whose consequences can be so grave?

How also can one fail to be astonished at seeing Mr. Le Roy make his moral explication of dogmas rest upon the absolutely unheard-of theory that dogmatic formulae have a purely negative meaning? According to him, in the order of pure thought, dogmas affirm nothing; they merely deny.

> The dogma has a negative force. It excludes and condemns certain errors rather than determining the truth in a positive way.[57]

55. *Bulletin de la Société française de philosophie* (May 1905): 160f.
56. St. Thomas Aquinas, *Summa theologiae*, I, q. 1, a. 7
57. Le Roy, "Qu'est-ce qu'un dogme," 512.

From a strictly intellectual point of view, it seems to me that dogmas only have the negative and prohibitive meaning of which I have been speaking.[58]

Here again, we can only adopt as our own the criticism made by Mr. Wehrlé:

No, I do not believe that one can say without grave peril to reason that being is to be understood in function of non-being, and that affirmation takes its force from the negation opposed to it. *This is a total reversal of metaphysics and of logic.*

Who, indeed, fails to realize that every negation is at bottom an affirmation? When you say that God does not change, does not die, you are affirming in God a property opposed to change and death.

Nevertheless, it is this ruinous principle of purely negative dogma that Mr. Le Roy makes the foundation for all apologetics—for what objection could even a [ferocious anticlerical like] Séailles or Buisson raise against dogmas that affirm nothing?

The only radical way to cut short all objections-in-principle against dogmas is to conceive them as we have done, as being indefinable as speculative propositions except in relation to prior doctrines upon which they pronounce an unexplained judgment.[59]

But when the foundation collapses, all of apologetics will collapse with it.

And to justify this paradox, how far into the realm of the improbable does this learned philosopher allow himself to be led? Against the most incontestable evidence, he will maintain that dogmatic formulas limit themselves to pronouncing a veto, limit themselves to declaring that "such and such a system does not fit, without otherwise ever indicating why it should not be accepted *or what to replace it with*." In that case, one has never read a collection of the Councils, not even the decrees of the Councils of Trent or Vatican I!

If we challenge him with the blatant positive definitions of Nicaea and Constantinople on the consubstantiality of the Son or of the procession of the Holy Spirit *a Patre Filioque*, he answers, "It is only the grammatical form that is affirmative here; the deeper issue is errors to exclude, rather than theories to formulate." How can one debate such claims?

Ditto for the Apostles' Creed. There, as Mr. Le Roy recognizes, we find nothing negative—but, he adds, nothing properly intellectual and theo-

58. Ibid., 516.
59. Ibid.

retical, nothing relating to the order of speculative knowledge, in a word, nothing that resembles the statement of a theorem. It is a *profession* of faith, a declaration of attitude.

One is truly stupefied by such assertions. Thus to affirm one God, the Creator of Heaven and earth, Jesus the only Son of the Father, His virgin birth, His resurrection, the last judgment, the holy Catholic Church, eternal life—all of that bears no relation to the order of speculative knowledge! And then, after admitting that "the apostolic *Credo affirms the existence of realities* of which it gives no representative theory, not even a rudimentary one," he concludes from this that "its only role in relation to abstract and reflective knowledge is the following: to posit objects and hence problems."[60] As if the mere *affirmation* of these great realities—God, creation, the sonship of Christ, the resurrection—had not been already an entire, sublime doctrine, a treasury of understanding, before it inspired in practice attitudes of the heart.

It remains to point out a final illusion of the partisans of moral dogmatism, the illusion upon which these partisans base their big objection, their invincible objection. "If you keep your intellectualism and your old dogmas, you will have no influence upon the minds of our time. People do not want to hear anymore about absolute truth, immutable truth. You have to choose." Well, for our part, we are never going to choose. How naïve it is to believe that one will have more influence when one has adopted the going agnosticism and thereby reduced oneself to complete powerlessness! To tear down reason under the pretext of going to God through the heart or, as they love to say these days (in a sense that was not Pascal's), "through reasons that the head does not know," is a dangerous game, whose inevitable results we are seeing all too clearly. Maintaining that the existence of God, of the soul, of the future life, is unprovable, outside the scope of our intelligence, is ruining all religion and all faith at its foundation. The experience is upon us, with terrible lessons.

No doubt the new school wants to establish its balance sheet of conquests. We see plenty of Catholics whose faith has been troubled or whose convictions have been weakened by this school. We are still looking for unbelievers whom it has converted. Also, if belonging to our age meant accepting the dominant ideas outside the Church, we should not be going to

60. Ibid., 514.

the philosophy of Mr. Le Roy or Mr. Blondel. We should be going to the serene atheism that is the bottom line of modern philosophy. One should reread with attention the conclusions of Paul Desjardins, or the sad little book of Mr. Hébert on religious *evolution*. Moral dogmatism is nothing but a *last idol*, which logic will overthrow with all the others.

On the contrary, when one contemplates the magnificent mission of Catholic philosophy, the truly unique role that it has been called to play in history up until this very hour, and one sees so many of its well-intentioned representatives using the marvelous resources of their minds to destroy reason, a poignant sorrow pierces one's heart. Never, indeed, have circumstances prepared for Christian philosophy a more glorious triumph than the one offered to us by the frightful disarray of minds outside the Church and the worldwide ruin of all metaphysics and all philosophy.

Ah, who could have told us sixty years ago, when rationalism reproached us so unjustly with putting limits on human intelligence and forbidding it to touch the supernatural mysteries—who could have told us that a day would come when we, the Catholic thinkers, would be almost the only ones to defend reason against its enemies, to take in hand the cause of philosophy, to reclaim for it not only a place in the symphony of human sciences but a special place, the first place, and therefore to avenge philosophy against the sophisms of an entire generation that exiled her from science into the region of dreams and poetic fictions?

And yet such is the true situation. Outside of our ranks, is there a school that fails, in the name of criticism, to cast a stone at human reason? There is no more truth; there is no more philosophy, because there is no more reason. At the 1900 congress for higher education, in the section on philosophy, I took part in a discussion with the most distinguished representatives of the philosophy of our time. The problem was this: should one teach philosophy in the schools? And I heard the masters of contemporary thought proclaim their own decline by proclaiming the decline of all philosophy. There is no more philosophy, they said; there are only *philosophies*. There is no more truth; there are only successive truths. Therefore we do not need to teach philosophy but the history of philosophies, much as a historian unrolls the series of dynasties buried in the necropolises of Egypt or Assyria. I got the sense of the magnificent role that has fallen to our lot, to us Christian philosophers: to enter into the souls of our contemporaries, study their state of unjustified disloyalty to reason; protect ourselves from what may be excessive in certain forms of intellectualism; give back to people the sense of the value of human reason; leave them to recognize, even for moral reasons, a personal God, the provident and supreme legislator of the world; and to lead them from there to faith in Jesus, the God-Man, the founder of the Church—and thus save faith and reason at the same time.

✳

What a splendid role! We wish to hope that it will tempt the noble minds of Messrs. Le Roy, Fonsegrive, Blondel, and their friends. It is certainly not too high for their rare talent and their Christian conviction.

Revue biblique 14 (1905): 323–49

11

"ON THE NATURE OF DOGMA"

J. Wehrlé

When he published in *La Quinzaine* last April 16 an article entitled, "What Is a Dogma?" Mr. Édouard Le Roy claimed that he was formulating a simple question. If he was also the first to propose an answer to it—which he presents as a trial essay—he certainly agrees and perhaps even desires not to remain the only person to take part in the debate he has opened. So, he cannot take it badly that we discuss the theory he outlined, that we contest its rightness and certitude, and that we produce a palpably different solution from the one he suggests.

Also, I am not embarrassed to say up front that the conception of dogma that he advances seems unacceptable to me from a Catholic point of view. But this impression, clear and deep as it may be in me, is not the main reason that convinced me to contradict the distinguished mathematician, who, for some years now, has rightly been attracting the attention of informed minds through his publications in the philosophical field. In the last analysis, it would be untimely for us to reproach him for the part of his recent article that presents itself as constructive, and we would have little ground to be upset about it if we could take it in itself and isolate it from the considerations introducing it. Since it has been offered to us as a free speculation, open to searching critique, it would be easy to replace it, if we find it unfitting, with another, better established, and more satisfying solution. And in fact this is not where the danger is.

What is grave is the attitude that Mr. Le Roy adopts at the outset; for his attitude renders flatly impossible all solutions that are not (under illusory changes of form) of the same species as his own. To be sure, he proclaims that we are not obliged to follow him on the path he is taking, to escape the unbelievers who press him with their arguments. But he only takes this path after having taken care to close all the paths that would lead to a different, liberating outcome. By taking as his own, in the precise form in which he presents them, the difficulties that he takes to be the necessary and legitimate expression of the modern mentality, and by affirming that the modern mind's summary and absolute rejection of dogma stems from genuine rights and from facts no longer disputable, he covertly imposes upon us as ineluctable the position he proposes to us overtly as a pure hypothesis.[1] In short, the problem is formulated in such a way that it is solved in advance, in an incurably negative way, in the very statement of the problem. We are taking hold here of the only genuinely positive datum in the whole article, and we are putting our finger on the genuine danger that it implies—a danger imminent enough and grave enough to alarm many believers who are otherwise wide-open to all the contemporary preoccupations and who are sincerely desirous of all the forms of progress worthy of that name. Well, it is precisely and first off these prejudicial "facts," declared irrefutable, that I contest. I readily grant that Mr. Le Roy's rapid and forcible exposé includes appreciable elements of truth. But I refuse, for my part, to accept it as it stands. The overall conclusion is weakened by a whole series of artificial simplifications, regrettable confusions, unacceptable concessions, and formal mistakes.

There you have the outline of the discussion that I should like to conduct. I shall try in the first place to show that we cannot and should not subscribe to the flat rejections [of dogma]. With the ground thus clear, I

1. [The alleged facts in question are (1) that dogma is unprovable with the proper sort of proof; (2) dogma is unacceptable because received merely on testimony; and (3) dogma is unintelligible because it uses outdated philosophical terminology to try to define the indefinable and because (4) it cannot be integrated with the human sciences.—Tr.]

will then undertake an examination of the theological doctrine proposed, with the intention of criticizing it and putting in its place a more positive and more comprehensive datum.

I

Before taking up individually the four objections that have been put to us, it is important to make some preliminary remarks that cover them all. In a little footnote that is attached to the passage in which he enters upon the topic of dogma (and that appears at the bottom of the third page of his article: 497n1), Mr. Le Roy instructs us "once and for all that by 'dogma' I understand above all the *dogmatic proposition*, the *dogmatic formula*, not at all the underlying reality." Given this declaration, it is impossible to avoid calling his attention to two things.

First of all, in the actual development of the first two "grounds of rejection" attributed to modern thought (that is, up to the end of 503), it is not quite correct to say that the dogmatic formula alone is put into question. In reality, it is the very substance of all Christian dogma that is enmeshed in controversy, compromised, and finally found unacceptable. If I am not mistaken, things go the same in the paragraph that serves to present the fourth and last objection (505). If the argument invoked in these pages of his are admitted as valid, what needs to be modified or renounced is not just this or that doctrinal formulation of revelation but the very object of this Revelation. The object is discarded; it is condemned, and one can no longer adhere to it without committing intellectual suicide. What is at stake, then, is no longer the partial or total bankruptcy of a certain system of obsolete definitions; rather, it is the bankruptcy of the Faith itself insofar as it claims to attain supernatural realities distinctly.

In the second place, it is illegitimate in principle to open up a dichotomy that consists in putting a certain knowable reality on one side and putting on the other side, apart from this known reality, the proposition that conveys it to our knowledge, as if one could envision these two items independently of one another, and as if one could thereby occupy oneself with the second while abstracting from the first. To proceed in this way is to set up the intellectual expression as an entity distinct from the thing expressed, separable and separated from its ontological raison d'être, discussable and discussed in itself as having a consistency of its own and an independent existence. Who can fail to see that, under the banner of reacting against intellectualism, such a dialectic renews and consecrates all the abuses of intellectualism (whose basic vice is to attribute to verbal definitions a sort of real, intrinsic value)? No doubt, Le Roy does not suppress all relation of the sign to the thing signified, and he does not locate the essence of a dogma solely in a series of conceptual constructs that are frankly arbitrary and void of all objective content. He limits himself to understanding by "dogma" *above all* the "dogmatic proposition" or "dogmatic formula" and not at all the underlying reality. But what I am incriminating is precisely this "above all," and the corresponding thought process is what I am denouncing as vitiating the inquiry at its outset and as reversing the genuine order of things by giving preponderance to the sign over the thing signified. Thus he begins by obeying an unconscious intellectualist impulse, and he uses at the outset, in the very posing of the problem, the essential procedure of the intellectualism that he pretends to combat. In a word, he places before us an object that is purely ideational, almost exclusively verbal, and it is this artifact that he holds up to our eyes as the surrogate of dogma, and he invites us to pronounce upon this surrogate, as if what was at stake was not the living and holy reality that it was supposed to express and of which he voided it in advance. It is hardly surprising that it became easy to make us take sides against this ridiculous and detestable idol, which is nothing but a skeleton without muscles, without warmth, without life, without soul. And it is to this that one will be inevitably drawn by a rebound of the inner dynamism whose swing has been determined by an unconscious intellectualism when it touched its spring. Here is the upshot. As one is profoundly anti-intellectualist by deliberate plan and conscious volition, as one therefore counts for little or nothing the abstract formula that one had started out unconsciously making everything, one believes sincerely that one can treat the formulas as puppets in a wholesale slaughter, and one remains persuaded that when one undoes them under the blows of one's criticism, one has made no attack upon the underlying reality. But since in the order of knowledge, where the debate has been placed, the sign is radically inseparable from the thing signified, as the formula cannot be detached from its living origins except by an artificial maneuver that reduces it to a nonentity, it turns out (by the power of a logic more powerful than all one's intentions) that one inevitably attacks and wounds (behind the expressive definition) the very reality that it was expressing and that one wished to spare. The illusion of the good anti-intellectualist faith put at the service of a spontaneous intellectual procedure only absolves the author at the cost of aggravating the disaster to which he comes as to a fatal end result. The mistake in such a case is thinking that the artificial distinction produced at the outset in our mind has the power to dissociate effectively the elements united and welded together, without a backlash in objective reality. Try as you will to say that you mean by "dogma" primarily the dogmatic formula and not at all the underlying reality, this "primarily" and this "not at all" cannot hang together consistently, and one has to clarify the precise sense of this vague reservation he has made on behalf of the reality.[2] If he means to say by this that the transcendent realities have, in themselves, an absolute existence that cannot be subordinated in any case to the knowledge of finite and contingent minds, he has taken a lot of trouble to express a sheer truism in philosophy. If, on the other hand, he calls into question the "underlying reality" insofar as it is knowable and known, if he thus touches upon the conscious relation that can unite us to it, then that reality, whatever one makes of it, remains the very essence of the formula and vanishes with it, if the formula falls. To be sure, the formula remains dependent upon the knowable reality, but the knowable reality is no less linked indissolubly to the formula. The destiny of the one will follow the destiny of the other, as the fate of our thought follows the fate of the wording that expresses it. And hence the dichotomy conceived and worked out by a subjective artifice can have none but a subjective effect. It can safeguard the conscience of the one who practices it, but it cannot take the links that it has severed by an imaginary, fictitious cut and prevent them from subsisting objectively and forming again spontaneously in other minds, on which one cannot impose the same constraint as one does upon oneself. This is why the discredit cast upon the formula entails the ruin of the dogma.

There is more: one will not escape unscathed the servitude of this vio-

2. I cannot fail to insist on the fundamental inconsistency and contradiction of this nevertheless crucial indication that I am handling. The "primarily" and the "not at all" exclude one another inevitably, and hence one must choose between two diametrically opposed meanings. If one maintains the "primarily," the "not at all" is evicted; the result is that (1) the "underlying reality" remains at stake in the debate—and carries incalculable consequences—and (2) that it is implicated secondarily—which is obviously illogical. If, on the other hand, one has the wisdom and the prudence to want to salvage the "not at all," then there is nothing in front of us except formulas that do not refer to any reality and that can neither enhance nor compromise any reality; and thus one arrives at utter insignificance; one enters a battle against phantoms.

lence against nature that one has inflicted upon oneself by a preoccupation to which one must elsewhere pay respect. The inevitable linkage will reform unconsciously in the very mind and under the very pen of the man who cuts the knot. And one will return to putting the reality into the formula, as I indicated above in my critique of the "fact" that corresponds mainly to the first and second objections. The substitution of the dogmatic substance for the formula of the dogma will take place mechanically, and it will turn out in the end that, although one thinks one has not exceeded the limits of a verbal contestation, one will have ruined the whole intellectual edifice of religion.

Under the beneficial influence of these remarks, let us examine the four "grounds of repulsion" that modern thought has against dogma. I hope I do not weaken their force by summarizing them at the outset, so as to provide an overview. Dogma, we are told, is indemonstrable because it is not susceptible to a rational justification that is direct, homogeneous, and decisive;—dogma is unacceptable because the external proof-by-testimony that is provided for it is not of the same nature as the content it is supposed to guarantee;—dogma is unintelligible because it borrows from a philosophical language (which is contestable, obsolete, and already discarded) the terminology for the definitions that try (uselessly) to formulate an inconceivable object;—dogma is incommensurable with the other elements of human knowing—that is, cannot enter into composition with the positive sciences to make a contribution to the general progress of intellectual life. There you have the complete series of arguments invoked. Let us now take them up one by one to make our critique.

1. It is absolutely true that dogma cannot be "proved" in the sense meant here. But there is really no relation between the kind of proofs demanded and the nature of the truths at stake here. The justification demanded is only possible in mathematics and in the sciences strictly bound to mathematics, like physics. Already biology, natural history, geology (to take a few examples) offer notable differences of procedure, and their assertions are no longer verifiable in the fashion of theorems of geometry. Philosophy, which the progress of its own technical organization is more and more turning into a science properly so called, cannot establish its metaphysical and moral data with a rigor sufficient to compel our adherence. "Ethics" presents in the linked series of its deductions a logical chain perhaps unique

in its kind; and yet it is not too much to say that (even if one grants Spinoza his premises) one can legitimately cast off the constraint of its urgent dialectic along the way. We are thus forced to admit in the immense field of human knowledge other types of science than mathematics and other proofs than geometrical demonstrations, but yet valid for a reason. But the objection that we are now criticizing supposes at the outset that there is only one kind of certitude. It implies secondly that the doctrinal affirmations of the Church should be compared to the propositions of the abstract sciences. This again is false. The dogmatic propositions conveying realities and facts that, while transcendent, are also concrete, are diametrically opposed to the ideal order of pure reasoning. We must include that, even if we consider the whole of Christianity as a simple hypothesis, it calls for an entirely different justification. And it is precisely the requirements of modern thought that call for differentiation. By acknowledging "specific" proofs for each intellectual discipline, contemporary reason should recognize a priori that the proofs of revealed religion, if this religion exists, have a distinctive character and belong to an order apart. It would thus be unjust to submit dogmatic affirmations to the "common law" of natural scientific truths, and it would be unjust again to prejudge that the supernatural cannot be an object of science under a special title.

I think that I am authorized, then, to protest from now on against the covert alternative of "all or nothing" that has been placed before us as an inevitable dilemma. We do not have to choose between science's allegedly adequate gnosticism and dogma's presumably radical agnosticism. The problem posed by the world and by life is complex in a different way, and the solution it needs is otherwise complex also. On the one hand, science does not exhaust its object and does not resolve the fundamental mystery opened like an abyss before the human mind by the phenomena that science apprehends and studies; on the other hand, religion cannot accept the summary judgment that forbids it to speak, as being incapable of knowing to any degree the secret of the Invisible and the Beyond. One is allowed to be astonished that Mr. Le Roy, of all people, gives so much credit to science, when he has preached elsewhere a conception of science that one may think far too nominalistic. If mathematics is, as he claims, really nothing but a series of well-connected conventions, if scientific facts and laws always keep a conditional and hypothetical character, it would be regrettable that he has no certitude higher than that which comes to us from this source of information. In reality, contrary to what has been insinuated, science neither proves nor disproves anything speculatively defined as absolute; science does not pretend to justify its postulates or to weaken dogmas. As for modern philosophy, it is very disputable whether it follows the Leibnizian precept to which people allude. It seems rather to distrust the attempts made to prove the axioms. For it senses quite well that, at the very beginning of life, above conscious reflection, there is an element of spontaneity that is in fact the "*primum movens*" of all intellectual and moral activity. The notional attaches to this without giving an adequate account of it. Its incalculable power renders the subject incommensurable with himself. I fail to see, therefore, from the most modern point of view, how one can contradict absolutely and without incoherence the following conclusion:

> It is not necessary these days to be a scholar or a philosopher in order to reject the content of dogma, and neither is it necessary to reject the very idea of dogma because one is a scholar or a philosopher.

It would not be critical thinking to deny a priori that a ray of supernatural light could shed a little clarity upon the enigma that we are to ourselves.

2. With the second objection, we are touching upon a genuine difficulty. One would have to be very ill-informed, indeed, to fail to know that this objection exists and is considerable. In any case, whatever one thinks about how matters should be, there exists a factual situation that one can no longer dispute. It is summed up in the following avowal:

> when we make contact with minds formed under the influence of modern methods, we see that the proofs of religion presented from the outside and by way of authority no longer suffice to win them over.

Mr. Leroy was not the first to be upset by this practical inefficacity or the first to discern its deep cause. He was also not the first, among the Catholics whose thinking counts for something, to understand and to say that, to cure the impotence of our apostolate toward unbelievers and to fulfill all of our duty toward the truth, it is becoming urgent to work for a renewal and an extension of apologetics. It was twelve years ago that Mr. Maurice Blondel gave us his book *Action*, because it was on June 7, 1893, that he submitted his thesis at the Sorbonne. In this first work, by an analysis of life carried out on the strictly philosophical level, he showed how the religious problem poses itself inevitably within each of us. It has been nine years since his "Letter on Apologetics" appeared. Speaking this time as a philosopher and a Catholic at once, he made it clear that the point of view of immanence (conforming to the requirements of modern thought and to the conclusions of a metaphysics of action) corresponds equally well to the a priori data of the Christian faith and to the twofold character (universal and obligatory) of the adult human person's supernatural vocation. The profound thinker and courageous Christian whom I have just named has never in my opinion, at least at bottom, gone beyond his rights as a philosopher and has never misunderstood his duties as a Catholic. Those who have taken the trouble to follow attentively the progressive development of his thought and its successive manifestations certainly do not think they are entitled to hold against him certain excesses of speech that were drawn out of him by an irritating and often unfair polemic. And if I allow myself these remarks, it is not to praise someone, but to indicate something more explicitly. I mean to establish that, in my humble opinion, there is an important element of truth in the point of view of immanence and a perfectly legitimate and orthodox way of adopting it. Nevertheless, the terrain one thereby traverses is perilous. There are limits that one cannot pass and that it is crucial to mark. This is why an explanation is needed to define, in the light of the Church's most formal teaching, the scope within which one may permissibly move.

To begin with, here are the terms in which the problem should be formulated. One must admit that the set of justifications exterior to us, which Catholicism claims for itself, is perfectly probative and even decisive. The integrity and demonstrability of the Object are not in question, then. What we are looking for is a scientific account of a relation between this Object and the human subject, a relation that holds universally, by its nature. For anyone who wishes to reflect carefully, this relation has to be established from the side of the subject. If the search is not motivated from within by an inner law of inadequacy, the search not only cannot succeed but cannot even be undertaken. Even for those who have in hand the Object distinctly revealed, the mere presentation of it cannot suffice, because the marvelous gift that it sets before us (real as it may be proved to be) remains just as "optional" as it is real. And yet we know that it is not optional. If one says that religious authority declares it obligatory by proving it true, one has not resolved the difficulty. In fact, this authority cannot have an intelligible right over the subject, unless the subject has already been converted to the Object, of which this authority itself is a part. The obligation that binds each individual conscience vis-à-vis the Object cannot reasonably exist, then, except on the condition that it is inwardly knowable to this conscience and is manifested in our conscience as applying to it. Thus, the search will set out from the subject, or it will not take place. It presupposes an inner situation that each of us bears within ourselves and that can thus become an object of knowledge. One thereby sees how the point of view of immanence is needed, but one also sees how it limits itself, because it deals only with discovering in the subject the origin and not the terminus of the subject's religious development.

Moreover, in determining this vital point of insertion into us of the objective supernatural, one must draw upon the static conception [of man]—that is to say, the medieval and Scholastic conception. Legitimate in itself, indispensable in its day, and still necessary today in its proper place, this way of looking at the human subject excludes all immanence. Considered as an abstract essence in the status of an ideal datum, or even as a real essence in the status of absolute unchangeability, human nature has no proportion to, and no possible continuity with, what is supernatural and divinizing. The point of view of immanence can only be introduced in the dynamical order. And let us note again with care that it cannot be merely the dynamism of thought or of the "life of the mind" that is in question, as Mr. Le Roy seems to admit. If the discussion is to succeed without impoverishing itself, it must embrace in an inexorable analysis the total development of our multiform activity. This is why Mr. Maurice Blondel called his book *Action* and gave it the subtitle *An Essay in the Critique of Life*. Taken thus in the fullness of its activity on earth, our humanity is no longer alone or purely natural. It continually implies in this very activity the inevitable collaboration of God—a collaboration that must somehow or other contribute to our de facto supernatural calling. Our activity is conditioned by the inheritances that dominate it, by the solidarity that penetrates it, by the destiny that surpasses it. It is precisely the conflict between the static datum and the dynamic exigency that opens the gap through which grace will pass and digs the abyss that grace alone can fill. Then when we name to our fellows, by His distinctly articulated Name, the God who is sending us to them to announce the good news and communicate to them the ineffable gift, the only thing they will have to do is place Him on the altar that every person of good will has had to dedicate in his heart to "the unknown God."

It now becomes easy to characterize the result to which the process I have just summarized should lead. If one chooses to take care, one will recognize that the method of immanence excludes a doctrine of the same name and yields an inevitable call for transcendence. What we are calling "immanent" in the subject is the postulation of this transcendence (at once obligatory for the subject and unachievable by him). The question has only been carried within him in order to force him the more surely to go outside himself. He must not enter back into himself until he has found the divine addition he was seeking. This mysterious reality cannot fulfill his hope unless it surpasses his hope prodigiously. It cannot fail to be, then, an "importation" (properly so called) into us of something infinitely original and sovereignly enriching. And to suggest that this new thing teaches us nothing new, that it gives nothing previously unsaid to our thought, that it puts nothing more-than-human into our action, or that because it is not from us it cannot be for us and claim residency among us—this is what we can never allow to be said without protest. This is what would certainly go beyond the limit that faith and reason alike forbid us to transgress.

Meantime, one must concede that the Sovereign Master of all things can subordinate the reception of the divine gifts to all the conditions it pleases Him to establish. If there exists, then, a normal and visible order in which one communes with transcendent reality under the guarantee of an authorized control and in the plenitude of an official dispensation; if this order commands and invisibly sustains all our unconscious initiatives and all our anonymous participations, the duty is to recognize it, and salvation is to accept it. One has no right to declare it indiscernible under the pretext that there is no passing from the spiritual element to the sensible element, no dependency of the individual datum upon the social datum. The discontinuity that people allege here is contradicted by the most easily observable and the most certainly ascertainable facts. Every day we see thought manifesting itself through material symbols and through an expressivity that we can sense. Every day we notice that particular interest is conditioned by collective organization. This mysterious continuity and this universal dependency impose themselves as a law of humanity. It is not permitted to exclude from it the supernatural, which is just a different and higher specification of the spiritual order. When people quote us that "reality is not made up of distinct slices juxtaposed" and that "everything is interior to everything else," they have to be consistent with these principles and not eliminate the supernatural from reality. In this way, the difficulty that people pose to us, by observing that testimonial or miraculous proof is heterogeneous to what it seeks to confirm, falls to the ground. The Incarnation has established the effective continuity of the Intelligible with the sensible, of the Absolute with the relative. By the same token, the Incarnation has revealed and communicated the supernatural through the social action of a tangible case of human nature that has forever unified, centralized, solidarized all of our contingent cases of human nature. The twofold divine process, at once sensible and social, employed by Jesus and consecrated in Jesus, continues to perpetuate itself in the Church. One cannot maintain that it is not legitimate, coherent, efficacious, and intelligible.

3. There are two parts in the third objection: (A) People tell us first that the dogmatic formulae are bound to certain philosophies by a bond so tight as to make them tributaries of that philosophy. This regrettable dependency is supposed to make our adherence to dogma depend upon a prior conversion to human doctrines that are disputable or false.—One must make bold to respond that this is an obvious exaggeration. On any hypothesis, it will always be necessary to distinguish the verbal conveyance from the meaning conveyed. If one confuses these, one must immediately claim that the same thought cannot be translated into several languages. And indeed, one does not see how an obsolete scientific terminology or a term borrowed from a dead language can impede our discerning the definite meaning that they had in the minds of those who used them. There is no question, then, of converting to philosophies; rather, we need to conserve and comprehend the truth that the systemizing and the vocabulary of those philosophies allowed people to formulate with higher precision than they could with their empirical vocabulary. It would also be important not to lump together under the same critique both the fundamental data of the faith and the sometimes trivial details of theological explication.—(B) On top of this first complaint, people add that (even from the point of view of the philosophy used in a dogmatic definition) the dogmatic expression can have no value but that of a metaphor (since the reality that this expression undertakes to convey in concepts

is literally unthinkable).—If the theological considerations that I am about to invoke can establish anything, they will show precisely how unacceptable and false is such a manner of conceiving dogma. But for the moment, I call attention again to the purely logical and intellectualist alternative of all or nothing that is being imposed upon us. Between the two extremes of this sort of religious mathematics, there is a middle position that allows us to discover the genuine solution. No, to be sure, we cannot think the dogma adequately and intrinsically; but it is false to say that a dogma is not thinkable "at all" and that the converging efforts of religious life and theological reflection will not succeed in clarifying the dogma's content progressively. I continue to believe that plenty of believers are in a position to "define with precision what they affirm and what they deny."

4. The final difficulty, drawn from the incommensurability of dogmas, will not seem very solid if one ponders the fact that the transcendent character of the reality they express takes away any constrictive tendency that their immutability would suggest. One might as well say that God cannot be taken as an object of knowledge without becoming an obstacle to progress. Moreover, the objection overlooks totally the complex relation (and the reciprocal solidarity) that permit us to unite, in a vital synthesis achieved by action, intellectual data pertaining to different levels. This latter point of view shows even better the injustice of the reproach hurled against us. For, on the one hand, the believer finds his adherence to dogma no obstacle to the free scientific research that is by hypothesis of another order; he can thus concur with all his might toward the progress of human knowing, and he can contribute his part to the development of the very dogma whose content he lives without ever exhausting its meaning but rather discovering ever new riches in it. On the other hand, since dogma is not a source of knowledge except by being a source of action, as the transcendent knowledge it represents should normally translate itself into more-than-human virtue, dogma is a source of moral fecundity; the believer who actualizes his faith thereby renders an appreciable service to a society that exists not merely to know the secrets of nature but that can only know those secrets on the condition that it [the society] exists and that only truly exists through self-denial, devotion, and love. Finally, it is important to clear away anything that looks like an equivocation on the specific raison d'être of the religion in which dogma forms an integral part. Religion has as its proper, direct, and

main goal to prepare people for eternity and to conduct them to heaven. It is no surprise, then, that dogma, insofar as it is a knowledge, is oriented toward the invisible world, which cannot coincide at every point with the world in which we live. So then, one must either disavow religion as illegitimate or else accept the fact that dogma renders only indirect services to *this* world's "intellectual life."

The preceding considerations suffice to show why I refuse, for my part, to concede Mr. Le Roy any of the points that he regards as settled. When he proclaims that he is going to expound the current objections of modern thought in "all their force," he does not say enough. He gives them a great deal more force than they have. Instead of combating the prejudices and clearing up the misunderstandings that they presuppose, he aggravates the blind hostility whence they proceed by presenting the object that they attack under a false light. Yes, it seems incontestable that people on our side have committed regrettable intellectualist abuses in their exposition and their defense of Catholicism. Denouncing these abuses is just doing a useful service. In this case, the good strategy would have been to show the mistake of those who attribute to abstract knowledge a preponderant role and an independent value. It would have been necessary above all to discard their compromising apologetics, which does not commit the Church and which even betrays the genuine spirit of the great Thomist theology to which they appeal. In place of the strategy just indicated, Le Roy and company start out by positing the most violently intellectualist notion of dogma that one can imagine, as if it were the only genuine notion, or even the only possible notion. From this original theme, already exaggerated, they then draw by abstract reasoning deductions that are more outrageous still. From that there comes a doctrinal reaction in the opposite direction, which condemns religion to being nothing more than an intellectual agnosticism and a moral empiricism. Such is in fact the twofold conclusion of the article we are studying. It remains for me to discuss the value of those conclusions.

II

Mr. Le Roy thought he had established that Catholic believers and their opponents found common ground in that they both admitted (without noticing it) "a neatly intellectualist conception" of dogma. Thereafter, he did not have to examine whether this reproach is well-founded and to what extent he had gratuitously created the object he criticizes by the way he presents the public with these "sides" and their anonymous theories. If there is intellectualism, I heartily join him in deploring it. But let us now leave aside the facts that each side interprets in its own way so as to make them complacent and docile supports for the cause defended. Let us likewise set aside the expressions that are incurably likely to stir up a pejorative meaning, such as this unhappy "intellectualism," which names an abuse in any case. By dwelling on the excesses or deformations of thought, one may end up suggesting that the human mind is incapable of justice and balance, like those professors of psychopathology who, haunted by the sight of their patients, end up losing the notion of sanity and denying its existence. Let us rather turn our attention to a new objective, and let us take up the perspective of a sound judgment regarding a question of right. Here is how I am transposing the statement of the problem:

Yes or no, when one tries to define the nature of dogma, is one right or is one wrong to view it as the intelligible expression (and hence the intellectual expression) of a set of realities or facts belonging to the order of revealed religion?

So formulated, the question subdivides into two distinct parts and calls for two successive examinations. We need to know first whether Revelation teaches us anything. If it seems that we must answer in the affirmative, it will remain for us to see whether this "something" it teaches us can have a meaning for us.

I posit first-off, as a fact, that "God has spoken," literally. I take issue with the tenor of the footnote appearing at the bottom of page 509, where Le Roy declares that this way of speaking is a metaphor. To be sure, the theophanies of the Old Testament are not all to be interpreted literally and put on the same level. Nevertheless, unless one implicitly denies biblical inspiration, one must perforce admit that even in Israel's history prior to Christ there was a manifestation of God's thoughts and feelings. That this occurred under forms appropriated to our humanity and assimilable by us, that these forms constitute a discursive and temporal rendering of what is pure and eternal Act in the Infinite Being—[there is] no doubt about it. Even so, it remains true that the Church, by making us say and sing that "the Holy Spirit spoke by the prophets," intends to indicate a positive divine locution. I will ultimately abandon, if you insist, everything pertaining to the Old Testament and so needing a more delicate, more complicated, and more controversial exegesis. I prefer to cut matters short, going straight to what is more clear and more certain. The Incarnation fulfills in a transcendent fact the strict truth of the "anthropomorphic" formula Le Roy incriminates as having a figurative sense difficult to unravel. The absolute Divinity of Christ makes the fact that "God has spoken" sensible, a fact of this world, in an immediate way. So if there is a "difficulty" hereabouts, it does not reside in the fact that God used human lips to speak to human beings in a human language, but lies rather in the fact that this distinct and articulated word rang out at a definite point in space and time, causing a group of Jews with a definite mentality to understand truths that hold good universally, eternally, and absolutely.

But this aspect of the problem is not currently under discussion. It is rather the content of the divine message that we have to define. In the all-merciful and gratuitous communication to which God has resorted, [which of the following is the case?] has He unveiled what we could not acquire by the sole effort of our mind, or, in conversing with us, has He said nothing for which we did not already have a presentiment and an implicit notion? Once again, this is what we must now clarify. However, it is easy to discern within the revealed teaching three distinct and ascending orders of truths. First of all, we are admitted to penetrate the secret of God's intimate life, and He has allowed us to see in the very bosom of the indivisible Unity a mysterious Trinity of relations. Apprehension of this absolute ontological datum is radically inaccessible to human reason left to its own devices. When we pass on from this first order to the second, we see one of these Three-who-are-One descend to earth by taking to Himself an individual nature identical to our own. The Absolute establishes Himself directly in the relative. This divine Act, which achieves the synthesis of the Infinite with the finite, is the revelatory act *par excellence*. However, it can only be revelatory on the condition that it is itself revealed. And, as the object manifested and at the same time the source of the manifesting, it constitutes a new datum inaccessible to our grasp. No doubt, the Incarnation offers at first a metaphysical aspect by which it claims the attention of philosophy. But on the other hand, it is not knowable as a fact except through a supernatural promulgation—that is to say, by the religious path. And I remark in passing that we are touching here upon the exact point that will someday serve, perhaps, as the locus for the linkage of philosophy and religion. Still, and this suffices for our present inquiry, the Incarnation is a reality impenetrable to rational investigation, which we apprehend as a new thing through revealed teaching. Finally, there is a third order of transcendent truths. The Son of God espoused our humanity only in order to permit us to share eternally in His Divinity. He only descended to us in order to make us rise up to Him. The condescensions of infinite Love that have come to us on a prevenient basis have effected a transposition of the creature to a level to which created things could have no access. Destined by nature to be irremediably subjected to God, a slave, a stranger, an alien, the creature has become filial, participant, received, assimilated. This merciful design puts us in possession of a gift so transcendent that, even when it is present in us, it cannot be known by us except through an explicit notification from God. We need an authentic and official certificate of our adoption, without which it will always be unknown to us. Until our Creator tells us that He is our Father, He remains for us solely our Master. Jesus alone could place upon human lips the ineffably tender expression that begins the greatest of prayers. Still today, hearts formed by the Church are the only ones that can put into their language the right note and the deep accent of this filial confidence. But one finds that this mystery of our divinization commands and embraces all the other elements of Catholic doctrine: grace, the fall, redemption, the sacraments, the Church. All these data that together form the third order are thus again unpublished matter that could only be published for us through a supernatural publication. One may say, then, that from the beginning to the end of this catalogue of the three orders, it is a question of truths such that "God has reserved to Himself alone the right to teach them to us."[3] The phraseology is from Pascal, and it consecrates what I should like to establish—namely, that God has taught us something.

Are we in a position to discover a meaning in it? This is the second part of the question. People tell us that these realities are so far above us that the propositions that try to convey them are inadequate to their object. We are all in agreement on this point. The Church is more zealous than anyone to maintain the incomprehensibility of the Christian mysteries. This is precisely why she calls them mysteries. She proclaims aloud that "by their very nature they surpass created understanding" and that they always remain

3. Pascal, *Pensées*, a. 24.

for us here below "enveloped, as it were, in a certain obscurity." Nevertheless, the Vatican Council that formulated these indispensable reservations is also quite positive about the relative intelligibility of these same truths. "Reason," it says, "enlightened by the faith, when it searches with care, piety, and discretion can arrive by the help of God at a certain very fertile understanding of the mysteries." If I am not mistaken, this amounts to saying that one must not confuse the two notions of being-incomprehensible and being-unintelligible. Human knowing can attain an object effectively without having an "adequate" [that is, exhaustive] apprehension of it. Between knowing nothing and penetrating to the bottom, there is thus a middle level capable of giving satisfaction to the mind.

I must observe furthermore that at least some of the reflections that people bring forward go further than they seem to realize. The passage from the *Summa contra Gentiles* that Mr. LeRoy quotes (513) is about defining the divine substance. But it seems to me that there is a question of theodicy here, which has helped and can still help the natural effort of purely philosophical speculation. As soon as human thought turns to the First Cause, it has before it the abyss of the infinite Being whose "*quid proprium*," special characteristic, is aseity. Catholic dogmatics is in no way to blame for the immeasurable depth of this problem, which belongs to the natural order before it belongs to the revealed order. If such depth is the reason one slaps an interdict on theology, philosophy must be equally condemned. Likewise, the personhood of God is a badly chosen example for putting dogma on trial. The question raised by it is susceptible to being studied anterior to any revealed proposition. Reason has a perfect right to work on this matter. Vatican I has implicitly declared that reason's effort in this direction is not sterile. The Council says that "by the natural light of human reason, one can know in a certain way the one and true God, our Creator and Master." Well, this notion of God that the Council says our understanding has the natural power to form—does it not presuppose personhood? The idea of personhood implies above all two elements whose realization can provide ever so many degrees and that we assume to be realized infinitely in God: namely, self-consciousness and independence. It is difficult to admit that God is truly the author and sovereign of His creatures, as the previously quoted text affirms, if one does not admit at the same time that He has a clear consciousness of Himself and a total independence. In a word, according to the

Council, as best as I can judge, reason is supposed to be capable of conceiving Him as personal. Hence, and once again, to declare that the notion of personhood applied to God is completely meaningless is to put reason on trial as much as the Faith; it is to attack philosophy as well as dogma.

A second remark is needed about the mode of human knowledge relating to revealed dogmas. People seem to forget that, for the believer at least, it is not naked reason that tries to find a meaning in the mysteries. The supernatural economy does not consist exclusively of proposing an object from without but also of activating the subject from within. In both cases, the procedure used is supernatural. When put in the presence of a truth that surpasses us, we are helped to perceive it in a manner suited to it. Also, when Vatican I declares the mysteries intelligible to some extent, the Council takes care to specify that it is "reason enlightened by the faith" that can arrive at knowing them a bit. Conversely, the human mind left to its own strength and placed in front of revealed doctrine can remain blocked and fail to see clearly. Jesus Christ spoke to his disciples about many topics that remained a closed book for them. It had to come to pass that "the Consoler, the Holy Spirit, sent by the Father in His Name, should teach them all things and intimate to them the meaning of all that He had said" (Jn 14:26). So even when Christians fail to make everyone understand the hidden sense of the truths they profess, one is not authorized to conclude that those truths mean nothing for them and that they do not possess a partial understanding of them.

To be sure, one must maintain that human reason, even when enlightened by the faith, can never perceive the Christian mysteries "in the mode of the real things which constitute their proper object."[4] But to penetrate the mystery to some extent, we have at our disposal the means to which the previously mentioned Council often draws our attention, very judiciously. Analogy permits us to compare the realities of the supernatural order with the realities of the natural order that we perceive directly. Moreover, we have every ability to connect the different data of revelation one to another and to relate them all together to the ultimate end of man. There you have a very complex task, which I am not undertaking to analyze here. One will find valuable indications on this subject in the opusculum that St. Thomas

4. Vatican I, Constitution *Dei filius*, c. 4. [Denzinger, nos. 3015–20; 3041–43].

Aquinas devoted to Boethius's book on the Trinity.[5] The results that one achieves by such work secure for the human mind at least the beginnings of satisfaction. Analogy well employed gives an intelligible meaning to each of the articles of the Catholic faith. The synthesis of all these elements, a synthesis in which some elements compensate for others, forms in the end a perfectly coherent and balanced system. One finds in it answers to the most serious questions we can ask ourselves. If science explains to some extent the visible world, religion thus understood explains in turn the invisible underpinnings of universal reality. It goes further: it gives some presentiment of what will be someday "new heavens and a new earth" for us,[6] which "the whole visible creation" is preparing "in groans and labor pains."[7] The process of analogy even allows the Christian who uses all his reason and all his faith to know something, if not of God's substance, then at least of what we may call His attributes. One must beware of using the pretext that He is incomprehensible to declare unintelligible the One who is naturally and supernaturally the source of all intelligibility. For, as Mr. Ollé-Laprune remarks, "if the human serves to symbolize the divine, the divine alone renders the human intelligible."[8] Having this truth of divine priority in mind will be enough to give these formulas of Leibniz their full value as contributing to the knowledge of God: "Minds are images of the Divinity itself, or of the very Author of nature; each mind is like a Divinity in its own area."[9] There is thus a real analogy that goes from God to us, and our conceptual analogy only retraces it by a movement in the opposite direction. For us, this analogy is twofold, because it embraces at once the order of nature and the order of grace. Also, when we in Christian language describe God as Master, King, Father, Friend, and Spouse, we are saying something true and intelligible about Him. We are conceiving Him under real aspects of His real relation with us, and these different aspects, far from excluding or supplanting each other, complement each other to enrich our knowledge. It is not just metaphysical meditation on the Trinity that sheds a glimmer of light on the supreme mystery. Of course, human sight, however enlightened by grace, will never be able to pierce the veil that hides, at

5. Aquinas, *In Boethii de Trinitate*, q. 2, on the manifestation of God's knowledge.

6. Is 65:17, 66:22. 2 Pt 3:13; Rv 21:1.

7. Rom 8:22.

8. Léon Ollé-Laprune, *La philosophie et le temps présent* (Paris: 1890), chap. 1.

9. Gottfried Wilhelm Leibniz, *Monadology* (1714), §83.

the center of the eternal temple, the holy of holies. But by the same token one cannot say that the Christian will remain inevitably in the court of the Gentiles and that he will never have any access to the quarters reserved for the children of the house.

Thus I think I am authorized from now on to affirm that the divine message has a meaning for us. Insofar as dogma is an intellectual expression of revealed realities, it must be held to be intelligible. It remains for us to describe the knowledge to which dogma gives rise. Shall we mark the result thus obtained with the sign for positive quantities or with the sign for negative ones? The answer to this last question is implicitly contained in the whole set of considerations I have just been making. No, I do not think one can say, without grave danger to reason, that being should be conceived in function of nonbeing and that an affirmation draws its value from the negation to which it is opposed. That is a complete reversal of metaphysics and of logic. The claim that error may often provide the occasion, in all branches of knowing, that determines a more decisive or more explicit manifestation of the truth, I admit without difficulty. But this concession must not be extended to the very bottom of things and must not apply to the real movement of thought. One must resolutely allocate to dogmatic conceptions and propositions the plus sign. Also, people should not allow themselves to be misled by the negative form presented outwardly by the canons of the Councils. In a *relatio* of Msgr. Gasser, bishop of Brixen—a *relatio* included in the full dossier of Vatican I—he clearly specified that between the dogma presented in the chapters of the dogmatic constitution and the doctrine in the canons attached at the end, there is no difference but the mode of declaration. The positive form of the doctrine in the body of the Constitution is fully obligatory for the belief of the faithful. Indeed, it takes all the resources of Mr. Le Roy's dialectic and talent to even try to maintain that the Apostles' Creed has as its clearest result the "posing of problems." The first preachers of the Gospel were conscious of giving very firm and very enlightening answers to the questions posed by the religious conscience of humanity. If the idea of a problem could have arisen in their mind, it would have been to produce there the certitude that they held the solution. This is why they gave Christian affirmation the absolute character it has kept ever since and that it cannot ever lose without destroying itself. They handed over to the Church's first believers all the substance of the sacred deposit, which is not a meteorite but a living truth. Hence it would be strange if interior experience and theological speculation working on these original and fundamental data were to give them a negative character. Quite the contrary, by bringing more and more to light the inexhaustible richness of the divine treasure, living experience and speculation have yielded more and more positive explications. I think there is no more reason to believe that the results should bear a minus sign when people let themselves believe that the results are gotten by the *via negationis*. It is easy to understand that what is negative in this "way" is the procedure and not the conception that it yields. The things that get denied here are themselves negations, and in the end one always poses a stronger affirmation of a richer reality. Far, then, from minimizing the formulas and dissolving their content into a ruinous indefiniteness, one must always enlarge the formulas in the precise direction of their statement and maximize their content in the definite direction of the perspectives opened up before us. In the last analysis, I maintain that the revealed dogmas not only have a meaning for us but also that this meaning is formally positive.

Turning now to a consideration of the examples invoked to sustain the thesis of doctrine's negative intellectual value, I start with the first. It deals with God's being a person. I explained previously why the choice of this specific example seems debatable to me. But now I am taking it up as it stands. We have seen that the notion of personhood involves above all two elements: self-consciousness and independence. In our experience of life, we acquire a quite clear idea of each of these two elements. At the same time, the same living experience shows us that we possess the one and the other imperfectly and to variable degrees. We therefore conceive distinctly that there can exist an open-ended increase in consciousness of one's own being and in independence from other beings. Given that much, we affirm two things about the infinite Being: first, that He has self-consciousness and is independent of all other beings; second, that this consciousness, infinite as He Himself is, perfectly matches His Being, and that His independence vis-à-vis everything created is sovereign and absolute. Doesn't one have the right to say that these are positive data, having a precise meaning for our mind and having sufficient meaning to ensure that, when divine personhood is mentioned, we are not debating with ourselves in the shadows, without a ray of light?

In the resurrection of Christ, which is dealt with in the next example, people see nothing but "a simple metaphor impossible to convert into precise ideas."—But the initial issue is not to imagine a resurrected body as one perceives by the eye a mortal body. Before all else, one must pronounce on a different point of capital importance. Prior to all speculation over how to conceive an essence, we have to take a stand on the affirmation of an existence. We can form later the best idea we can of the reality, but we have to say beforehand whether, apart from all subjective representation, this reality exists as real. In a word, we must know whether we admit that Christ is risen and that we shall rise again one day after His example. But if, for Christ and for us, the resurrection is not a regaining of the body, then it is nothing at all, and there should be no more talk about it. By teaching us distinctly that, on the one hand, we have an immortal soul and, on the other hand, that our body is reserved for the resurrection, the Church indicates that the immortality of the soul is one thing and that the resurrection of the body is another. The resurrection is thus a physical and corporeal reality, or else it is nothing but a metaphorical transposition of the immortality of the soul—that is, a pure nothing. Hence, what collapses is our faith, once we subtract the mystery that, according to St. Paul, serves as its foundation.—Now, how should we conceive a resurrected body? People tell us that this is the thing that is unintelligible for us. So suppose we hang back a minute from this difficulty, which has been declared insurmountable. Will we be any better off? We will still have to conceive the immortality of the soul, which is too positive a reality to be reducible to a metaphor. Will this be easier? I doubt it. The idea of a body made marvelously subtle seems easier to admit for creatures with senses than the idea of a soul continuing to exist independently of its body.—Now let us go back to the resurrection and see if it is really impossible to conceive. What I notice is that Mr. Le Roy takes as essential signs and factors of physical life all the scars and flaws that are its earthly limitation. If we take vulnerability to suffering and death as the complete and supreme expression of every bodily organism, we arrive perforce at an impasse, and we can no longer find any satisfying notion of a glorified body. This is why it would seem logical to work in the other direction. Then we will take pains to eliminate one after another all of the ideas that represent deficient elements of physical life. We shall put aside the grossness and heaviness of our flesh, fatigue, sickness, old age, and the many needs that press upon our flesh like a yoke of servitude. Then, we shall conceive more and more positively that there can exist a more elevated state of corporeal matter. We shall begin to glimpse a situation of perfect harmony in which the sensory energies grouped into an organism will be submitted to the domination of the soul, like a numerous and docile people. We shall glimpse finally that this marvelous equilibrium can last eternally. Once again, by the *via negationis*, we shall have stripped away limits and reached a positive result. And if we are not fully satisfied, it suffices to remind ourselves that the resurrection is a mystery.

I come now to the third example. It is drawn from Eucharistic doctrine. People seem to think that the Church has limited herself to affirming the real presence of Christ without making the notion more precise in any way. This is a factual error. The modality of the real presence has certainly been specified by the conciliar definitions of Trent. Canon 1 from Session XIII deals mainly with the theory of the "Sacramentarians," who reduced the Eucharist to being a symbol or figure. Nevertheless, this first canon does a great deal more than condemn Zwingli and Oecolampadius; it reproves explicitly the conception of Calvin, who professed a "dynamic presence"; and the canon affirms that Christ is present in the whole of His reality. Is this the end of it? No. The Lutheran theories of impanation and consubstantiation do not exclude the notion of the real presence, and yet Canon 2 from the same session explicitly disavows them. If one thinks, then, that the obligatory definition of faith touches only upon the fact of the real presence, one is deceiving oneself. The definition equally addresses the modality of the fact.—On another front people exaggerate the relation of dependency between the doctrine of transubstantiation and Scholastic philosophy. Leave aside for the moment "substance," because it can easily become a bugbear. Let us summarize what is really implied by the solemn decisions of the Church. (1) The reality of the bread ceases to exist; (2) the reality of the Body of Christ begins to exist; (3) between these two successive facts, there is an intimate connection of reciprocal final causality (the reality of the bread ceasing to be because Christ is produced, and Christ being produced or beginning to be sacramentally because the reality of the bread ceases to be); (4) after the Body of Christ has been produced, the sensible appearances of the bread remain. If we admit that a passage from the first of these points to the second cannot take place without "a marvelous change," we have thereby accepted all of the obligatory doctrine. I want to know what is the substantialist or realist philosophy (apart from pantheism) that cannot accommodate these essential data.—Finally, the "conceptual" notion that we have of a being's presence is constituted by something quite different from the distinctly perceived empirical characteristics of physical action or of a spiritual influence. For the Eucharist as for the resurrection, people are forgetting that the affirmation of the fact is itself a concept. I repeat that one can know existences of things without knowing intrinsically the essences of the things one affirms to be real. True human knowledge is synthetic, global, and practical; and the certitude that it brings with it, however difficult it may be to theorize about, is nevertheless decisive and sure. We know that a human being is standing in front of us, without needing to define scientifically what a human being is, and what local presence is. One can know, then, in the proper sense of "know" that Jesus is there without perceiving adequately all that He is and how He is there.

To be sure, there has been progress in the theological systematization of the faith. For the doctrine of the Eucharist in particular, one can (if one works at it) distinguish a first period, which was like the primary state of the dogma, and a second period, which would stand to the dogma as its secondary state. If Mr. Le Roy just wishes to say that the spiritual efficacity of the revealed object should not be measured by the philosophical precision of our knowledge, he is perfectly right. The earliest Christians, using formulas that seem to us imperfect or implicit in some regards, communicated in the divine reality as much as our contemporaries do and as much as the disciples of St. Thomas Aquinas did. On a different level of ideas, certain dogmas can have been fitted into formulas whose original redaction underwent the influence, perhaps, of cosmic conceptions now thoroughly discredited by the progress of science. The "descent" into hell is a case in point and could give rise to a long dissertation. But it will always be easy to disengage a substantial and properly religious datum, which one makes independent of the obsolete element in the formula that served to express it. Likewise, by declaring that Jesus "ascended" into heaven with his glorified humanity, the Church does not oblige us to profess the outdated theory of the empyrean heaven of the ancients. The difficulties that people try to throw at us on this subject are not ones capable of ruining Catholicism. Rather, it was the far more gratuitous difficulties mentioned previously that persuaded Le Roy to propose a moral and practical interpretation of dogmas. The affirmation of God's personhood is thus supposed to mean, "Behave in your relations with God as you do in your relations with a human person." It would be truly useless to combat metaphysical anthropomorphism by falling into a moral anthropomorphism just as bad. I do not see what we gain by this new formula. The resurrection is supposed to signify mainly that we should conduct ourselves toward Jesus as we do toward a person living in the current life. To say the least, that is requiring of us altogether too much or too little. From the Eucharistic doctrine, he draws an analogous conclusion: it is enough for us to take up "an attitude towards the consecrated host identical to the one we would take towards Jesus made visible." There is no need to dwell on the danger that would come with adopting such a proposition.

Such dangerous concessions—would they at least establish and safeguard the *primacy of action*? I do not think so. Le Roy admits in effect that the moral attitudes or cultic procedures previously defined by the Church should be adopted by us as a matter of obligation. But then what is the basis for this obligation? It is the *knowledge* of a dogmatic proposition published by the Church, behind which one admits that there is a reality capable of justifying the required practices. The relation between the reality addressed by a formula and a formula that promulgates it without manifesting it is already a strange relation—as is the relation between that reality and a proposition that expresses it in words, even though these words fail to present a precise and intelligible meaning. What is even more astonishing is that a formula that has become powerless to grasp and convey its divine object keeps the regulatory power to put the human subject under a law of blind obedience. Worst of all, however, is the shipwreck of the primacy of action, which despite everything goes down with all hands in this adventure. For the knowledge of dogma (whose description as "diminished knowledge" does not prevent it from remaining knowledge) is what sets our whole religious life in motion. It remains the "*primum movens*" of our morality and of our ritual. By an otherwise profitless abandonment, Le Roy has thus left standing a priority and a supremacy of knowledge over action. He has eliminated from dogma all intelligible data and removed from our knowledge all intellectual value, without having succeeded in removing the fact that dogma determines morality and commands practice. Where is the primacy of action in all of that?

It is important, nevertheless, to respect and defend (if not the primacy, then) at least the legitimate rights of action. These rights protect the interests of knowledge, because action is the crucible in which true human knowledge is built up—living and vivifying knowledge because it is experiential and lived. Why not divulge my whole thought? What seems to me most regrettable in the work of Mr. Le Roy (otherwise inspired as it is by sincere and noble concerns) is that it compromises the cause it wants to serve. The agnostic and indefinable praxis-ism that he proposes raises justified alarms. How can one not mistrust the consequences of this half-blind moral empiricism, whose individualism ruins the social organization of Catholicism? Le Roy is thus paving the way for a counteroffensive by intellectualism—while Maurice Blondel has so happily opposed intellectualism with his metaphysical pragmatism. In this latter we find a remarkably balanced system that preserves the equilibrium between thought and action, knowledge and practice, metaphysics and morals, dogma and religious experience. Le Roy and company destroy the harmony of this complex synthesis by a one-sided doctrine that is excessive and visibly dangerous.

Given the many and intertwining problems that are in play here, I am going to allow myself in conclusion just to pick out a certain number of propositions that seem to me to be settled and sure.

If we adopt a point of view uninfluenced by any immediate religious preoccupation, and we examine the whole dynamism of our interior life from that point of view, we shall ascertain the following points.

(1) When we keep the words "action" and "thought" in their vague and current meaning, there is neither a primacy of action in our life nor a primacy of thought, but an alternating rhythm of action and thought in which action sometimes goes ahead of thought, and sometimes thought precedes action. This oscillating movement is a sufficient guarantee that neither of these factors ever retains the upper hand, and neither remains the only one at stake. (2) When we look more closely, there is not action and thought but thought and thought. Action is an unconscious or vague thought in motion toward the reflective and distinct idea that will reveal the content it originally had. The idea in turn is just an intellectual fulfillment of action. The genuine problem confronting a philosophy of action will thus be the relation of spontaneous and enacted thought to willed and acting thought. (3) In this alternating series of successive unstable balances, each moment,

viewed in its relation to the preceding moment, represents a synthesis that goes beyond the empirical datum of the component elements from which it was born. Thus, no new synthesis is entirely reducible to the antecedent states; none can be viewed legitimately as the "sum" in an addition in which the anterior states provided the summands. While appearing to arise from below, the idea thus also and already is proceeding from above. Hence again, there is within us the collaboration of an Other who causes us continually to discover what He already knows. A metaphysic of action is thus possible, and this metaphysic, as a fruit of life, is called to become a source of transcendent life. But up to this point, everything is going on within our interior and is nothing but the putting to work of continuous and subjective data.

The level of perspectives is quite different when one moves on to our conscious relation with Christian Revelation. This time, the knowledge, even the primitive knowledge, no longer builds itself up in our immanence but penetrates positively into us from outside and constitutes an "importation" properly so-called. Nevertheless, action is going to resume its rights. The only reason supernatural truth is proposed to us intellectually is so that it might be lived by us totally; it is admitted from the outside solely in order to make us become consubstantial [with it] under the action of an interior principle of assimilation; it only sheds light on us in order to have light shone on it in turn by us. Also, when the Church defines it, she acts in reality with the vital concurrence of all her children. Revelation, initially a source of individual knowing, and then a source of action and life, finishes up by becoming a source of organized knowledge. This supreme outcome is obtained by the immense effort of the Christian collectivity in its entirety. This holy society is always causing the living deposit received from God to bear fruit, and it is always making the inexhaustible truth of Christ rise higher above the horizon of humanity.

BIBLIOGRAPHY

Aquinas, Thomas. *Divi Thomae Aquinatis Opera omnia*. 34 vols. Paris: Vivès, 1871–80. Hereafter: *Opera*.

———. *Summa theologiae: Prima pars*. In *Opera*, vol. 1 (1871).

———. *Summa theologiae: Secunda secundae*. In *Opera*, vol. 3 (1872).

———. *Summa contra Gentiles*. In *Opera*, vol. 12 (1874).

———. *In Boethii de Trinitate*. In *Opera*, vol. 28 (1875).

———. *Quaestiones disputatae de potentia Dei*. In *Opera*, vol. 13 (1875).

———. *Quaestiones disputatae de veritate*. In *Opera*, vol. 15 (1875).

Augustine. *Epistola 238*. In Patrologia latina, ed. Jacques-Paul Migne. Vol. 33. Paris: Vrayet, 1841ff. Hereafter: PL.

———. *Sermones 212–16*. In PL, vol. 38.

———. *De fide rerum quae non videntur*. In PL, vol. 40.

———. *De Trinitate*. In PL, vol. 42.

Bainvel, Jean Vincent. *La foi et l'acte de foi*. Paris: Lethielleux, 1898.

Batiffol, Pierre. "L'Idée de l'église dans le Nouveau Testament." *Revue biblique* 5 (1896): 360–380.

———. "À propos de Richard Simon." *Bulletin de littérature ecclésiastique* 2 (1900): 257–268.

———. "L'Évangile et l'Église." *Bulletin de littérature ecclésiastique* 5 (January, 1903): 3–15. English translation in this volume.

———. "Jésus et l'église." *Bulletin de littérature ecclésiastique* 5 (1903): 27–61. English translation in this volume.

———. Jésus et l'histoire. Paris: Lecoffre, 1904.

———. *Études d'histoire et de théologie positive*. Vol. 2, *L'Eucharistie: La présence réelle et la transsubstantiation*. Paris: Lecoffre, 1905.

———. *L'Enseignement de Jésus*. Paris: Bloud et Cie, 1909.

———. and Alfred Vacant, "Apôtres (Symbole des)." Vacant, Alfred., Eugène Mangenot, and Émile Amann, eds. *Dictionnaire de théologie catholique*. Volume I/2. Paris: Letouzey et Ané, 1900.

Beillevert, Paul, ed. *Laberthonnière: L'homme et l'oeuvre, introduction à sa pensée*. Paris: Beauchesne, 1972.

Blanchette, Oliva. *Maurice Blondel: A Philosophical Life*. Grand Rapids, Mich.: Eerdmans, 2010.

Blondel, Maurice. *L'Action: Essai d'une critique de la vie et d'une science de la pratique*. Ph.D. diss. Paris: Sorbonne, 1893. Published in Paris by Alcan, 1893. Translated by Olive Blanchette as *Action*. Notre Dame: University of Notre Dame Press, 1984.

———. *Les premiers écrits de Maurice Blondel*. Paris: Presses Universitaires de France, 1956. Translated and edited by Alexander Dru and Iltyd Trethowan as *Maurice Blondel: The Letter on Apologetics and History and Dogma*. London: Harvill Press, 1964.

Bois, Henri. *Le dogme grec*. Paris: Fischbacher, 1893.

Boland, André. *La crise moderniste hier et aujourd'hui*. Paris: Beauchesne, 1980.

Bossuet, Jacques-Bénigne. *de Discours sur l'histoire universelle*. Paris: Librairie Firmin Didot, 1871.

Bousset, Wilhelm. *Der Antichrist*. Göttingen: Vandenhoek and Ruprecht, 1895.

———. "Review of Wrede, *Das Messiasgeheimnis*." *Theologische Rundschau* (August, 1902).

Bremond, Henri. *Newman: Psychologue de la foi*. Paris: Bloud, 1905.

Broglie, August-Théodore-Paul de. *Religion et critique*. Paris: Lecoffre, 1896.

Bruneau, Joseph. *Synopse évangélique*. Paris: Lecoffre, 1901

Brunetière, Ferdinand. *Sur les chemins de la croyance*. Paris: Perrin, 1905.

Caird, Edward. *The Evolution of Religion*. Glasgow: James Maclehose and Sons, 1893.

Cavallera, Ferdinand. "Portalié, Eugène." In *Dictionnaire de théologie catholique*, vol. 12, cols. 2590–93.

Charles, R. H. *The Apocrypha and Pseudepigrapha of the Old Testament*. Oxford: Clarendon Press, 1913. Reprinted in 1964.

Chauvin, Amédée. *Le père Gratry*. Paris: Bloud et Barral, 1901.

Colin, Pierre. *L'audace et le soupçon: La crise moderniste dans le catholicisme français 1893–1914*. Paris: Desclée de Brouwer, 1997.

Delehaye, Hippolyte. *L'oeuvre des Bollandistes à travers trois siècles 1615–1915*. Brussels: Société des Bollandistes, 2000.

Denzinger, Henricus, and Schönmetzer, Adolphus. *Enchiridion Symbolorum, Definitionum et Declarationum de rebus fidei et morum*. 36th ed. Freiburg im Breisgau: Herder, 1976.

Desjardins, Paul. *Catholicisme et critique: Réflexions d'un profane sur l'affaire Loisy*. Paris: Cahier de la Quinzaine, 1905.

d'Hulst, Maurice. "La question biblique." *Le Correspondant* n. s. 134 (1893): 201–51.

Dimnet, Ernest. *La pensée catholique dans L'Angleterre contemporaine*. Paris: Lecoffre, 1906.

Doumergue, Émile. *L'autorité en matière de foi et la nouvelle école*. Paris: Fischbacher, 1892.

Duchesne, Louis-Marie-Olivier. *Témoins anténicéens du dogme de la Trinité*. Amiens: 1883.

———. *Origines du culte chrétien: Étude sur la liturgie latine avant Charlemagne*. Paris: Ernest Thorin, 1903.

Fitzer, Joseph, ed. *Romance and the Rock: Nineteenth-Century Catholics on Faith and Reason*. Minneapolis: Fortress Press, 1989.
Fonsegrive, George. "A propos d'exégèse." *La Quinzaine* (December 16, 1903).
———. "A propos du centenaire de Kant." *La Quinzaine* (March 1, 1904).
———. "Catholicisme et libre pensée." *La Quinzaine* (May 1, 1905); (May 16, 1905).
Fontaine, Julien. *Les infiltrations protestants et l'exégèse du Nouveau Testament*. Paris: Victor Retaux, 1905.
Franon, Eugène. "Un nouveau manifeste catholique d'agnosticisme." *Bulletin de littérature ecclésiastique* 5 (June, 1903): 157–166. English translation in this volume.
———. "Un scholastique anti-intellectualiste." *Bulletin de littérature ecclésiastique* 7 (1905); English translation: "An Anti-Intellectualist Scholastic." In this volume.
———. "La philosophie religieuse du P. Tyrrell." *Bulletin de littérature ecclésiastique* 8 (1906): 157–166. English translation: "The Religious Philosophy of Fr. Tyrrell." In this volume.
Franzelin, Johannes Baptista. *Tractatus de divina traditione*. Rome: Ex Typographia Polyglotta, 1882.
Gayraud, Hippolyte, O.P. "L'Évangile et l'Église." *Univers* (February 15, 1903).
Gensac, Henri de. "Eugène Portalié." In *Dictionnaire du monde religieux dans la France contemporaine*. Vol. 1, *Les jésuites*. Paris: Beauchesne, 1985, 217–18.
Gertz, Karl-Peter. *Joseph Turmel (1859–1943): Ein theologiegeschichtlicher Beitrag zum Problem der Geschichtlichkeit der Dogmen*. Frankfurt am Main: Peter Lang, 1975.
Goichot, Émile. *Alfred Loisy et ses amis*. Paris: Les Éditions du Cerf, 2002.
Goyau, Georges. *L'Allemagne religieuse*. 2 vols. Paris: Librairie Académique Didiet Perrin, 1901.
Grandgeorge, L. *St. Augustin et le néo-platonisme*. Paris: Ernest Leroux, 1896.
Grandmaison, Léonce de. "Théologiens scholastiques et théologiens critiques." *Études* 74 (1898): 27–50.
———. "L'élasticité des formules dogmatiques." *Études* 76 (August 5 and 10, 1898): 341–58; 478–99.
———. "Le Christ de M. Harnack." *Études* 90 (1902): 731–62.
———. "L'Essence du Christianisme." *Études* 92 (1902): 696–700.
———. "L'Évangile et l'Église." *Études* 94 (1903): 145–174; 288.
———. "L'Expansion du Christianisme d'après M. Harnack." *Études* 96 (1903): 300–29; 459–76.
———. "Qu'est-ce qu'un dogme?" *Bulletin de littérature ecclésiastique* 7 (1905): 187–221; 8 (1906): 21–27. English translation in this volume.
Gratry, August Joseph Alphonse. *De la connaissance de Dieu*. 2 vols. Paris: Douniol, 1854.
———. *Logique*. 2 vols. Paris: Douniol, 1855.
———. *De la connaissance de l'âme*. Paris: Douniol, 1857.
Hahn, August. *Bibliothek der Symbole und Glaubensregeln der alten Kirche*. 3rd ed. Breslau: Morgenstern, 1897.
Harnack, Adolf von. *Dogmengeschichte*. Freiburg im Breisgau: Mohr, 1888.
———. *Das Wesen des Christentums*. Leipzig: Hinrichs'sche Buchhandlung, 1902. French translation: *L'essence du christianisme*. Paris: Fischbacher, 1902.

———. *Mission und Ausbreitung des Christentums.* Leipzig: Hinrichs'sche Buchhandlung, 1902.

———. *Das Christentum und die Geschichte.* Leipzig: Hinrichs'sche Buchhandlung, 1906

Harvey, Van. *The Historian and the Believer.* Toronto: Macmillan, 1969.

Headlam, Arthur C. *The Sources and Authority of Dogmatic Theology.* London: Macmillan, 1903.

Hill, Harvey, Louis-Pierre Sardella, and C. J. T. Talar. *By Those Who Knew Them: French Modernists Left, Right, and Center.* Washington, D.C.: The Catholic University of America Press, 2008.

———. *The Politics of Modernism: Alfred Loisy and the Scientific Study of Religion.* Washington, D.C.: The Catholic University of America Press, 2002.

Holtzmann, H. J. *Lehrbuch der Neutestamentlichen Theologie.* 2 vols. Freiburg im Breisgau: Mohr, 1896.

Hort, F. J. A. *The Christian Ecclesia.* London: Macmillan, 1897.

Houtin, Albert. *Un prêtre symboliste: Marcel Hébert (1851–1916).* Paris: F. Rieder, 1926.

James, William. *The Varieties of Religious Experience.* London: Longmans Green, 1902. French translation: *L'expérience religieuse.* Translated by Frank Abauzit. Paris: Alcan, 1906.

Joassart, Bernard. *Hippolyte Delehaye: Hagiographie critique et modernisme.* 2 vols. Brussels: Société des Bollandistes, 2000.

Jodock, Darrell, ed. *Catholicism Contending with Modernity: Roman Catholic Modernism and Anti-Modernism in Historical Context.* Cambridge: Cambridge University Press, 2000.

Jülicher, Adolf. *Die Gleichnisreden Jesu.* 2nd ed. 2 vols. Tübingen: Akademische Verlagsbuchhandlung J. C. B. Mohr, 1888.

Klein, Félix. *Le fait religieux et la manière de l'observer.* Paris: Lethielleux, 1903.

La Barre, André de. *La vie du dogme catholique.* Paris: Lethielleux, 1898.

Laberthonnière, Lucien. *Essais de philosophie religieuse.* Paris: Lethielleux, 1903.

Lagrange, Marie-Joseph, OP. "L'Évangile et l'Église." *Revue biblique* 12 (1903): 292–313. English translation in this volume.

———. *La méthode historique: Surtout à propos de l'Ancien Testament.* Paris: Victor Lecoffre, 1903. English translation: *Historical Criticism and the Old Testament.* London: Catholic Truth Society, 1905.

———. "Jésus et la critique des Évangiles." *Bulletin de littérature ecclésiastique* 5 (1903): 1–26. English translation in this volume.

———. *Le père Lagrange: Au service de la bible; Souvenirs personnels.* Paris: Les Éditions du Cerf, 1967. Translated by Henry Wansbrough as *Père Lagrange: Personal Reflections and Memoirs.* New York: Paulist Press, n.d.

Laplanche, François, ed. *Alfred Loisy: La crise de la foi dans le temps présent.* Turnhout: Brepols, 2010.

Larkin, Maurice. *Church and State after the Dreyfus Affair: The Separation Issue in France.* New York: Macmillan, 1974.

Lebreton, Jules. *Le père Léonce de Grandmaison.* Paris: Gabriel Beauchesne, 1932.

Le Roy, Édouard. "Qu'est-ce qu'un dogme?" *La Quinzaine* (April 16, 1905): 495–527.

———. *Dogme et critique*. Paris: Librairie Bloud et Cie., 1907.

Lescoeur, Louis. *La théodicée chrétienne d'après les pères de l'église, ou essai philosophique sur le traité de Deo du P. Thomassin*. Paris: Remquet, 1861.

Lévy-Bruhl, Lucien. *La philosophie de Jacobi*. Paris: Alcan, 1894.

Lightfoot, Joseph Barber. *Colossians*. London: Macmillan, 1875.

Loisy, Alfred. *Les évangiles synoptiques*. 2 vols. Amiens; J. Rousseau, 1896–1897.

———. "L'apocalypse synoptique." *Revue biblique* 5 (1896): 173–98 and 335–59.

———. [A. Firmin]. "Le développement chrétien d'après le Cardinal Newman." *Revue du clergé français* 17 (1898): 5–20.

———. [A. Firmin]. "La définition de la religion," *Revue du clergé français* 18 (1899): 193–209.

———. [A. Firmin]. "La théorie individualiste de la religion." *Revue du clergé français* 17 (1899): 202–15.

———. [A. Firmin]. "L'idée de la révélation," *Revue du clergé français* 21 (1900): 250–71.

———. [A. Firmin]. "Les preuves et l'économie de la révélation," *Revue du clergé français* 22 (1900): 126–53.

———. [A. Firmin]. "La religion d'Israël." *Revue du clergé français* 24 (1900): 337–63.

———. *Études évangéliques*. Paris: Picard, 1902.

———. *L'évangile et l'église*. Paris: Picard, 1902. English translation *The Gospel and the Church*, translated by Christopher Home. London: Isbister, 1903. Reprinted by Fortress Press, 1976.

———. *Autour d'un petit livre*. Paris: Alphonse Picard et fils, Éditeurs, 1903.

———. *Le quatrième évangile*. Paris: Picard, 1903.

———. Le discours sur la montagne. Paris: Picard, 1903.

———. *Choses passées*. Paris: Émile Nourry, 1913. English translation by Richard Wilson Boynton, *My Duel with the Vatican*. New York: Greenwood Press, 1968.

———. *Mémoires pour servir à l'histoire religieuse de notre temps*. 3 vols. Paris: Émile Nourry, 1930–31.

———. *Prelude to the Modernist Crisis: The "Firmin" Articles of Alfred Loisy*. Translated by Christine Thirlway. Oxford: Oxford University Press, 2010.

Lubac, Henri de. *Maurice Blondel-Joannès Wehrlé: Correspondance*. Paris: Aubier, 1969.

Mansini, Guy. *"What Is a Dogma?": The Meaning and Truth of Dogma in Edouard Le Roy and His Scholastic Opponents*. Rome: Editrice Pontificia Università Gregoriana, 1985.

Margival, Henri. *Essai sur Richard Simon et la critique biblique au XVIIe siècle*. Paris: Maillet, 1900.

Mayeur, Jean-Marie, and Madeleine Rebérioux. *The Third Republic from its Origins to the Great War 1871–1914*. Translated by J. R. Foster. Cambridge History of Modern France. Cambridge: Cambridge University Press, 1984.

Mignot, Archbishop Eudòxe-Irénée-Edouard. "L'évolutionnisme religieux." *Le Correspondant* (April 10, 1897): 85ff.

Montagnes, Bernard. *Naissance de la méthode critique*. Paris: Les Éditions du Cerf, 1992.

———. *Le père Lagrange (1855–1938): L'exégèse catholique dans la crise moderniste*. Paris: Les Éditions du Cerf, 1995. Translated by Benedict Viviano as *The Story of Father Marie-Joseph Lagrange: Founder of Modern Catholic Bible Study*. New York: Paulist Press, 2006.

———. *Marie-Joseph Lagrange: Une biographie critique.* Paris: Les Éditions du Cerf, 2004.
Pascal, Blaise. *Pensées et opuscules.* Ed. Brunschveig. Paris: Alcan, 1905.
Petre, Maude. *Autobiography and Life of George Tyrrell.* 2 vols. London: Edward Arnold, 1912.
Poincaré, Henri. *La valeur de la science.* Paris: Flammarion, 1905. English translation: *The Value of Science: Essential Writings of Henri Poincare.* New York: Modern Library, 2001.
Portalié, Eugène. "Dogme et histoire." *Bulletin de littérature ecclésiastique* 6 (1904): 62–90; 7 (1904): 91–143. English translation: "History and Dogma." In in this volume.
———. "L'Exposition morale des dogmes. Réponse à la Quinzaine." *Études* 103 (July 1905):147–173; (August, 1905):315–342. English translation "On the Moral Exposition of Dogmas." In this volume.
Poulat, Émile. *Histoire, dogme et critique dans la crise moderniste* [1962]. Tournai: Casterman, 1979.
———. *La question religieuse et ses turbulences au XXe siècle.* Paris: Berg International, 2005.
Prudhomme, René Sully. *La vraie religion selon Pascal.* Paris: Alcan, 1905.
Puniet, Pierre de. *Les trois homélies catéchétiques du Sacramentaire Gélasien.* Louvain: Peeters, 1905.
Rafferty, Oliver, ed. *George Tyrrell and Catholic Modernism.* Dublin: Four Courts Press, 2010.
Reardon, B. M. G. *Roman Catholic Modernism.* Stanford: Stanford University Press, 1970.
Rivière, Jean. *Monseigneur Batiffol (1861–1929).* Paris: J. Gabalda, 1929.
Robinson, John A. T. *Redating the New Testament.* Philadelphia: Westminster Press, 1976.
Rose, Fr. Vincent. *Études sur les évangiles.* Paris: H. Welter, 1902.
Rush, Ormond. *Still Interpreting Vatican II.* New York: Paulist, 2004.
Ryle, Herbert E., and Montague R. James. *Psalms of the Pharisees Commonly Called the Psalms of Solomon.* Cambridge, 1891.
Sabatier, August. *Esquisse d'une philosophie de la religion.* Paris: Fischbacher, 1897. English translation: *Outlines of a Philosophy of Religion Based on Psychology and History.* Harper Torchbooks 23. Harper and Row, 1970.
———. *Les religions d'autorité et la religion de l'esprit.* Paris: Fischbacher, 1903. English translation: *The Religions of Authority and the Religion of the Spirit.* London: Williams and Norgate; New York: McClure and Phillips, 1910.
Sagovsky, Nicholas. *"On God's Side": A Life of George Tyrrell.* Oxford: Clarendon Press, 1990.
Saleilles, R. *La méthode historique et la Bible.* Geneva: Imprimerie Schautz et Cie., 1903.
Scheeben, Matthias Josef. *Handbuch der katholischen Dogmatik.* Freiburg im Breisgau: Herder, 1873. Translated by Abbé Paul Bélet as *La Dogmatique.* Paris: Victor Palmé, 1882.
Schultenover, David. *George Tyrrell: In Search of Catholicism.* Shepherdstown, W.Va.: Patmos Press, 1981.

Schwalm, M. B. "Les illusions de l'idéalisme et leurs dangers pour la foi." *Revue Thomiste* 4 (1896): 413–41.
Seeberg, Alfred. *Der Katechismus der Urchristenheit.* Leipzig: Deichert, 1903.
Semeria, Giovanni. *Dogma, gerarchia e culto nella Chiesa primitiva.* Rome: 1902.
Sertillanges, Antonin Dalmace. Letter to the Editor. *La Quinzaine* (June 1, 1905): 412–19.
———. *Les sources de la croyance en Dieu.* Paris: Librairie Perrin et Cie., 1905.
Somerville, James M. *Total Commitment: Blondel's "L'action."* Washington, D.C.: Corpus, 1968.
Talar, C. J. T. "Innovation and Interpretation." In *Catholicism Contending with Modernity: Roman Catholic Modernism and Anti-modernism in Historical Context*, edited by Darrell Jodock. Cambridge: Cambridge University Press, 2000.
———. "Le moderniste malgré lui: Pierre Batiffol." In *By Those Who Knew Them: French Modernists Left, Right, and Center*, edited by Harvey Hill et al. Washington, D.C.: The Catholic University of America Press, 2008.
———, ed. *The Modernist as Philosopher: Selected Writings of Marcel Hébert.* Washington, D.C.: The Catholic University of America Press, 2011.
———. "Rehabilitating Richard Simon, Legitimating Alfred Loisy." In *The Rise of Historical Consciousness among the Christian Churches*, edited by Kenneth L. Parker and Eric H. Moser, 47–63. Lanham, Md.: University Press of America, 2013.
Thomassin, Louis. *Dogmata theologica.* 3 vols. Paris: Vivès, 1865ff.
Tixeront, Joseph. *Histoire des Dogmes.*3 vols. Paris: Lecoffre, 1905.
Turmel, Joseph. *Comment j'ai donné congé aux dogmes* (1935); *Comment l'église romaine m'a donné congé* (1939). Translated by C. J. T. Talar and Elizabeth Emery as *"Martyr to the Truth": The Autobiography of Joseph Turmel.* Eugene, Ore.: Pickwick, 2012.
Tyrrell, George. *Nova et Vetera.* London: Longmans Green, 1902.
———. ["Ernest Engels"]. *Religion as a Factor of Life.* Exeter and London: William Pollard and Company, n.d.
———. *Lex Orandi or Prayer and Creed.* London: Longmans Green, 1904.
———. "Semper eadem." *The Month* (January 1904), 5–8.
Vacant, Alfred., Eugène Mangenot, and Émile Amann. *Dictionnaire de théologie catholique.* 15 vols. in 30. Paris: Letouzey et Ané, 1899–1950.
Vanot, Jean. "Une grande entreprise théologique." *Études* 90 (1902): 405–9.
Vasquez, Gabriel. *Commentariorum et disputationum in S. Thomae Summam theologiae tomus primus.* Alcala: 1598.
Vidler, Alec R. *Prophecy and Papacy: A Study of Lamennais, the Church and the Revolution.* New York: Charles Scribner's Sons, 1954.
———. *A Variety of Catholic Modernists.* Cambridge: Cambridge University Press, 1970.
Vincent of Lerins. *Commonitorium.* PL 50.
Vincent, Louis-Hugues. *Le père Marie-Joseph Lagrange: Sa vie et son oeuvre.* Paris: Éditions Parole et Silence, 2013.
Virgoulay, René. *Blondel et le modernisme.* Tournai: Casterman, 1979.
Waché, Brigitte. *Monseigneur Louis Duchesne (1843–1922).* Rome: L'École Française de Rome, 1992.
Wendt, Hans Hinrich. *Die Lehre Jesu.* Göttingen: Vandenhoek and Ruprecht, 1901.

Wehrlé, Johannès. "De la nature du dogme." *Revue biblique* 14 (1905): 323–349. English translation in this volume.

Wernle, Paul. *Anfänge unserer Religion*. Tübingen: Mohr, 1901. English translation by G. A. Bienemann, *The Beginnings of Christianity*. London: Williams and Norgate; New York: Putnam, 1904.

Westcott, Brooke Foss. *The Epistles of St. John*. Cambridge: Macmillan, 1886.

Wetzer, Heinrich Josef, and Benedikt Welte. *Kirchenlexicon*. 13 vols. 2nd ed. Freiburg im Breisgau: Herder, 1881.

Wrede, Wilhelm. *Das Messiasgeheimniss in den Evangelien*. Göttingen: Vandenhoeck und Ruprecht, 1901.

Yzermans, Vincent A., ed. *All Things in Christ: Encyclical Letters and Selected Documents of Saint Pius X*. Westminster, Md.: Newman Press, 1954.

INDEX OF BIBLICAL AND PSEUDEPIGRAPHAL VERSES

GENERAL INDEX

Defending the Faith: An Anti-Modernist Anthology was designed in Garamond with Hypatia Sans display and composed by Kachergis Book Design of Pittsboro, North Carolina. It was printed on 60-pound Natural Recycled Book and bound by McNaughton & Gunn of Saline, Michigan.